D0941222

VOLUME 6

UNIVERSE'S FINEST

BATMAN/SUPERMAN

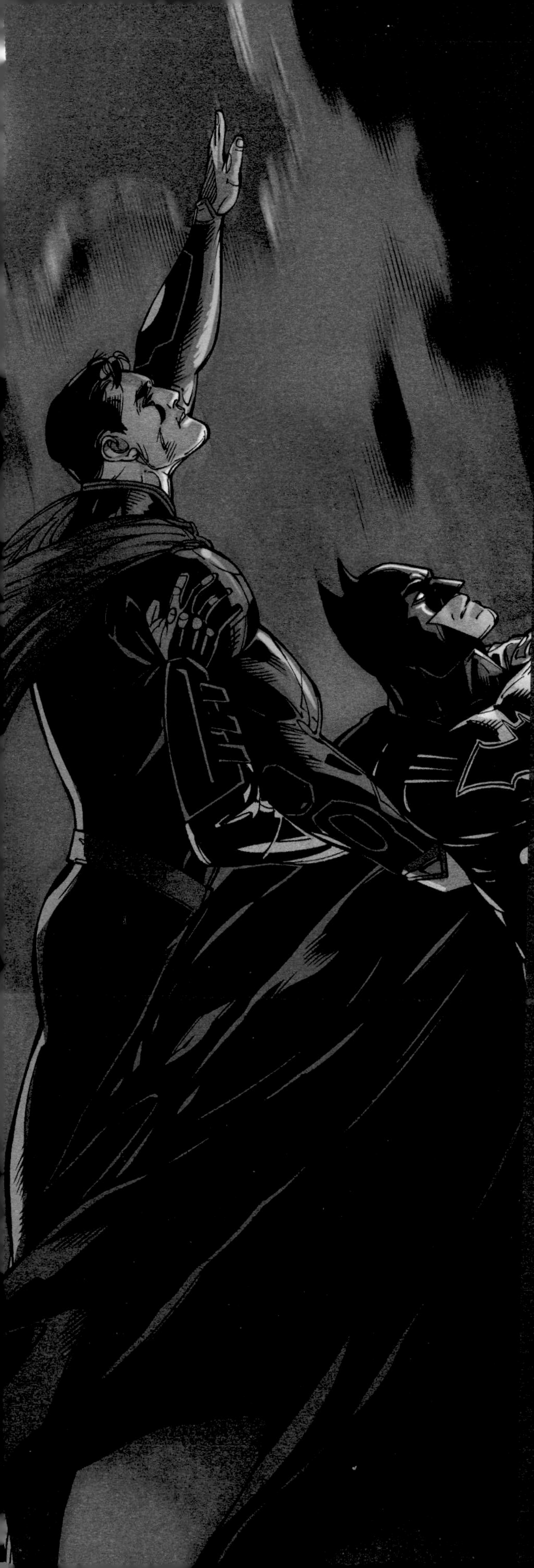

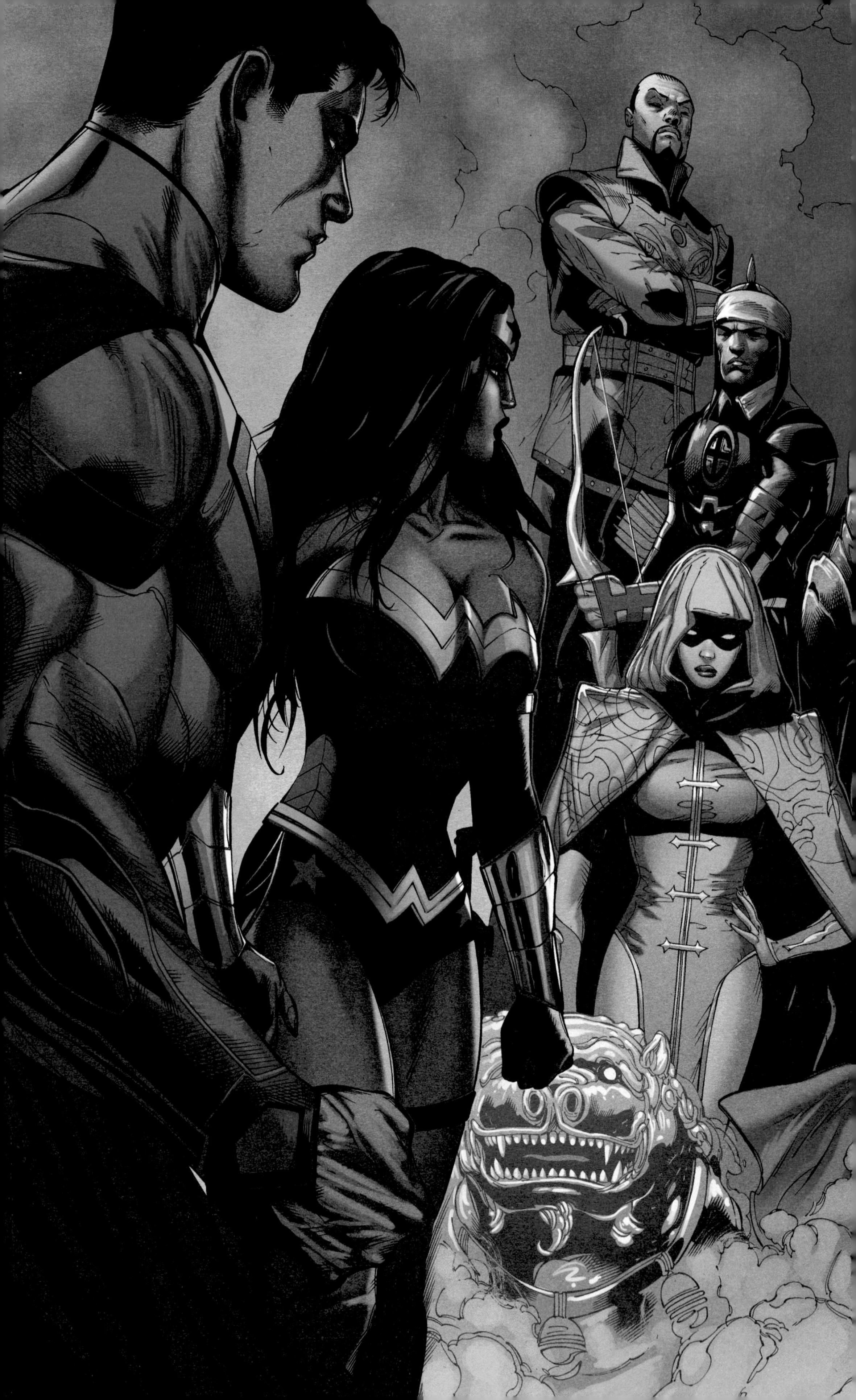

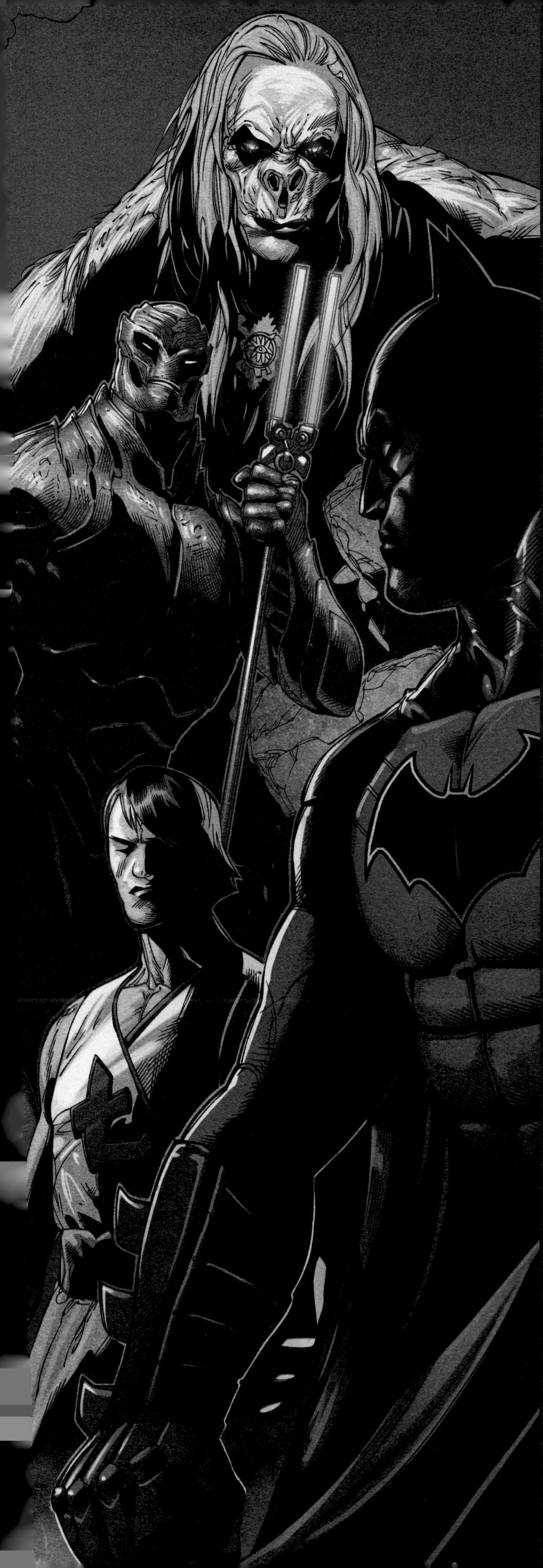

BATMAN/SUPERMAN

VOLUME 6
UNIVERSE'S FINEST

WRITTEN BY
TOM TAYLOR
PETER J. TOMASI
FRANK TIERI

PENCILS BY
ROBSON ROCHA
DOUG MAHNKE
ALEX KONAT
ELIA BONETTI
GIUSEPPE CAFARO

INKS BY
DEXTER VINES
WADE VON GRAWBADGER
NORM RAPMUND
JULIO FERREIRA
JAY LEISTEN
JAIME MENDOZA
CHRISTIAN ALAMY
JOHN LIVESAY
TOM NGUYEN
ROB HUNTER
MATT BANNING
MARK ROSLAN
ELIA BONETTI
GIUSEPPE CAFARO

COLOR BY
BLOND
WIL QUINTANA
LEE LOUGHRIDGE
WES HARTMAN

LETTERS BY
ROB LEIGH
TRAVIS LANHAM

COLLECTION COVER BY
YANICK PAQUETTE WITH
NATHAN FAIRBAIRN

SUPERMAN CREATED BY
JERRY SIEGEL & **JOE SHUSTER**
SUPERGIRL BASED ON
THE CHARACTERS CREATED BY
JERRY SIEGEL & **JOE SHUSTER**
BY SPECIAL ARRANGEMENT WITH
THE JERRY SIEGEL FAMILY

BATMAN CREATED BY
BOB KANE WITH **BILL FINGER**

ANDREW MARINO Assistant Editor – Original Series
DAVID WOHL, MARIE JAVINS Editors – Original Series
EDDIE BERGANZA Group Editor – Original Series
JEB WOODARD Group Editor – Collected Editions
LIZ ERICKSON Editor – Collected Edition
STEVE COOK Design Director – Books
DAMIAN RYLAND Publication Design

BOB HARRAS Senior VP – Editor-in-Chief, DC Comics

DIANE NELSON President
DAN DiDIO Publisher
JIM LEE Publisher
GEOFF JOHNS President & Chief Creative Officer
AMIT DESAI Executive VP – Business & Marketing Strategy, Direct to Consumer & Global Franchise Management
SAM ADES Senior VP – Direct to Consumer
BOBBIE CHASE VP – Talent Development
MARK CHIARELLO Senior VP – Art, Design & Collected Editions
JOHN CUNNINGHAM Senior VP – Sales & Trade Marketing
ANNE DePIES Senior VP – Business Strategy, Finance & Administration
DON FALLETTI VP – Manufacturing Operations
LAWRENCE GANEM VP – Editorial Administration & Talent Relations
ALISON GILL Senior VP – Manufacturing & Operations
HANK KANALZ Senior VP – Editorial Strategy & Administration
JAY KOGAN VP – Legal Affairs
THOMAS LOFTUS VP – Business Affairs
JACK MAHAN VP – Business Affairs
NICK J. NAPOLITANO VP – Manufacturing Administration
EDDIE SCANNELL VP – Consumer Marketing
COURTNEY SIMMONS Senior VP – Publicity & Communications
JIM (SKI) SOKOLOWSKI VP – Comic Book Specialty Sales & Trade Marketing
NANCY SPEARS VP – Mass, Book, Digital Sales & Trade Marketing

BATMAN/SUPERMAN VOLUME 6: UNIVERSE'S FINEST

DC Comics, 2900 West Alameda Ave., Burbank, CA 91505
Printed by LSC Communications, Salem, VA. 3/3/17. First Printing.
ISBN: 978-1-4012-6819-0

Library of Congress Cataloging-in-Publication Data is available.

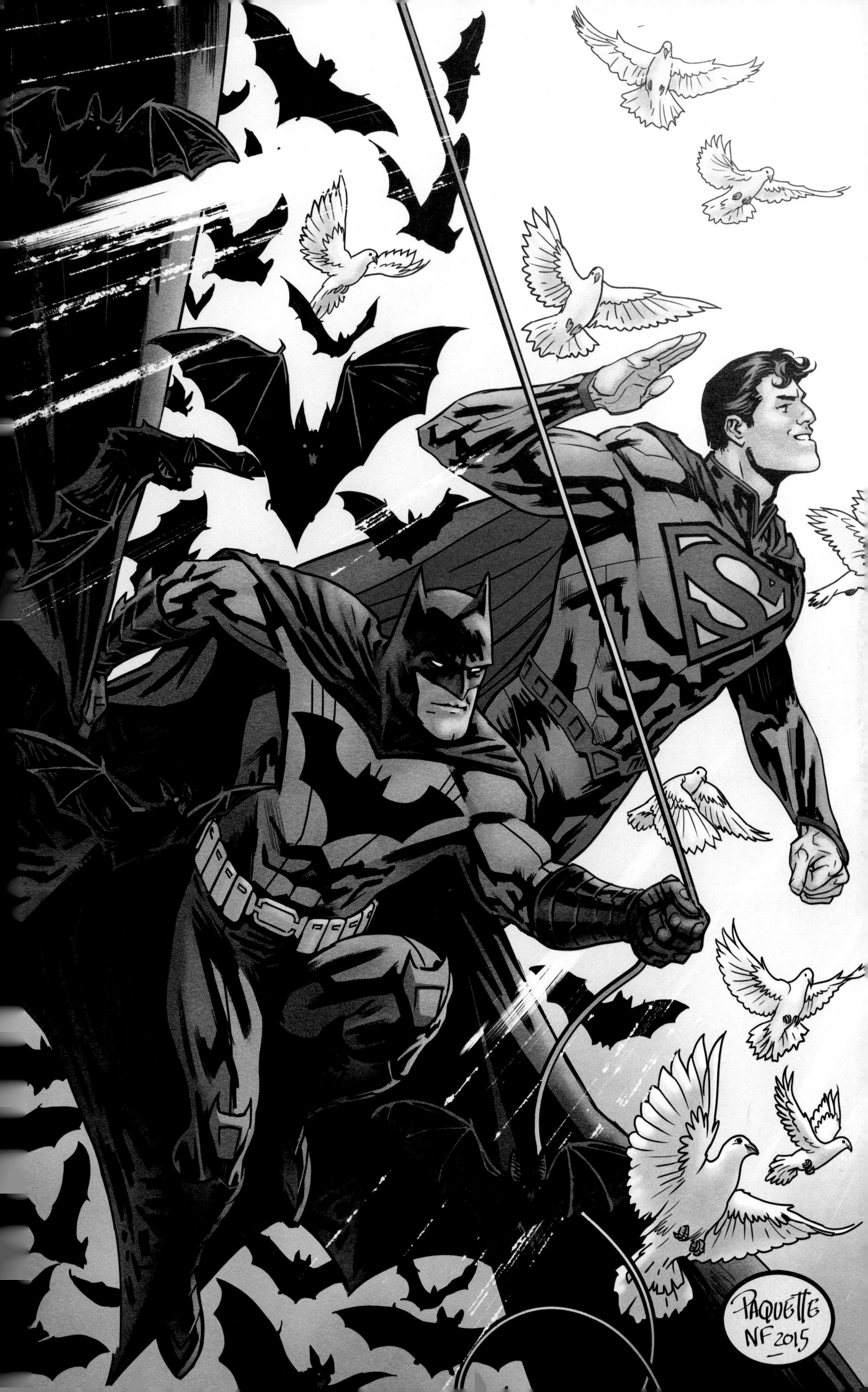
PAQUETTE
NF 2015

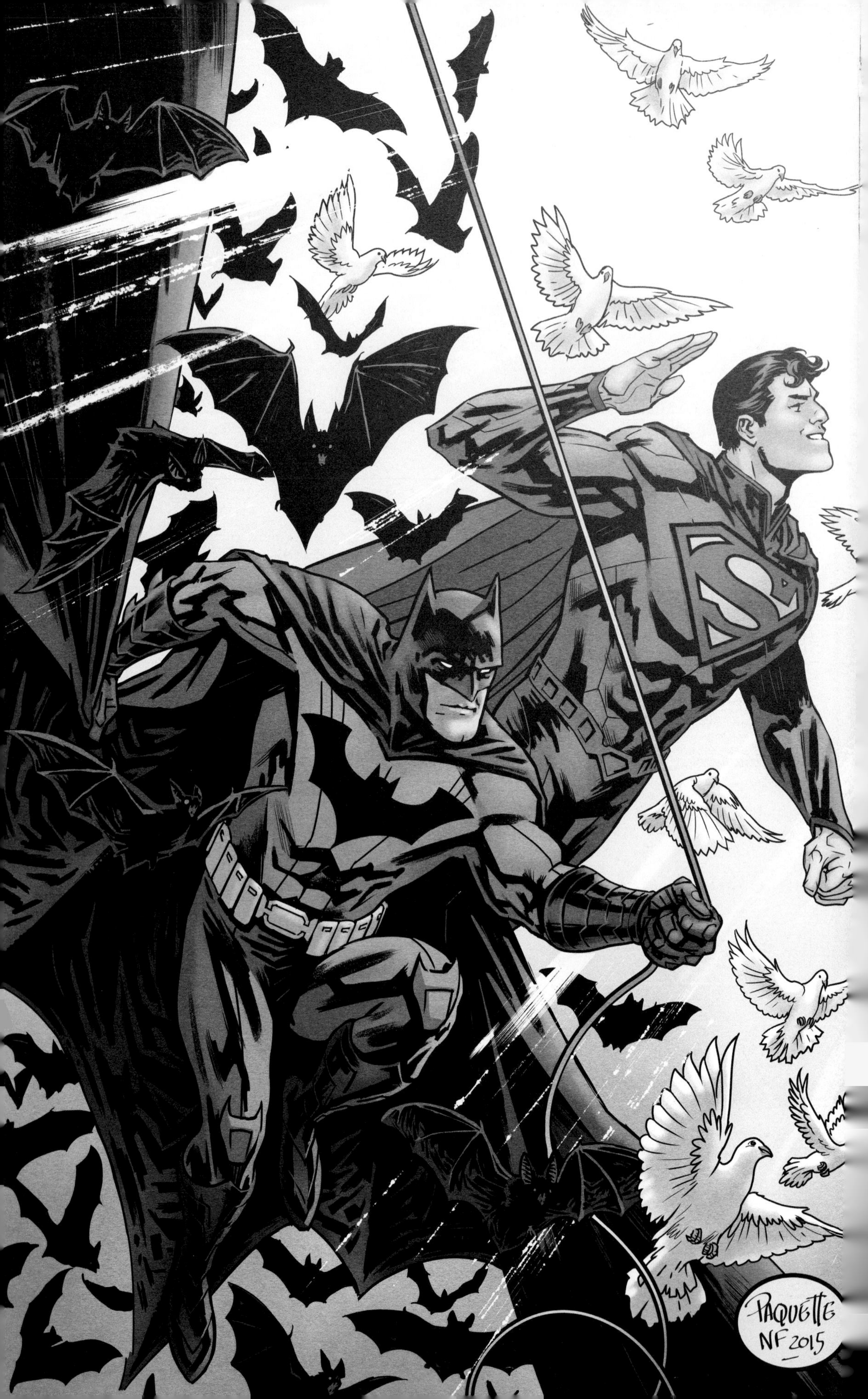
PAQUETTE
NF 2015

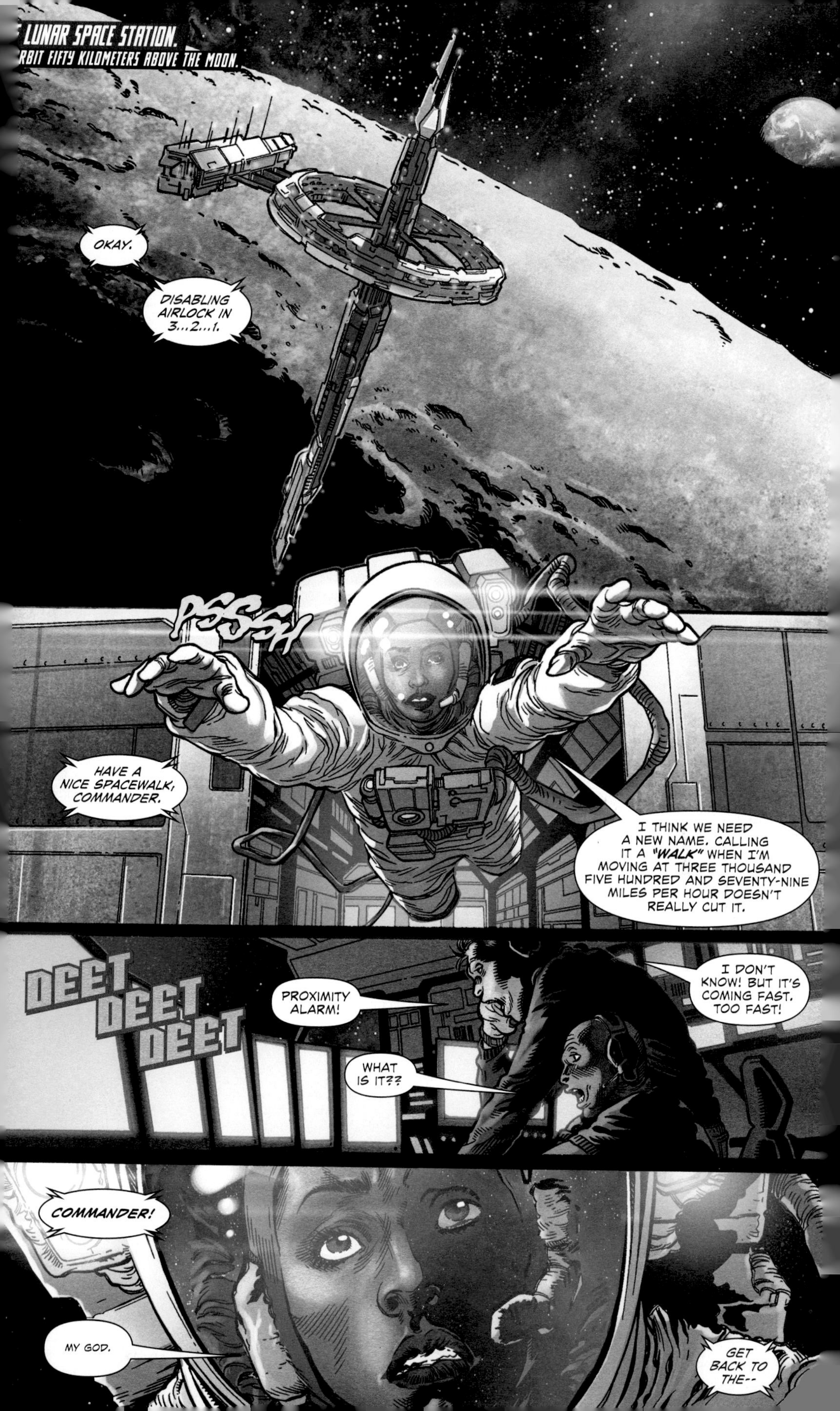

LUNAR SPACE STATION.
RBIT FIFTY KILOMETERS ABOVE THE MOON.
OKAY.
DISABLING AIRLOCK IN 3...2...1.
PSSSH
HAVE A NICE SPACEWALK, COMMANDER.
I THINK WE NEED A NEW NAME. CALLING IT A "WALK" WHEN I'M MOVING AT THREE THOUSAND FIVE HUNDRED AND SEVENTY-NINE MILES PER HOUR DOESN'T REALLY CUT IT.
DEET DEET DEET
PROXIMITY ALARM!
WHAT IS IT??
I DON'T KNOW! BUT IT'S COMING FAST. TOO FAST!
COMMANDER!
MY GOD.
GET BACK TO THE--

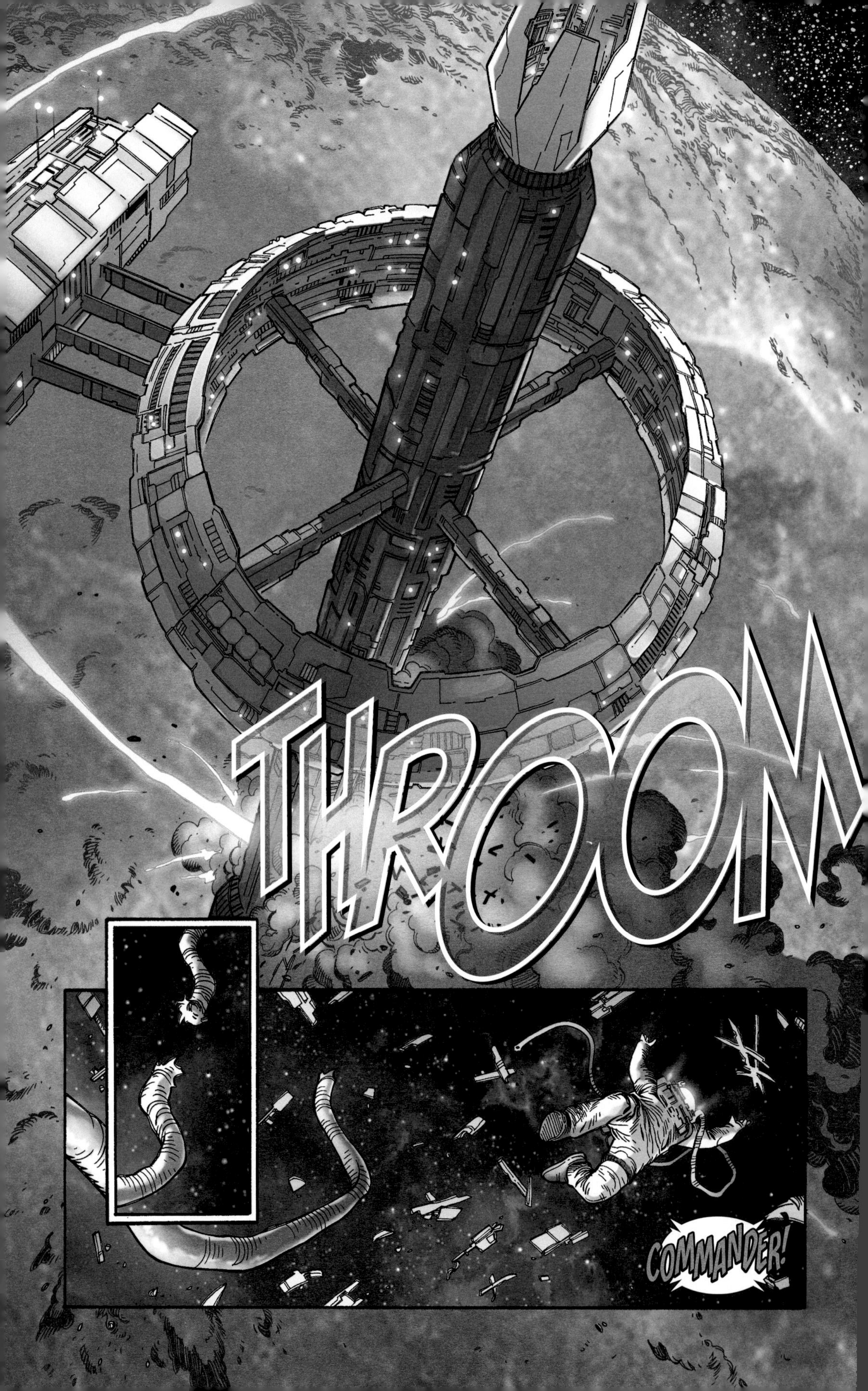
THROOM
COMMANDER!

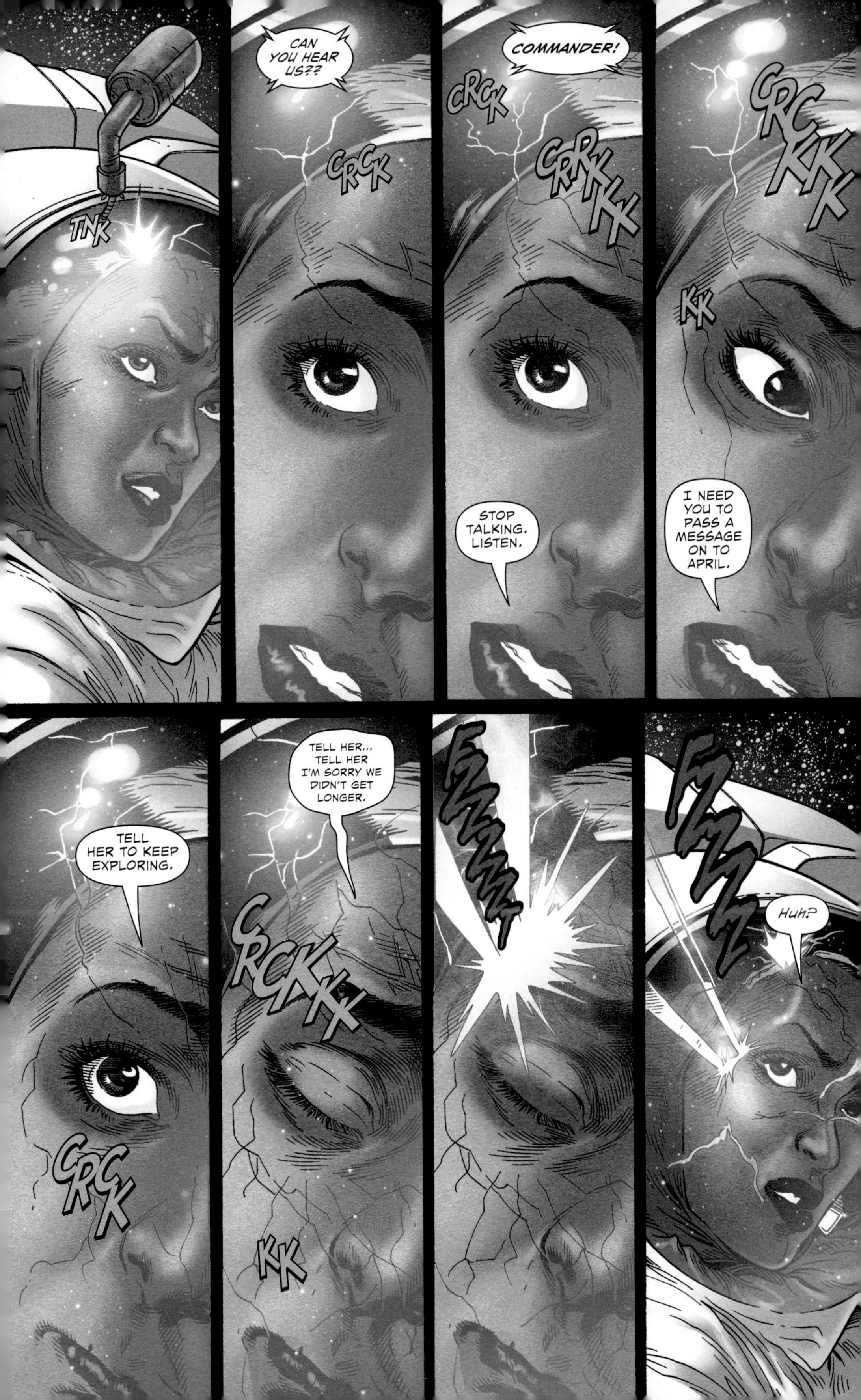
TNK
CAN YOU HEAR US??
CRCK
COMMANDER!
CRCK
CRRKKK
STOP TALKING. LISTEN.
CRCKKK
KK
I NEED YOU TO PASS A MESSAGE ON TO APRIL.
TELL HER TO KEEP EXPLORING.
CRCK
TELL HER... TELL HER I'M SORRY WE DIDN'T GET LONGER.
CRCKKK
KK
FZZZZZT
FZZZZ
Huh?

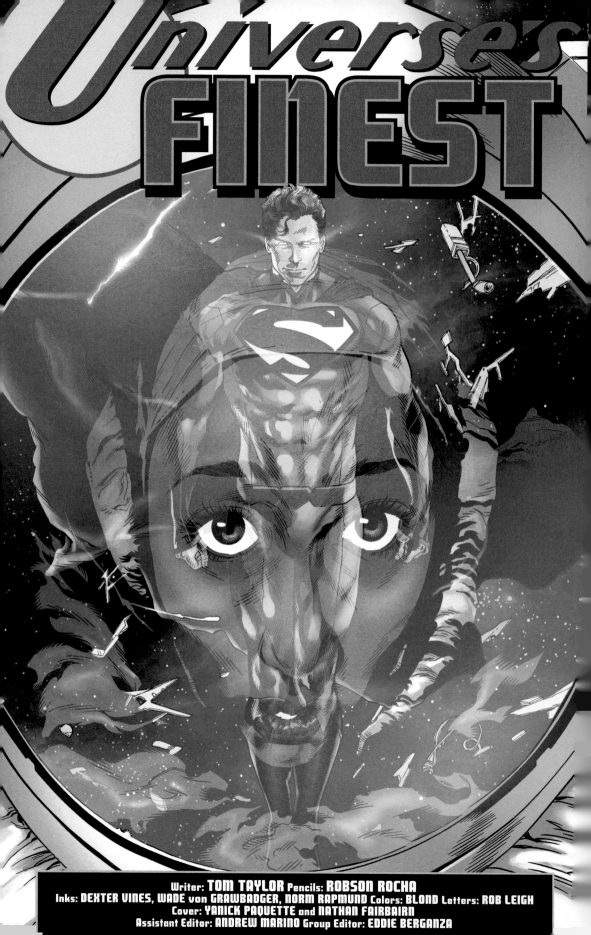

Universe's FINEST

Writer: **TOM TAYLOR** Pencils: **ROBSON ROCHA**
Inks: **DEXTER VINES, WADE von GRAWBADGER, NORM RAPMUND** Colors: **BLOND** Letters: **ROB LEIGH**
Cover: **YANICK PAQUETTE** and **NATHAN FAIRBAIRN**
Assistant Editor: **ANDREW MARINO** Group Editor: **EDDIE BERGANZA**

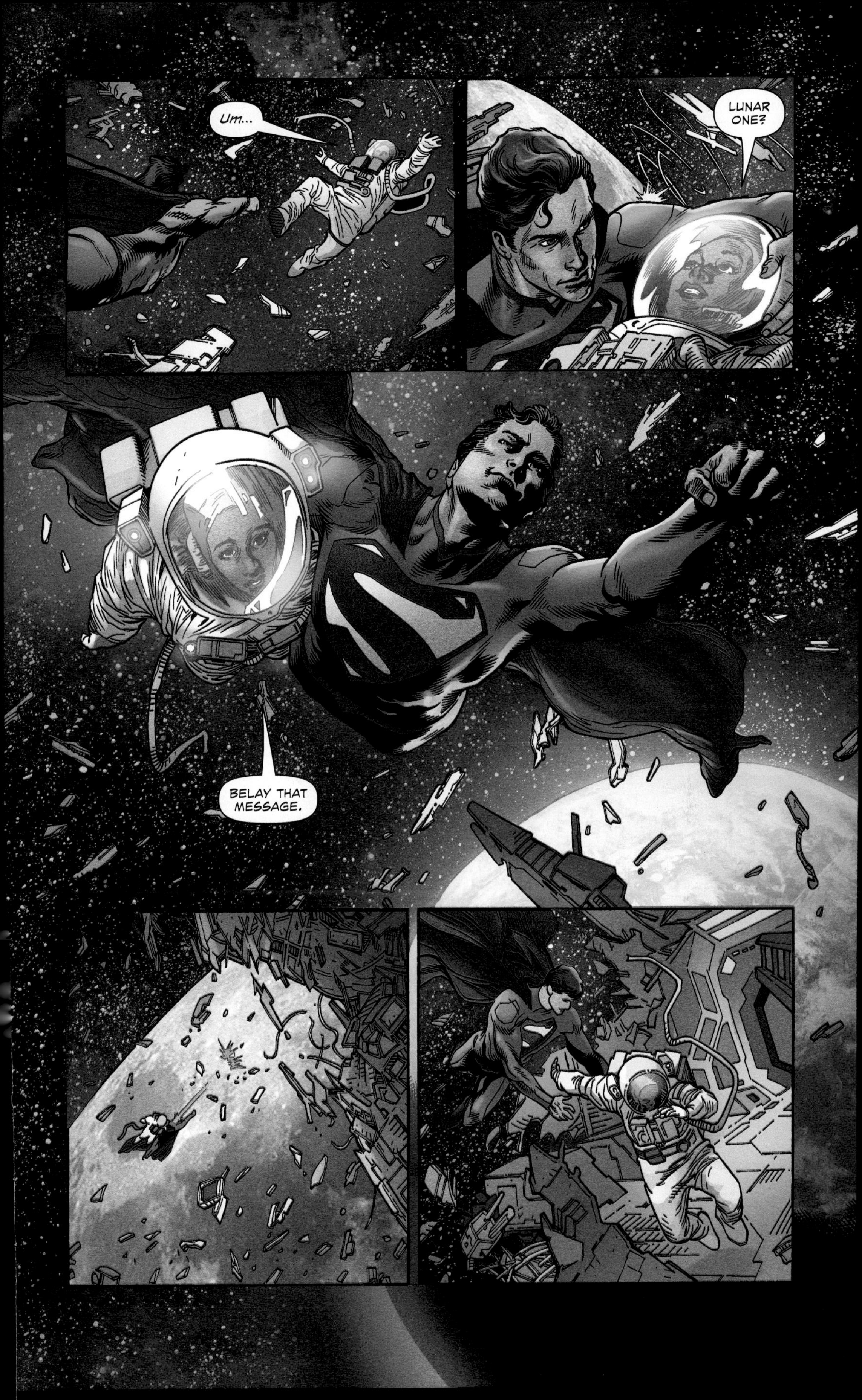
Um...
LUNAR ONE?
BELAY THAT MESSAGE.

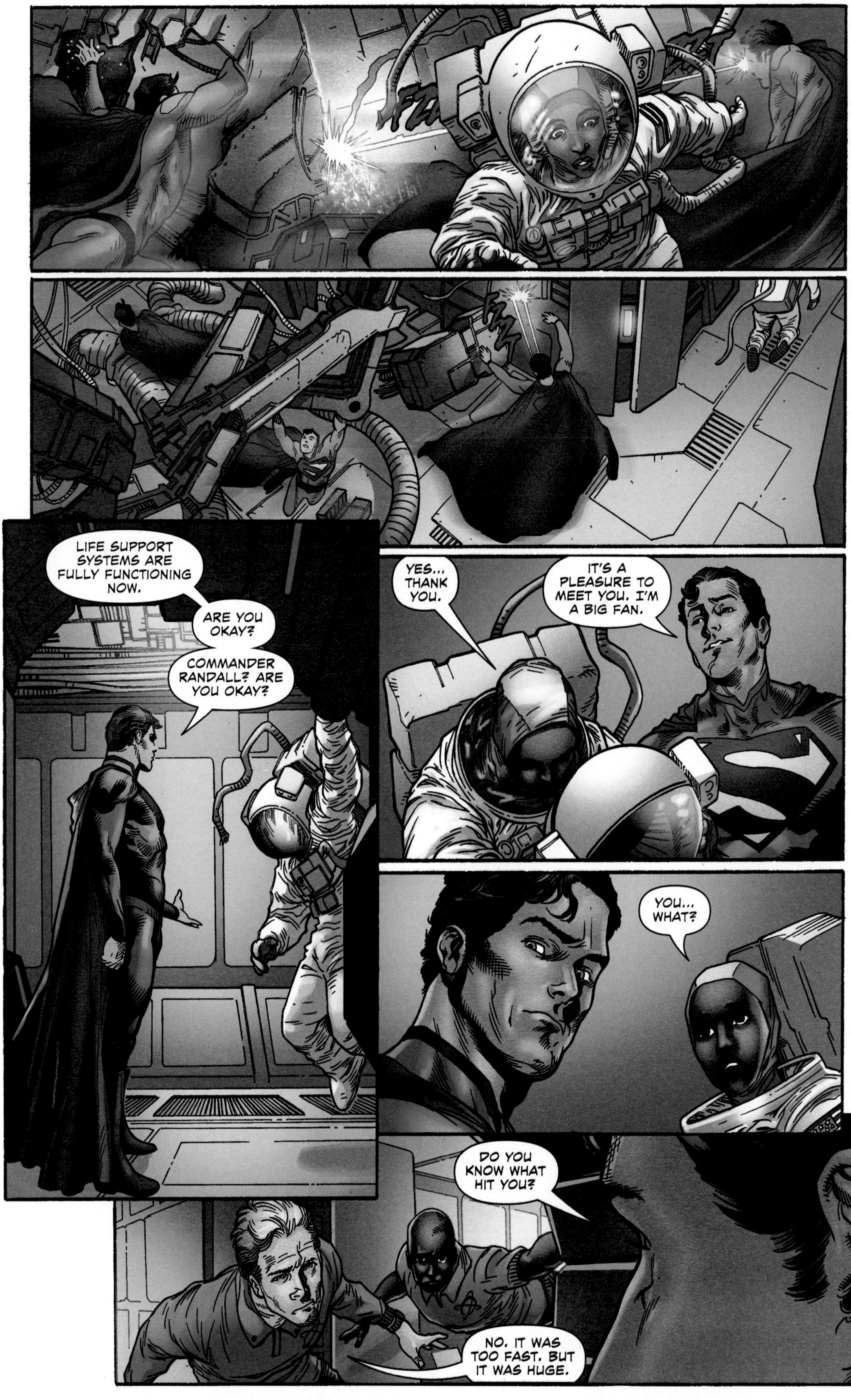

FZZ
FZZZ
LIFE SUPPORT SYSTEMS ARE FULLY FUNCTIONING NOW.
ARE YOU OKAY?
COMMANDER RANDALL? ARE YOU OKAY?
YES... THANK YOU.
IT'S A PLEASURE TO MEET YOU. I'M A BIG FAN.
YOU... WHAT?
DO YOU KNOW WHAT HIT YOU?
NO. IT WAS TOO FAST. BUT IT WAS HUGE.

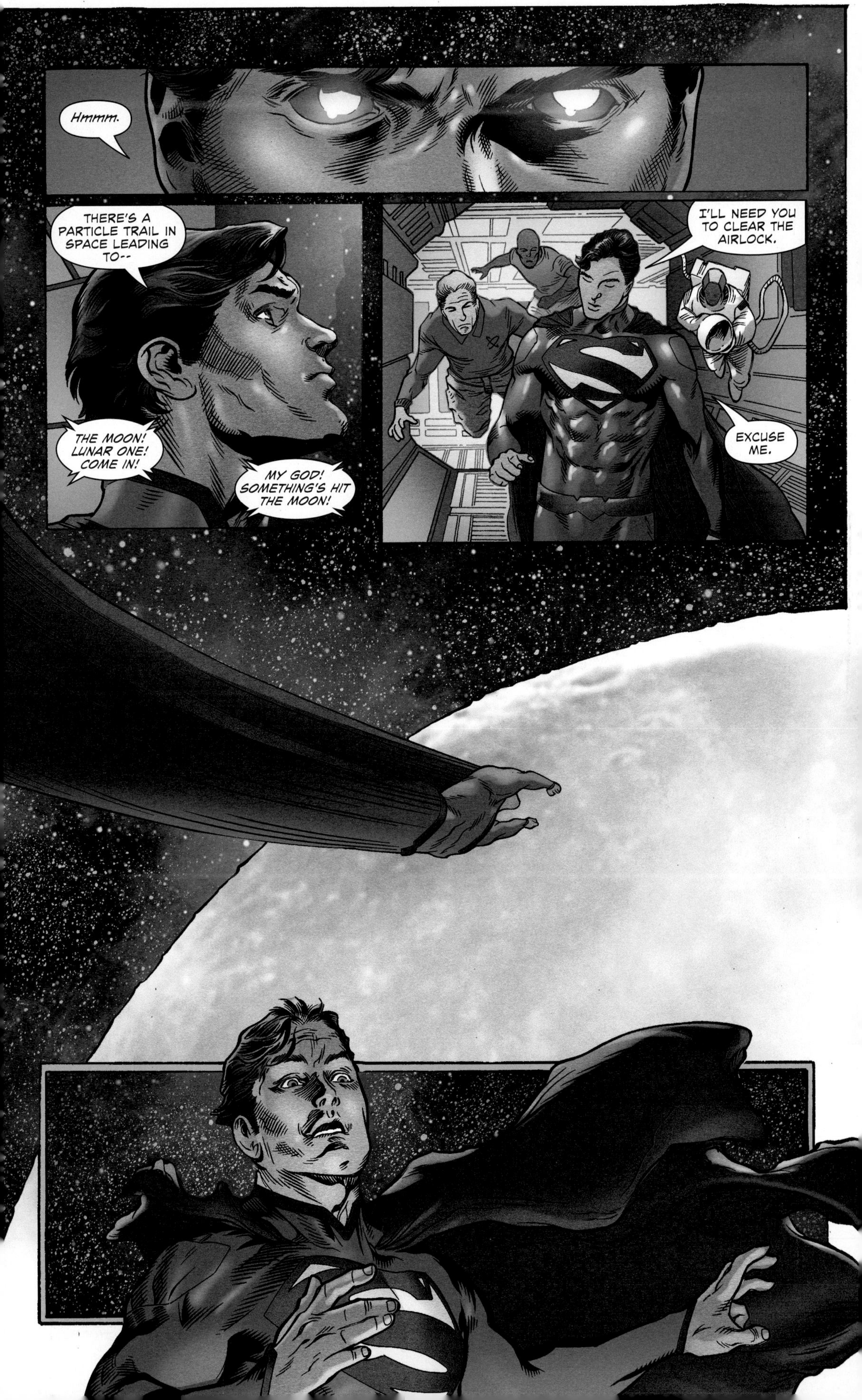
Hmmm.
THERE'S A PARTICLE TRAIL IN SPACE LEADING TO--
THE MOON! LUNAR ONE! COME IN!
MY GOD! SOMETHING'S HIT THE MOON!
I'LL NEED YOU TO CLEAR THE AIRLOCK.
EXCUSE ME.

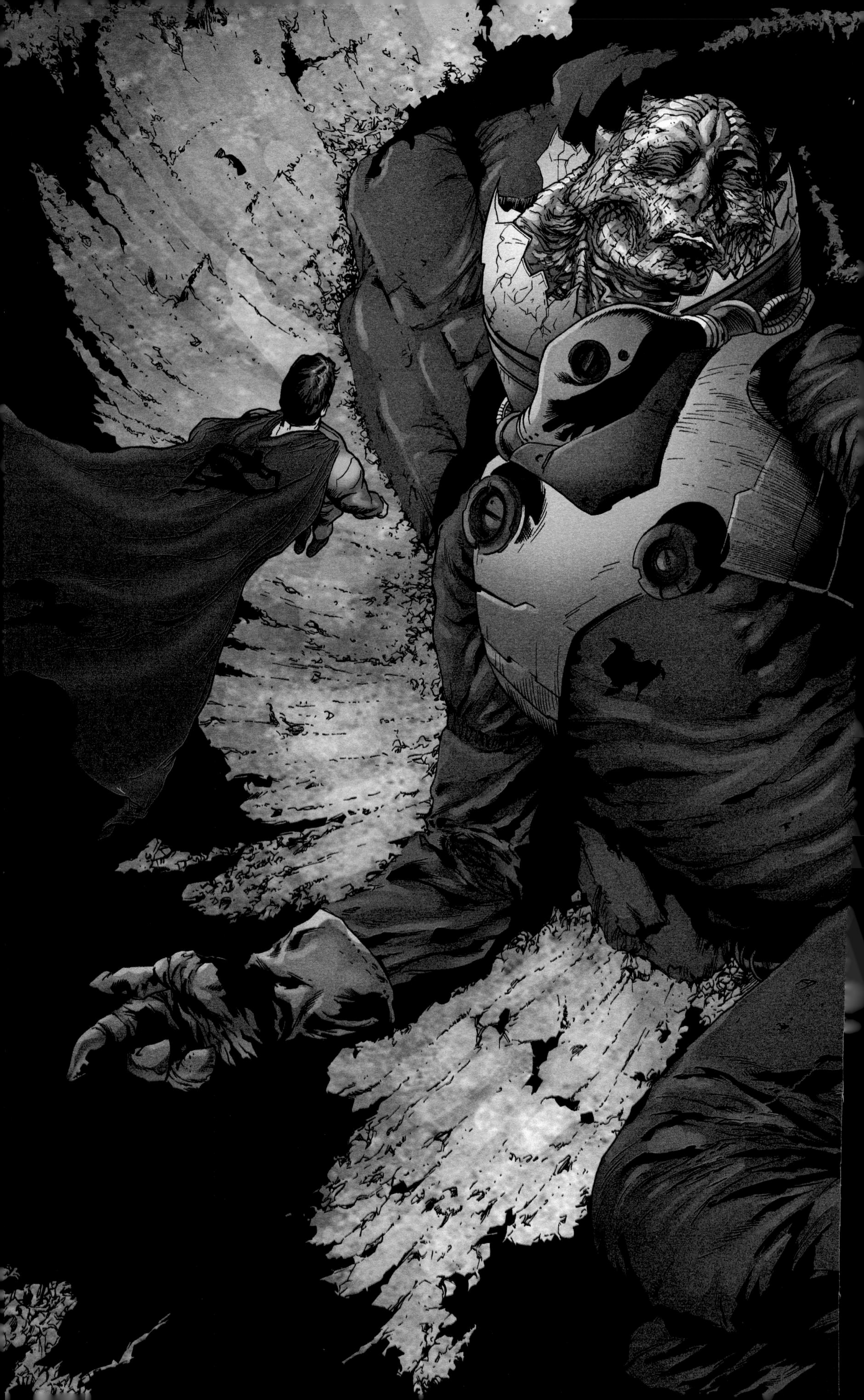

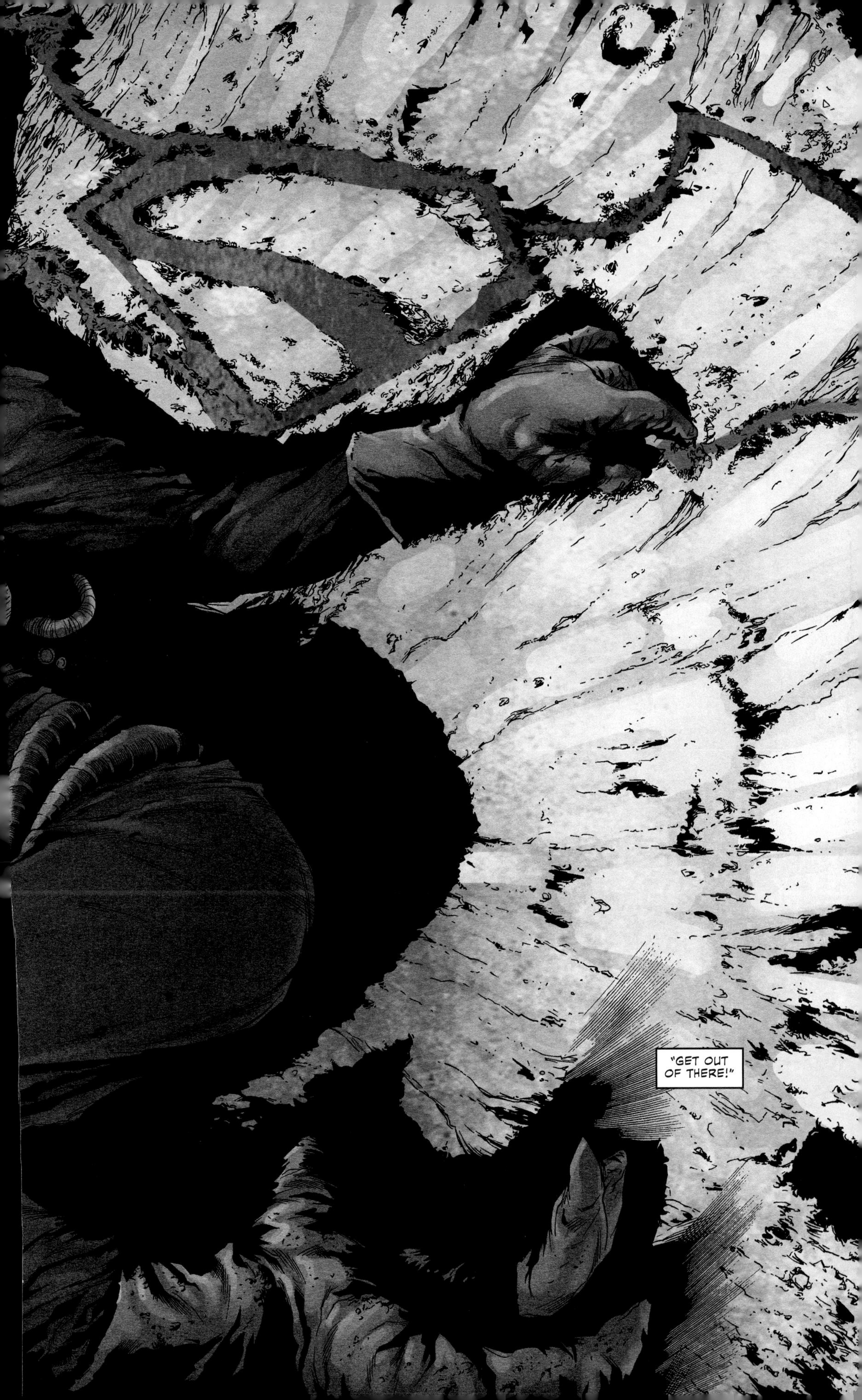
"GET OUT
OF THERE!"

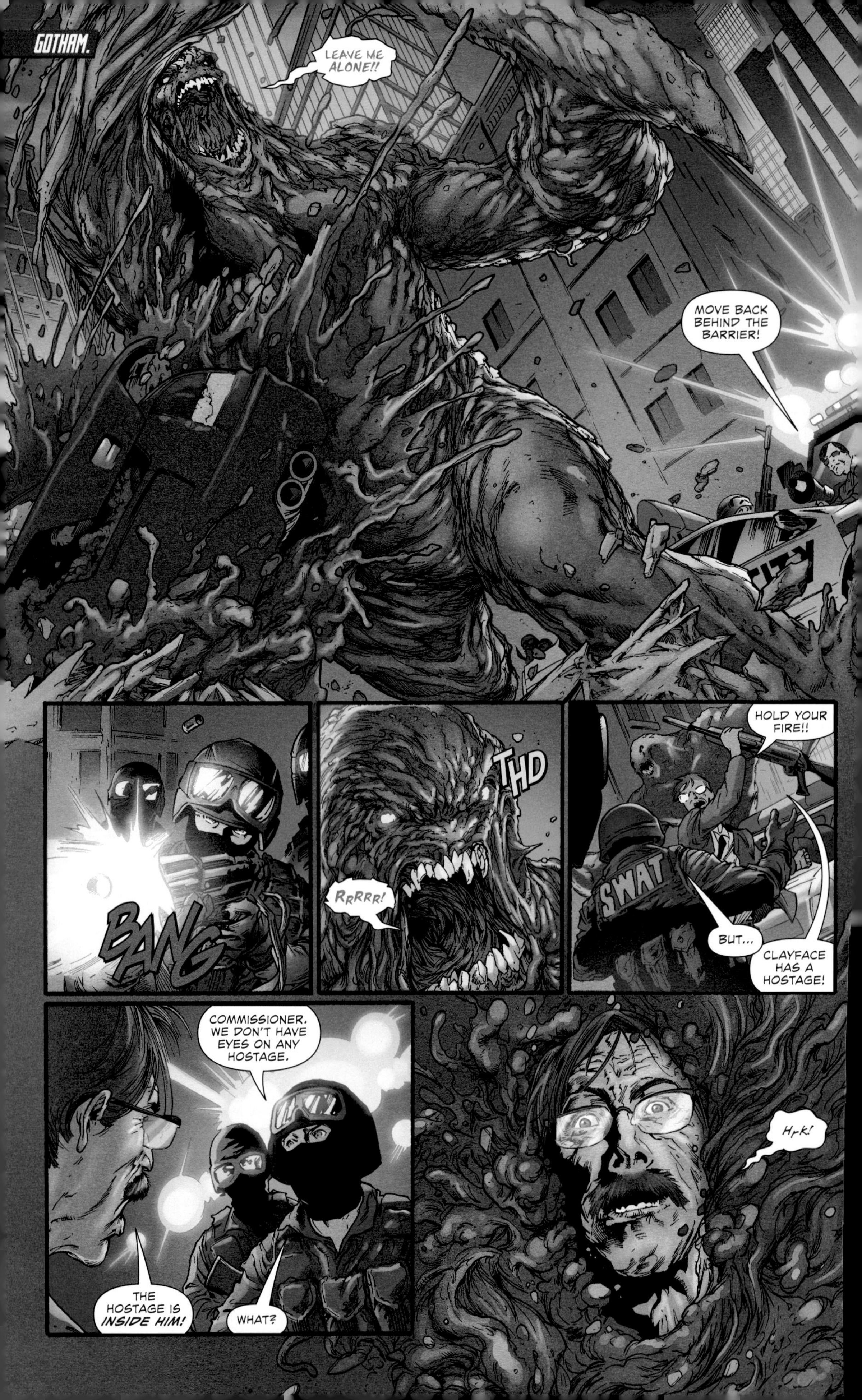
GOTHAM.
LEAVE ME ALONE!!
MOVE BACK BEHIND THE BARRIER!
BANG
THD
RRRRR!
HOLD YOUR FIRE!!
BUT...
CLAYFACE HAS A HOSTAGE!
COMMISSIONER. WE DON'T HAVE EYES ON ANY HOSTAGE.
THE HOSTAGE IS INSIDE HIM!
WHAT?
Hrk!

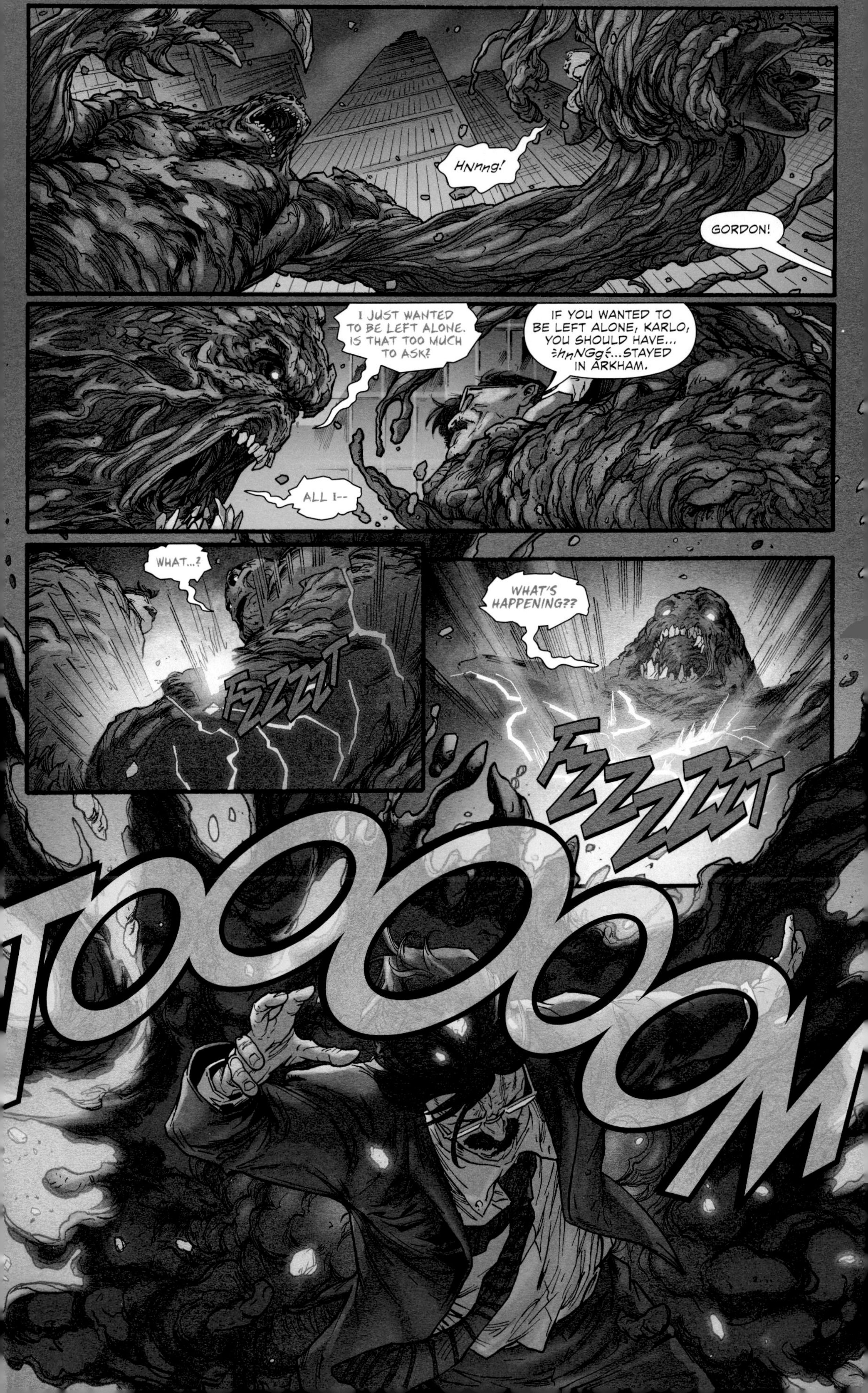
Hnnng!
GORDON!
I JUST WANTED TO BE LEFT ALONE. IS THAT TOO MUCH TO ASK?
IF YOU WANTED TO BE LEFT ALONE, KARLO, YOU SHOULD HAVE... hnNGg...STAYED IN ARKHAM.
ALL I--
WHAT...?
FZZZZT
WHAT'S HAPPENING??
FZZZZZT
TOOOOOOM

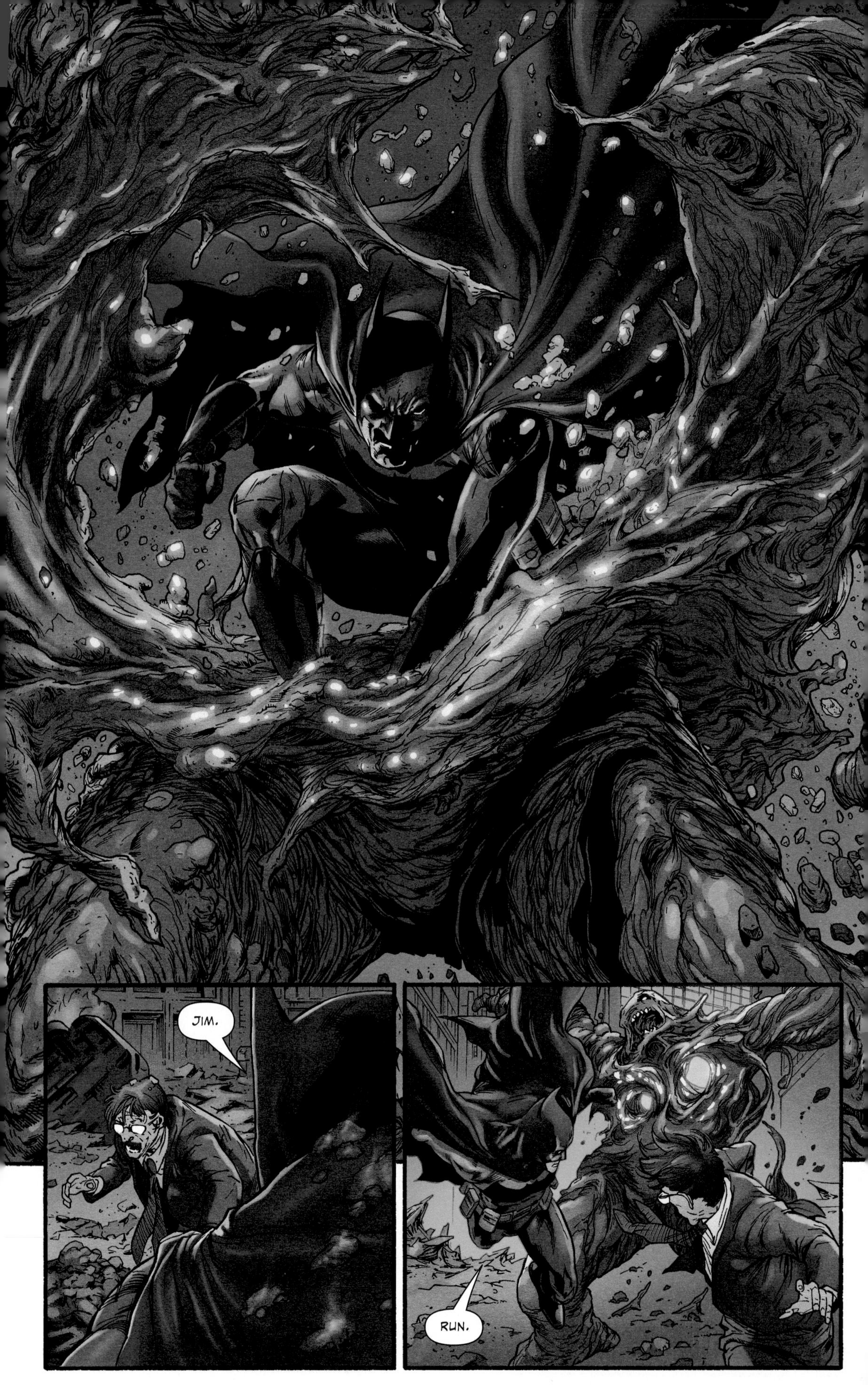
JIM.
RUN.

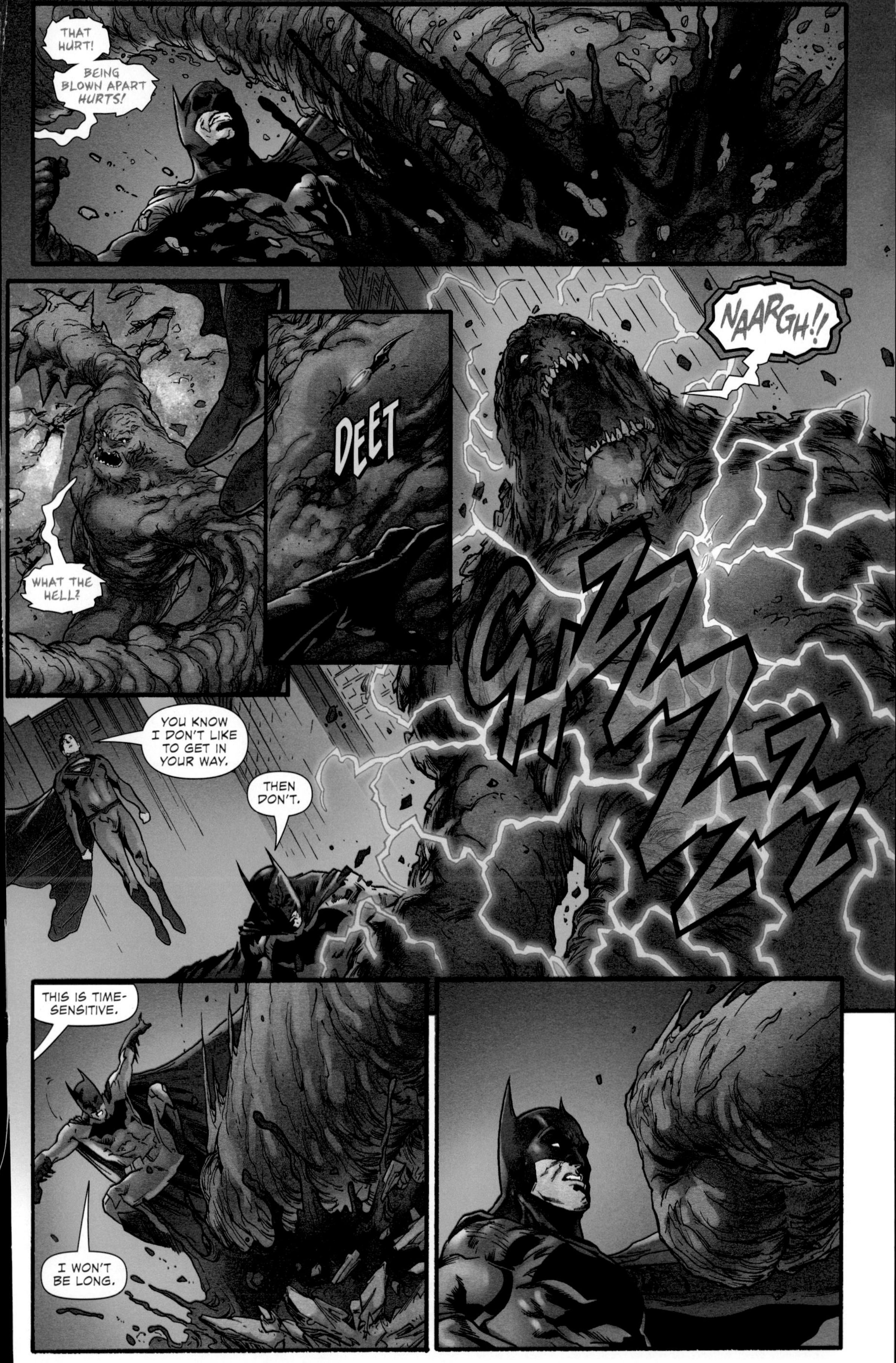
THAT HURT!
BEING BLOWN APART HURTS!
WHAT THE HELL?
DEET
NAARGH!!
YOU KNOW I DON'T LIKE TO GET IN YOUR WAY.
THEN DON'T.
THIS IS TIME-SENSITIVE.
I WON'T BE LONG.

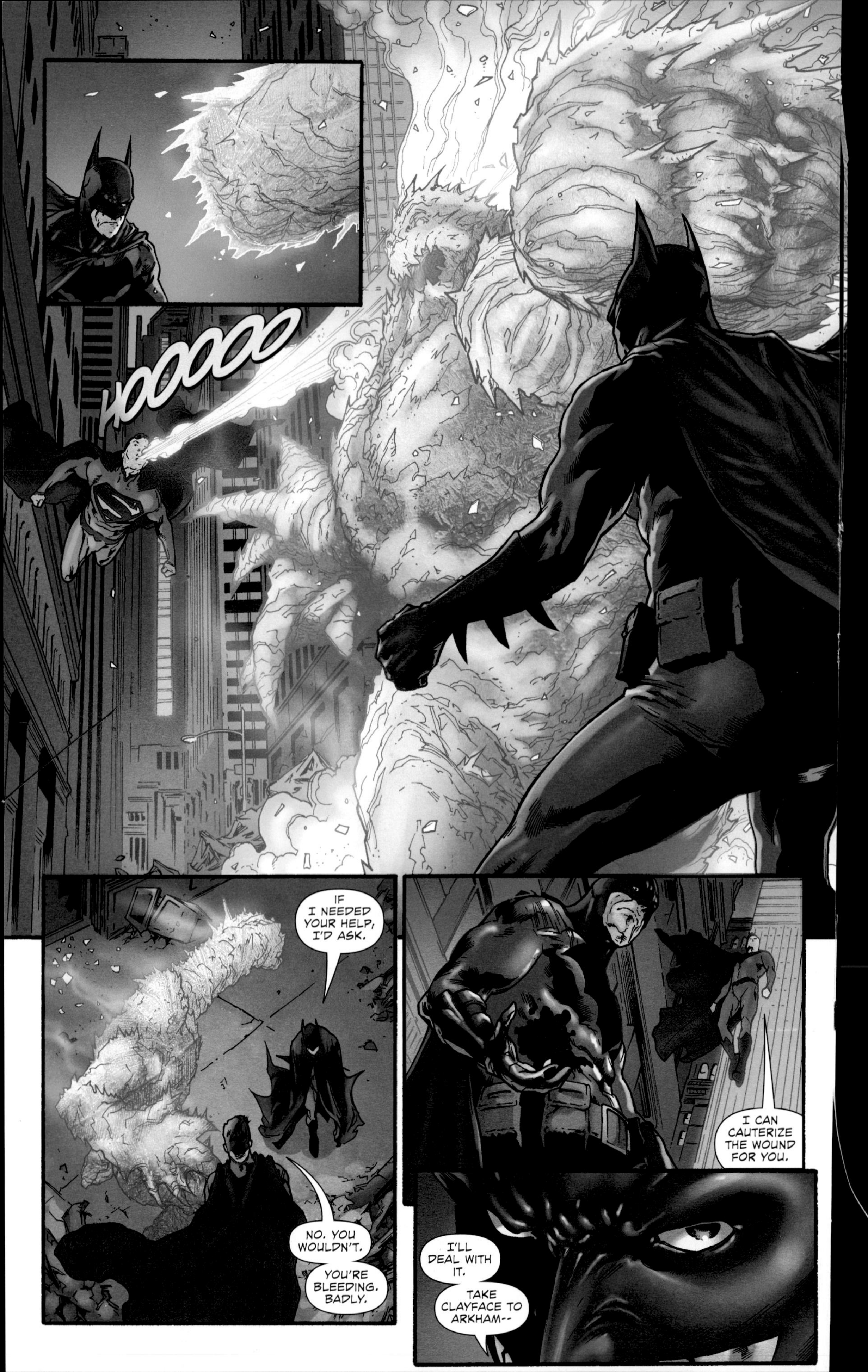
HOOOOOO
IF I NEEDED YOUR HELP, I'D ASK.
NO. YOU WOULDN'T.
YOU'RE BLEEDING. BADLY.
I CAN CAUTERIZE THE WOUND FOR YOU.
I'LL DEAL WITH IT.
TAKE CLAYFACE TO ARKHAM--

"--AND MEET ME AT THE CAVE."

MASTER WAYNE.

HE'S HERE, SIR.

YOU STOPPED FOR TEA?

I DIDN'T EVEN SEE ALFRED GIVE IT TO ME.

IT'S HIS SUPERPOWER.

I DELIVERED CLAYFACE. THE ARKHAM STAFF WERE VERY GRATEFUL.

I'D PREFER THEY WERE COMPETENT.

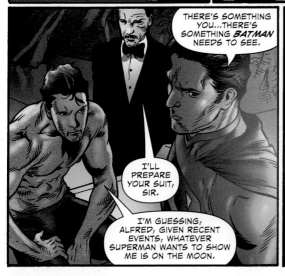

THERE'S SOMETHING YOU...THERE'S SOMETHING *BATMAN* NEEDS TO SEE.

I'LL PREPARE YOUR SUIT, SIR.

I'M GUESSING, ALFRED, GIVEN RECENT EVENTS, WHATEVER SUPERMAN WANTS TO SHOW ME IS ON THE MOON.

I'LL PREPARE YOUR *OTHER* SUIT, SIR.

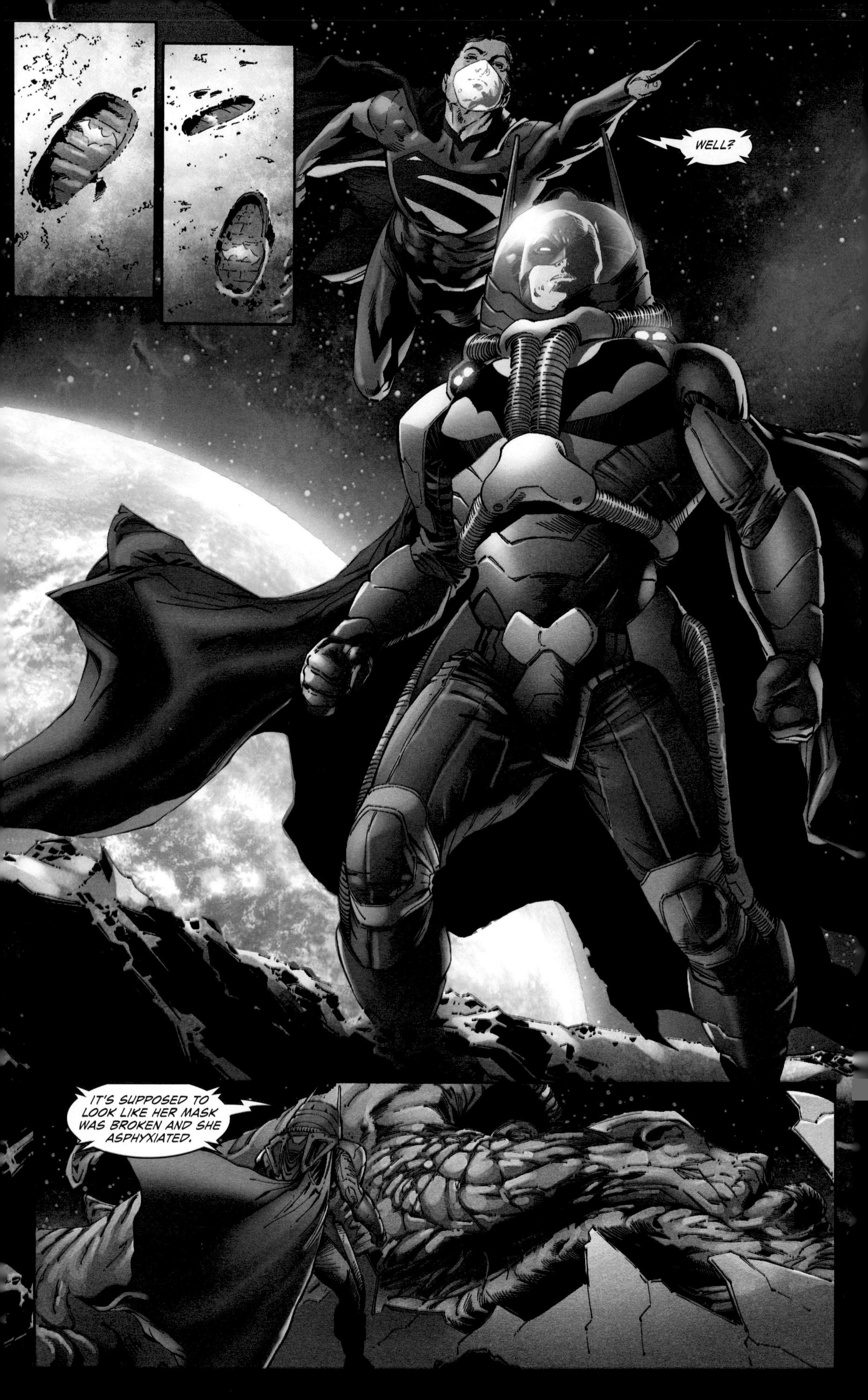
WELL?
IT'S SUPPOSED TO LOOK LIKE HER MASK WAS BROKEN AND SHE ASPHYXIATED.

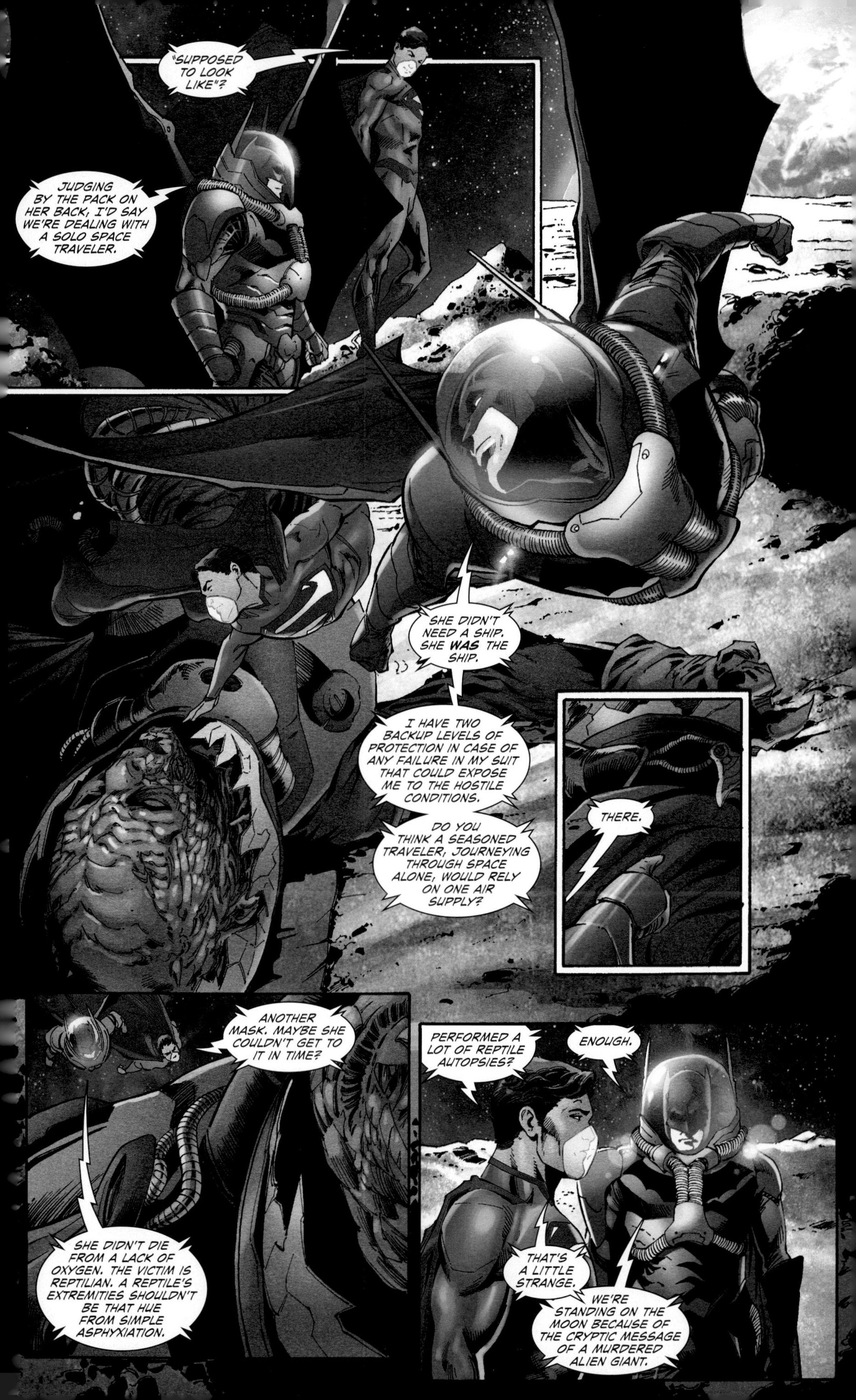
"SUPPOSED TO LOOK LIKE"?
JUDGING BY THE PACK ON HER BACK, I'D SAY WE'RE DEALING WITH A SOLO SPACE TRAVELER.
SHE DIDN'T NEED A SHIP. SHE WAS THE SHIP.
I HAVE TWO BACKUP LEVELS OF PROTECTION IN CASE OF ANY FAILURE IN MY SUIT THAT COULD EXPOSE ME TO THE HOSTILE CONDITIONS.
DO YOU THINK A SEASONED TRAVELER, JOURNEYING THROUGH SPACE ALONE, WOULD RELY ON ONE AIR SUPPLY?
THERE.
ANOTHER MASK. MAYBE SHE COULDN'T GET TO IT IN TIME?
SHE DIDN'T DIE FROM A LACK OF OXYGEN. THE VICTIM IS REPTILIAN. A REPTILE'S EXTREMITIES SHOULDN'T BE THAT HUE FROM SIMPLE ASPHYXIATION.
PERFORMED A LOT OF REPTILE AUTOPSIES?
ENOUGH.
THAT'S A LITTLE STRANGE.
WE'RE STANDING ON THE MOON BECAUSE OF THE CRYPTIC MESSAGE OF A MURDERED ALIEN GIANT.

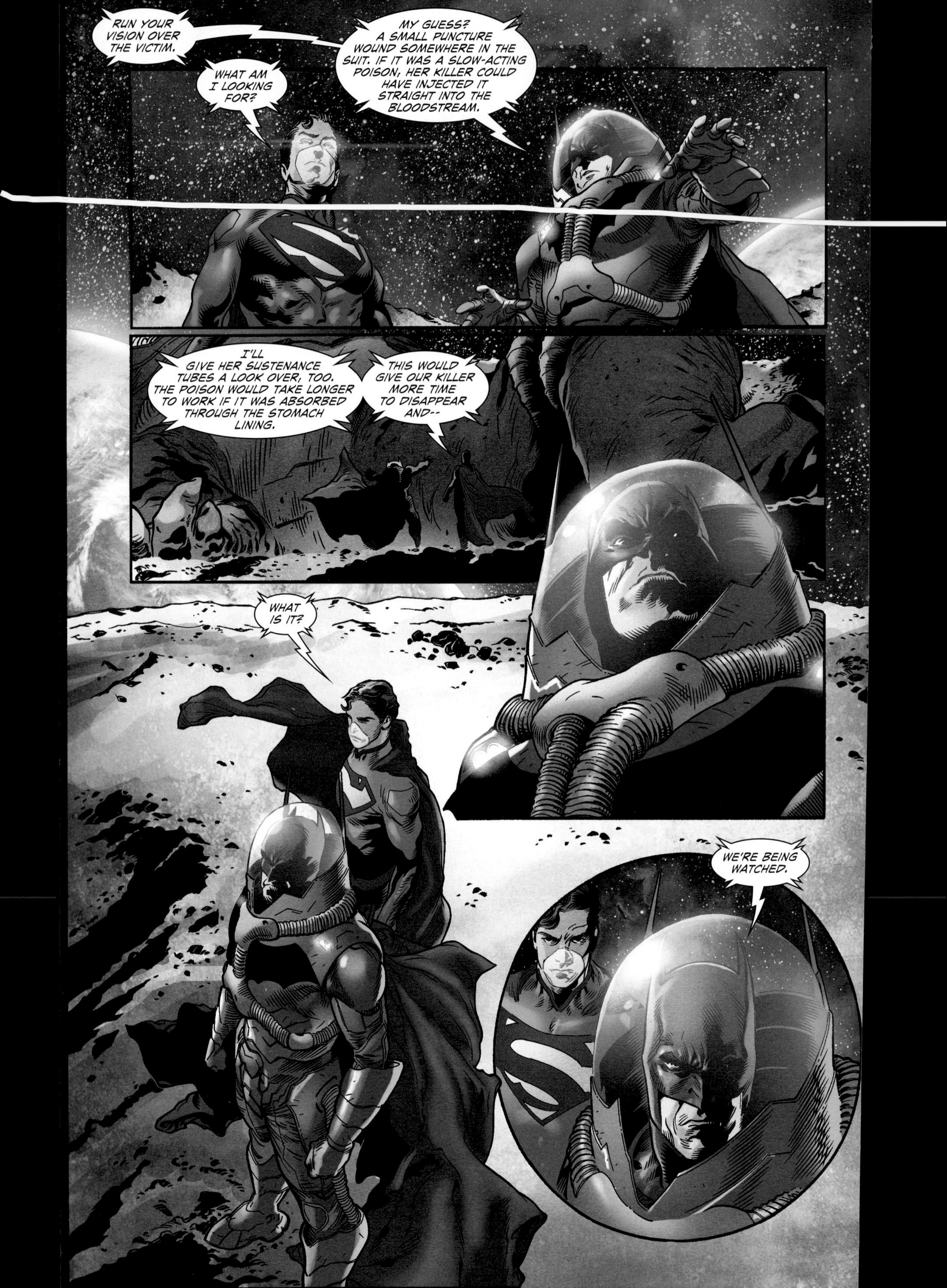
RUN YOUR VISION OVER THE VICTIM.
WHAT AM I LOOKING FOR?
MY GUESS? A SMALL PUNCTURE WOUND SOMEWHERE IN THE SUIT. IF IT WAS A SLOW-ACTING POISON, HER KILLER COULD HAVE INJECTED IT STRAIGHT INTO THE BLOODSTREAM.
I'LL GIVE HER SUSTENANCE TUBES A LOOK OVER, TOO. THE POISON WOULD TAKE LONGER TO WORK IF IT WAS ABSORBED THROUGH THE STOMACH LINING.
THIS WOULD GIVE OUR KILLER MORE TIME TO DISAPPEAR AND--
WHAT IS IT?
WE'RE BEING WATCHED.

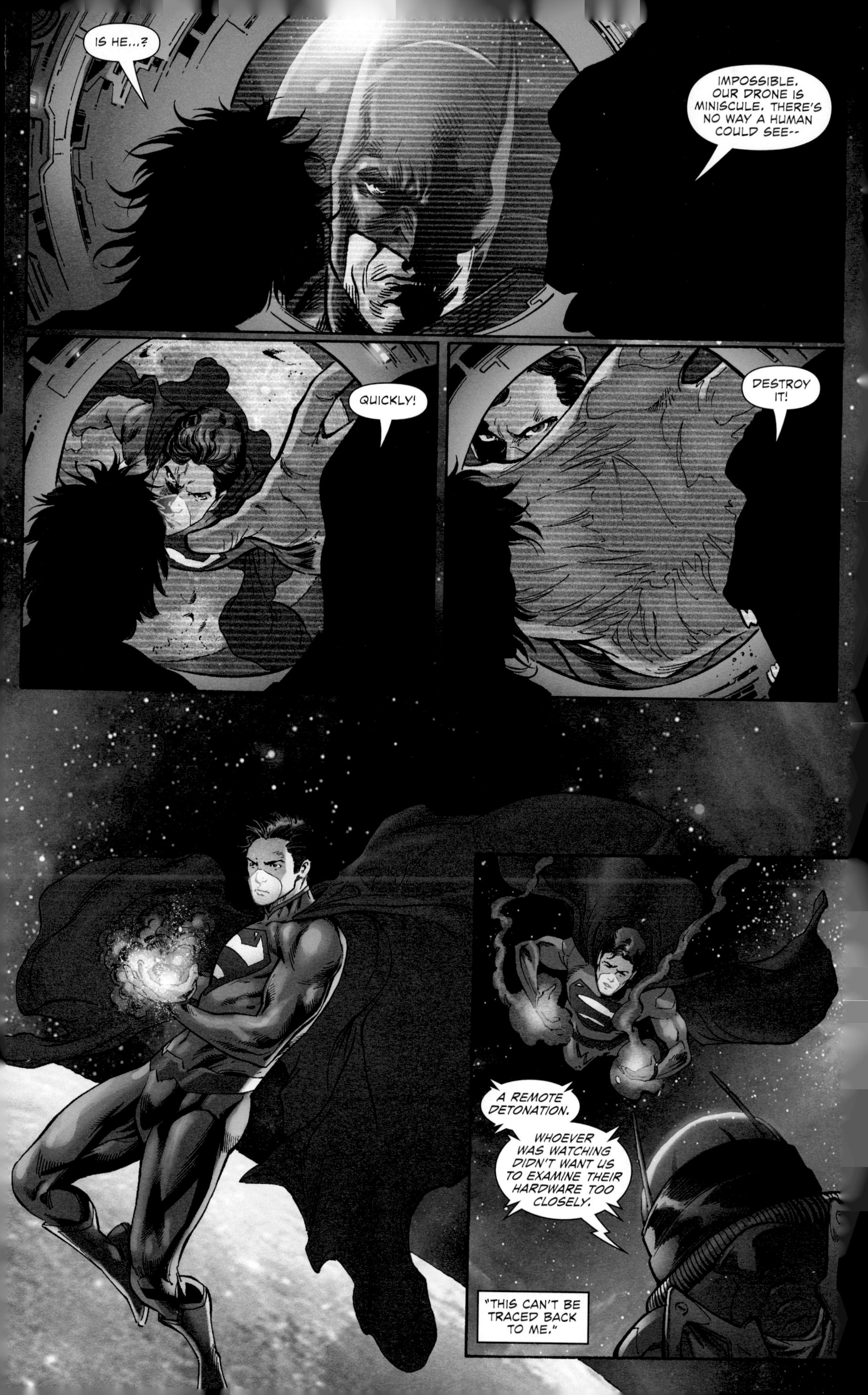
IS HE...?
IMPOSSIBLE. OUR DRONE IS MINISCULE. THERE'S NO WAY A HUMAN COULD SEE--
QUICKLY!
DESTROY IT!
A REMOTE DETONATION.
WHOEVER WAS WATCHING DIDN'T WANT US TO EXAMINE THEIR HARDWARE TOO CLOSELY.
"THIS CAN'T BE TRACED BACK TO ME."

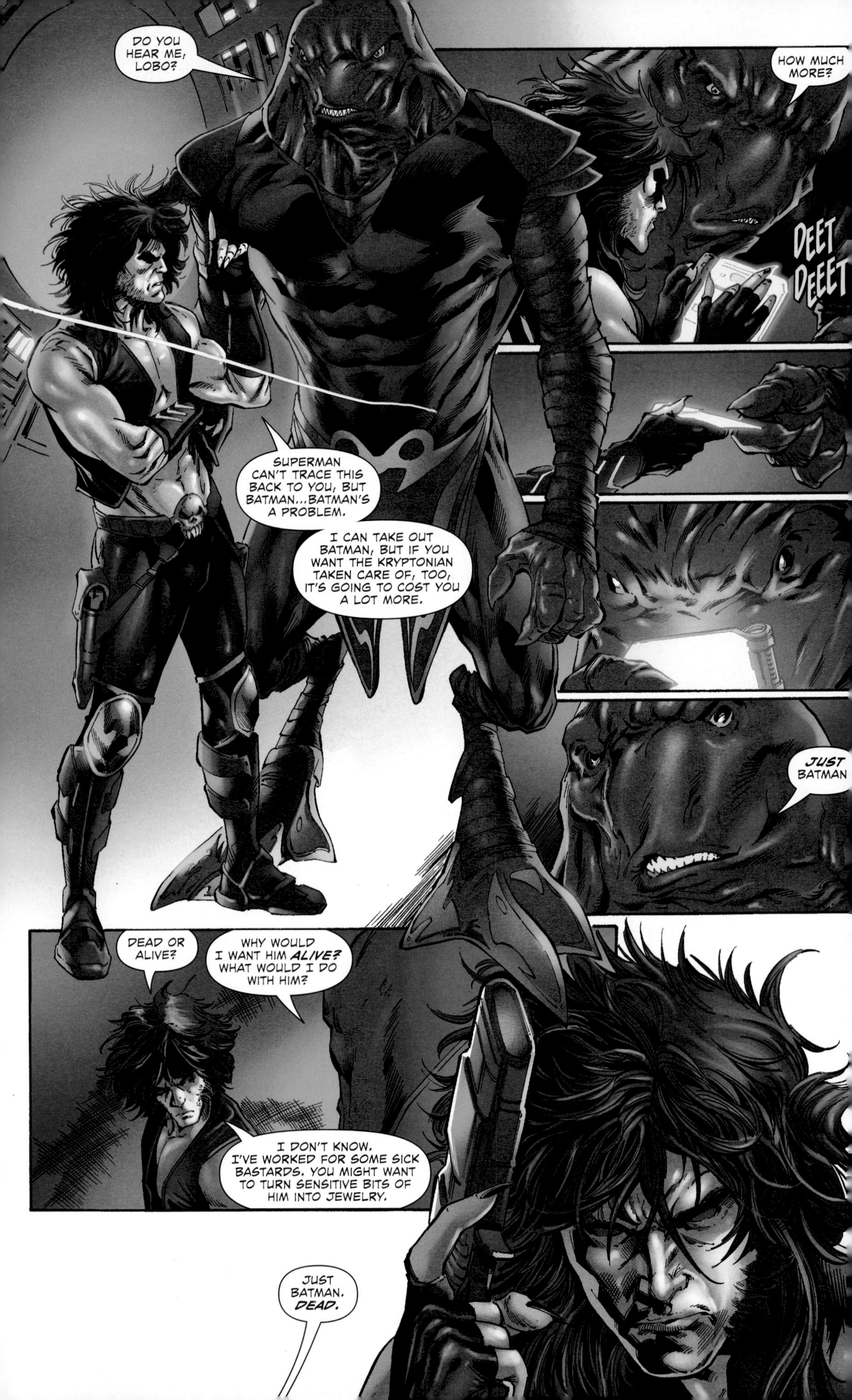
DO YOU HEAR ME, LOBO?
HOW MUCH MORE?
DEET DEEET
SUPERMAN CAN'T TRACE THIS BACK TO YOU, BUT BATMAN...BATMAN'S A PROBLEM.
I CAN TAKE OUT BATMAN, BUT IF YOU WANT THE KRYPTONIAN TAKEN CARE OF, TOO, IT'S GOING TO COST YOU A LOT MORE.
JUST BATMAN
DEAD OR ALIVE?
WHY WOULD I WANT HIM ALIVE? WHAT WOULD I DO WITH HIM?
I DON'T KNOW. I'VE WORKED FOR SOME SICK BASTARDS. YOU MIGHT WANT TO TURN SENSITIVE BITS OF HIM INTO JEWELRY.
JUST BATMAN. DEAD.

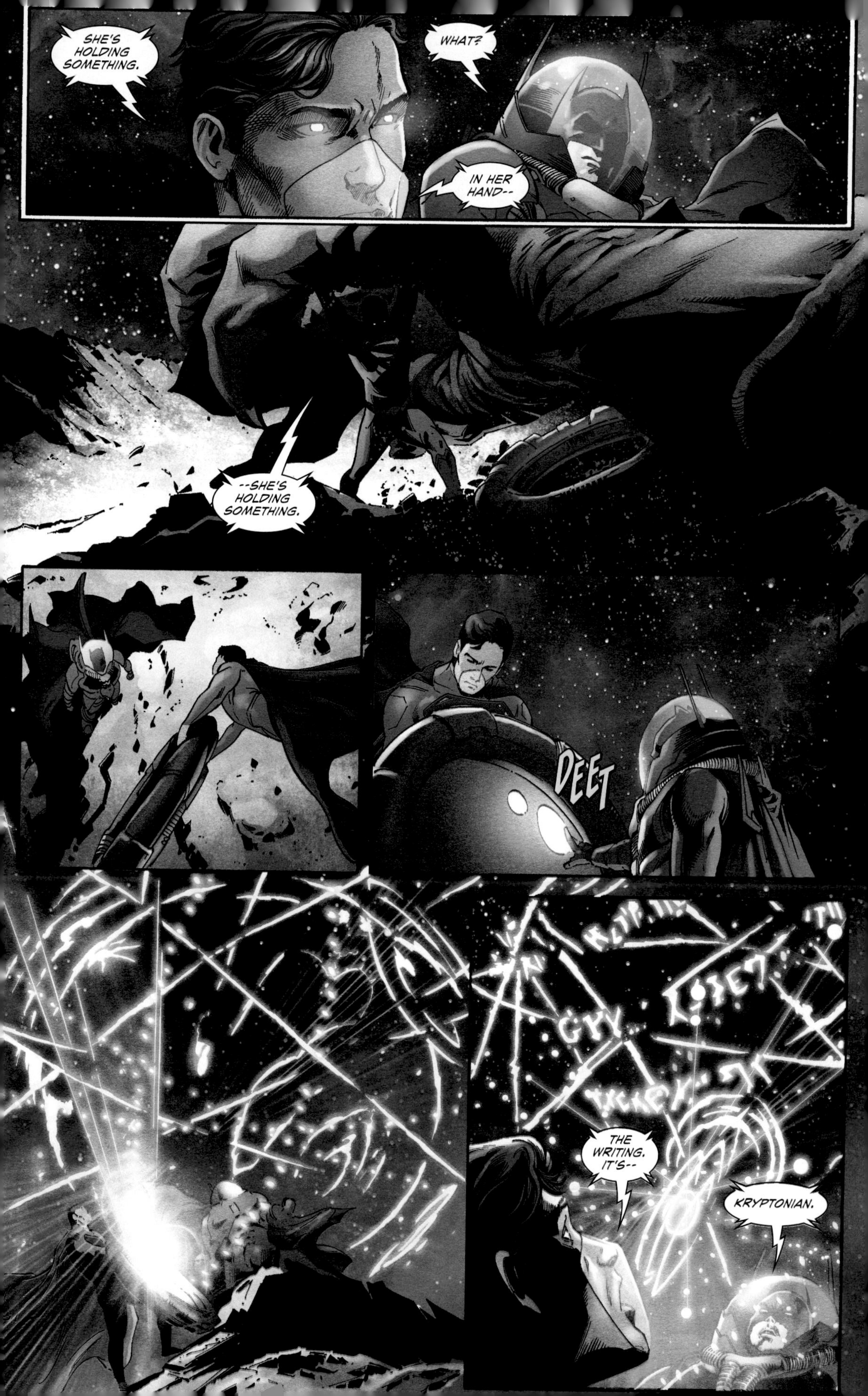
SHE'S HOLDING SOMETHING.
WHAT?
IN HER HAND--
--SHE'S HOLDING SOMETHING.
DEET
THE WRITING. IT'S--
KRYPTONIAN.

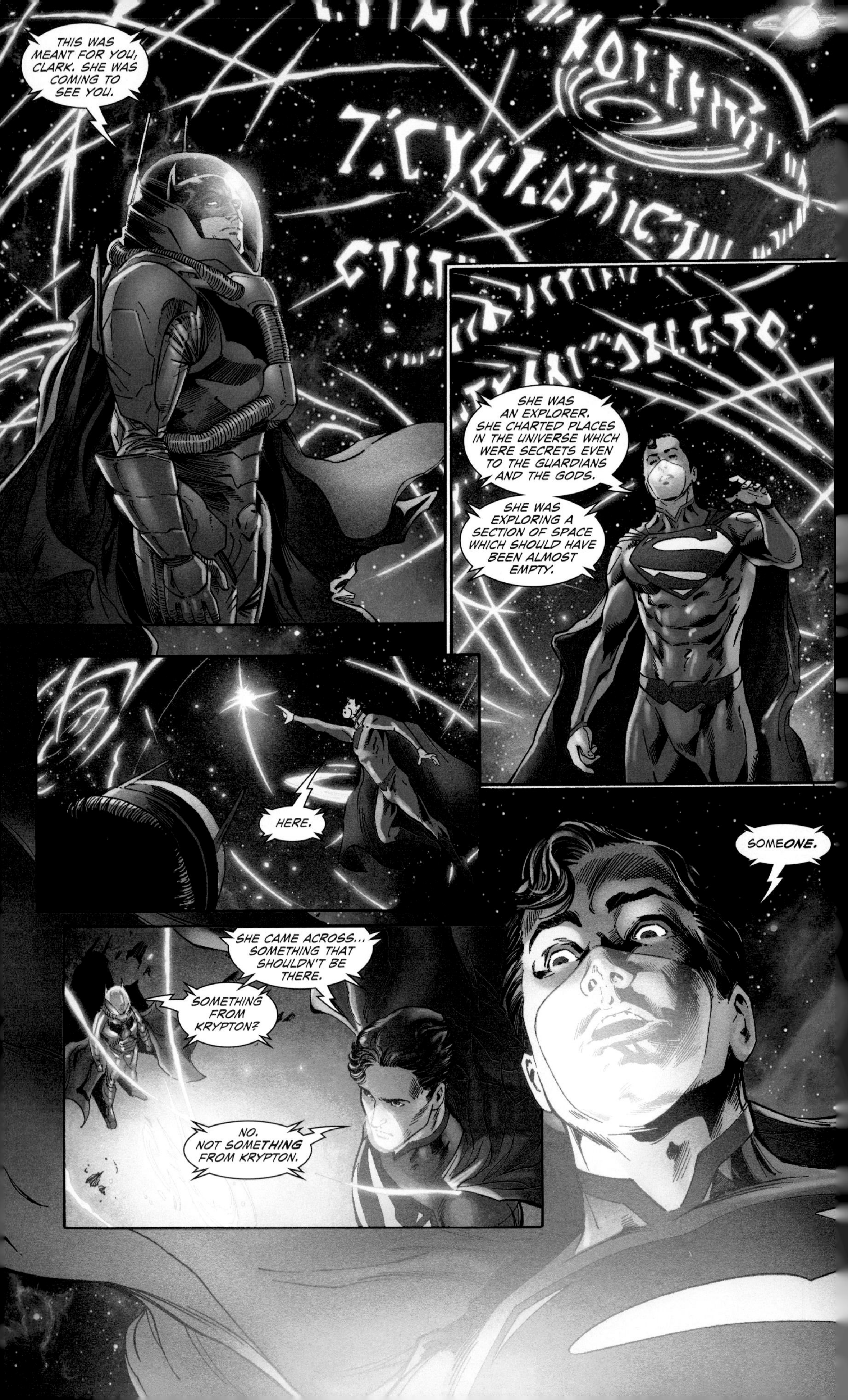
THIS WAS MEANT FOR YOU, CLARK. SHE WAS COMING TO SEE YOU.
SHE WAS AN EXPLORER. SHE CHARTED PLACES IN THE UNIVERSE WHICH WERE SECRETS EVEN TO THE GUARDIANS AND THE GODS.
SHE WAS EXPLORING A SECTION OF SPACE WHICH SHOULD HAVE BEEN ALMOST EMPTY.
HERE.
SHE CAME ACROSS... SOMETHING THAT SHOULDN'T BE THERE.
SOMETHING FROM KRYPTON?
NO. NOT SOMETHING FROM KRYPTON.
SOMEONE.

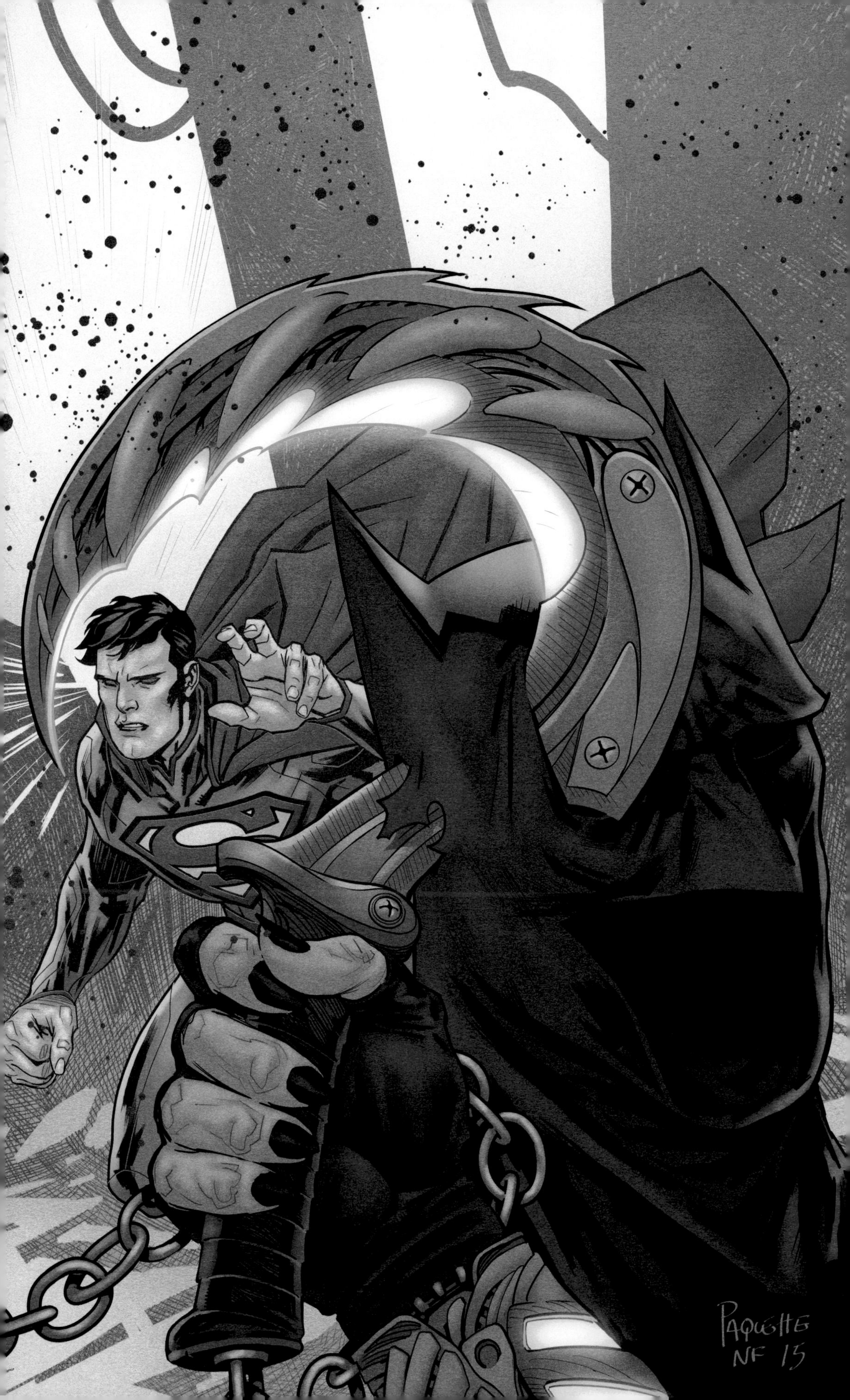
PAQUETTE
NF 15

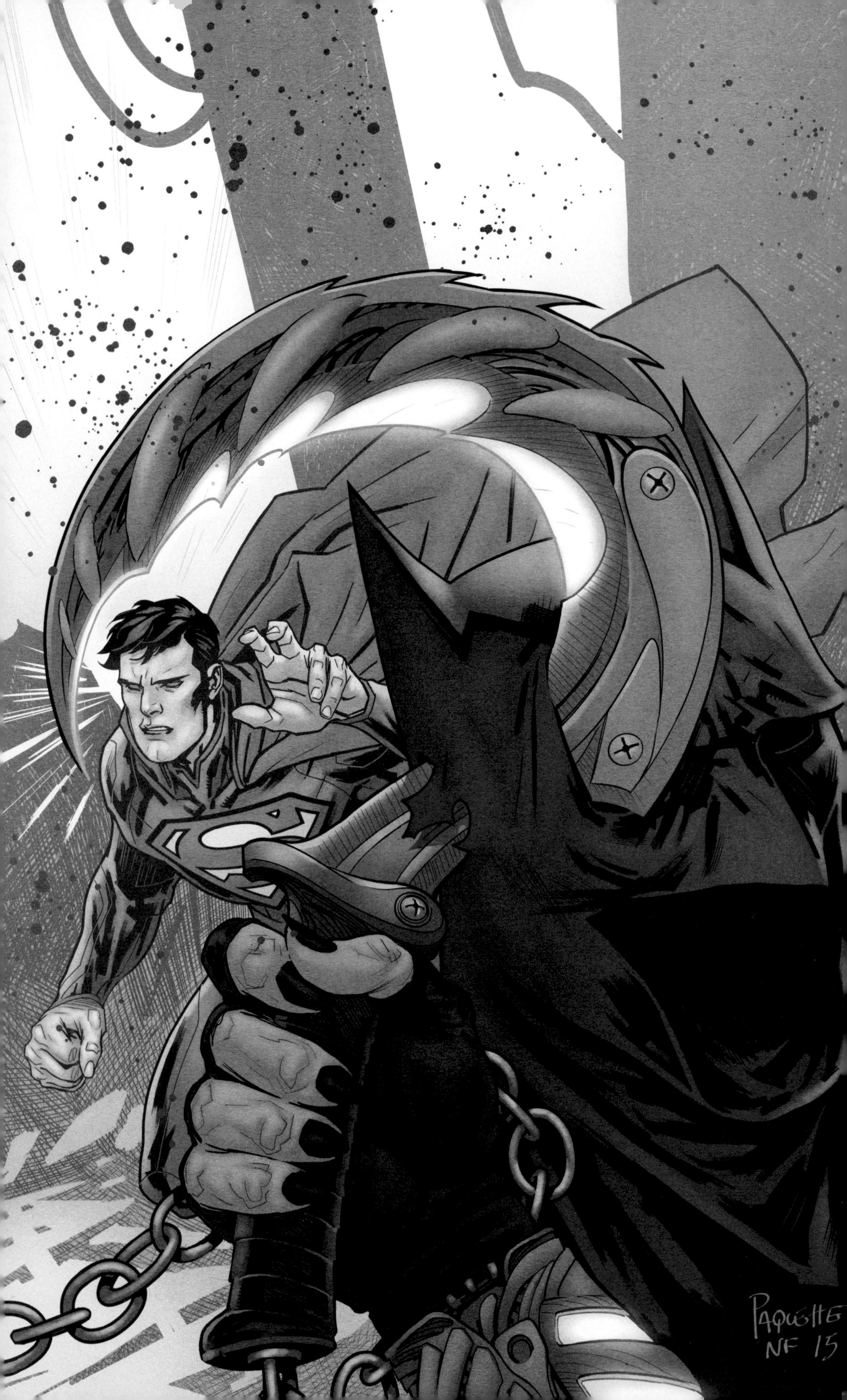

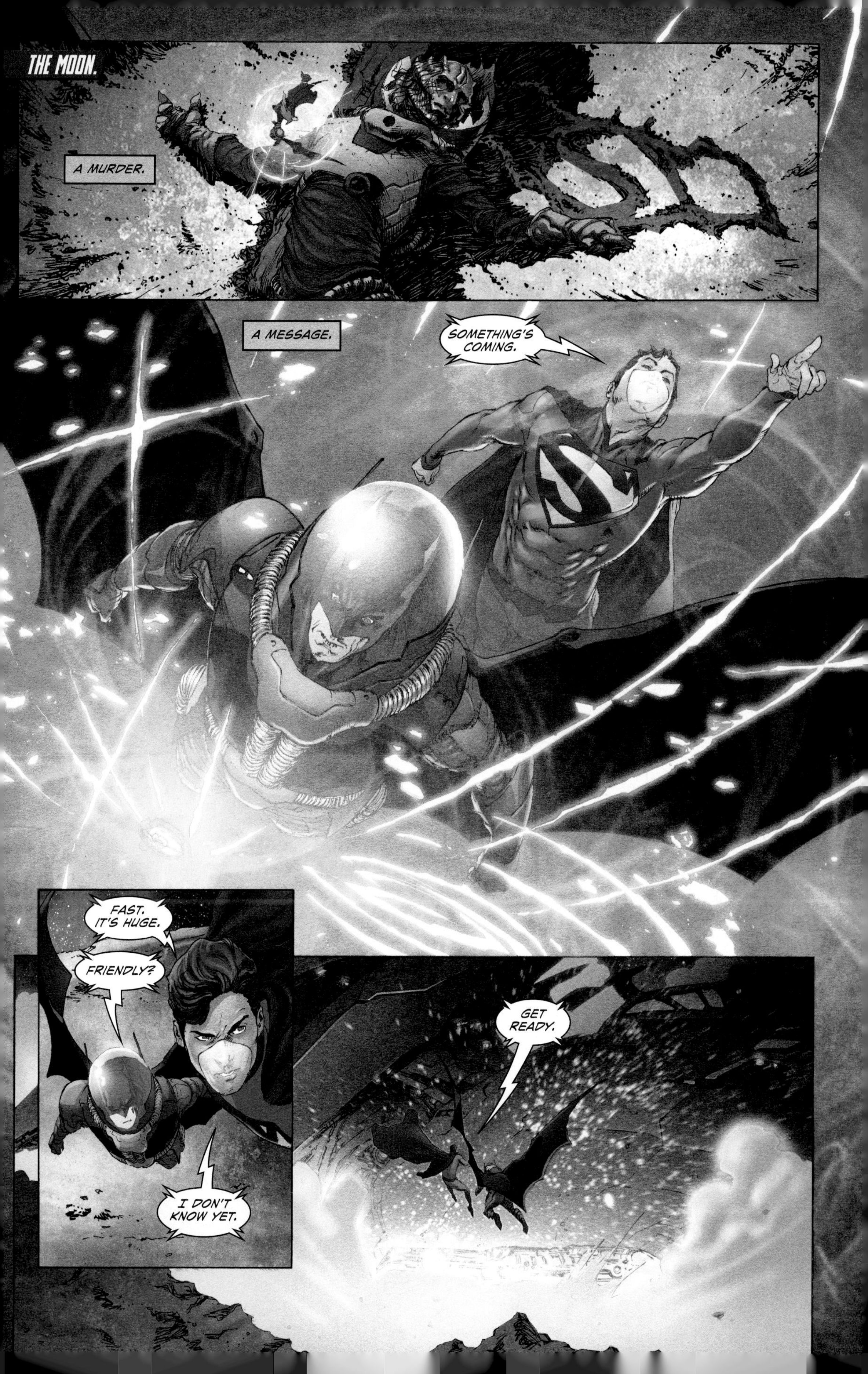
THE MOON.
A MURDER.
A MESSAGE.
SOMETHING'S COMING.
FAST. IT'S HUGE.
FRIENDLY?
I DON'T KNOW YET.
GET READY.

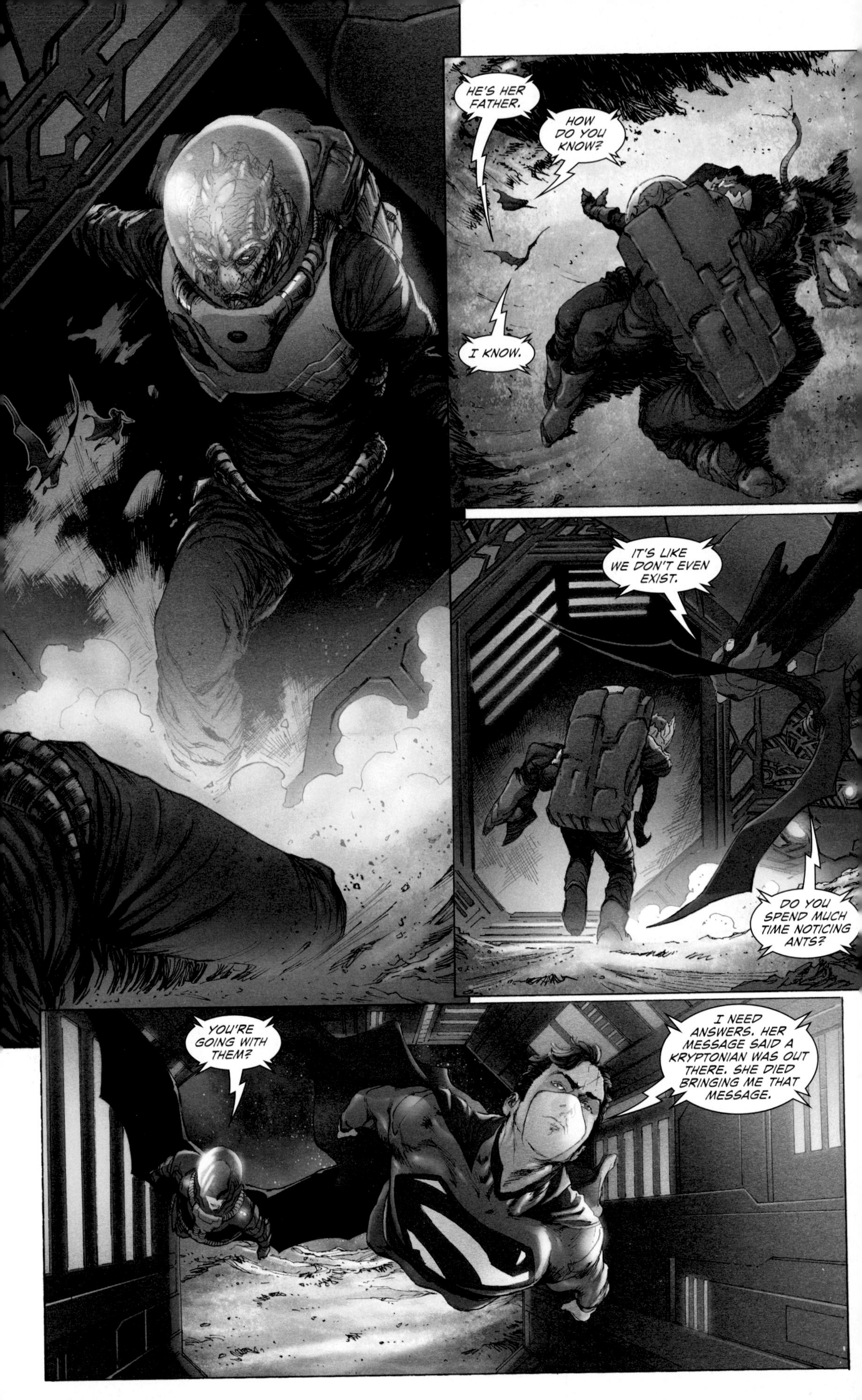
HE'S HER FATHER.
HOW DO YOU KNOW?
I KNOW.
IT'S LIKE WE DON'T EVEN EXIST.
DO YOU SPEND MUCH TIME NOTICING ANTS?
YOU'RE GOING WITH THEM?
I NEED ANSWERS. HER MESSAGE SAID A KRYPTONIAN WAS OUT THERE. SHE DIED BRINGING ME THAT MESSAGE.

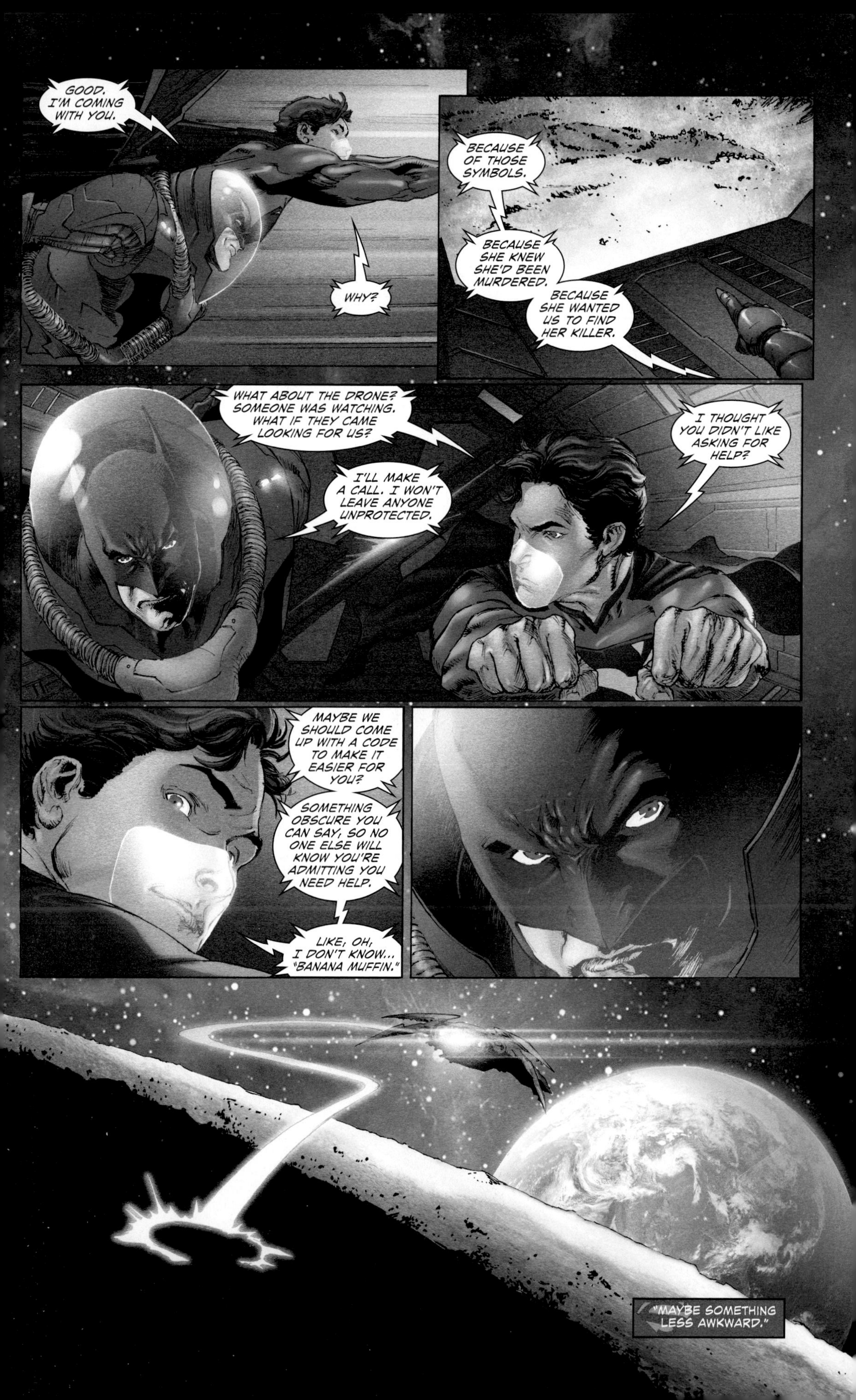
GOOD. I'M COMING WITH YOU.
WHY?
BECAUSE OF THOSE SYMBOLS.
BECAUSE SHE KNEW SHE'D BEEN MURDERED.
BECAUSE SHE WANTED US TO FIND HER KILLER.
WHAT ABOUT THE DRONE? SOMEONE WAS WATCHING. WHAT IF THEY CAME LOOKING FOR US?
I'LL MAKE A CALL. I WON'T LEAVE ANYONE UNPROTECTED.
I THOUGHT YOU DIDN'T LIKE ASKING FOR HELP?
MAYBE WE SHOULD COME UP WITH A CODE TO MAKE IT EASIER FOR YOU?
SOMETHING OBSCURE YOU CAN SAY, SO NO ONE ELSE WILL KNOW YOU'RE ADMITTING YOU NEED HELP.
LIKE, OH, I DON'T KNOW... "BANANA MUFFIN."
"MAYBE SOMETHING LESS AWKWARD."

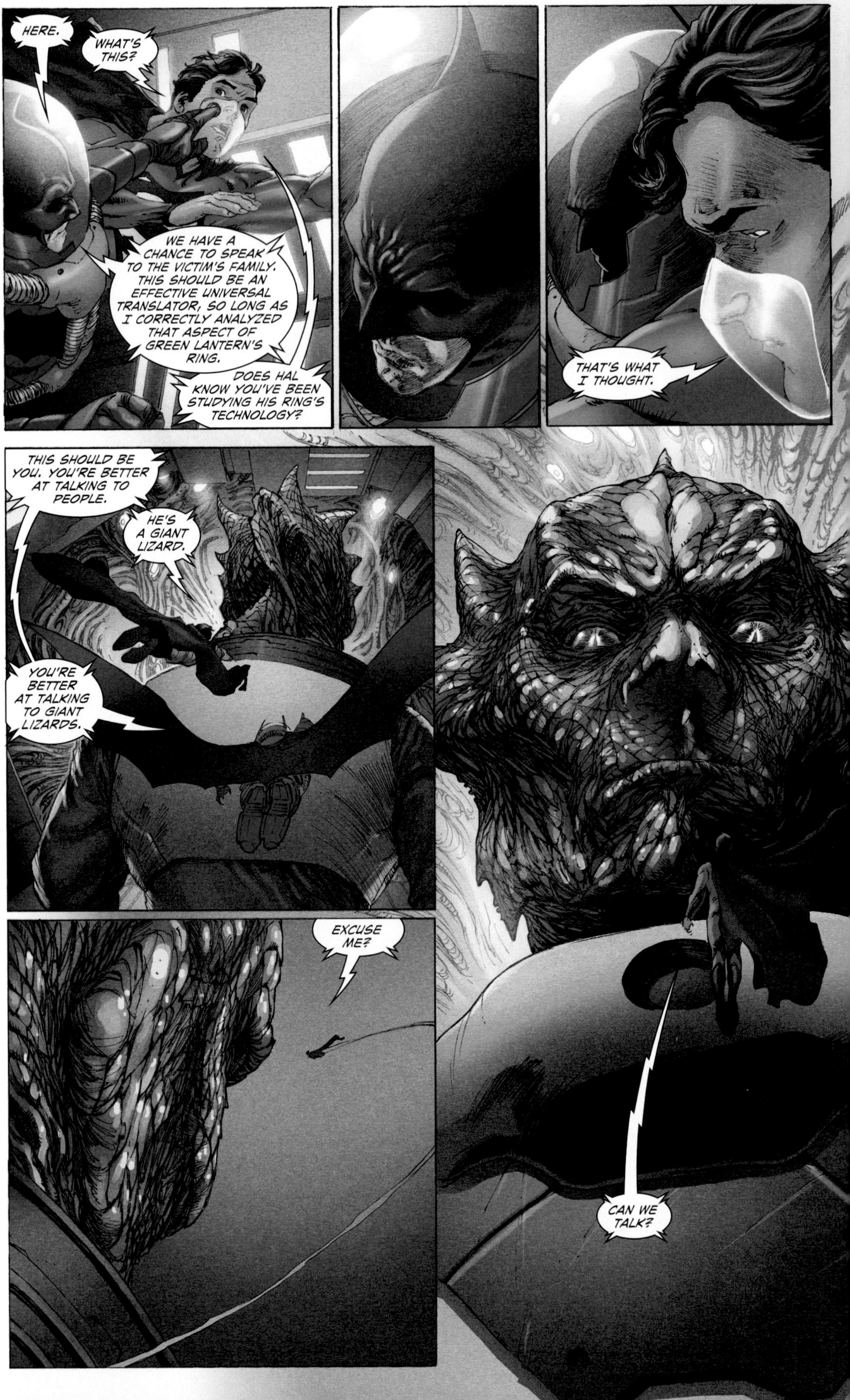
HERE.
WHAT'S THIS?
WE HAVE A CHANCE TO SPEAK TO THE VICTIM'S FAMILY. THIS SHOULD BE AN EFFECTIVE UNIVERSAL TRANSLATOR, SO LONG AS I CORRECTLY ANALYZED THAT ASPECT OF GREEN LANTERN'S RING.
DOES HAL KNOW YOU'VE BEEN STUDYING HIS RING'S TECHNOLOGY?
THAT'S WHAT I THOUGHT.
THIS SHOULD BE YOU. YOU'RE BETTER AT TALKING TO PEOPLE.
HE'S A GIANT LIZARD.
YOU'RE BETTER AT TALKING TO GIANT LIZARDS.
EXCUSE ME?
CAN WE TALK?

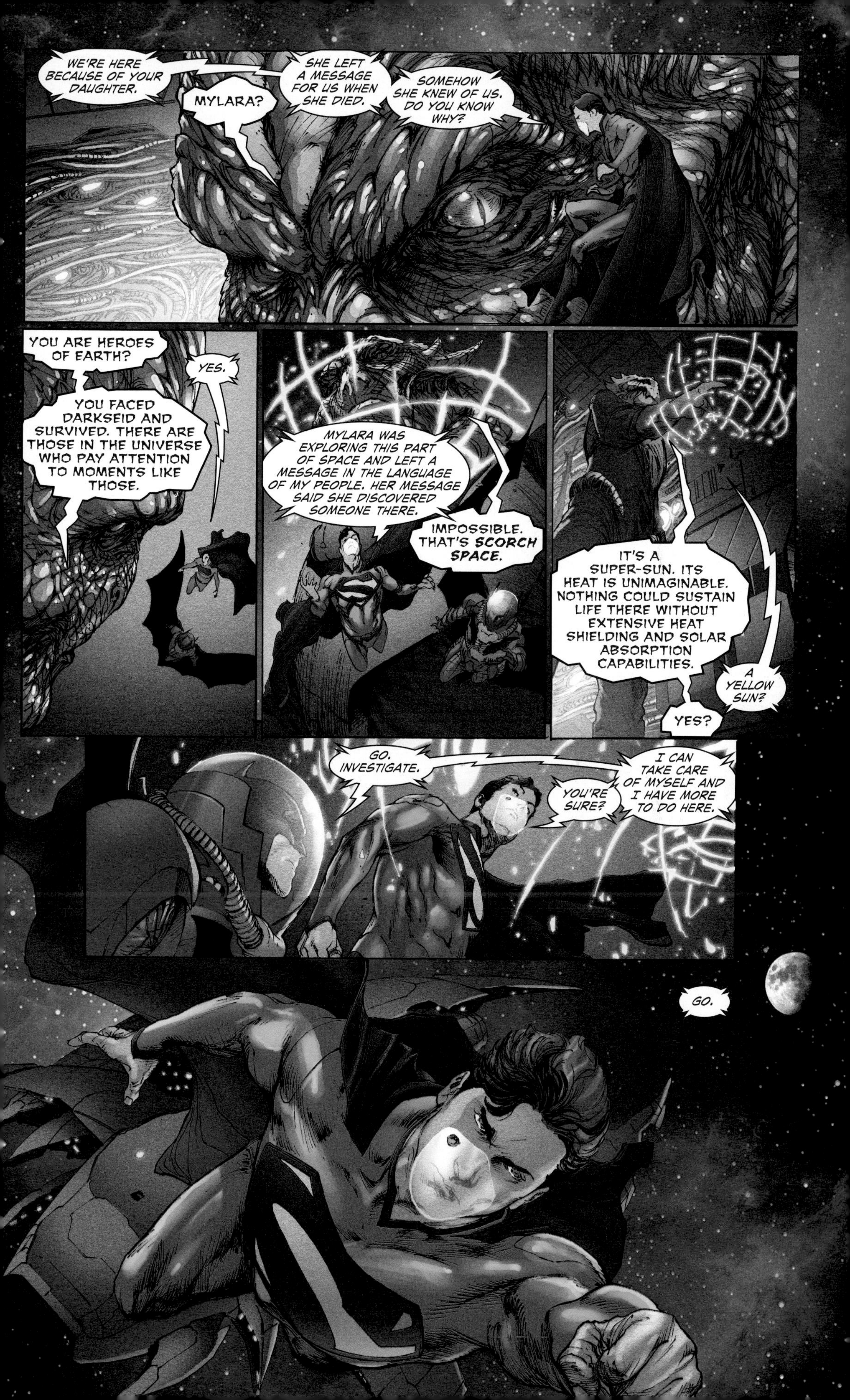
WE'RE HERE BECAUSE OF YOUR DAUGHTER.
MYLARA?
SHE LEFT A MESSAGE FOR US WHEN SHE DIED.
SOMEHOW SHE KNEW OF US. DO YOU KNOW WHY?
YOU ARE HEROES OF EARTH?
YES.
YOU FACED DARKSEID AND SURVIVED. THERE ARE THOSE IN THE UNIVERSE WHO PAY ATTENTION TO MOMENTS LIKE THOSE.
MYLARA WAS EXPLORING THIS PART OF SPACE AND LEFT A MESSAGE IN THE LANGUAGE OF MY PEOPLE. HER MESSAGE SAID SHE DISCOVERED SOMEONE THERE.
IMPOSSIBLE. THAT'S SCORCH SPACE.
IT'S A SUPER-SUN. ITS HEAT IS UNIMAGINABLE. NOTHING COULD SUSTAIN LIFE THERE WITHOUT EXTENSIVE HEAT SHIELDING AND SOLAR ABSORPTION CAPABILITIES.
A YELLOW SUN?
YES?
GO. INVESTIGATE.
YOU'RE SURE?
I CAN TAKE CARE OF MYSELF AND I HAVE MORE TO DO HERE.
GO.

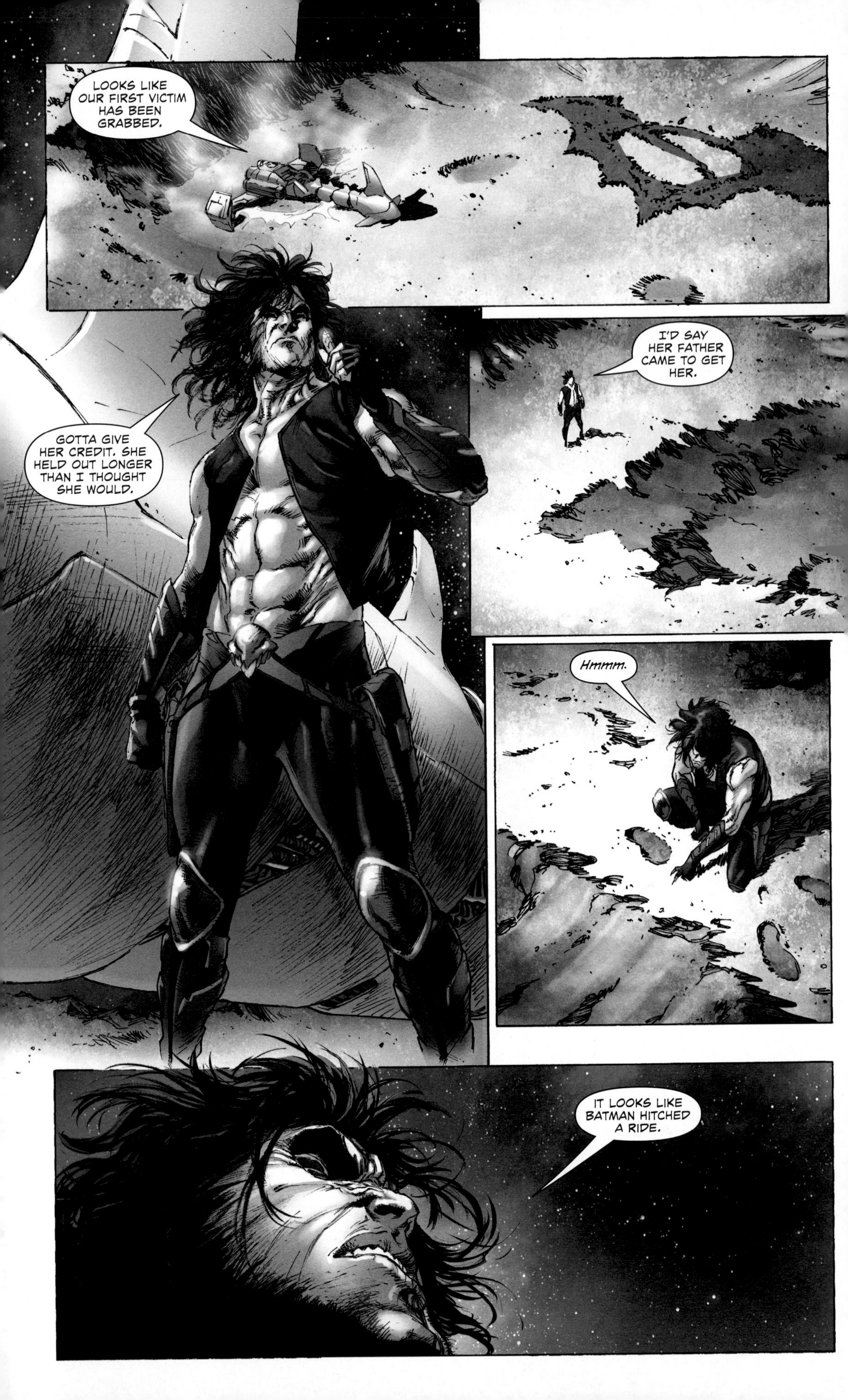
LOOKS LIKE OUR FIRST VICTIM HAS BEEN GRABBED.
GOTTA GIVE HER CREDIT. SHE HELD OUT LONGER THAN I THOUGHT SHE WOULD.
I'D SAY HER FATHER CAME TO GET HER.
Hmmm.
IT LOOKS LIKE BATMAN HITCHED A RIDE.

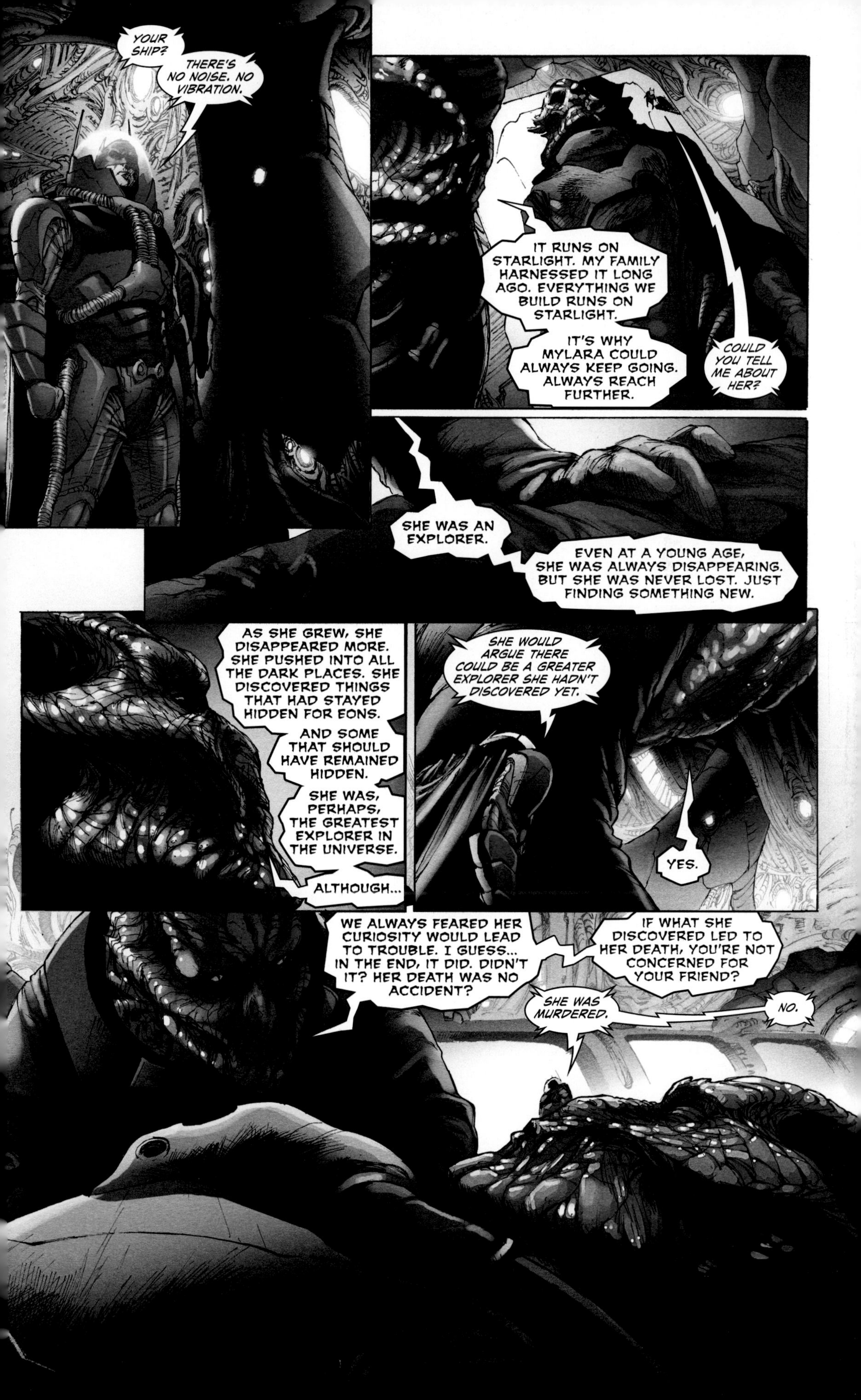
YOUR SHIP?
THERE'S NO NOISE. NO VIBRATION.
IT RUNS ON STARLIGHT. MY FAMILY HARNESSED IT LONG AGO. EVERYTHING WE BUILD RUNS ON STARLIGHT.
IT'S WHY MYLARA COULD ALWAYS KEEP GOING. ALWAYS REACH FURTHER.
COULD YOU TELL ME ABOUT HER?
SHE WAS AN EXPLORER.
EVEN AT A YOUNG AGE, SHE WAS ALWAYS DISAPPEARING. BUT SHE WAS NEVER LOST. JUST FINDING SOMETHING NEW.
AS SHE GREW, SHE DISAPPEARED MORE. SHE PUSHED INTO ALL THE DARK PLACES. SHE DISCOVERED THINGS THAT HAD STAYED HIDDEN FOR EONS.
AND SOME THAT SHOULD HAVE REMAINED HIDDEN.
SHE WAS, PERHAPS, THE GREATEST EXPLORER IN THE UNIVERSE.
ALTHOUGH...
SHE WOULD ARGUE THERE COULD BE A GREATER EXPLORER SHE HADN'T DISCOVERED YET.
YES.
WE ALWAYS FEARED HER CURIOSITY WOULD LEAD TO TROUBLE. I GUESS... IN THE END, IT DID. DIDN'T IT? HER DEATH WAS NO ACCIDENT?
SHE WAS MURDERED.
IF WHAT SHE DISCOVERED LED TO HER DEATH, YOU'RE NOT CONCERNED FOR YOUR FRIEND?
NO.

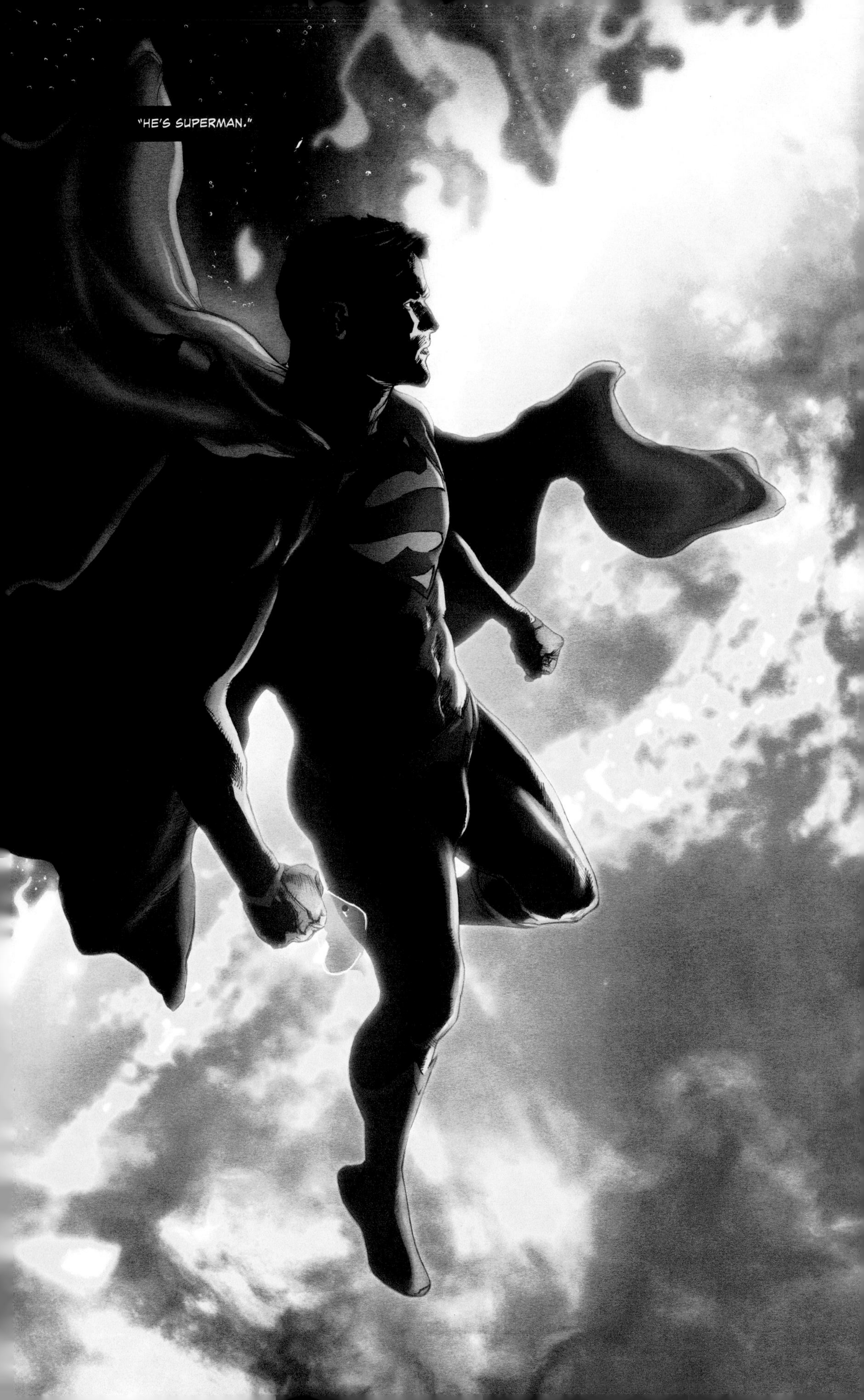
"HE'S SUPERMAN."

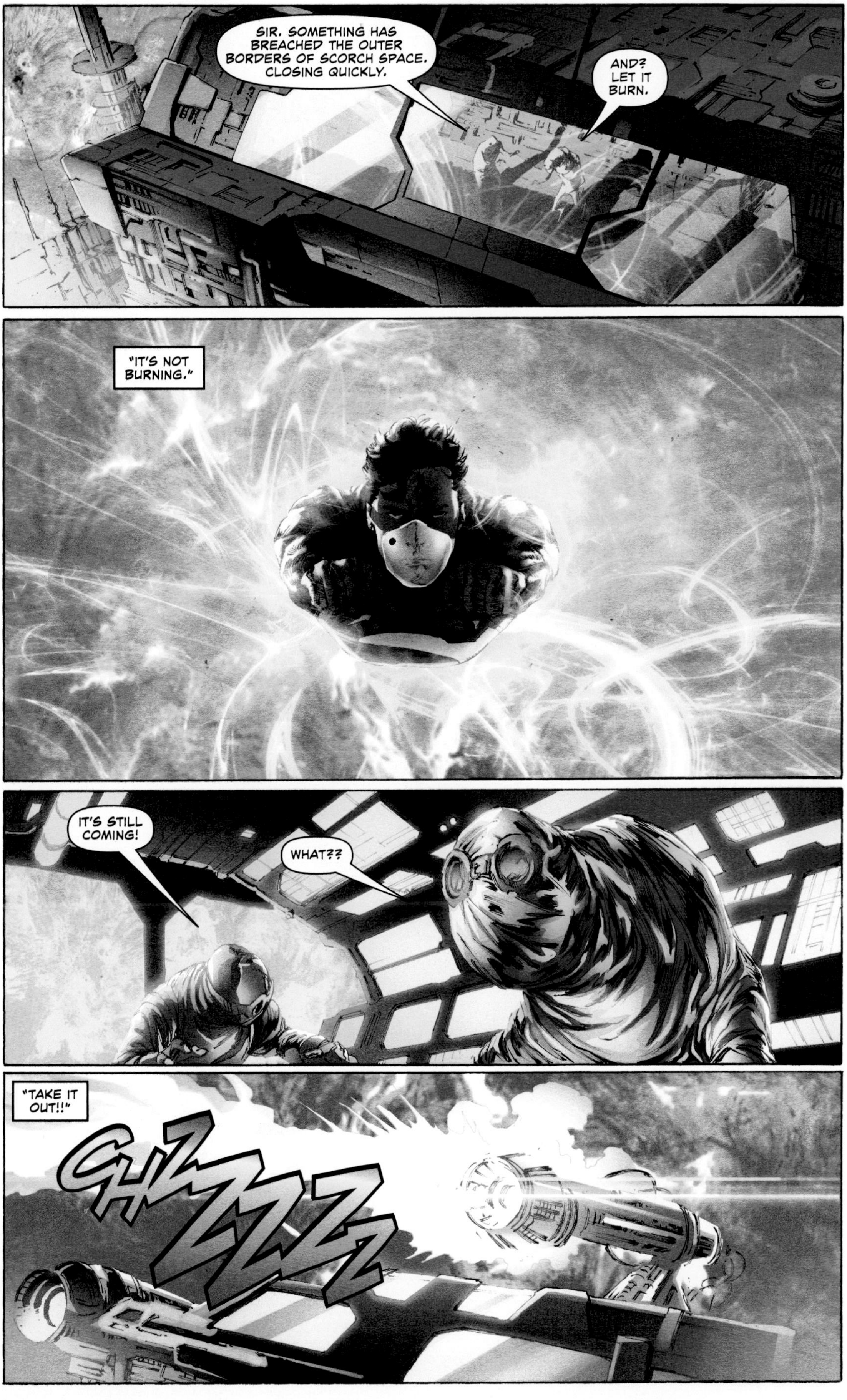
SIR. SOMETHING HAS BREACHED THE OUTER BORDERS OF SCORCH SPACE. CLOSING QUICKLY.
AND? LET IT BURN.
"IT'S NOT BURNING."
IT'S STILL COMING!
WHAT??
"TAKE IT OUT!!"
CHZZZZZ

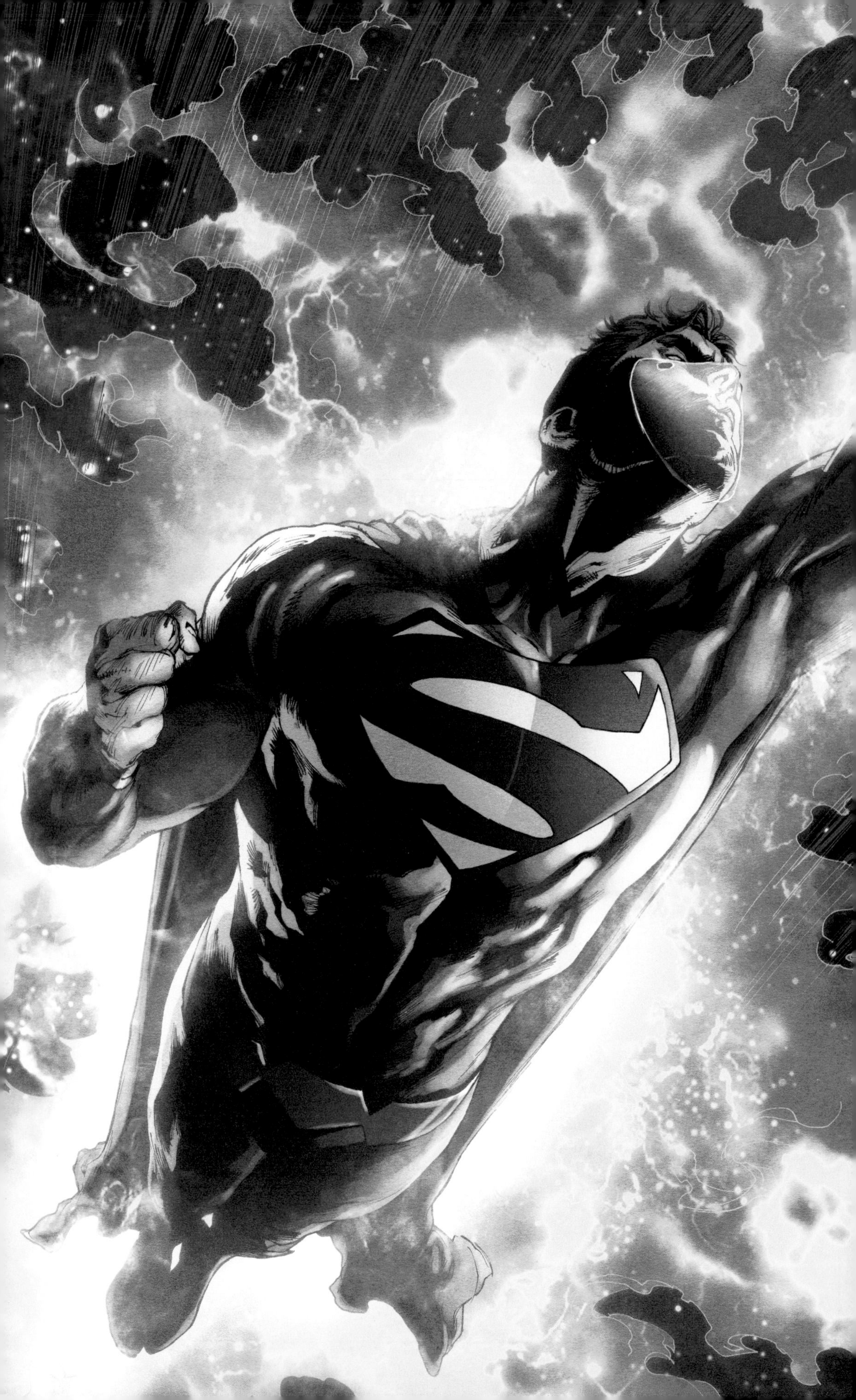

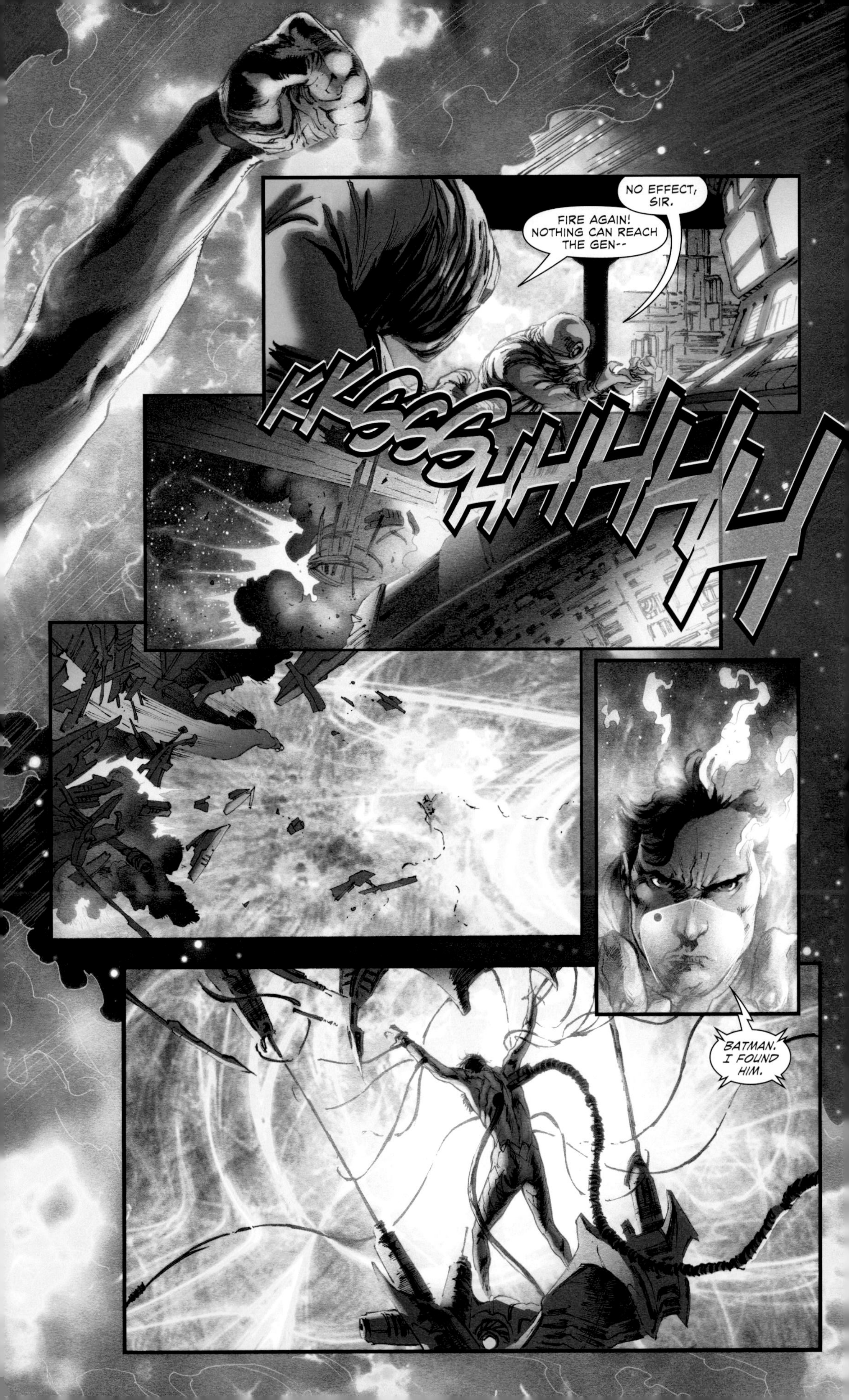
FIRE AGAIN! NOTHING CAN REACH THE GEN--
NO EFFECT, SIR.
KSSSHHHHH
BATMAN. I FOUND HIM.

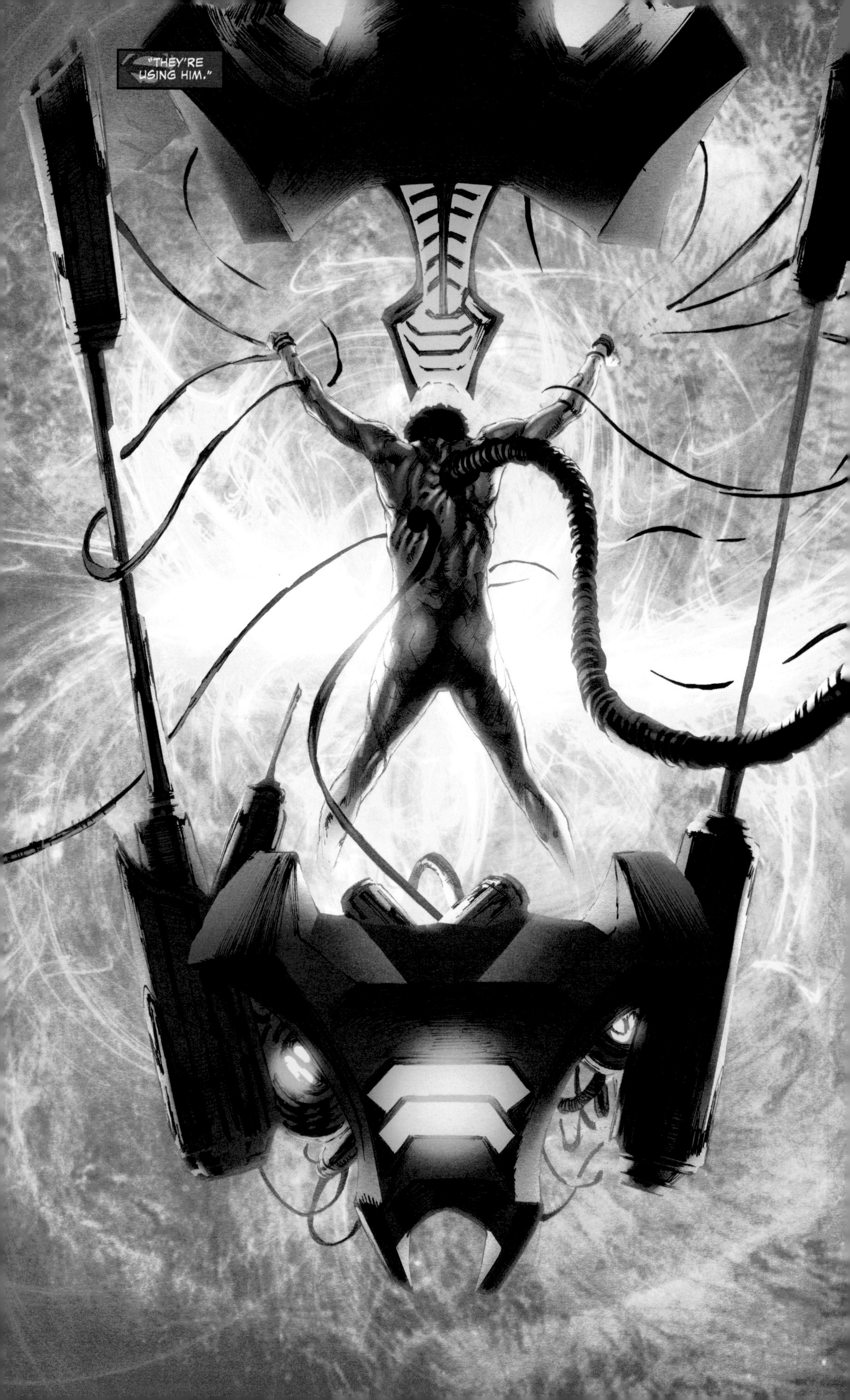
"THEY'RE USING HIM."

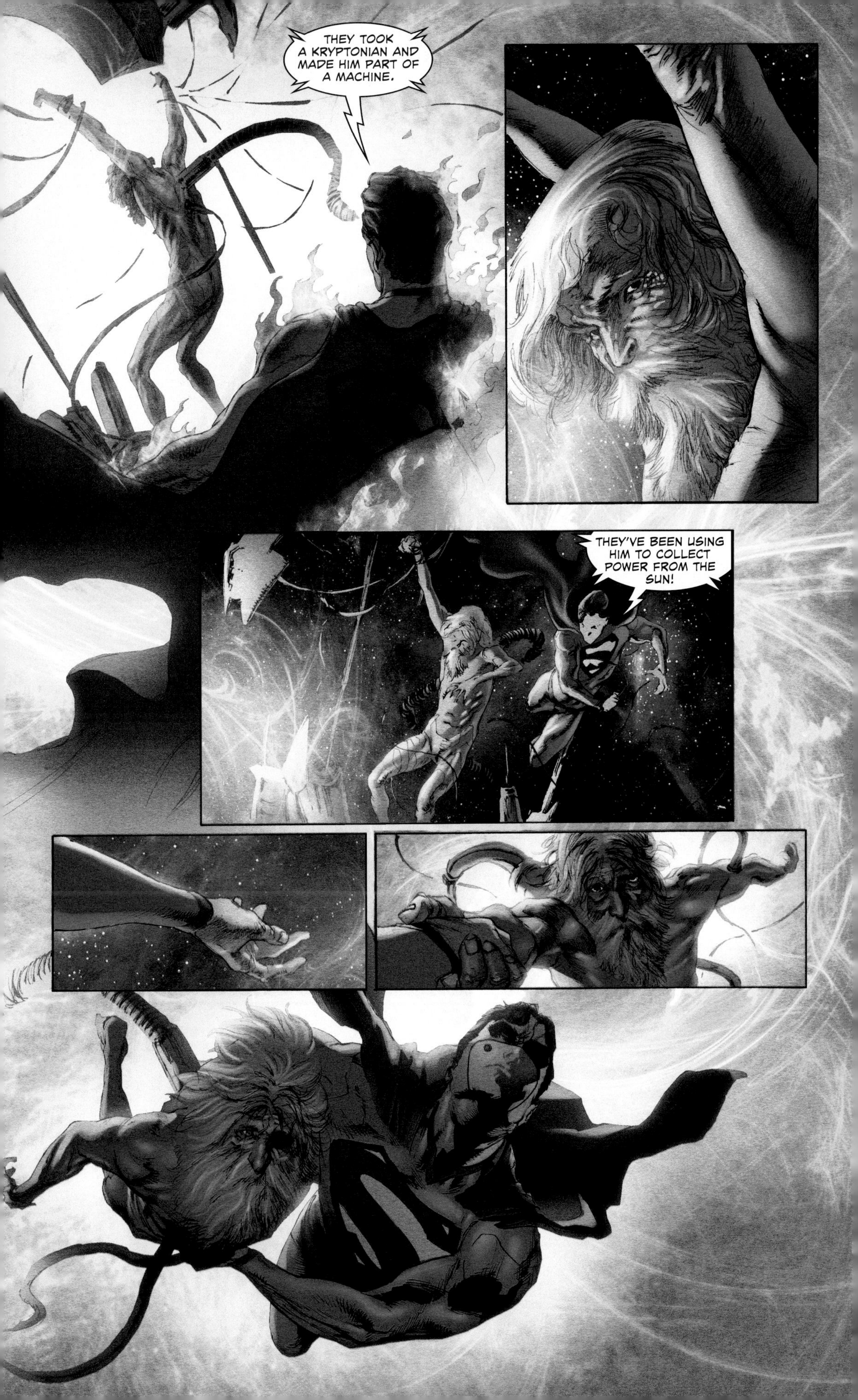
THEY TOOK A KRYPTONIAN AND MADE HIM PART OF A MACHINE.
THEY'VE BEEN USING HIM TO COLLECT POWER FROM THE SUN!

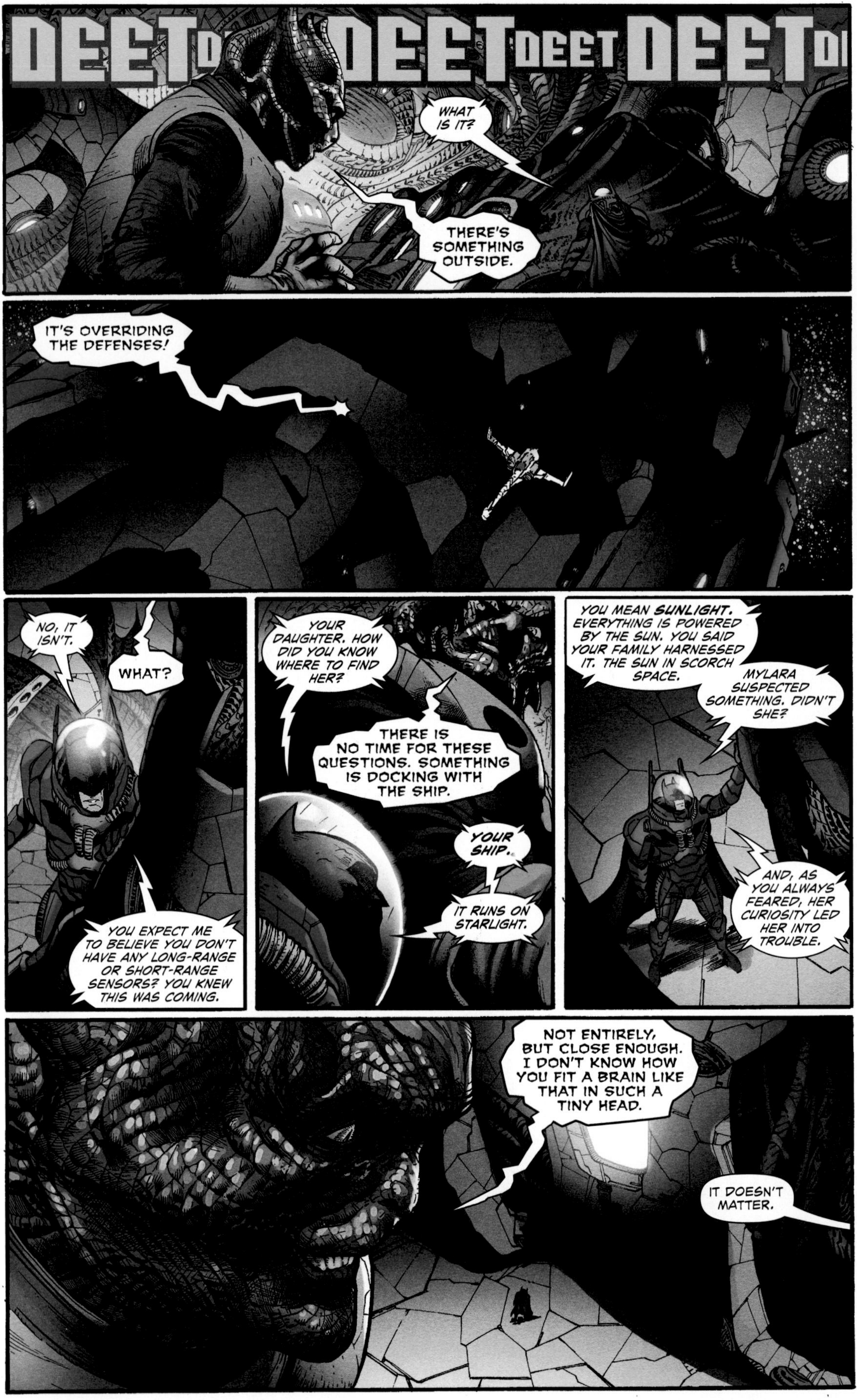

DEET DEET DEET DEET DEET
WHAT IS IT?
THERE'S SOMETHING OUTSIDE.
IT'S OVERRIDING THE DEFENSES!
NO, IT ISN'T.
WHAT?
YOU EXPECT ME TO BELIEVE YOU DON'T HAVE ANY LONG-RANGE OR SHORT-RANGE SENSORS? YOU KNEW THIS WAS COMING.
YOUR DAUGHTER. HOW DID YOU KNOW WHERE TO FIND HER?
THERE IS NO TIME FOR THESE QUESTIONS. SOMETHING IS DOCKING WITH THE SHIP.
YOUR SHIP.
IT RUNS ON STARLIGHT.
YOU MEAN SUNLIGHT. EVERYTHING IS POWERED BY THE SUN. YOU SAID YOUR FAMILY HARNESSED IT. THE SUN IN SCORCH SPACE.
MYLARA SUSPECTED SOMETHING. DIDN'T SHE?
AND, AS YOU ALWAYS FEARED, HER CURIOSITY LED HER INTO TROUBLE.
NOT ENTIRELY, BUT CLOSE ENOUGH. I DON'T KNOW HOW YOU FIT A BRAIN LIKE THAT IN SUCH A TINY HEAD.
IT DOESN'T MATTER.

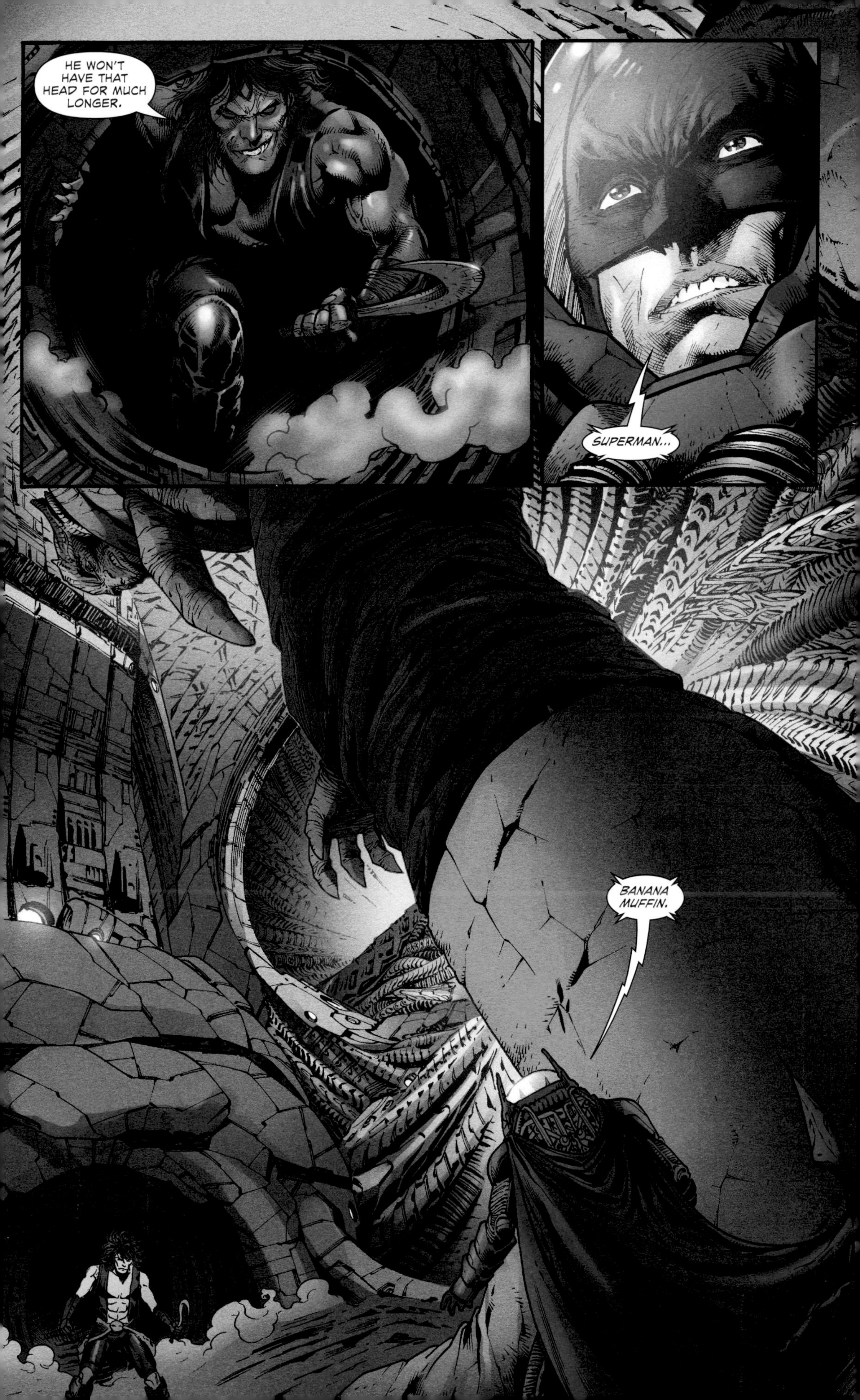
HE WON'T HAVE THAT HEAD FOR MUCH LONGER.
SUPERMAN...
BANANA MUFFIN.

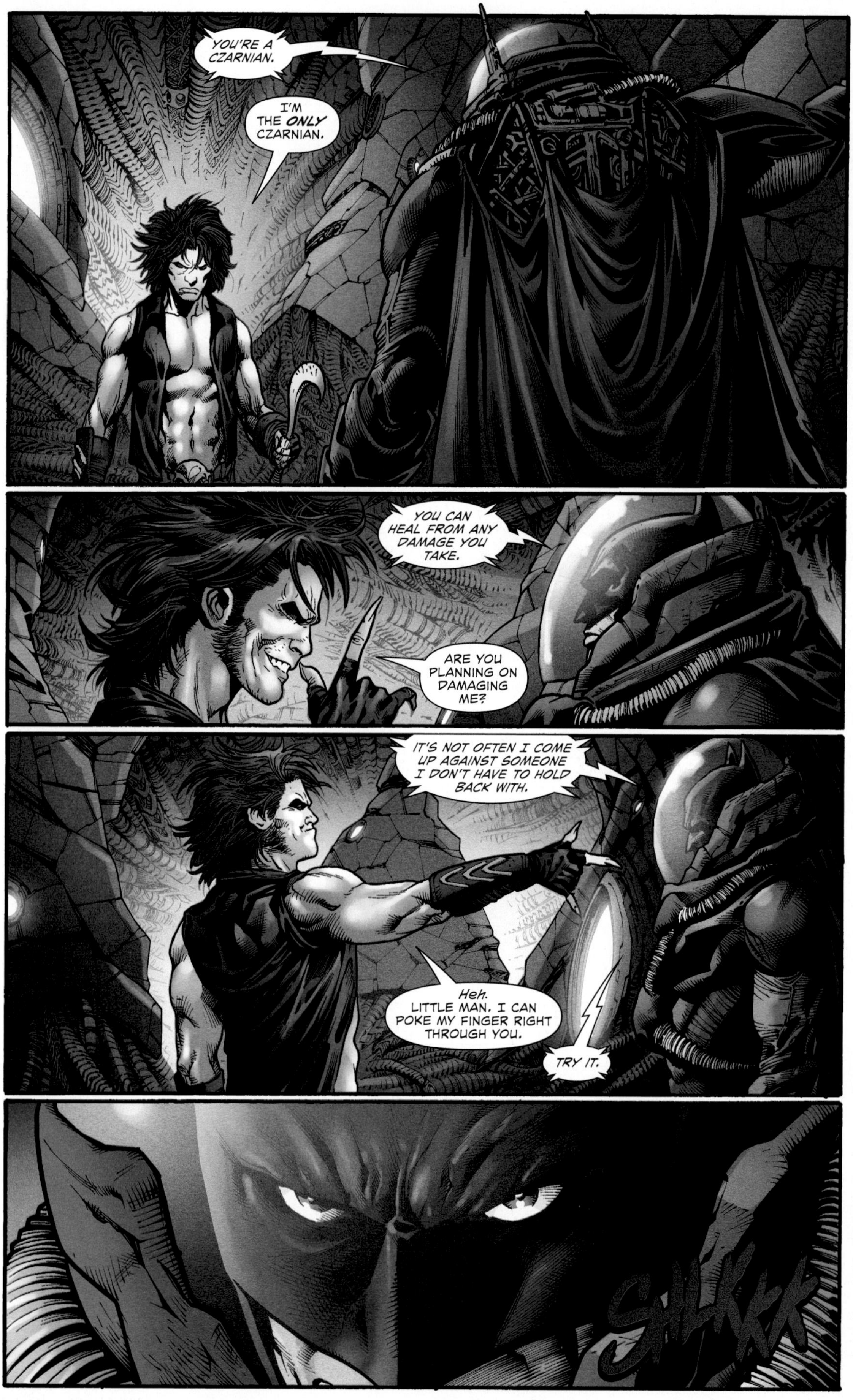
YOU'RE A CZARNIAN.
I'M THE ONLY CZARNIAN.
YOU CAN HEAL FROM ANY DAMAGE YOU TAKE.
ARE YOU PLANNING ON DAMAGING ME?
IT'S NOT OFTEN I COME UP AGAINST SOMEONE I DON'T HAVE TO HOLD BACK WITH.
Heh. LITTLE MAN. I CAN POKE MY FINGER RIGHT THROUGH YOU.
TRY IT.
SHKKK

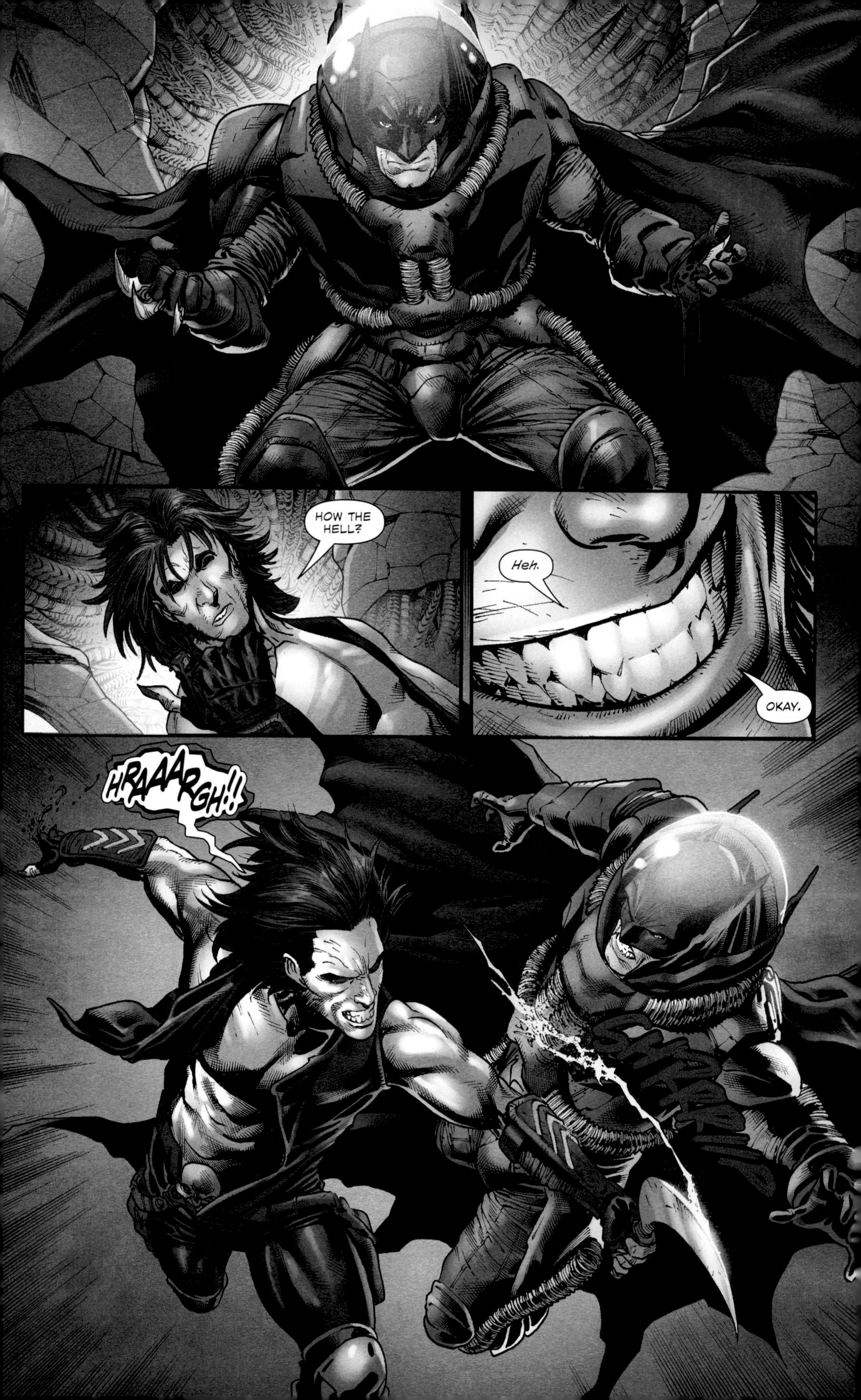
HOW THE HELL?
Heh.
OKAY.
HRAAARGH!!

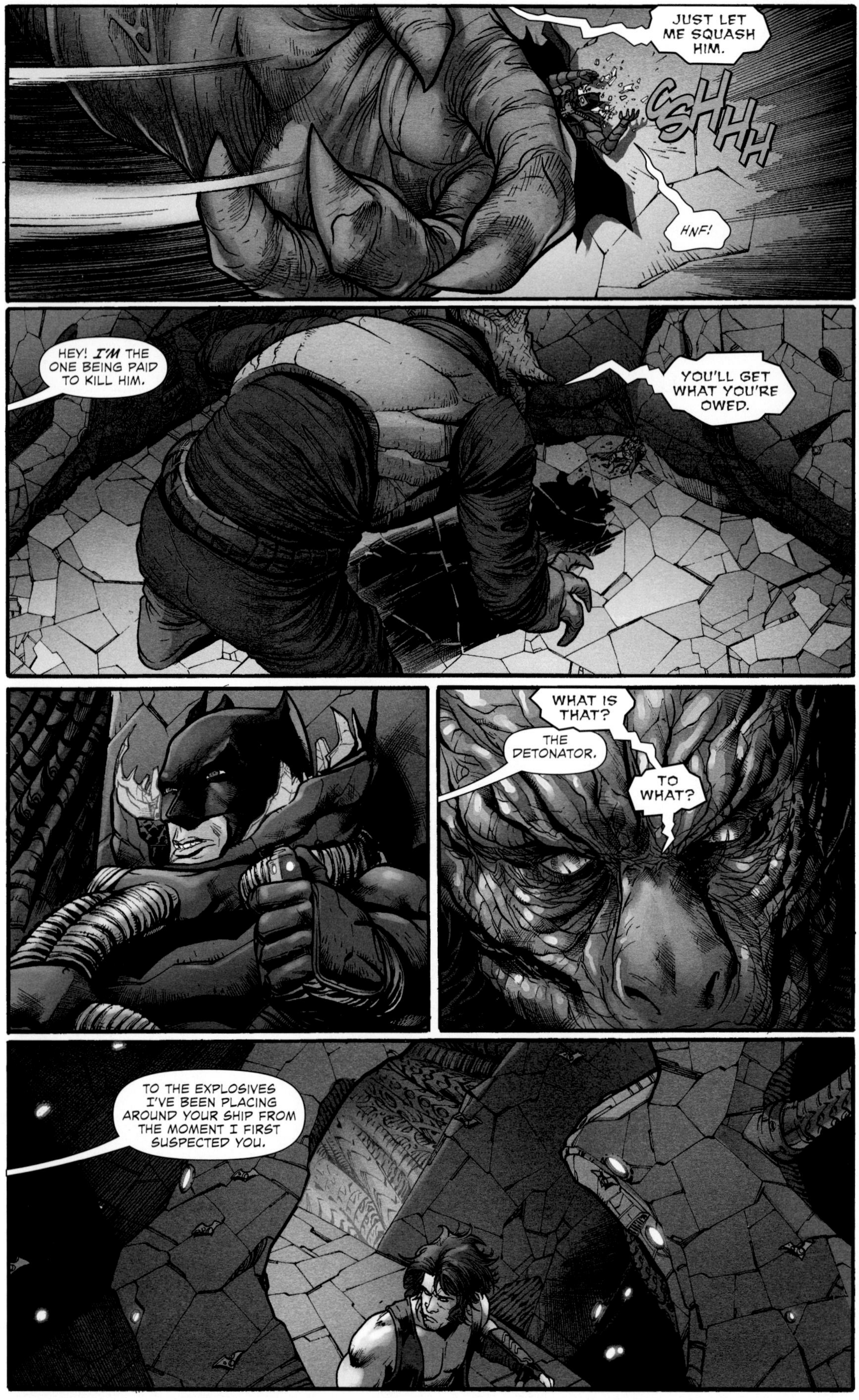
JUST LET ME SQUASH HIM.
CSHHH
HNF!
HEY! I'M THE ONE BEING PAID TO KILL HIM.
YOU'LL GET WHAT YOU'RE OWED.
WHAT IS THAT?
THE DETONATOR.
TO WHAT?
TO THE EXPLOSIVES I'VE BEEN PLACING AROUND YOUR SHIP FROM THE MOMENT I FIRST SUSPECTED YOU.

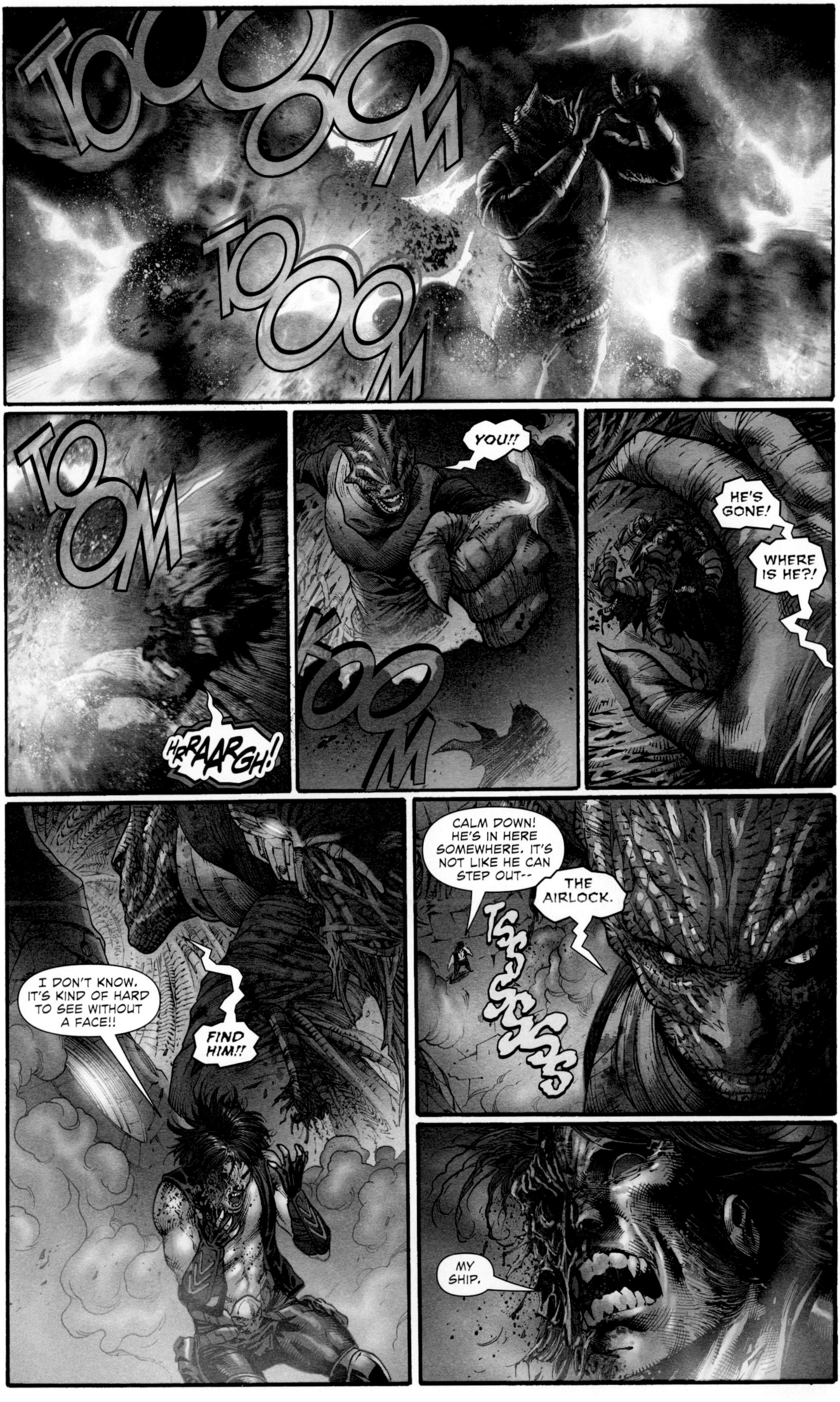
TOOOOOOM
TOOOOM
TOOOM
HRRAARGH!
YOU!!
KOOOM
HE'S GONE!
WHERE IS HE?!
I DON'T KNOW. IT'S KIND OF HARD TO SEE WITHOUT A FACE!!
FIND HIM!!
CALM DOWN! HE'S IN HERE SOMEWHERE. IT'S NOT LIKE HE CAN STEP OUT--
THE AIRLOCK.
TSSSSSSSS
MY SHIP.

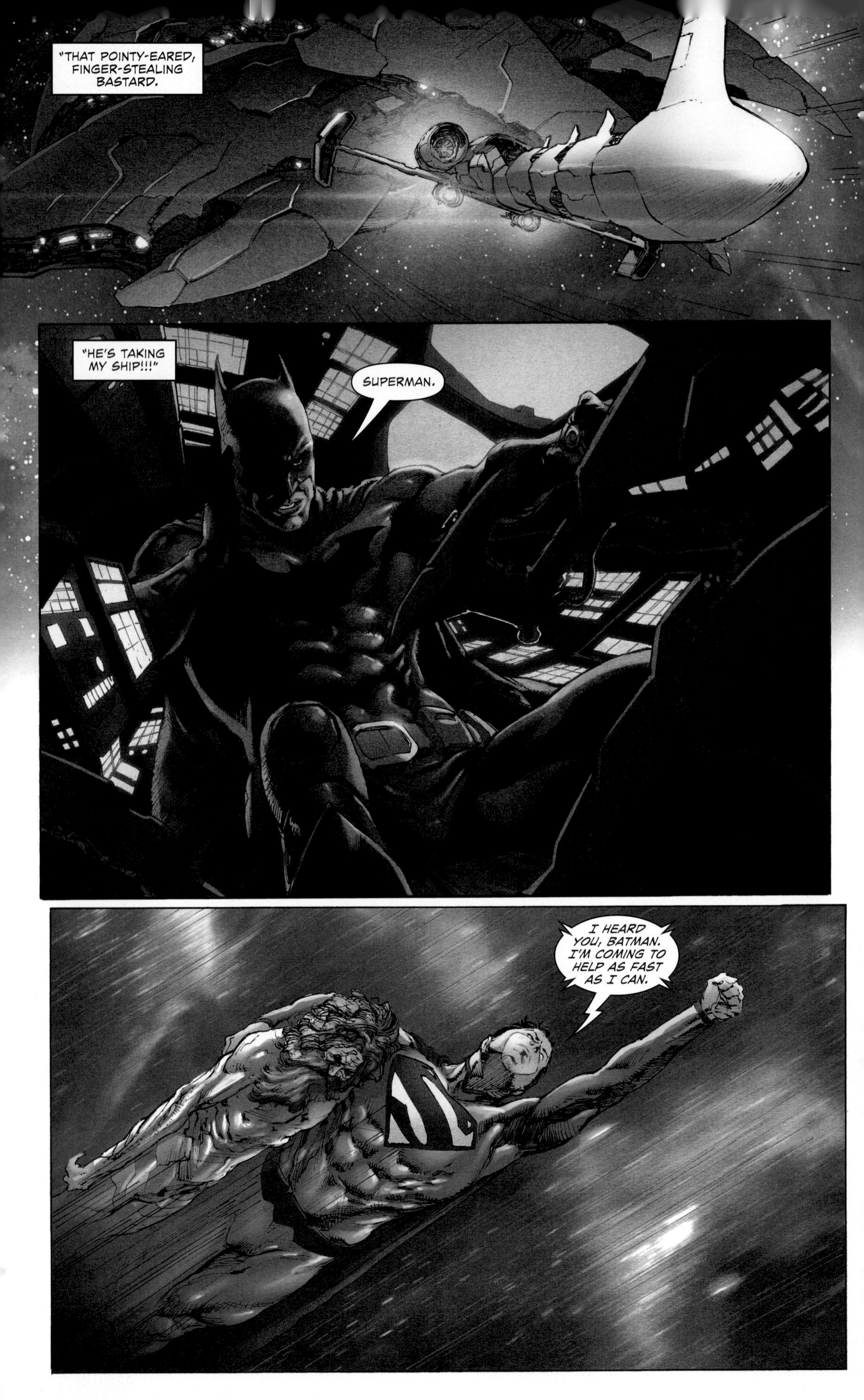
"THAT POINTY-EARED, FINGER-STEALING BASTARD.
"HE'S TAKING MY SHIP!!!"
SUPERMAN.
I HEARD YOU, BATMAN. I'M COMING TO HELP AS FAST AS I CAN.

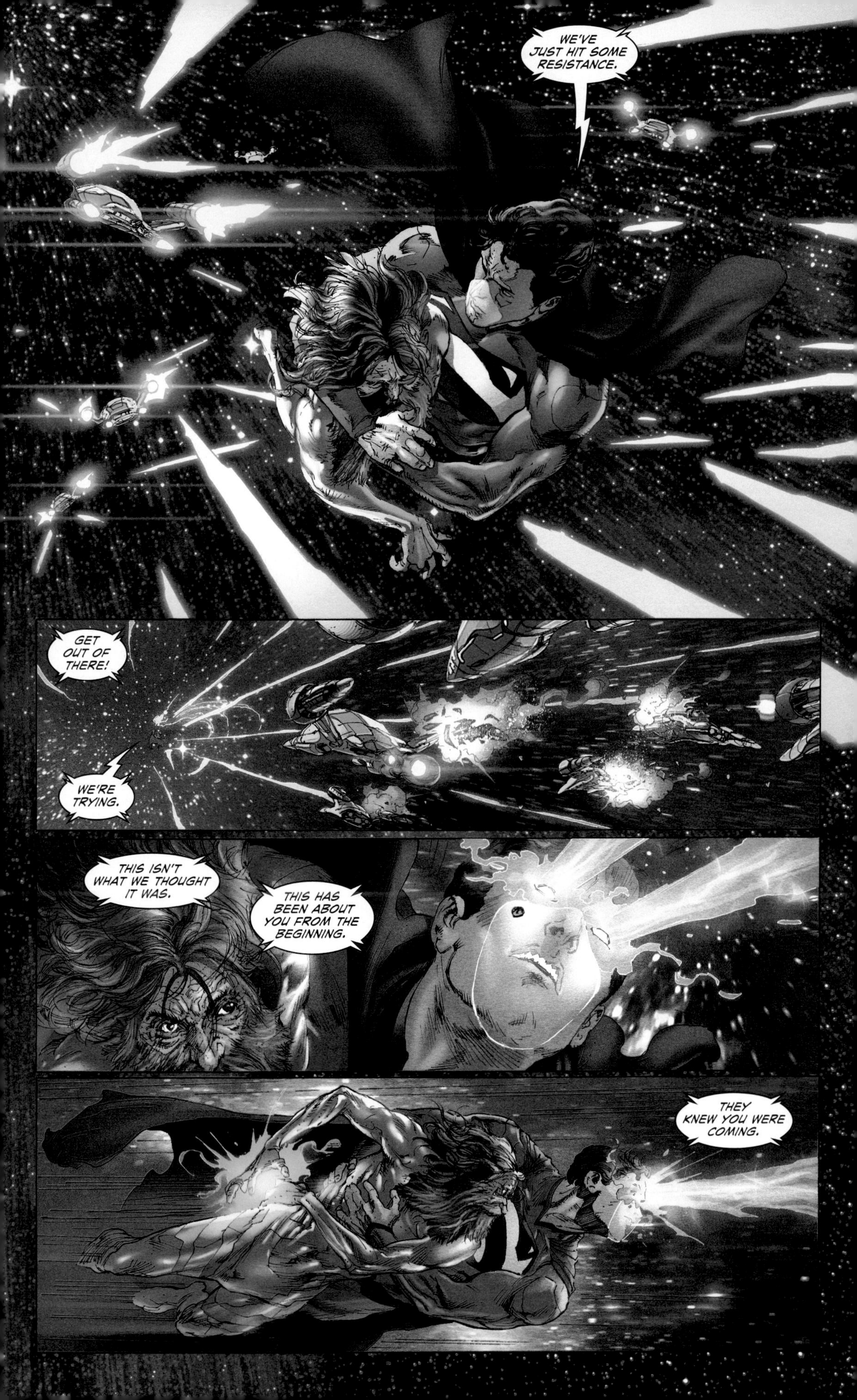
WE'VE JUST HIT SOME RESISTANCE.
GET OUT OF THERE!
WE'RE TRYING.
THIS ISN'T WHAT WE THOUGHT IT WAS.
THIS HAS BEEN ABOUT YOU FROM THE BEGINNING.
THEY KNEW YOU WERE COMING.

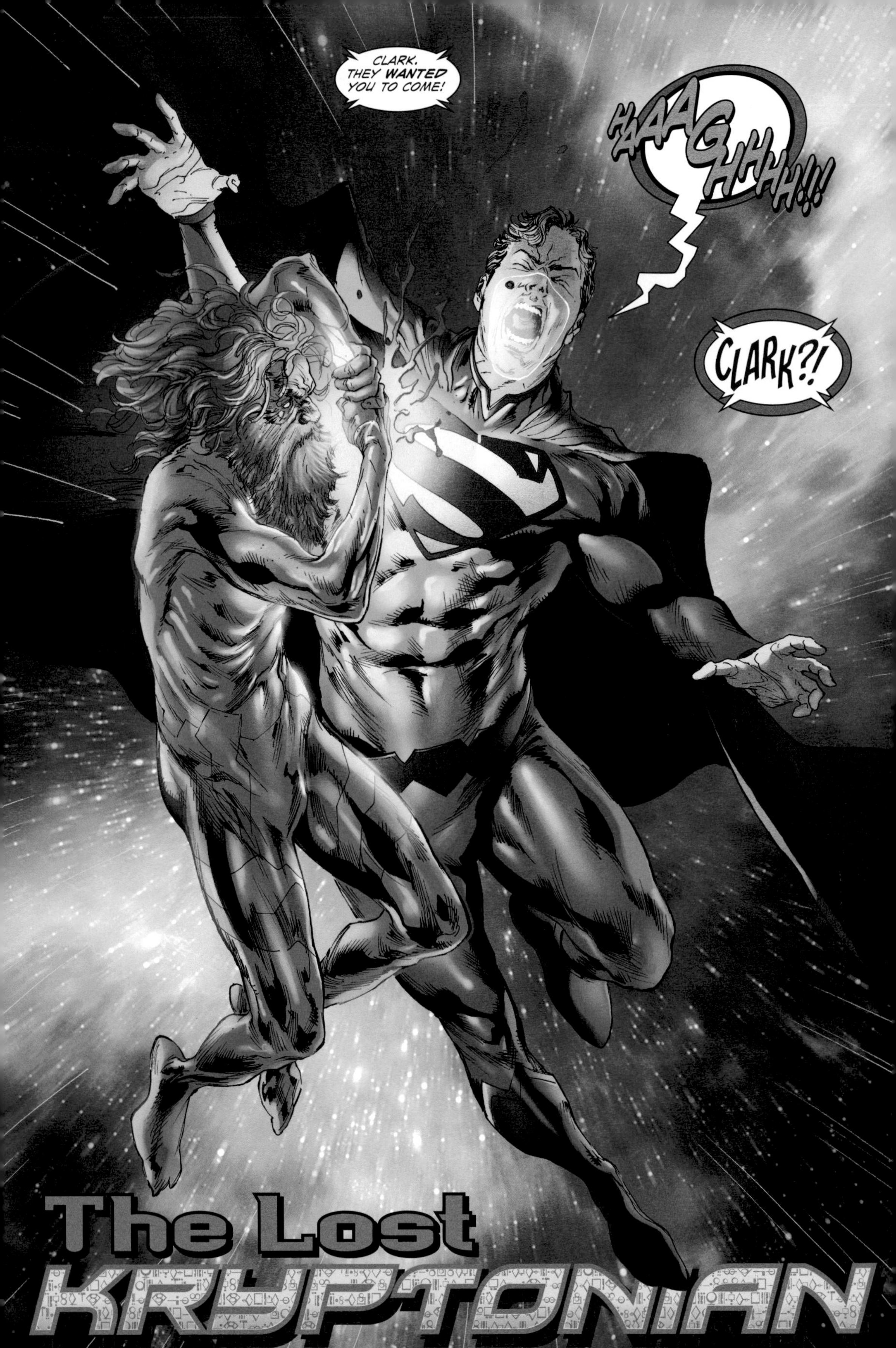
CLARK. THEY WANTED YOU TO COME!
HAAAGHHHH!!!
CLARK?!
The Lost KRYPTONIAN

Writer: TOM TAYLOR **Art:** ROBSON ROCHA & JÚLIO FERREIRA
Colors: BLOND **Letters:** ROB LEIGH **Cover:** YANICK PAQUETTE
Editor: DAVID WOHL **Group Editor:** EDDIE BERGANZA

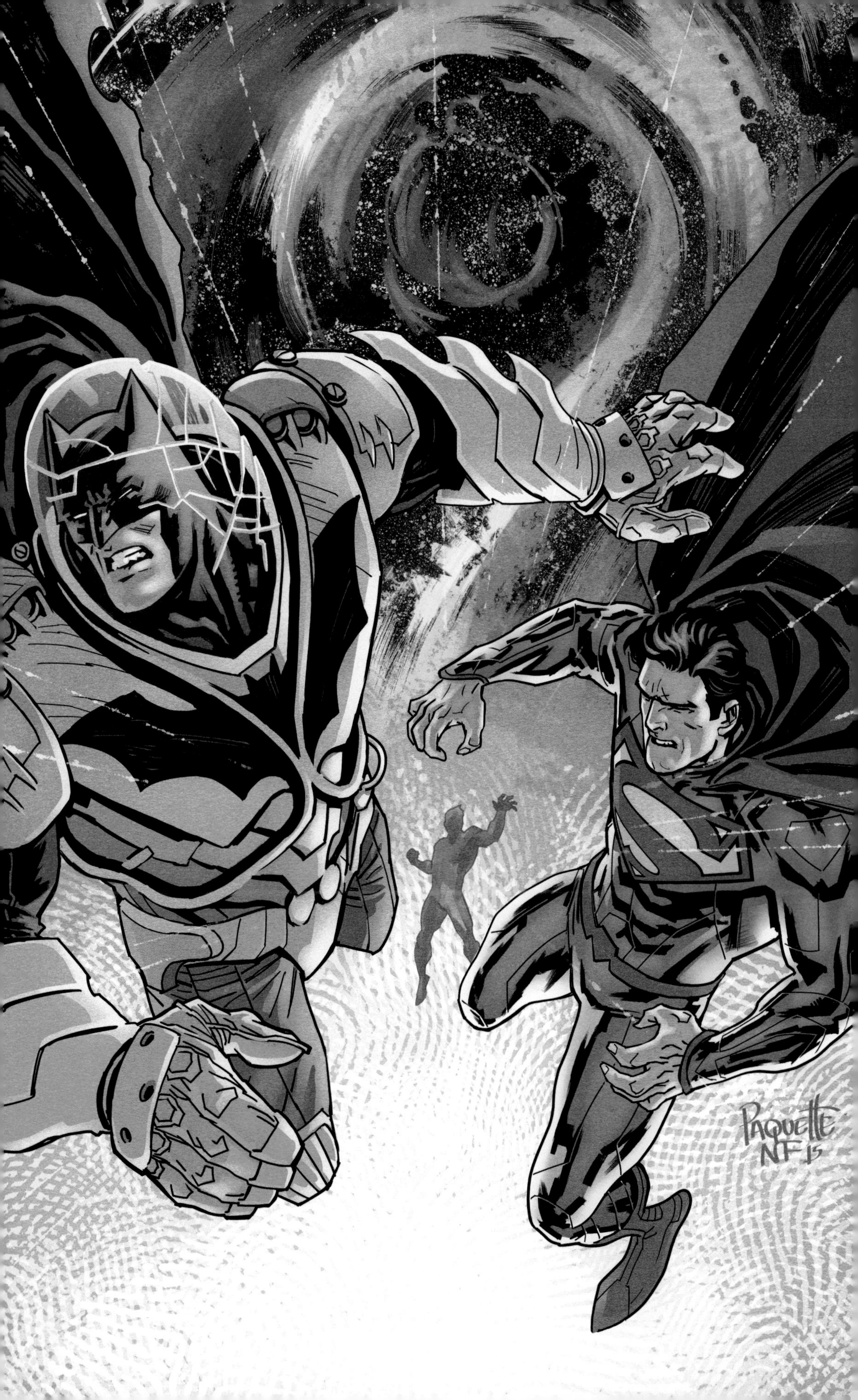
PAQUETTE
NF 15

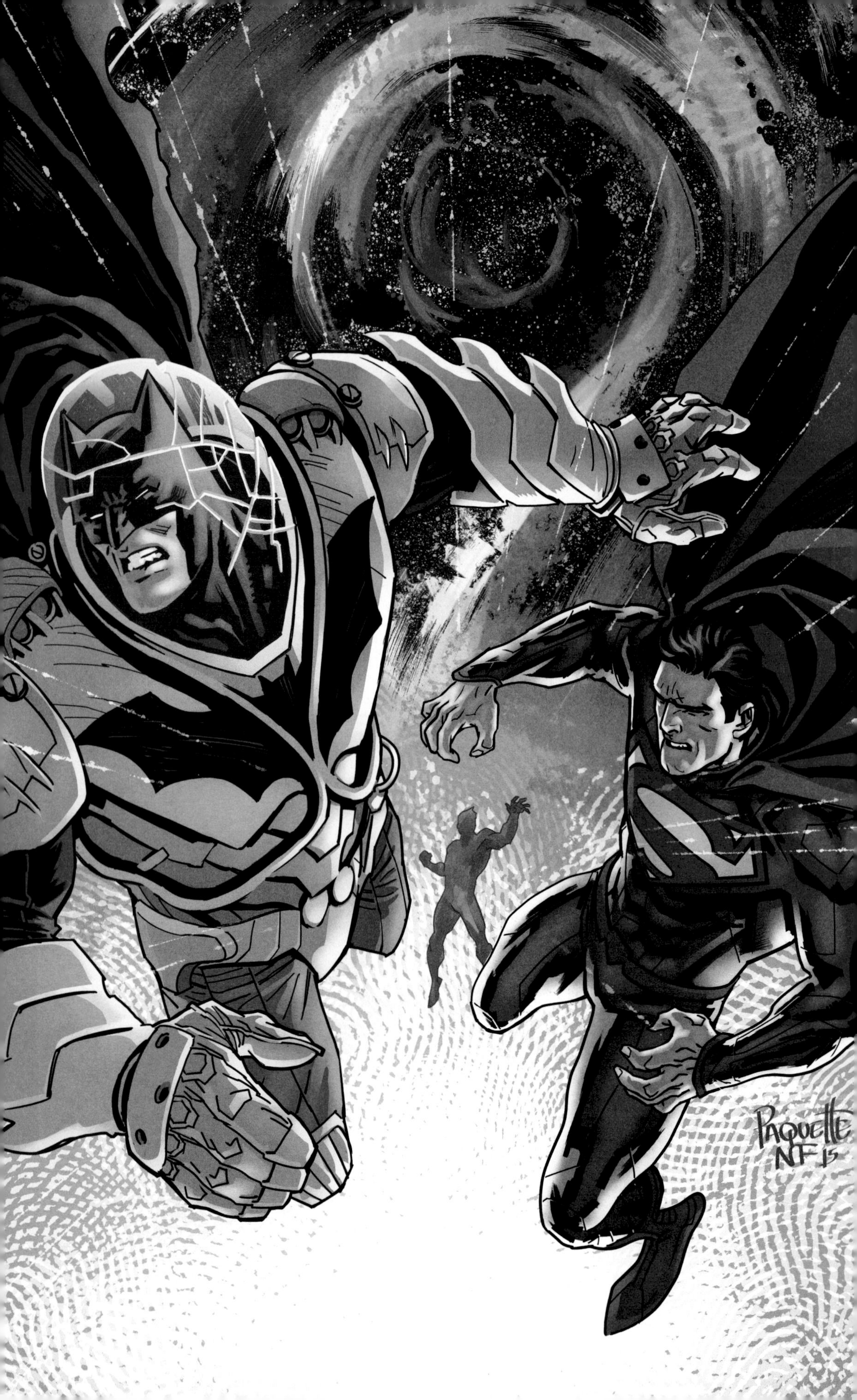
PAQUETTE
NF 15

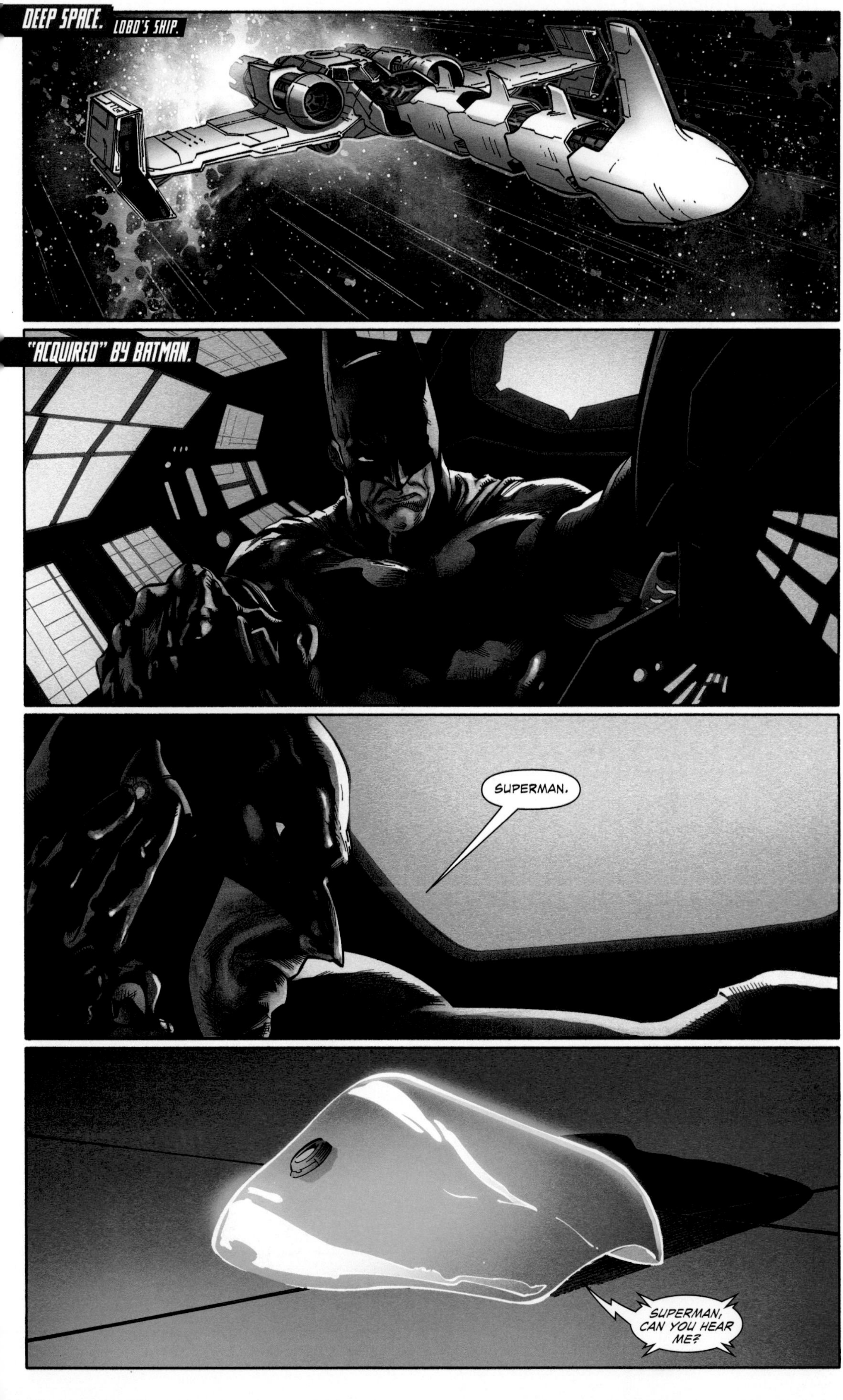
DEEP SPACE. LOBO'S SHIP.
"ACQUIRED" BY BATMAN.
SUPERMAN.
SUPERMAN, CAN YOU HEAR ME?

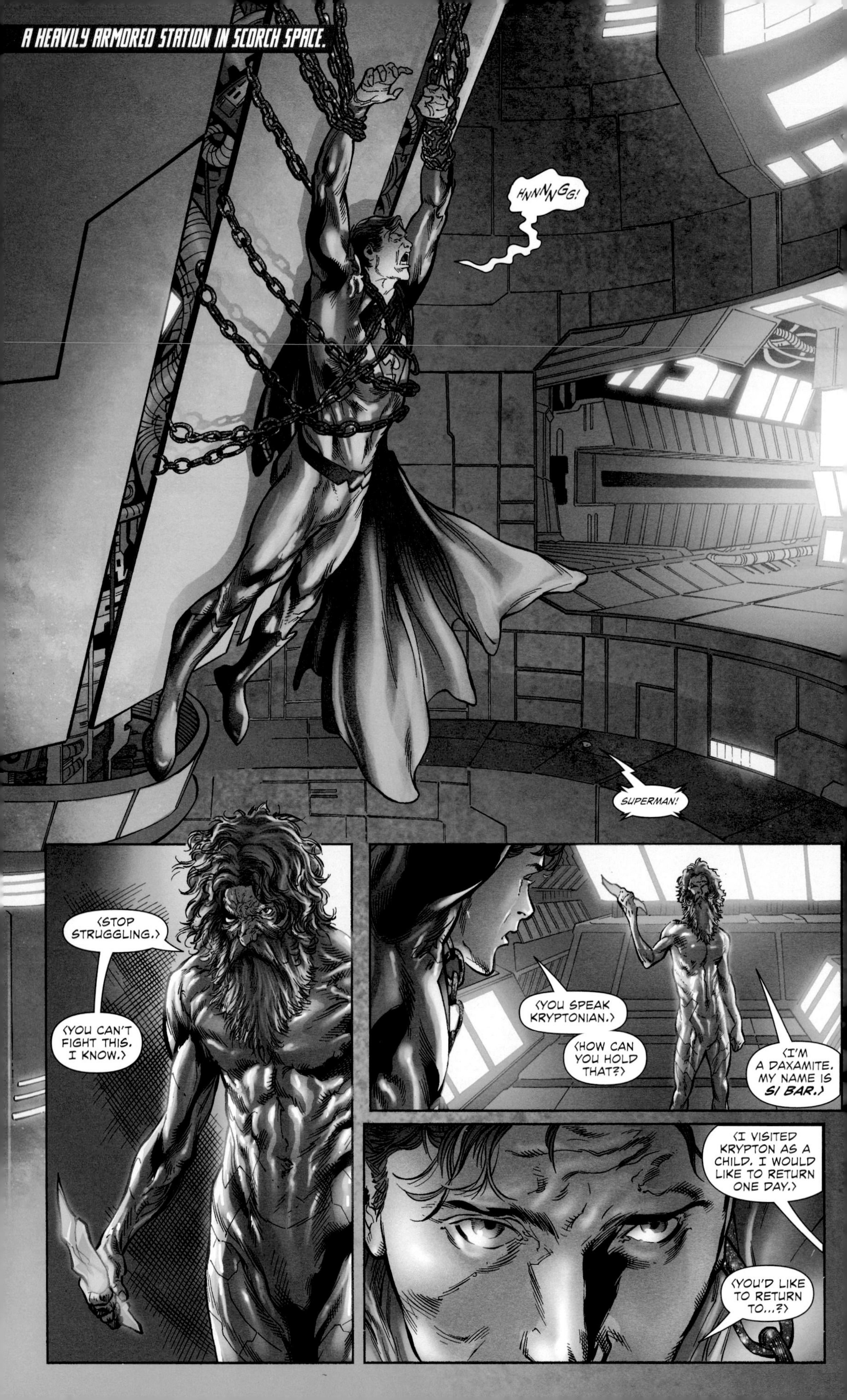
A HEAVILY ARMORED STATION IN SCORCH SPACE.
HNNNNGG!
SUPERMAN!
‹STOP STRUGGLING.›
‹YOU CAN'T FIGHT THIS. I KNOW.›
‹YOU SPEAK KRYPTONIAN.›
‹HOW CAN YOU HOLD THAT?›
‹I'M A DAXAMITE. MY NAME IS SI BAR.›
‹I VISITED KRYPTON AS A CHILD. I WOULD LIKE TO RETURN ONE DAY.›
‹YOU'D LIKE TO RETURN TO...?›

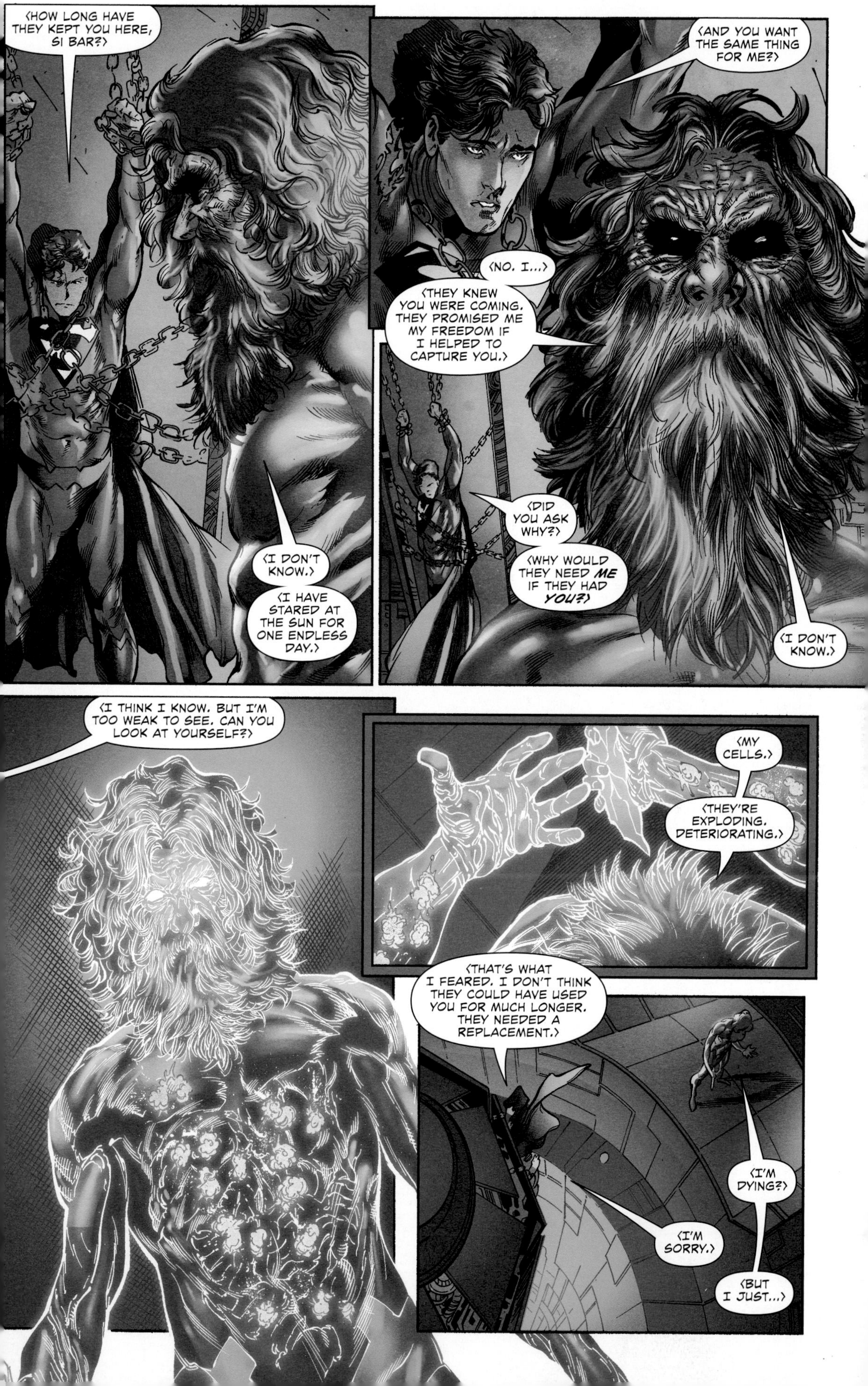

‹HOW LONG HAVE THEY KEPT YOU HERE, SI BAR?›
‹I DON'T KNOW.›
‹I HAVE STARED AT THE SUN FOR ONE ENDLESS DAY.›
‹AND YOU WANT THE SAME THING FOR ME?›
‹NO. I...›
‹THEY KNEW YOU WERE COMING. THEY PROMISED ME MY FREEDOM IF I HELPED TO CAPTURE YOU.›
‹DID YOU ASK WHY?›
‹WHY WOULD THEY NEED ME IF THEY HAD YOU?›
‹I DON'T KNOW.›
‹I THINK I KNOW. BUT I'M TOO WEAK TO SEE. CAN YOU LOOK AT YOURSELF?›
‹MY CELLS.›
‹THEY'RE EXPLODING. DETERIORATING.›
‹THAT'S WHAT I FEARED. I DON'T THINK THEY COULD HAVE USED YOU FOR MUCH LONGER. THEY NEEDED A REPLACEMENT.›
‹I'M DYING?›
‹I'M SORRY.›
‹BUT I JUST...›

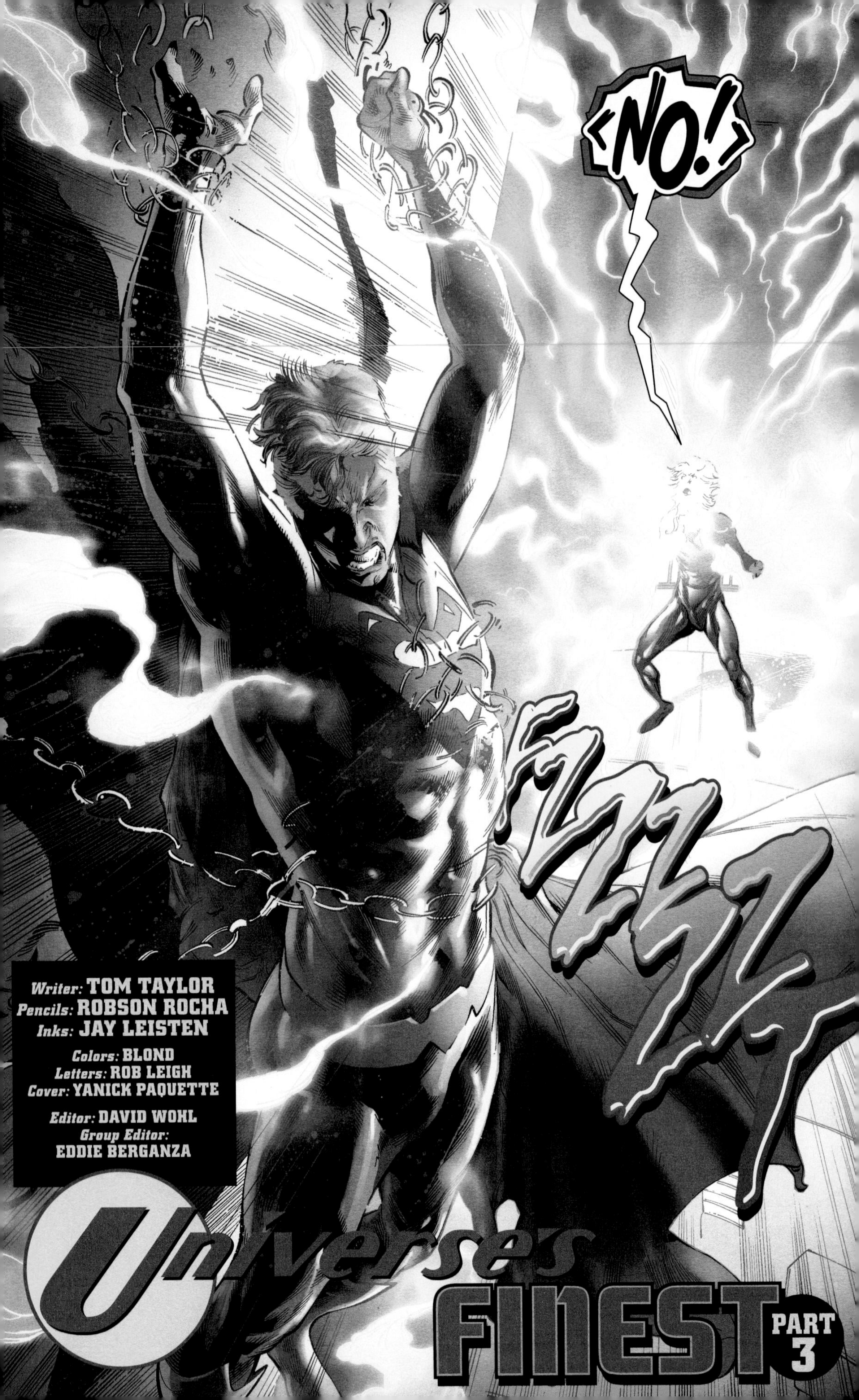

<NO!>
FZZZZZ
Writer: TOM TAYLOR
Pencils: ROBSON ROCHA
Inks: JAY LEISTEN
Colors: BLOND
Letters: ROB LEIGH
Cover: YANICK PAQUETTE
Editor: DAVID WOHL
Group Editor:
EDDIE BERGANZA
Universes FINEST PART 3

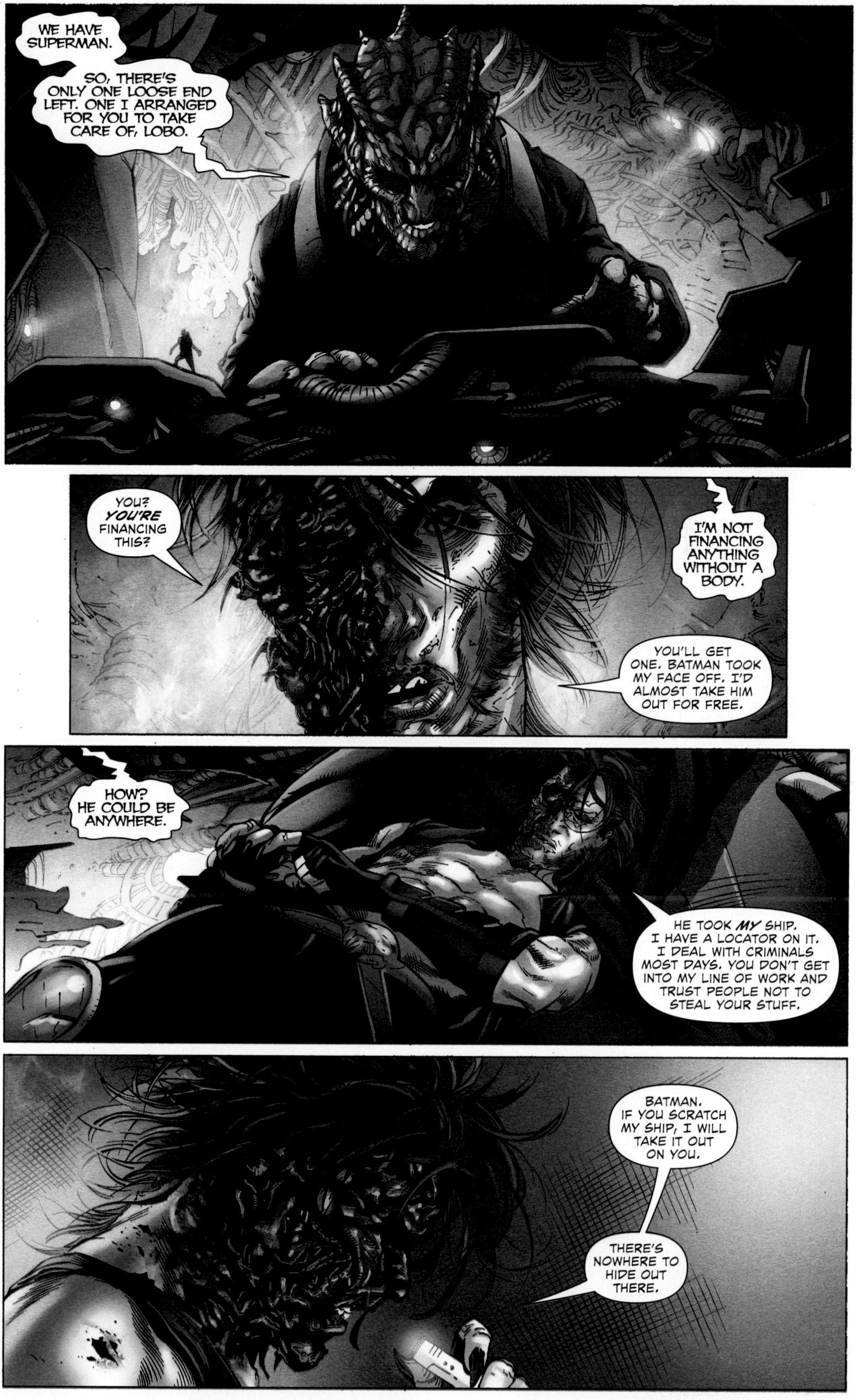
WE HAVE SUPERMAN.
SO, THERE'S ONLY ONE LOOSE END LEFT. ONE I ARRANGED FOR YOU TO TAKE CARE OF, LOBO.
YOU? YOU'RE FINANCING THIS?
I'M NOT FINANCING ANYTHING WITHOUT A BODY.
YOU'LL GET ONE. BATMAN TOOK MY FACE OFF. I'D ALMOST TAKE HIM OUT FOR FREE.
HOW? HE COULD BE ANYWHERE.
HE TOOK MY SHIP. I HAVE A LOCATOR ON IT. I DEAL WITH CRIMINALS MOST DAYS. YOU DON'T GET INTO MY LINE OF WORK AND TRUST PEOPLE NOT TO STEAL YOUR STUFF.
BATMAN. IF YOU SCRATCH MY SHIP, I WILL TAKE IT OUT ON YOU.
THERE'S NOWHERE TO HIDE OUT THERE.

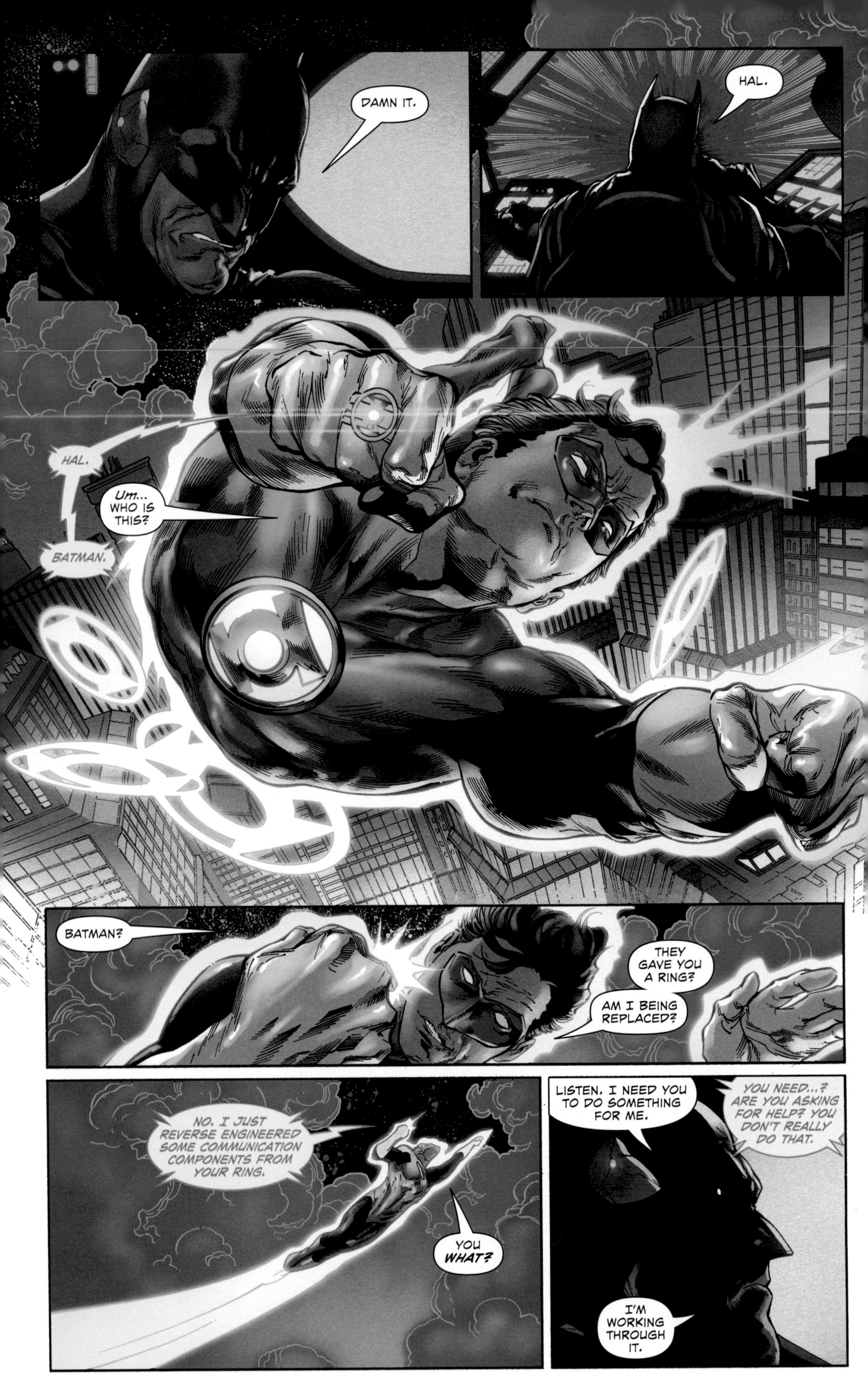
DAMN IT.
HAL.
HAL.
Um... WHO IS THIS?
BATMAN.
BATMAN?
THEY GAVE YOU A RING?
AM I BEING REPLACED?
NO. I JUST REVERSE ENGINEERED SOME COMMUNICATION COMPONENTS FROM YOUR RING.
YOU WHAT?
LISTEN. I NEED YOU TO DO SOMETHING FOR ME.
YOU NEED...? ARE YOU ASKING FOR HELP? YOU DON'T REALLY DO THAT.
I'M WORKING THROUGH IT.

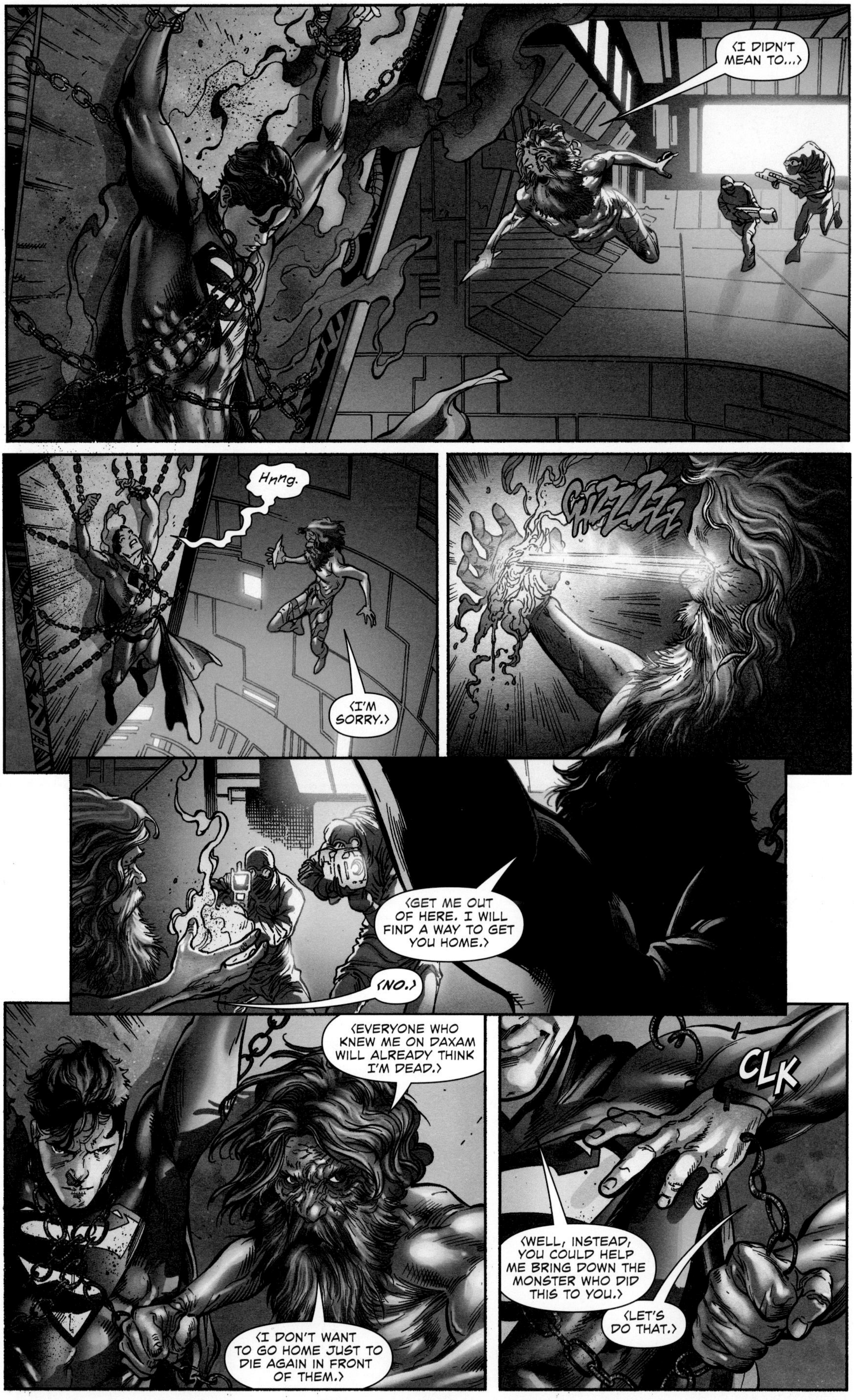

‹I DIDN'T MEAN TO...›
Hnng.
‹I'M SORRY.›
‹GET ME OUT OF HERE. I WILL FIND A WAY TO GET YOU HOME.›
‹NO.›
‹EVERYONE WHO KNEW ME ON DAXAM WILL ALREADY THINK I'M DEAD.›
‹I DON'T WANT TO GO HOME JUST TO DIE AGAIN IN FRONT OF THEM.›
CLK
‹WELL, INSTEAD, YOU COULD HELP ME BRING DOWN THE MONSTER WHO DID THIS TO YOU.›
‹LET'S DO THAT.›

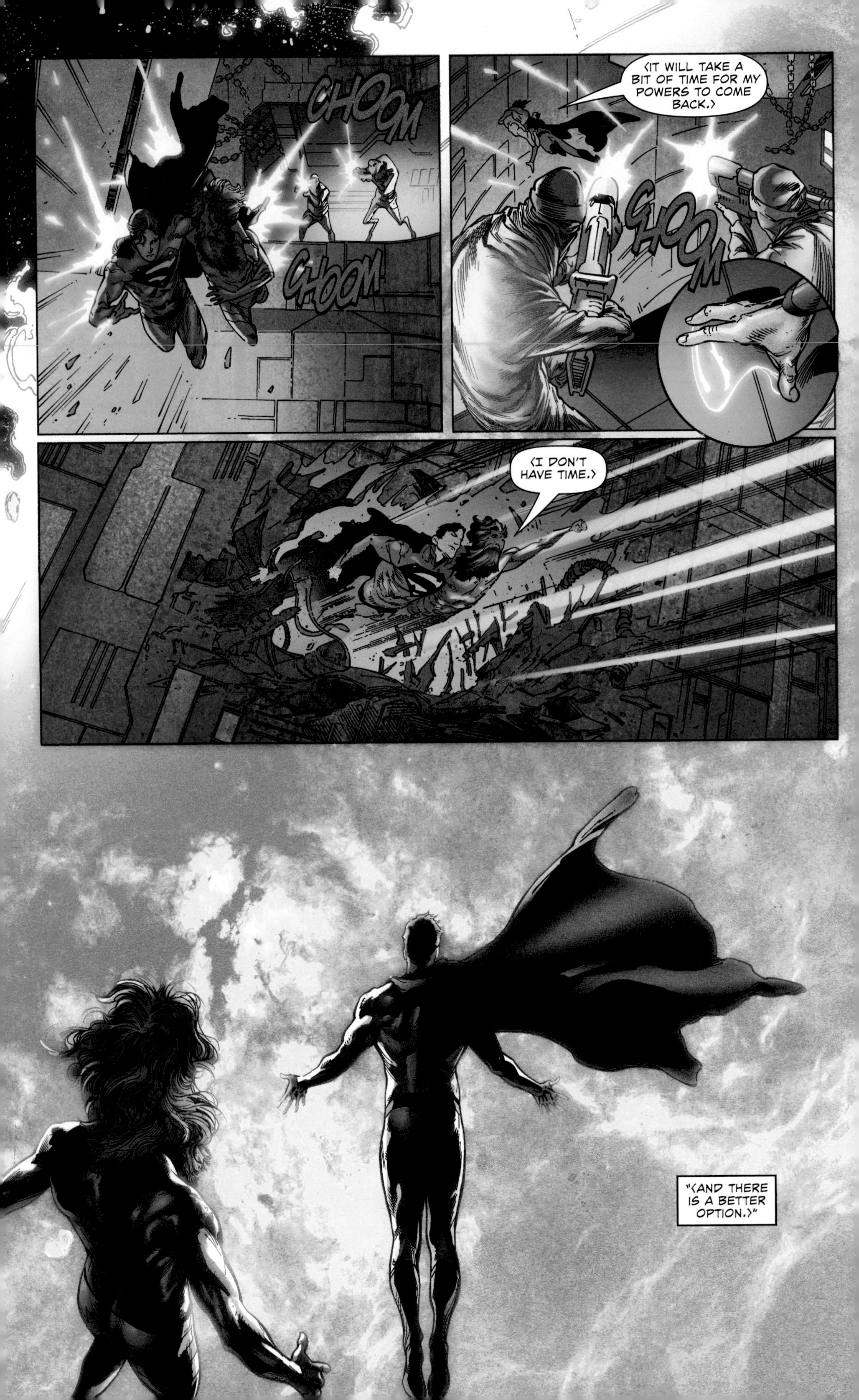
CHOOM
CHOOM
‹IT WILL TAKE A BIT OF TIME FOR MY POWERS TO COME BACK.›
CHOOM
‹I DON'T HAVE TIME.›
"‹AND THERE IS A BETTER OPTION.›"

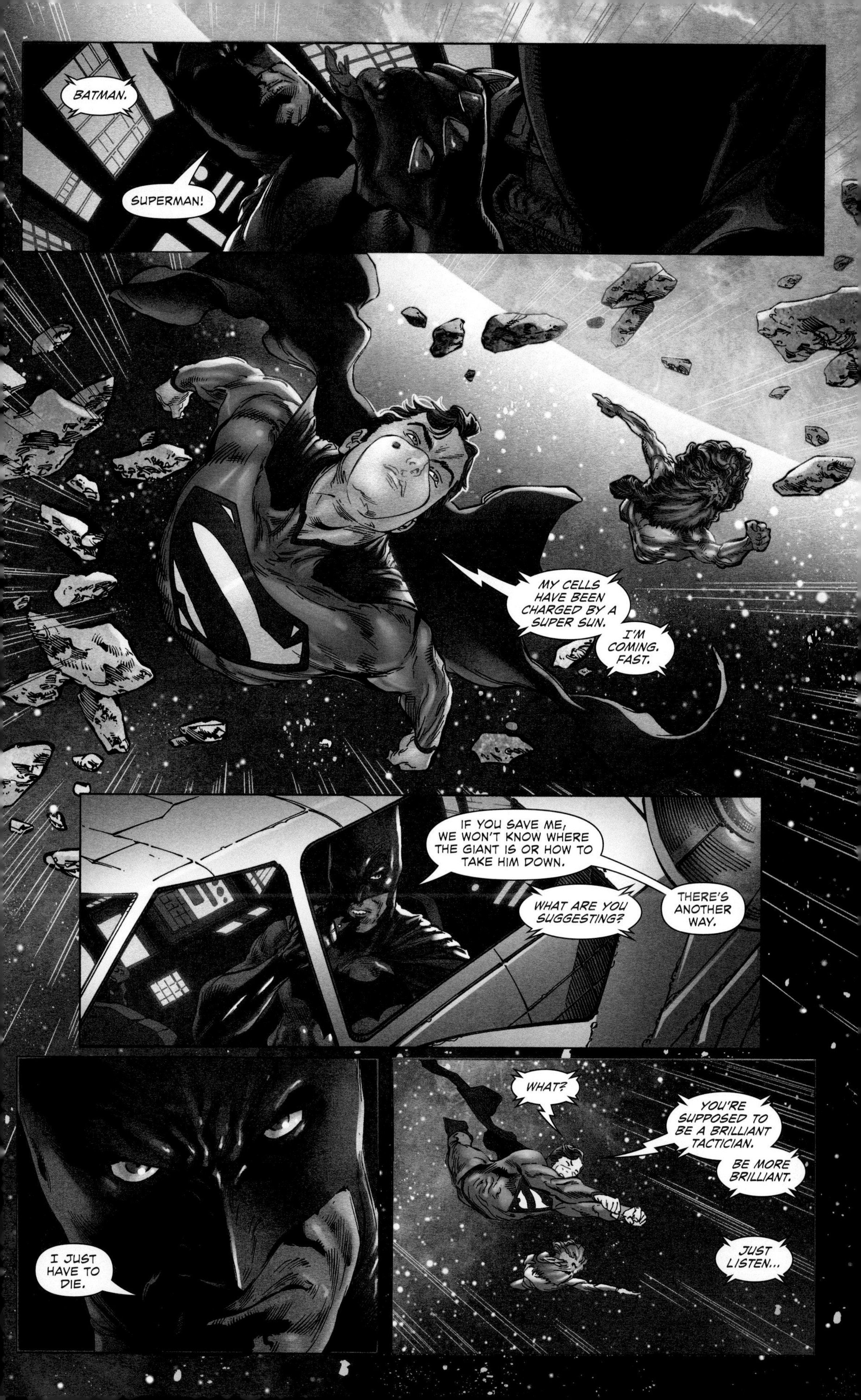
BATMAN.
SUPERMAN!
MY CELLS HAVE BEEN CHARGED BY A SUPER SUN.
I'M COMING. FAST.
IF YOU SAVE ME, WE WON'T KNOW WHERE THE GIANT IS OR HOW TO TAKE HIM DOWN.
WHAT ARE YOU SUGGESTING?
THERE'S ANOTHER WAY.
I JUST HAVE TO DIE.
WHAT?
YOU'RE SUPPOSED TO BE A BRILLIANT TACTICIAN.
BE MORE BRILLIANT.
JUST LISTEN...

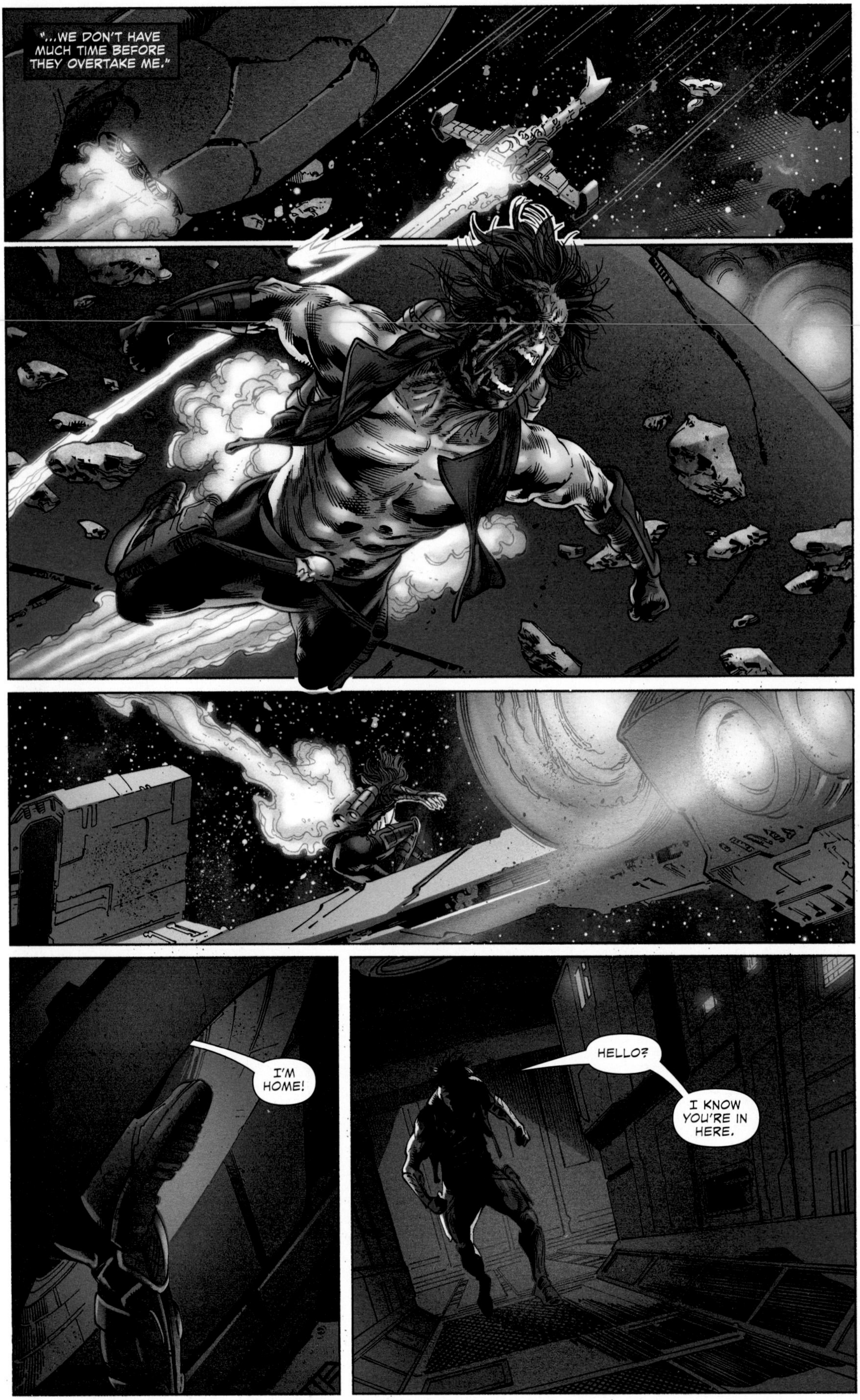
"...WE DON'T HAVE MUCH TIME BEFORE THEY OVERTAKE ME."
I'M HOME!
HELLO?
I KNOW YOU'RE IN HERE.

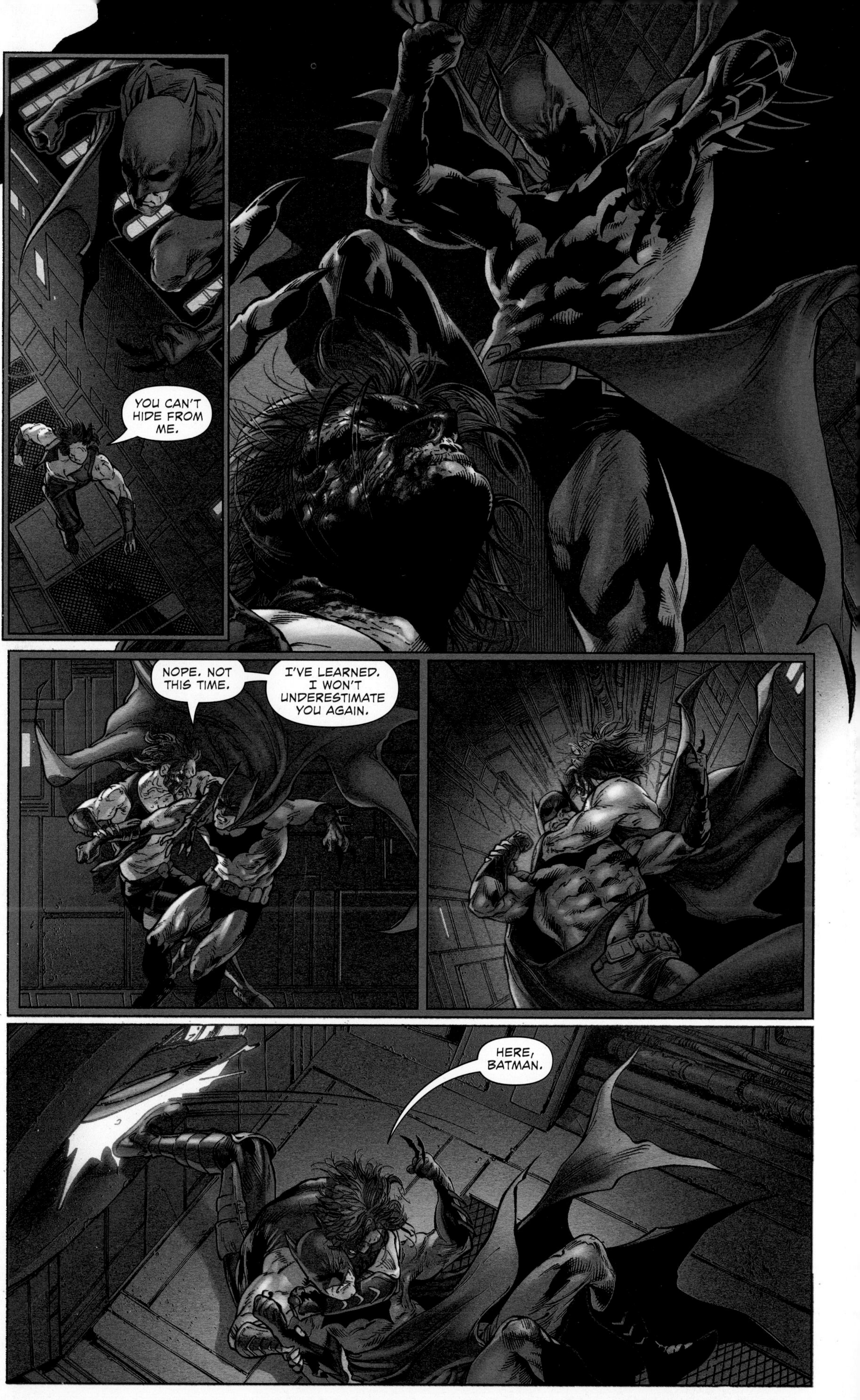
YOU CAN'T HIDE FROM ME.
NOPE. NOT THIS TIME.
I'VE LEARNED. I WON'T UNDERESTIMATE YOU AGAIN.
HERE, BATMAN.

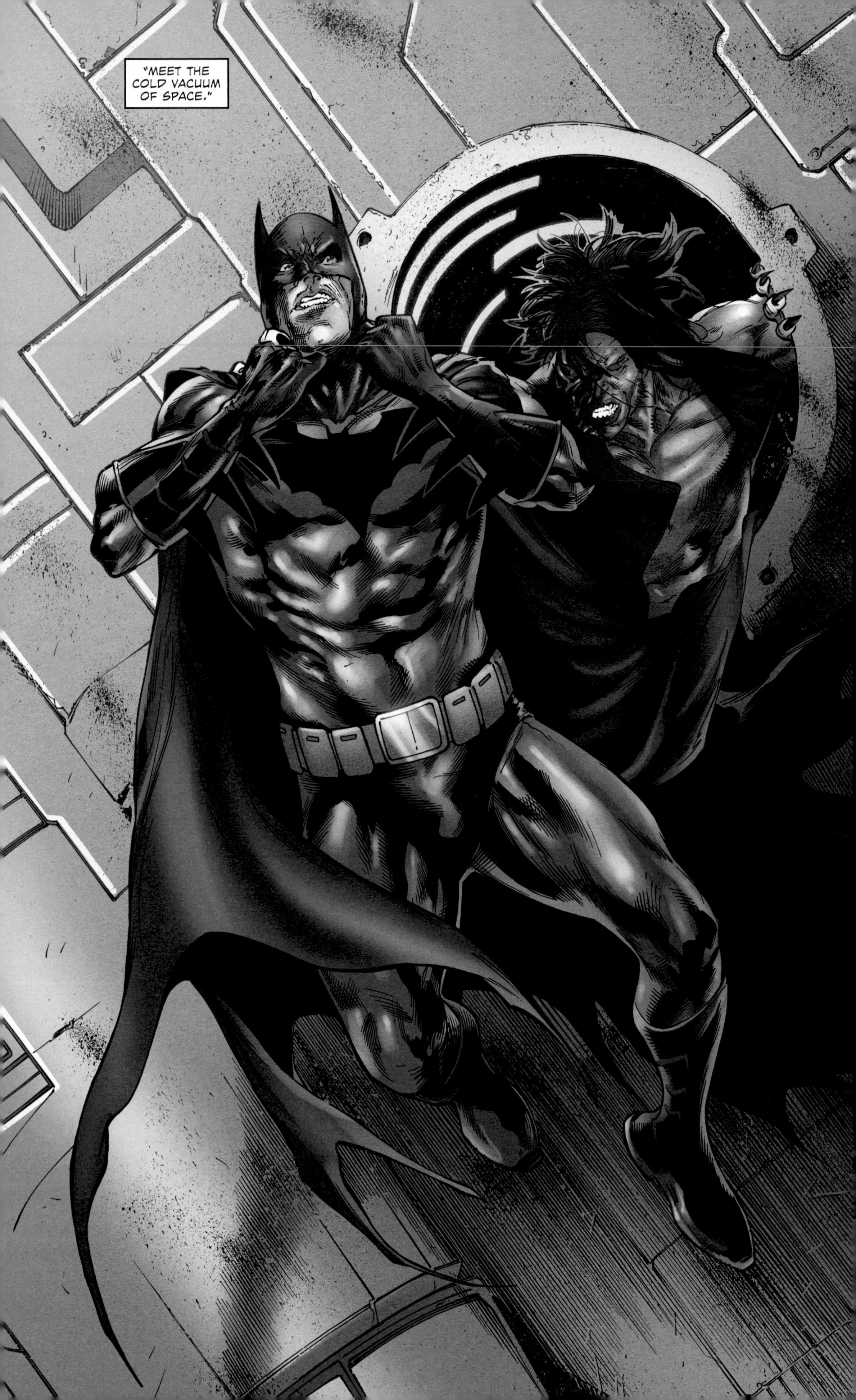
"MEET THE COLD VACUUM OF SPACE."

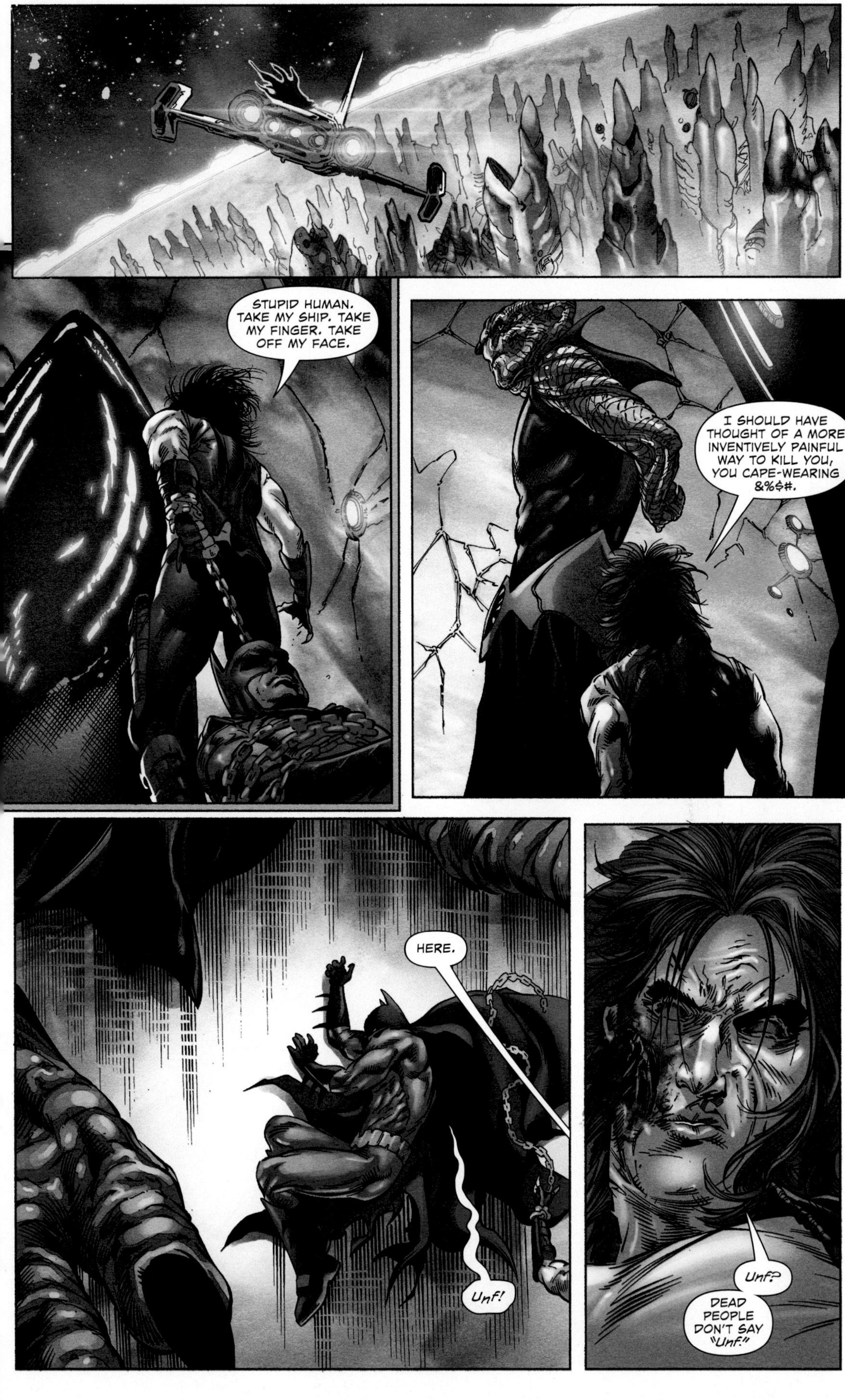
STUPID HUMAN. TAKE MY SHIP. TAKE MY FINGER. TAKE OFF MY FACE.
I SHOULD HAVE THOUGHT OF A MORE INVENTIVELY PAINFUL WAY TO KILL YOU, YOU CAPE-WEARING &%$#.
HERE.
Unf!
Unf?
DEAD PEOPLE DON'T SAY "Unf."

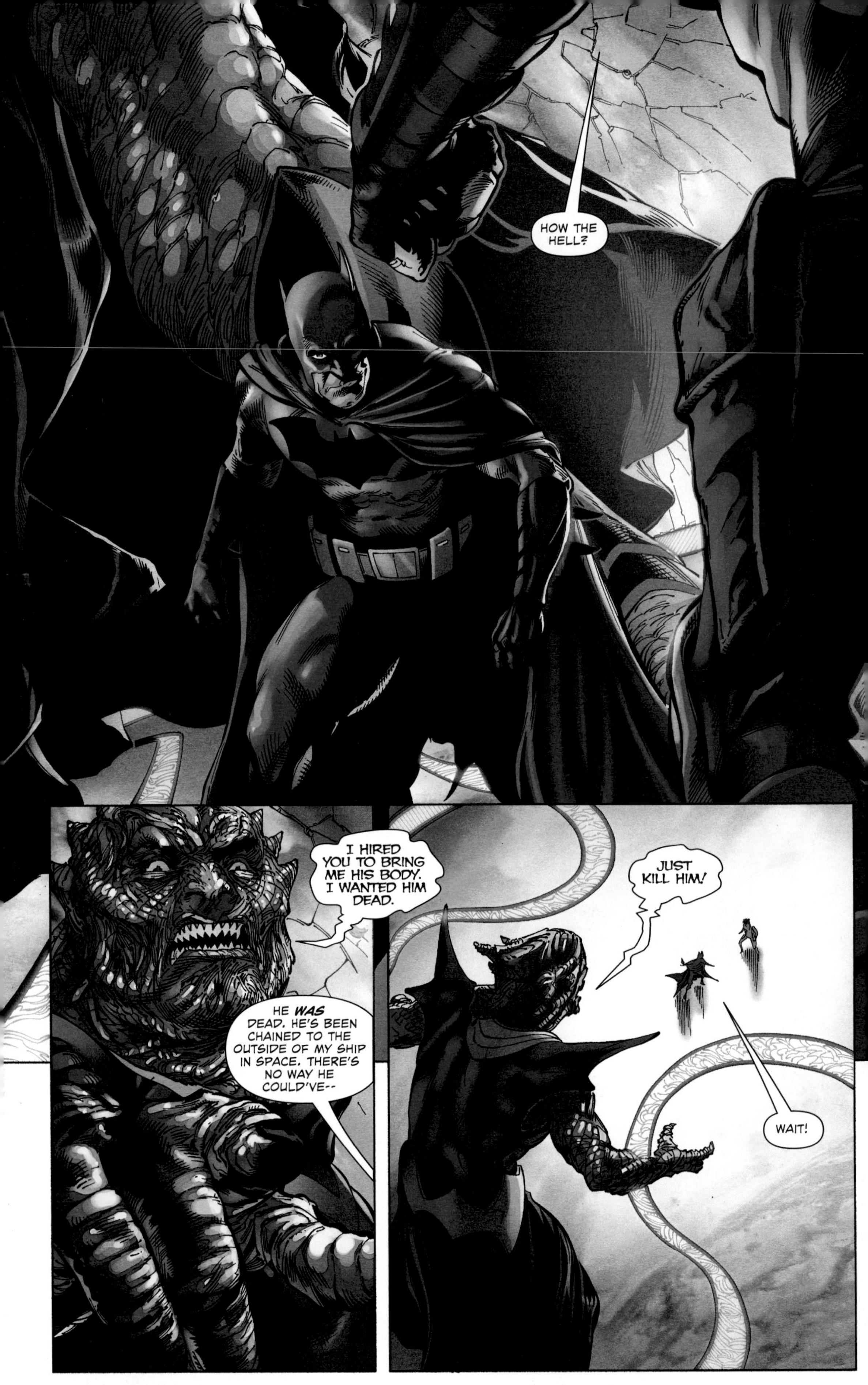
HOW THE HELL?
I HIRED YOU TO BRING ME HIS BODY. I WANTED HIM DEAD.
HE WAS DEAD. HE'S BEEN CHAINED TO THE OUTSIDE OF MY SHIP IN SPACE. THERE'S NO WAY HE COULD'VE--
JUST KILL HIM!
WAIT!

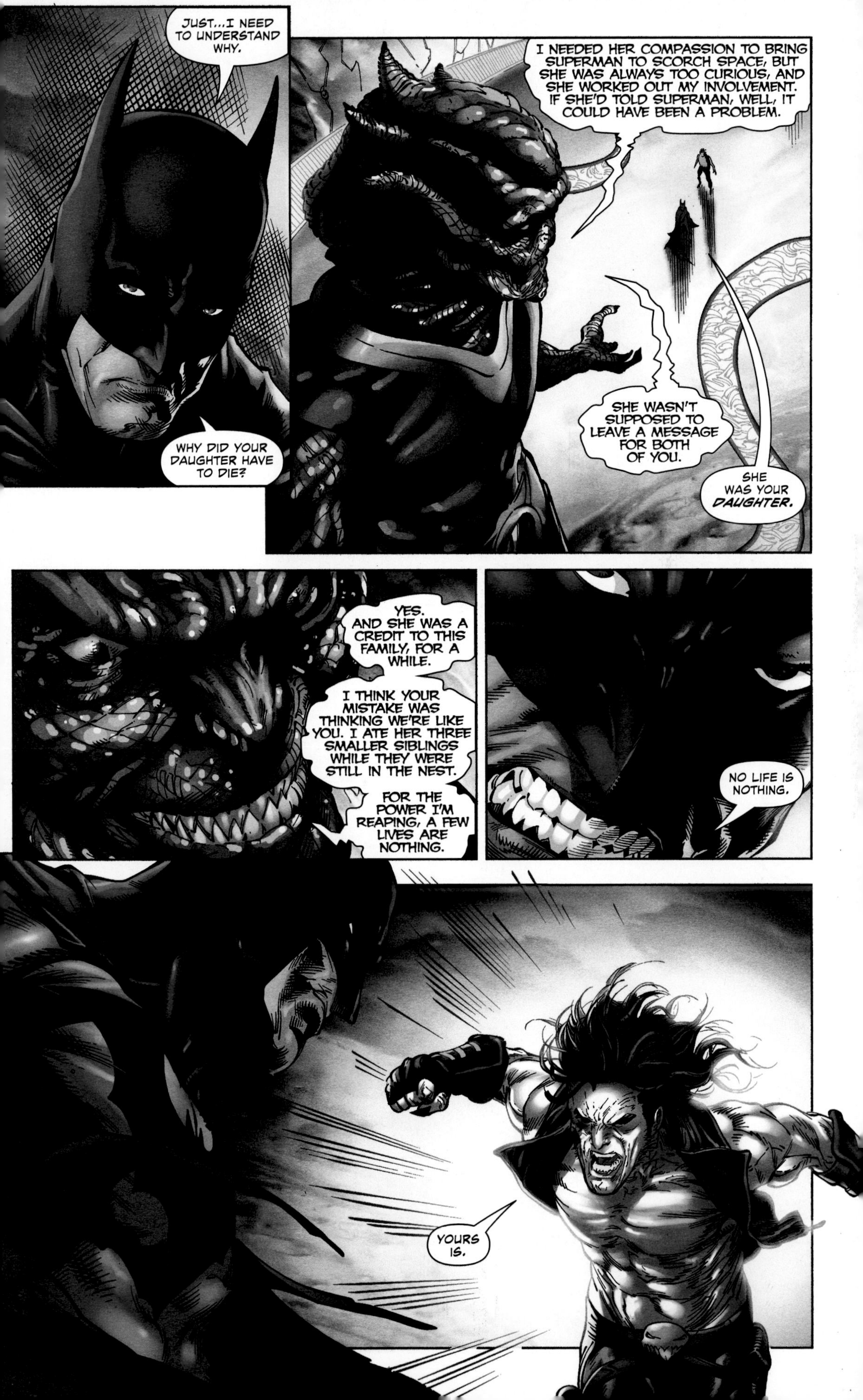
JUST...I NEED TO UNDERSTAND WHY.
WHY DID YOUR DAUGHTER HAVE TO DIE?
I NEEDED HER COMPASSION TO BRING SUPERMAN TO SCORCH SPACE, BUT SHE WAS ALWAYS TOO CURIOUS, AND SHE WORKED OUT MY INVOLVEMENT. IF SHE'D TOLD SUPERMAN, WELL, IT COULD HAVE BEEN A PROBLEM.
SHE WASN'T SUPPOSED TO LEAVE A MESSAGE FOR BOTH OF YOU.
SHE WAS YOUR *DAUGHTER.*
YES. AND SHE WAS A CREDIT TO THIS FAMILY, FOR A WHILE.
I THINK YOUR MISTAKE WAS THINKING WE'RE LIKE YOU. I ATE HER THREE SMALLER SIBLINGS WHILE THEY WERE STILL IN THE NEST.
FOR THE POWER I'M REAPING, A FEW LIVES ARE NOTHING.
NO LIFE IS NOTHING.
YOURS IS.

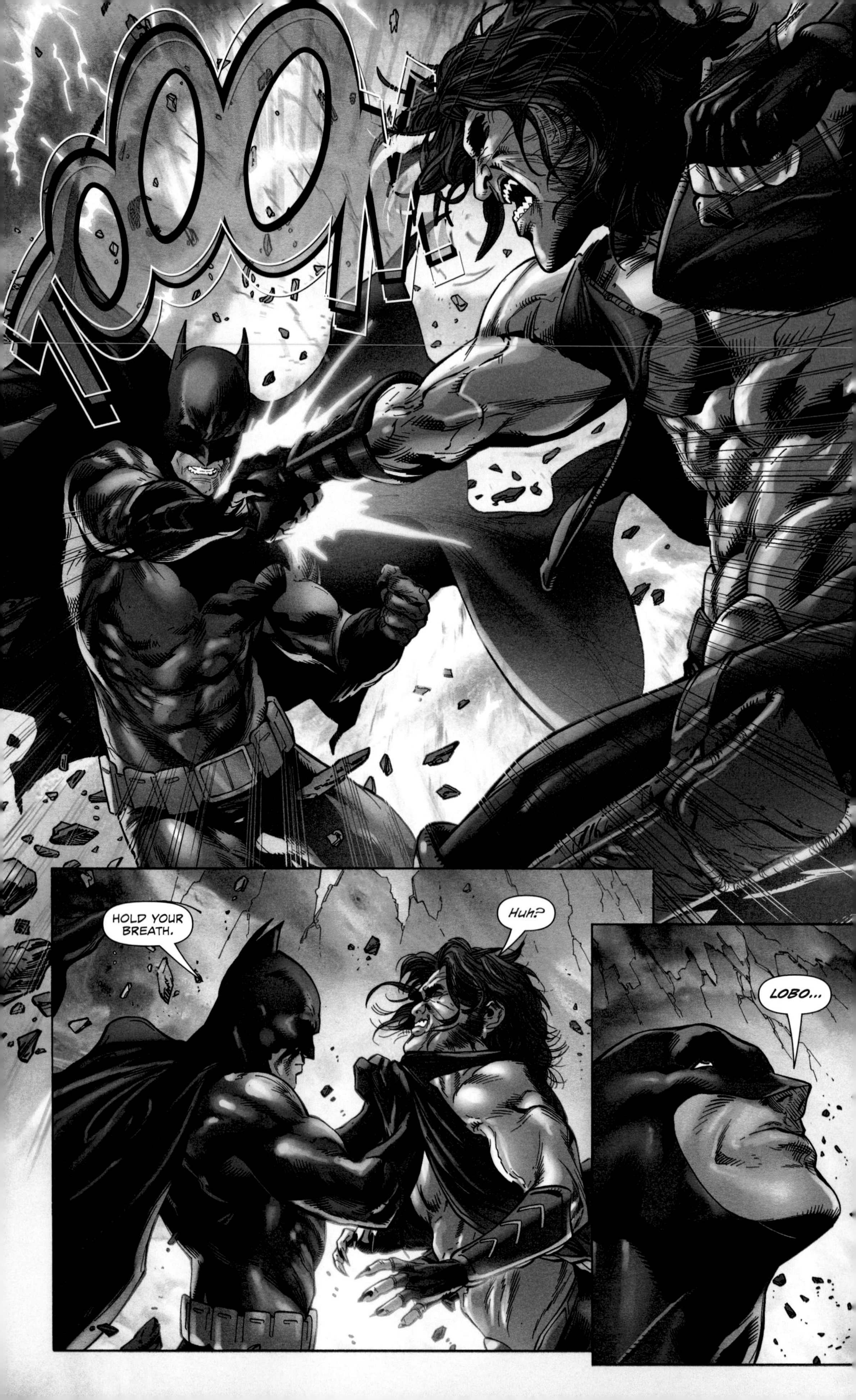
BOOOM!
HOLD YOUR BREATH.
Huh?
LOBO...

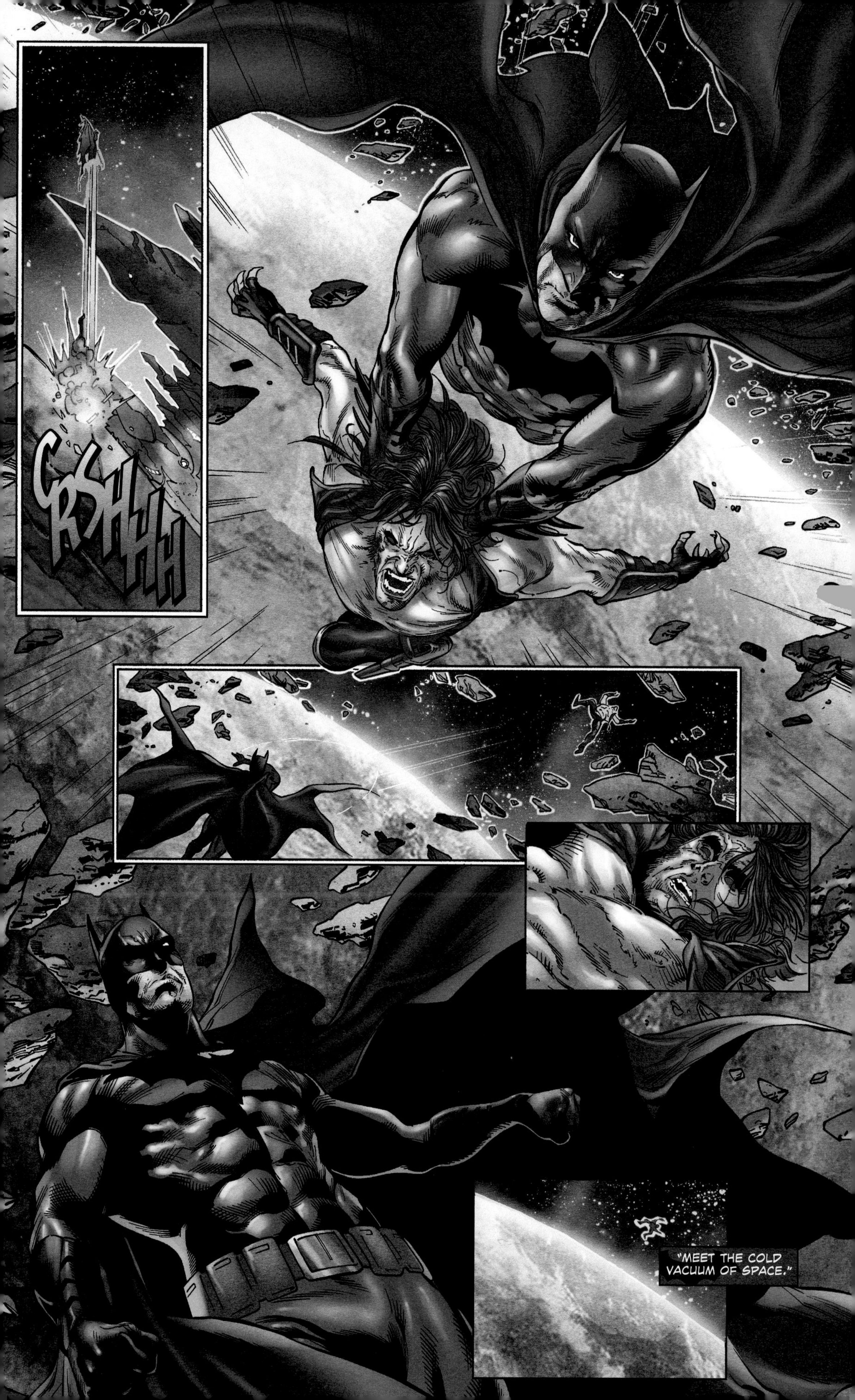
CRSHHH
"MEET THE COLD VACUUM OF SPACE."

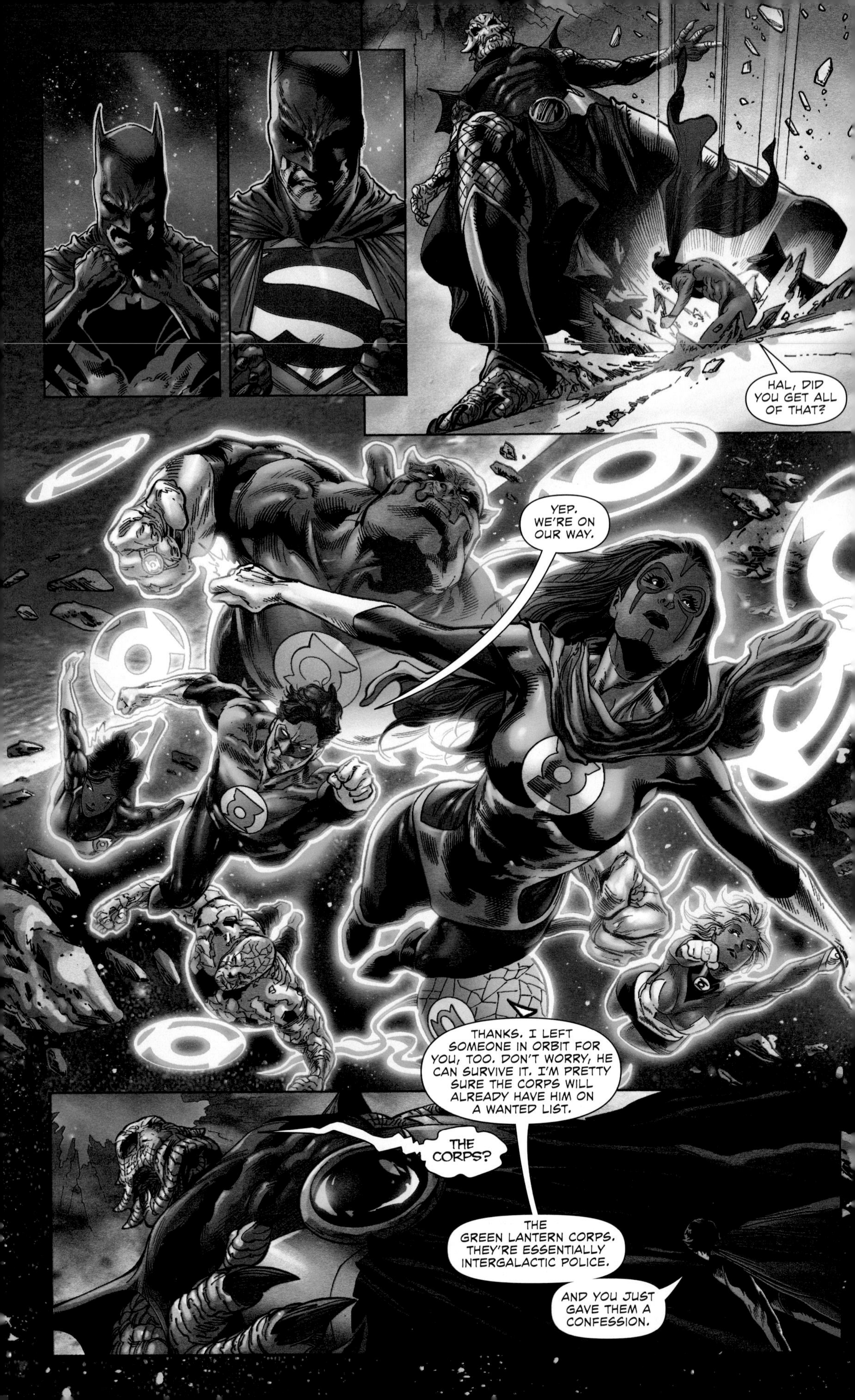
HAL, DID YOU GET ALL OF THAT?
YEP. WE'RE ON OUR WAY.
THANKS. I LEFT SOMEONE IN ORBIT FOR YOU, TOO. DON'T WORRY, HE CAN SURVIVE IT. I'M PRETTY SURE THE CORPS WILL ALREADY HAVE HIM ON A WANTED LIST.
THE CORPS?
THE GREEN LANTERN CORPS. THEY'RE ESSENTIALLY INTERGALACTIC POLICE.
AND YOU JUST GAVE THEM A CONFESSION.

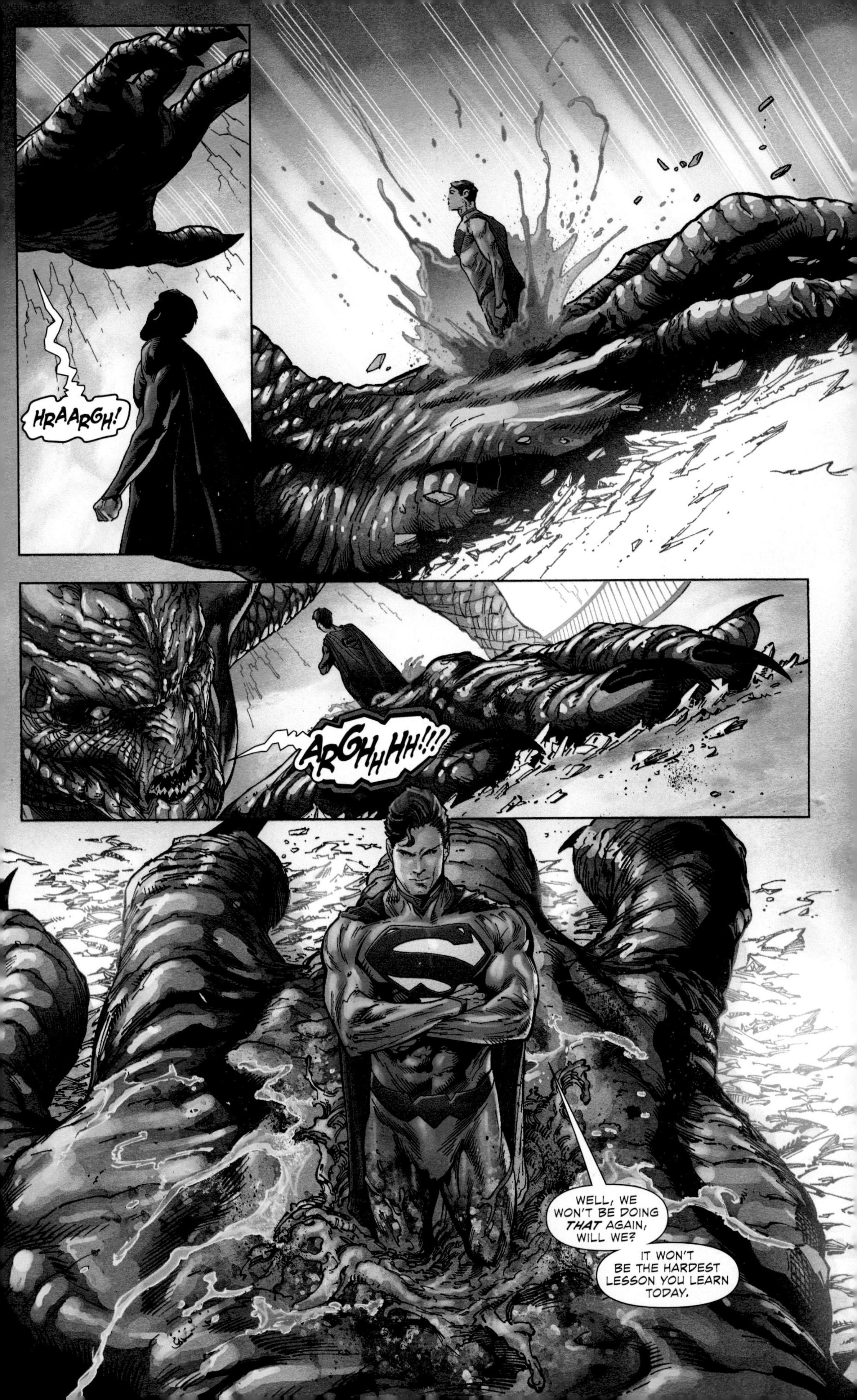
HRAARGH!
ARGHHHH!!!
WELL, WE WON'T BE DOING *THAT* AGAIN, WILL WE?
IT WON'T BE THE HARDEST LESSON YOU LEARN TODAY.

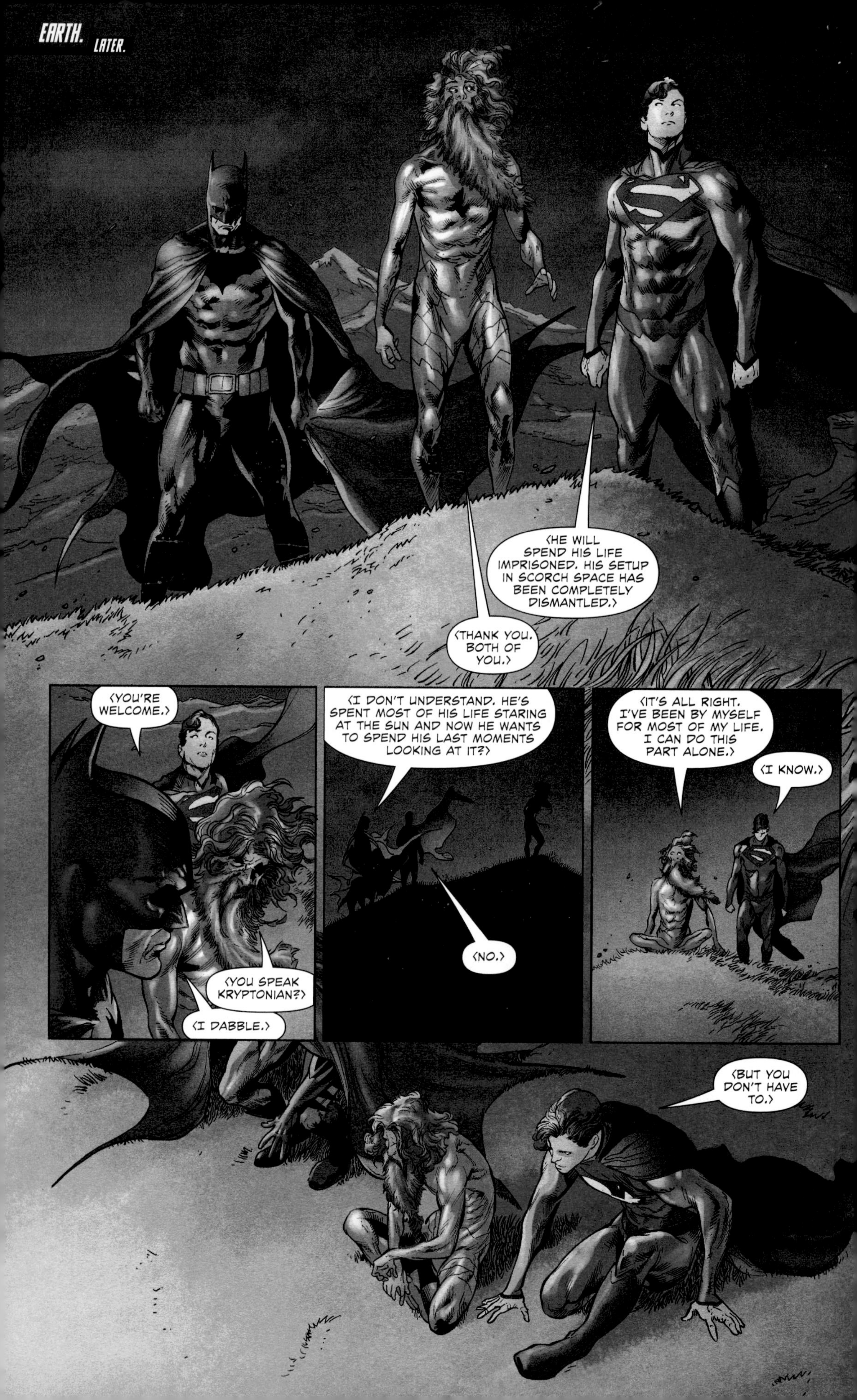
EARTH. LATER.
⟨HE WILL SPEND HIS LIFE IMPRISONED. HIS SETUP IN SCORCH SPACE HAS BEEN COMPLETELY DISMANTLED.⟩
⟨THANK YOU. BOTH OF YOU.⟩
⟨YOU'RE WELCOME.⟩
⟨YOU SPEAK KRYPTONIAN?⟩
⟨I DABBLE.⟩
⟨I DON'T UNDERSTAND. HE'S SPENT MOST OF HIS LIFE STARING AT THE SUN AND NOW HE WANTS TO SPEND HIS LAST MOMENTS LOOKING AT IT?⟩
⟨NO.⟩
⟨IT'S ALL RIGHT. I'VE BEEN BY MYSELF FOR MOST OF MY LIFE. I CAN DO THIS PART ALONE.⟩
⟨I KNOW.⟩
⟨BUT YOU DON'T HAVE TO.⟩

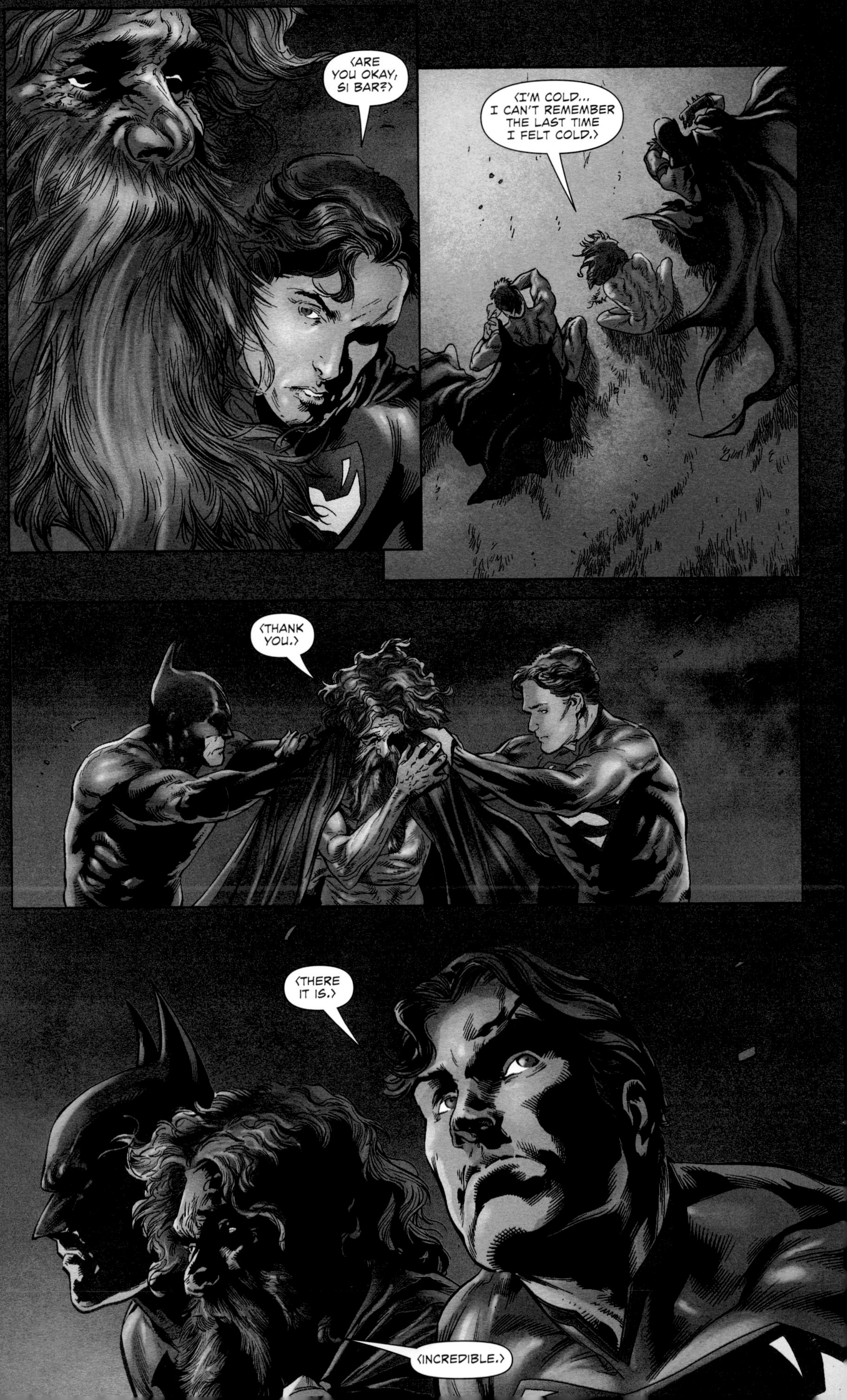

‹ARE YOU OKAY, SI BAR?›
‹I'M COLD... I CAN'T REMEMBER THE LAST TIME I FELT COLD.›
‹THANK YOU.›
‹THERE IT IS.›
‹INCREDIBLE.›

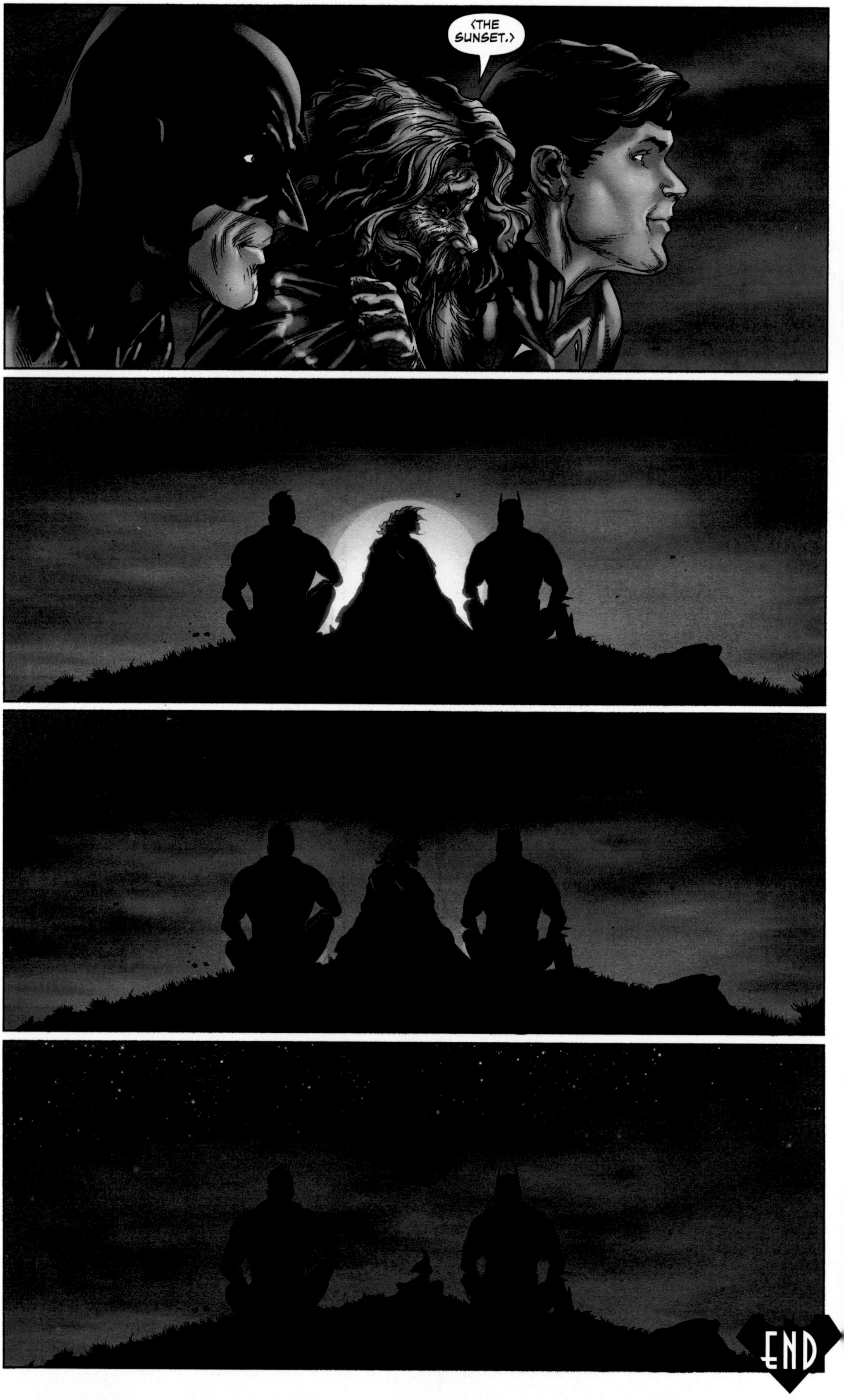
<THE SUNSET.>
END

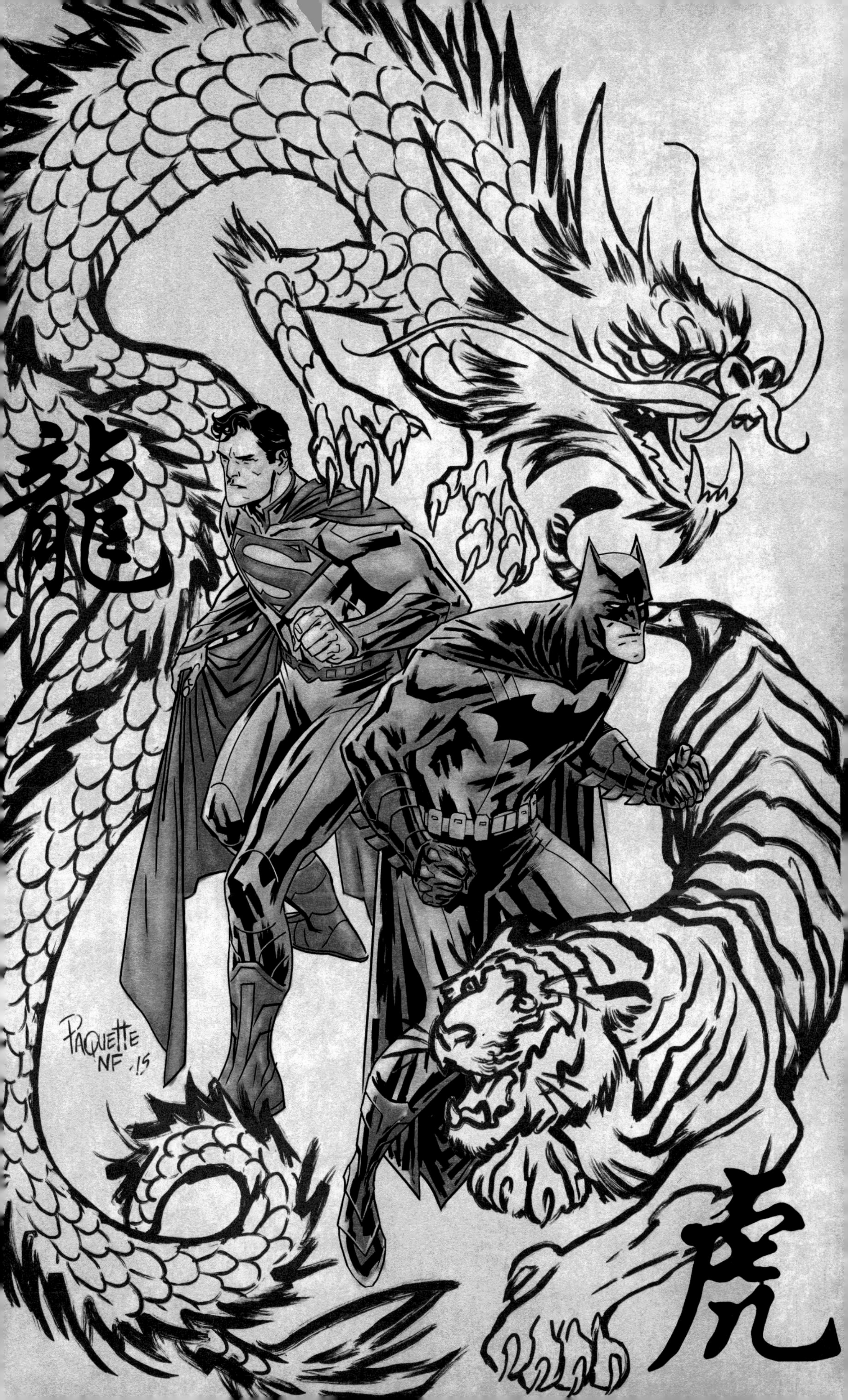

龍
PAQUETTE
NF '15
虎

Previously,
in SUPERMAN #51...

His never-ending battles have finally taken their toll on the Last Son of Krypton. After repeated exposure to Kryptonite and the fire pits of Apokolips, as well as encounters with the Kryptonian sun god, Rao, Superman faces an irrefutable diagnosis: he is dying.

With the time he has left, Superman chooses to say good-bye to those closest to him, and seeks to prepare the people of Earth for a future without their greatest hero. But even though he's getting sicker, there's always a job for Superman.

Halfway around the world in China, his residual solar energy flares become the source of mysterious tests conducted by Dr. Omen. And, closer to home, after being struck by a strange energy blast, an escaped convict begins manifesting unusual powers and believes himself to be none other than the Man of Steel...

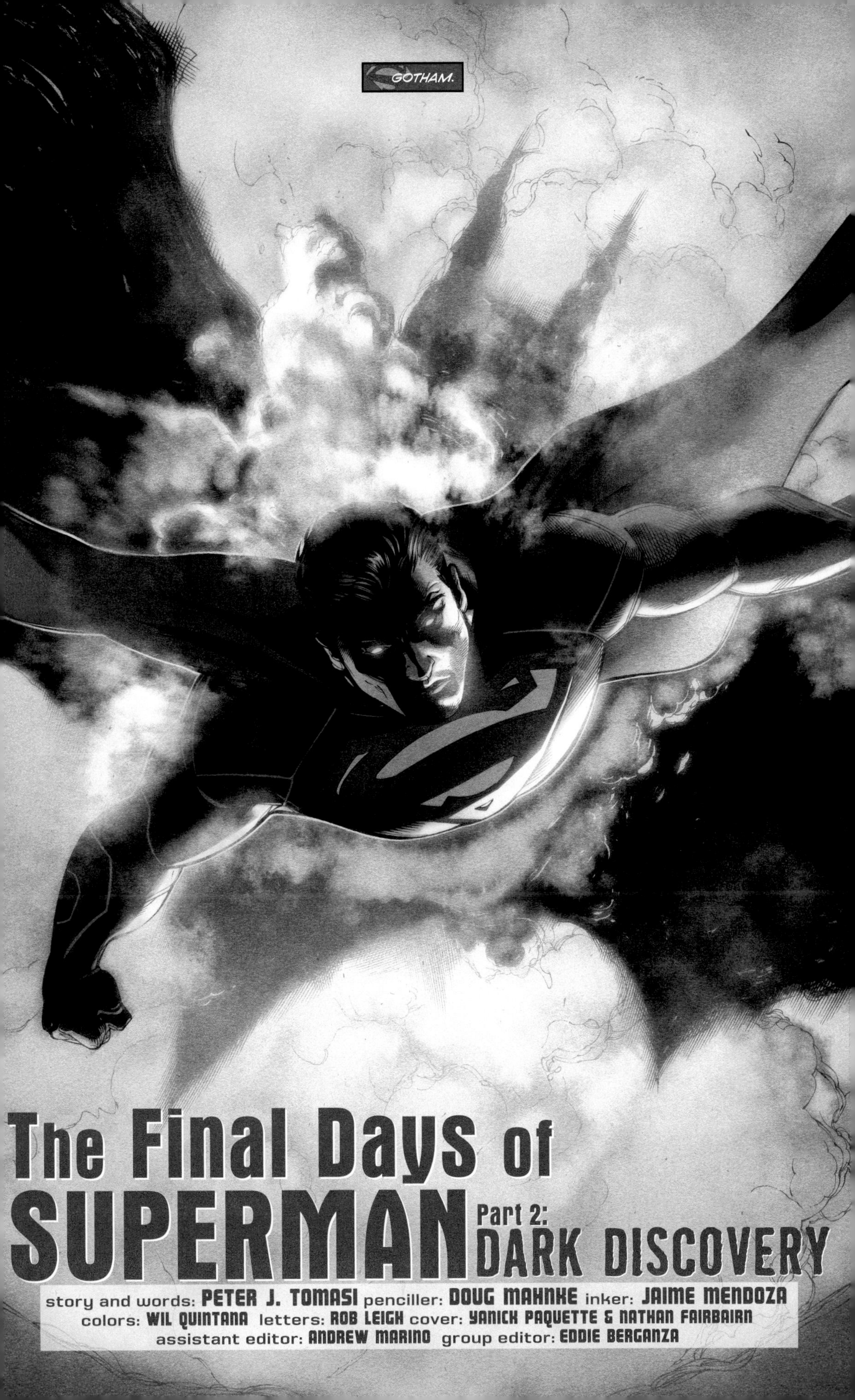
GOTHAM.
The Final Days of SUPERMAN
Part 2: DARK DISCOVERY
story and words: PETER J. TOMASI penciller: DOUG MAHNKE inker: JAIME MENDOZA
colors: WIL QUINTANA letters: ROB LEIGH cover: YANICK PAQUETTE & NATHAN FAIRBAIRN
assistant editor: ANDREW MARINO group editor: EDDIE BERGANZA

THE FIRST AND LAST PLACE YOU GO...
BUDDA BUDDA
BUDDA
TAKE HIM DOWN!
I'M GONNA GUT HIM FOR SCREWING UP THIS JOB!

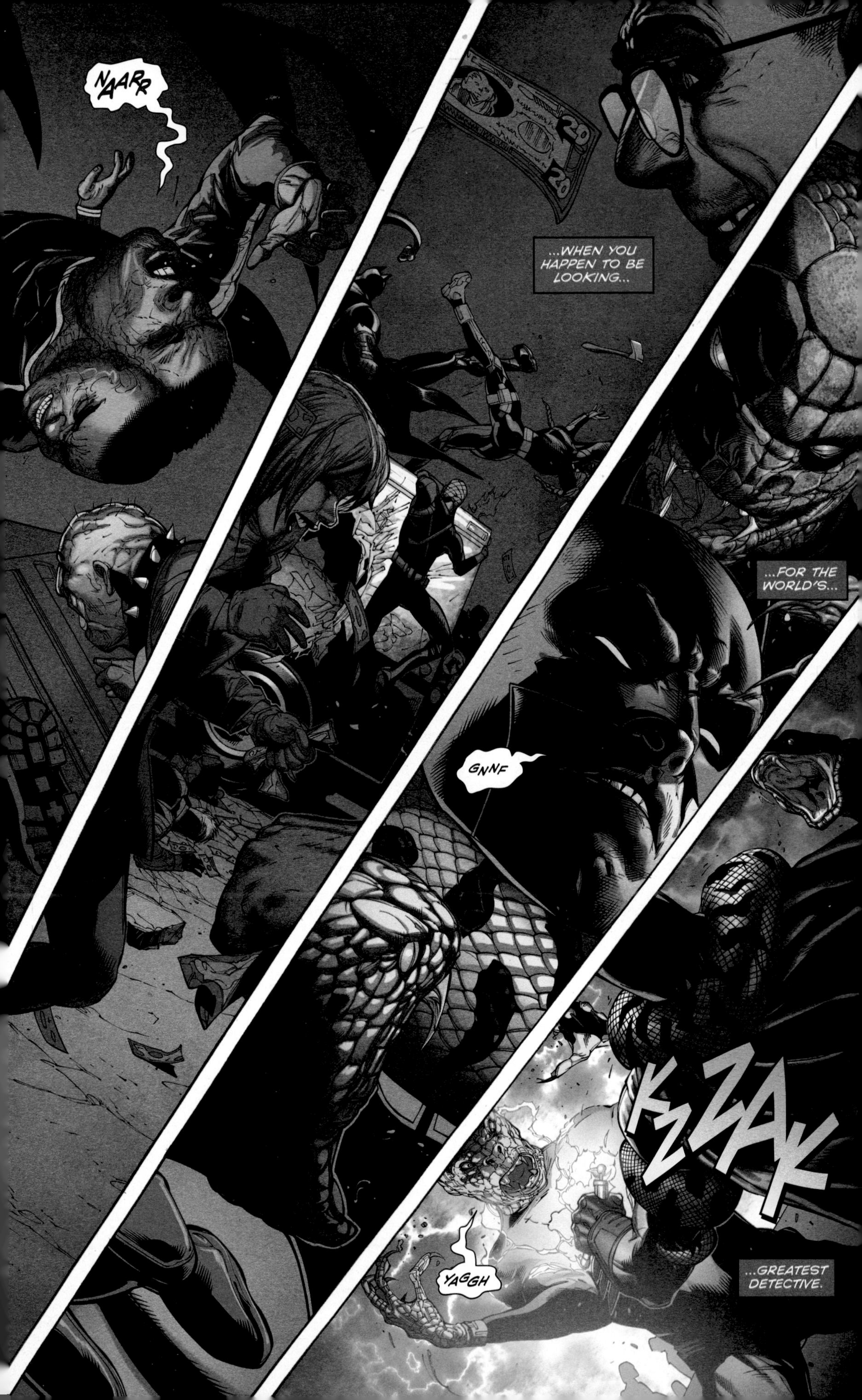
NAARR
...WHEN YOU HAPPEN TO BE LOOKING...
...FOR THE WORLD'S...
GNNF
KZZAK
YAGGH
...GREATEST DETECTIVE.

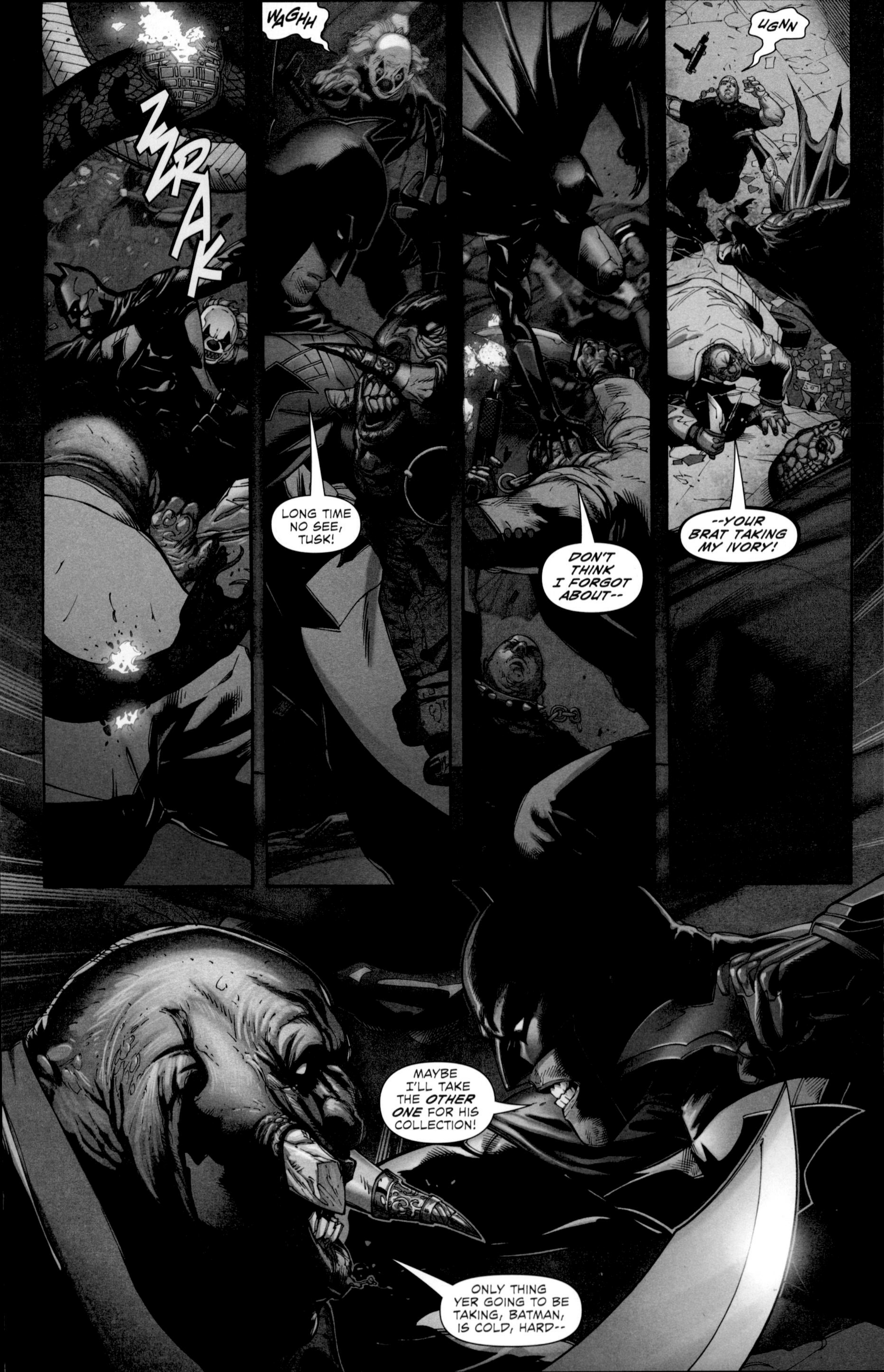
ZZRAK
WAGHH
LONG TIME NO SEE, TUSK!
DON'T THINK I FORGOT ABOUT--
UGNN
--YOUR BRAT TAKING MY IVORY!
MAYBE I'LL TAKE THE OTHER ONE FOR HIS COLLECTION!
ONLY THING YER GOING TO BE TAKING, BATMAN, IS COLD, HARD--

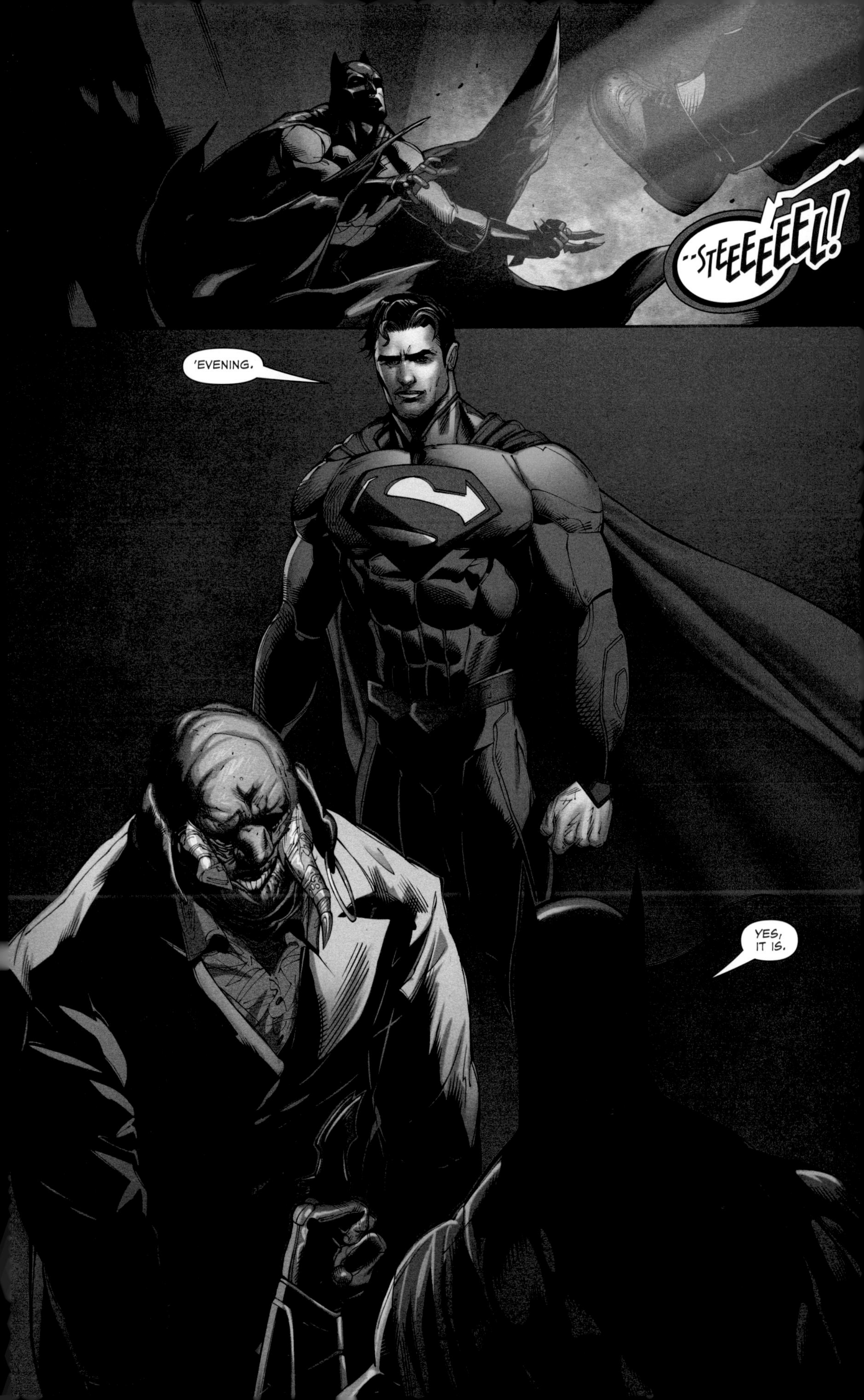
--STEEEEEEL!
'EVENING.
YES, IT IS.

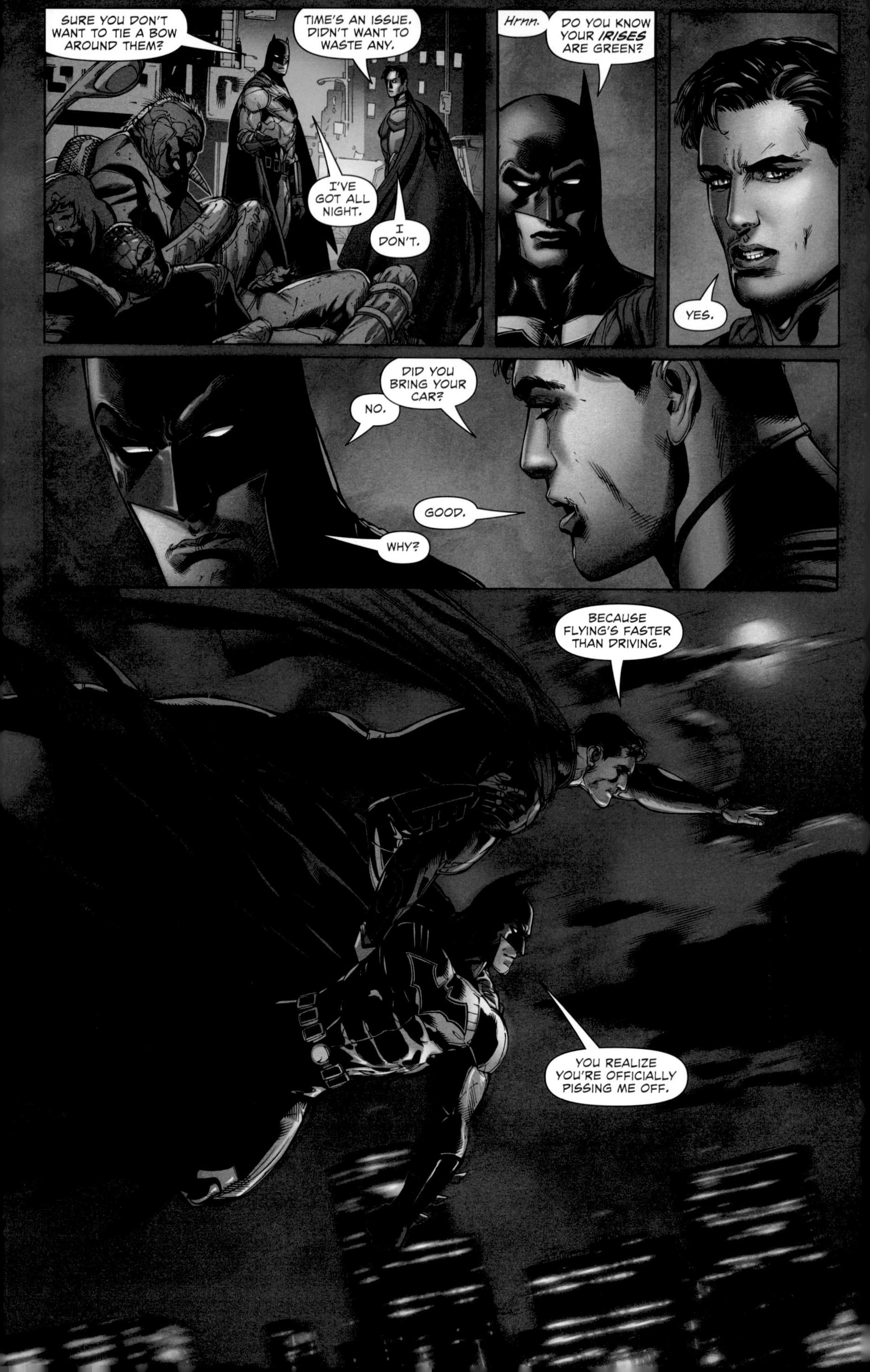
SURE YOU DON'T WANT TO TIE A BOW AROUND THEM?
TIME'S AN ISSUE. DIDN'T WANT TO WASTE ANY.
I'VE GOT ALL NIGHT.
I DON'T.
Hrnn.
DO YOU KNOW YOUR IRISES ARE GREEN?
YES.
DID YOU BRING YOUR CAR?
NO.
GOOD.
WHY?
BECAUSE FLYING'S FASTER THAN DRIVING.
YOU REALIZE YOU'RE OFFICIALLY PISSING ME OFF.

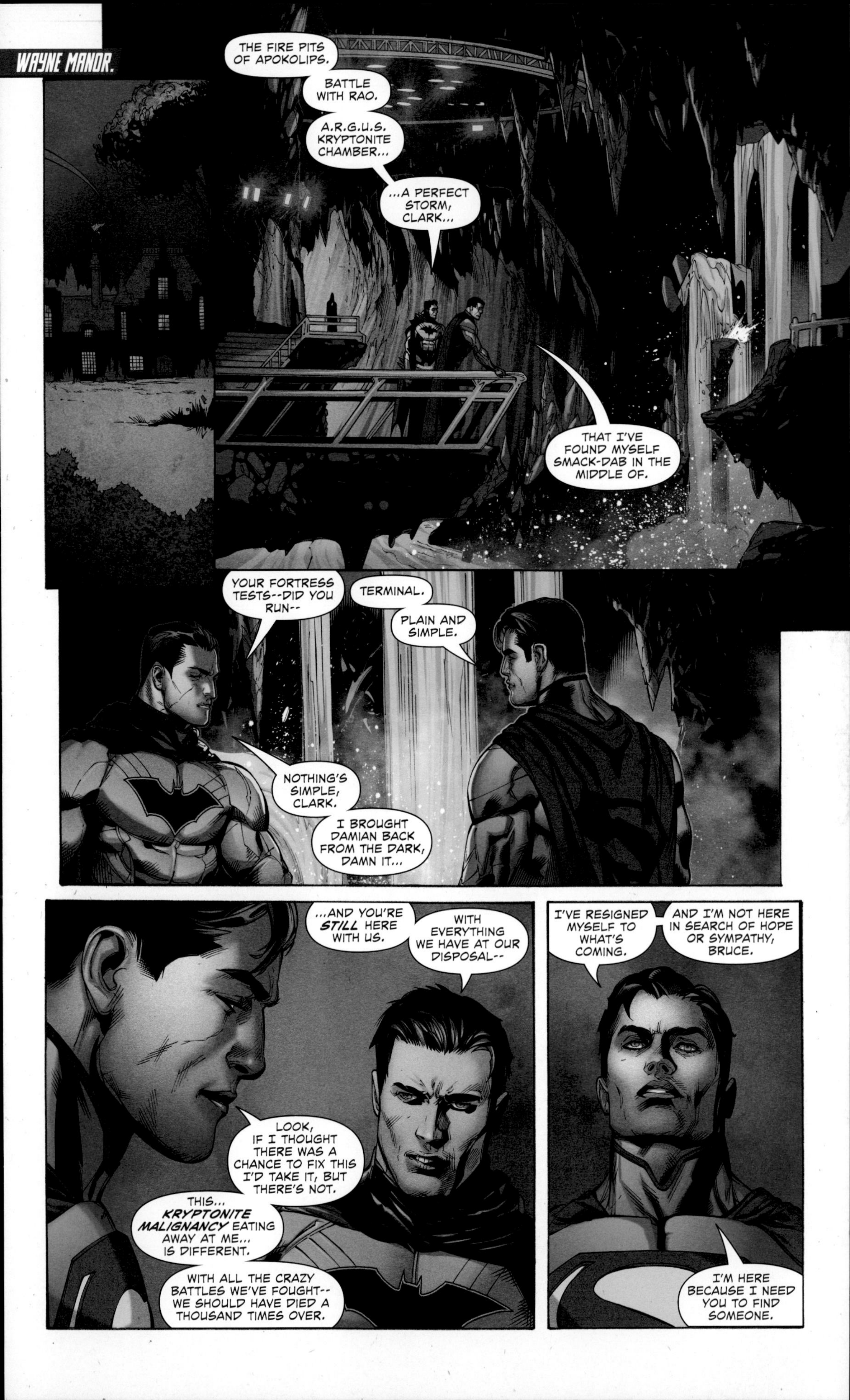
WAYNE MANOR.
THE FIRE PITS OF APOKOLIPS.
BATTLE WITH RAO.
A.R.G.U.S. KRYPTONITE CHAMBER...
...A PERFECT STORM, CLARK...
THAT I'VE FOUND MYSELF SMACK-DAB IN THE MIDDLE OF.
YOUR FORTRESS TESTS--DID YOU RUN--
TERMINAL.
PLAIN AND SIMPLE.
NOTHING'S SIMPLE, CLARK.
I BROUGHT DAMIAN BACK FROM THE DARK, DAMN IT...
...AND YOU'RE STILL HERE WITH US.
WITH EVERYTHING WE HAVE AT OUR DISPOSAL--
LOOK, IF I THOUGHT THERE WAS A CHANCE TO FIX THIS I'D TAKE IT, BUT THERE'S NOT.
THIS... KRYPTONITE MALIGNANCY EATING AWAY AT ME... IS DIFFERENT.
WITH ALL THE CRAZY BATTLES WE'VE FOUGHT--WE SHOULD HAVE DIED A THOUSAND TIMES OVER.
I'VE RESIGNED MYSELF TO WHAT'S COMING.
AND I'M NOT HERE IN SEARCH OF HOPE OR SYMPATHY, BRUCE.
I'M HERE BECAUSE I NEED YOU TO FIND SOMEONE.

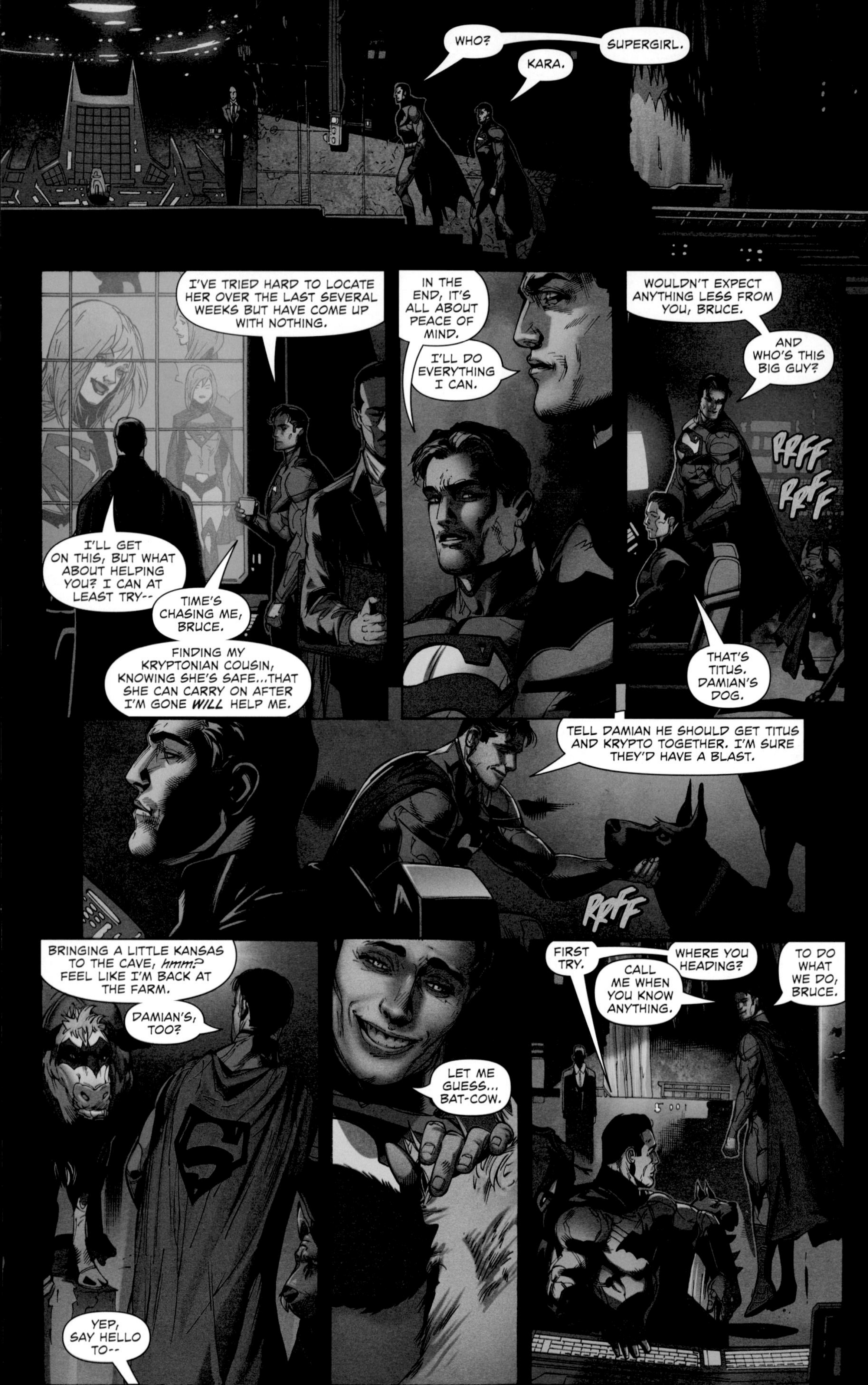
WHO?
SUPERGIRL.
KARA.
I'VE TRIED HARD TO LOCATE HER OVER THE LAST SEVERAL WEEKS BUT HAVE COME UP WITH NOTHING.
I'LL GET ON THIS, BUT WHAT ABOUT HELPING YOU? I CAN AT LEAST TRY--
TIME'S CHASING ME, BRUCE.
FINDING MY KRYPTONIAN COUSIN, KNOWING SHE'S SAFE...THAT SHE CAN CARRY ON AFTER I'M GONE WILL HELP ME.
IN THE END, IT'S ALL ABOUT PEACE OF MIND.
I'LL DO EVERYTHING I CAN.
WOULDN'T EXPECT ANYTHING LESS FROM YOU, BRUCE.
AND WHO'S THIS BIG GUY?
RRFF RRFF
THAT'S TITUS. DAMIAN'S DOG.
TELL DAMIAN HE SHOULD GET TITUS AND KRYPTO TOGETHER. I'M SURE THEY'D HAVE A BLAST.
RRFF
BRINGING A LITTLE KANSAS TO THE CAVE, hmm? FEEL LIKE I'M BACK AT THE FARM.
DAMIAN'S, TOO?
YEP, SAY HELLO TO--
LET ME GUESS... BAT-COW.
FIRST TRY.
CALL ME WHEN YOU KNOW ANYTHING.
WHERE YOU HEADING?
TO DO WHAT WE DO, BRUCE.

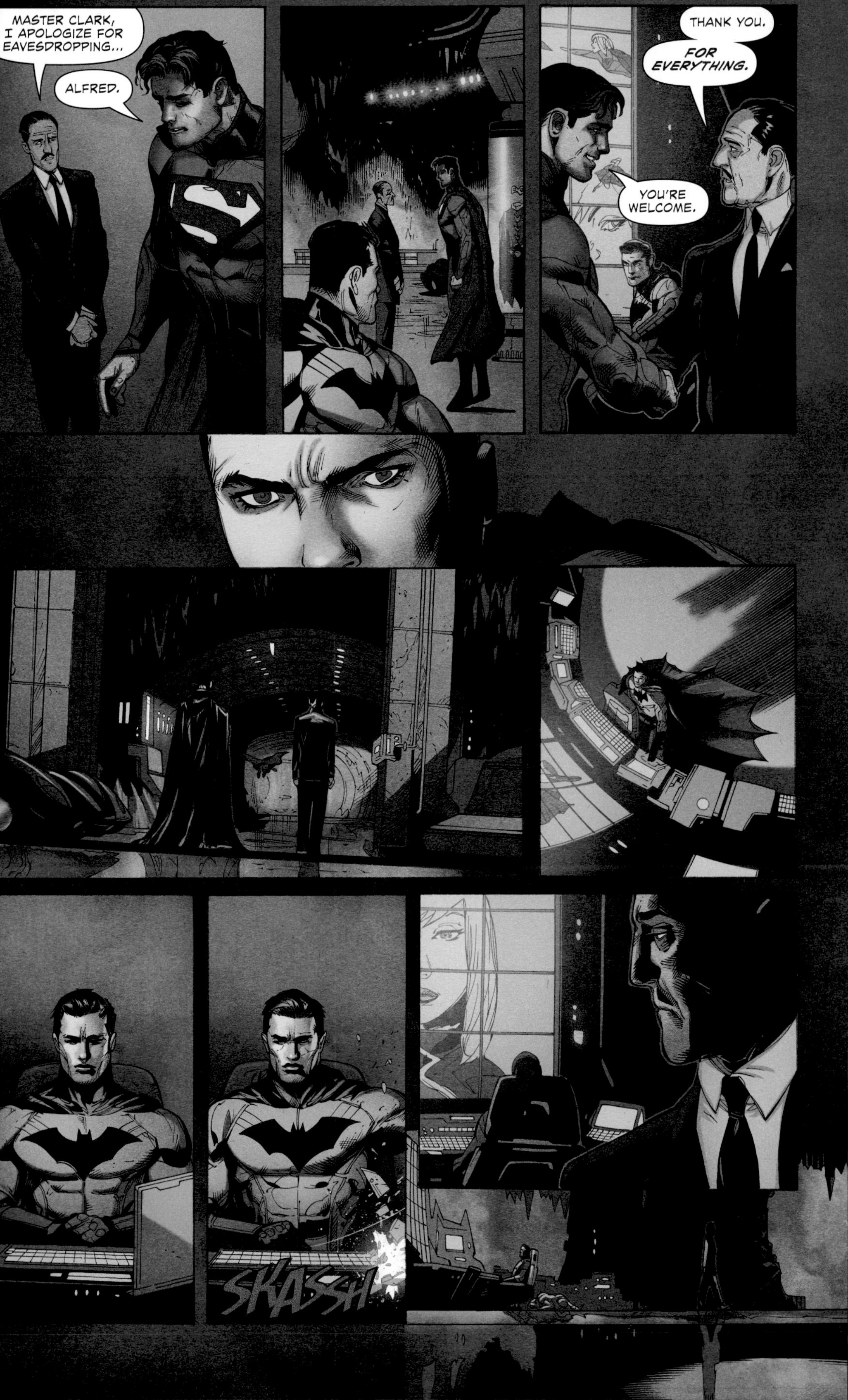
MASTER CLARK, I APOLOGIZE FOR EAVESDROPPING...
ALFRED.
THANK YOU.
FOR EVERYTHING.
YOU'RE WELCOME.
SKASSH

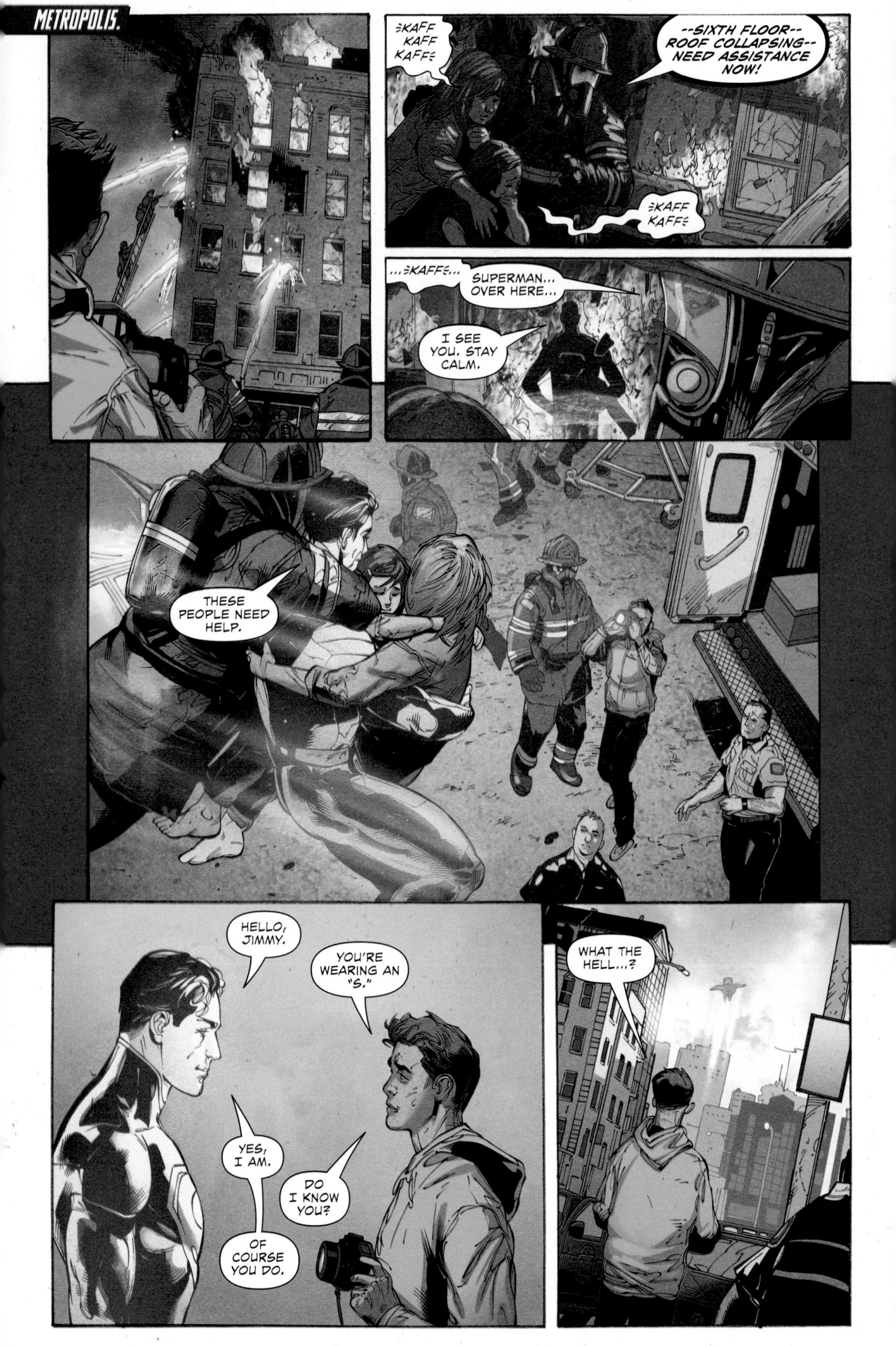
METROPOLIS.
KAFF KAFF KAFF
--SIXTH FLOOR-- ROOF COLLAPSING-- NEED ASSISTANCE NOW!
KAFF KAFF
...KAFF...
SUPERMAN... OVER HERE...
I SEE YOU. STAY CALM.
THESE PEOPLE NEED HELP.
HELLO, JIMMY.
YOU'RE WEARING AN "S."
YES, I AM.
DO I KNOW YOU?
OF COURSE YOU DO.
WHAT THE HELL...?

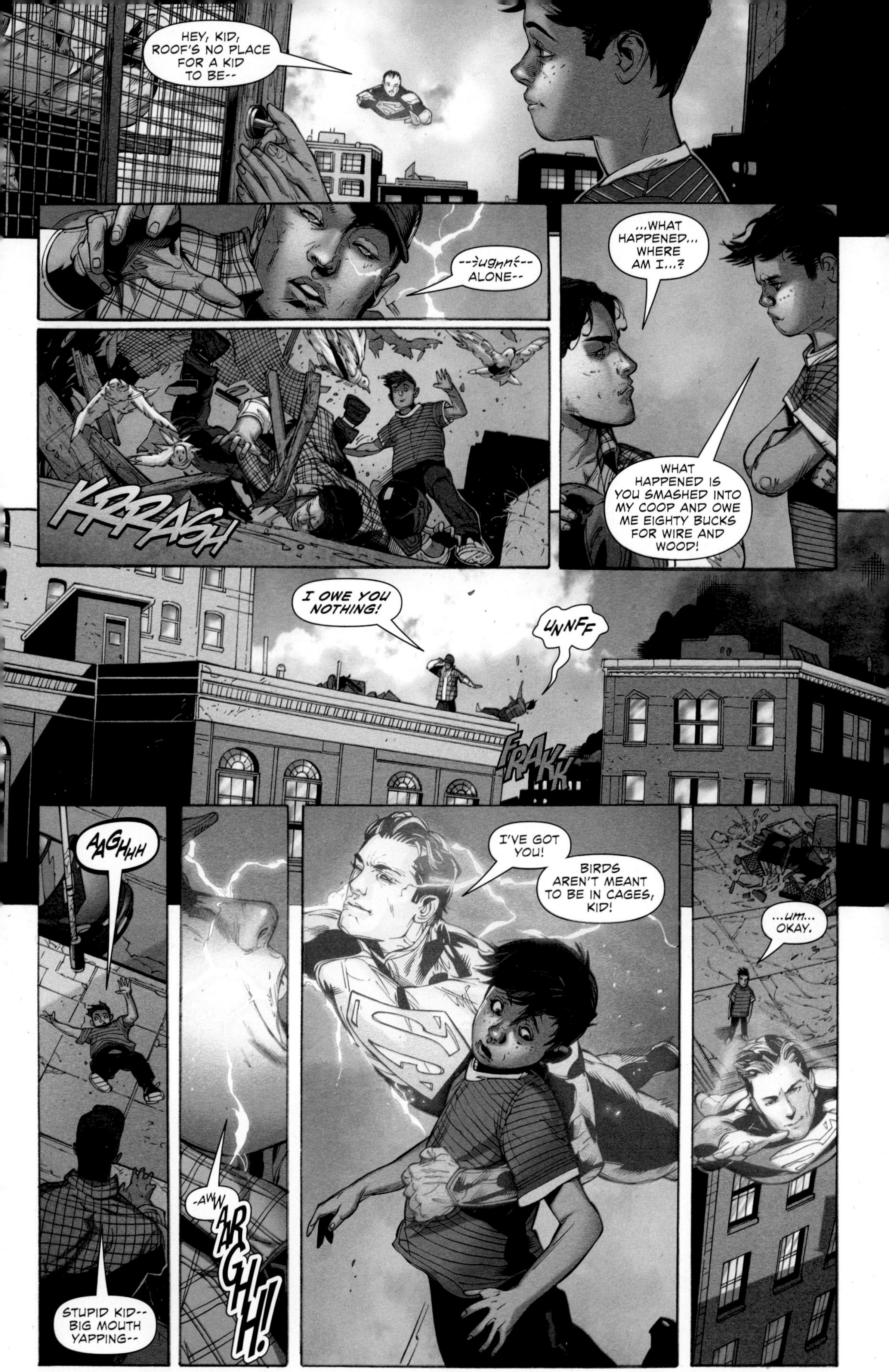
HEY, KID, ROOF'S NO PLACE FOR A KID TO BE--
--ugnn-- ALONE--
KRRASH
...WHAT HAPPENED... WHERE AM I...?
WHAT HAPPENED IS YOU SMASHED INTO MY COOP AND OWE ME EIGHTY BUCKS FOR WIRE AND WOOD!
I OWE YOU NOTHING!
UNNFF
FRAKKK
AAGHHH
STUPID KID-- BIG MOUTH YAPPING--
-AWWAARGHH!
I'VE GOT YOU!
BIRDS AREN'T MEANT TO BE IN CAGES, KID!
...UM... OKAY.

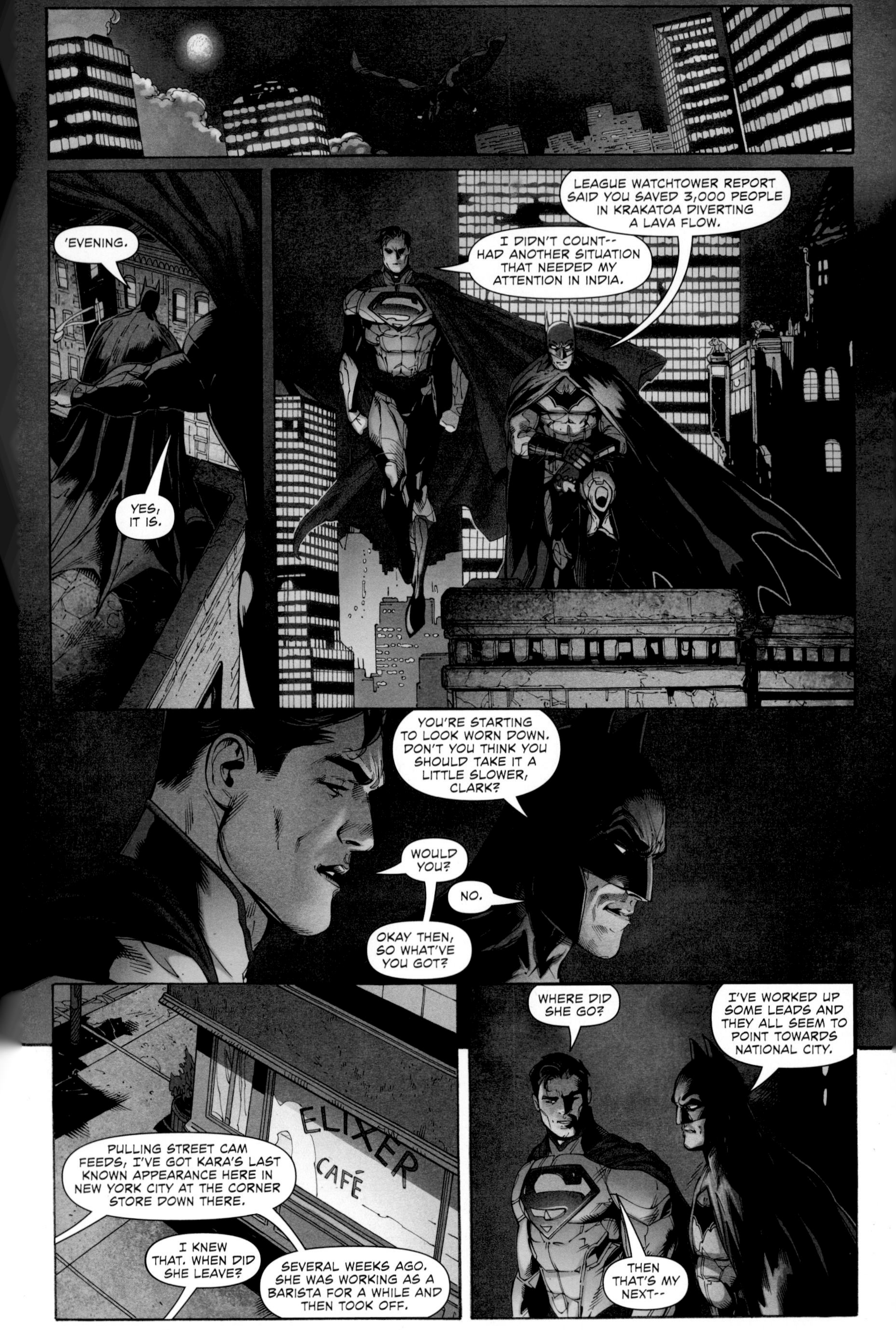
'EVENING.
YES, IT IS.
LEAGUE WATCHTOWER REPORT SAID YOU SAVED 3,000 PEOPLE IN KRAKATOA DIVERTING A LAVA FLOW.
I DIDN'T COUNT-- HAD ANOTHER SITUATION THAT NEEDED MY ATTENTION IN INDIA.
YOU'RE STARTING TO LOOK WORN DOWN. DON'T YOU THINK YOU SHOULD TAKE IT A LITTLE SLOWER, CLARK?
WOULD YOU?
NO.
OKAY THEN, SO WHAT'VE YOU GOT?
ELIXER
CAFÉ
PULLING STREET CAM FEEDS, I'VE GOT KARA'S LAST KNOWN APPEARANCE HERE IN NEW YORK CITY AT THE CORNER STORE DOWN THERE.
I KNEW THAT. WHEN DID SHE LEAVE?
SEVERAL WEEKS AGO. SHE WAS WORKING AS A BARISTA FOR A WHILE AND THEN TOOK OFF.
WHERE DID SHE GO?
I'VE WORKED UP SOME LEADS AND THEY ALL SEEM TO POINT TOWARDS NATIONAL CITY.
THEN THAT'S MY NEXT--

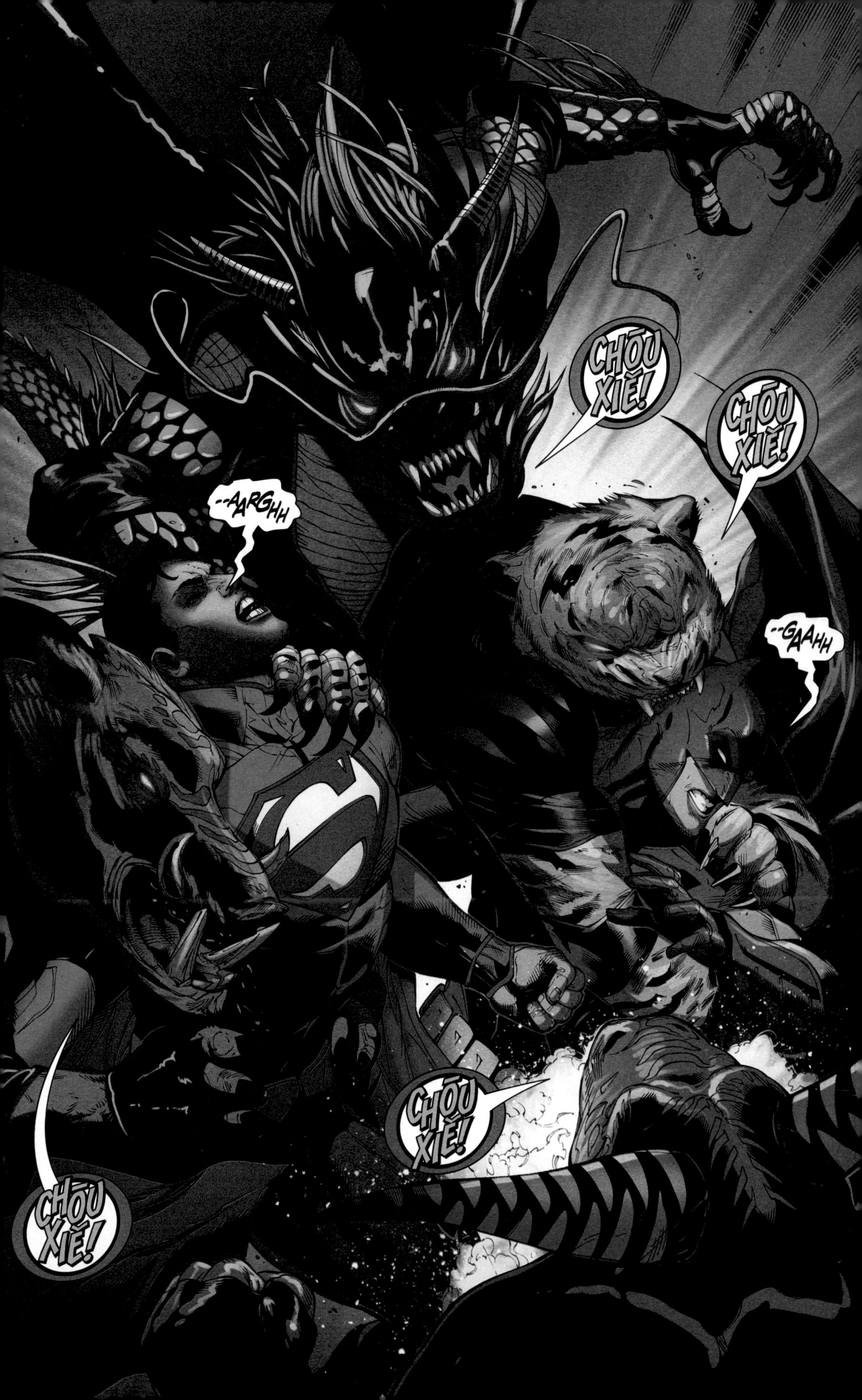
CHŌU XIÉ!
CHŌU XIÉ!
--AARGHH
--GAAHH
CHŌU XIÉ!
CHŌU XIÉ!

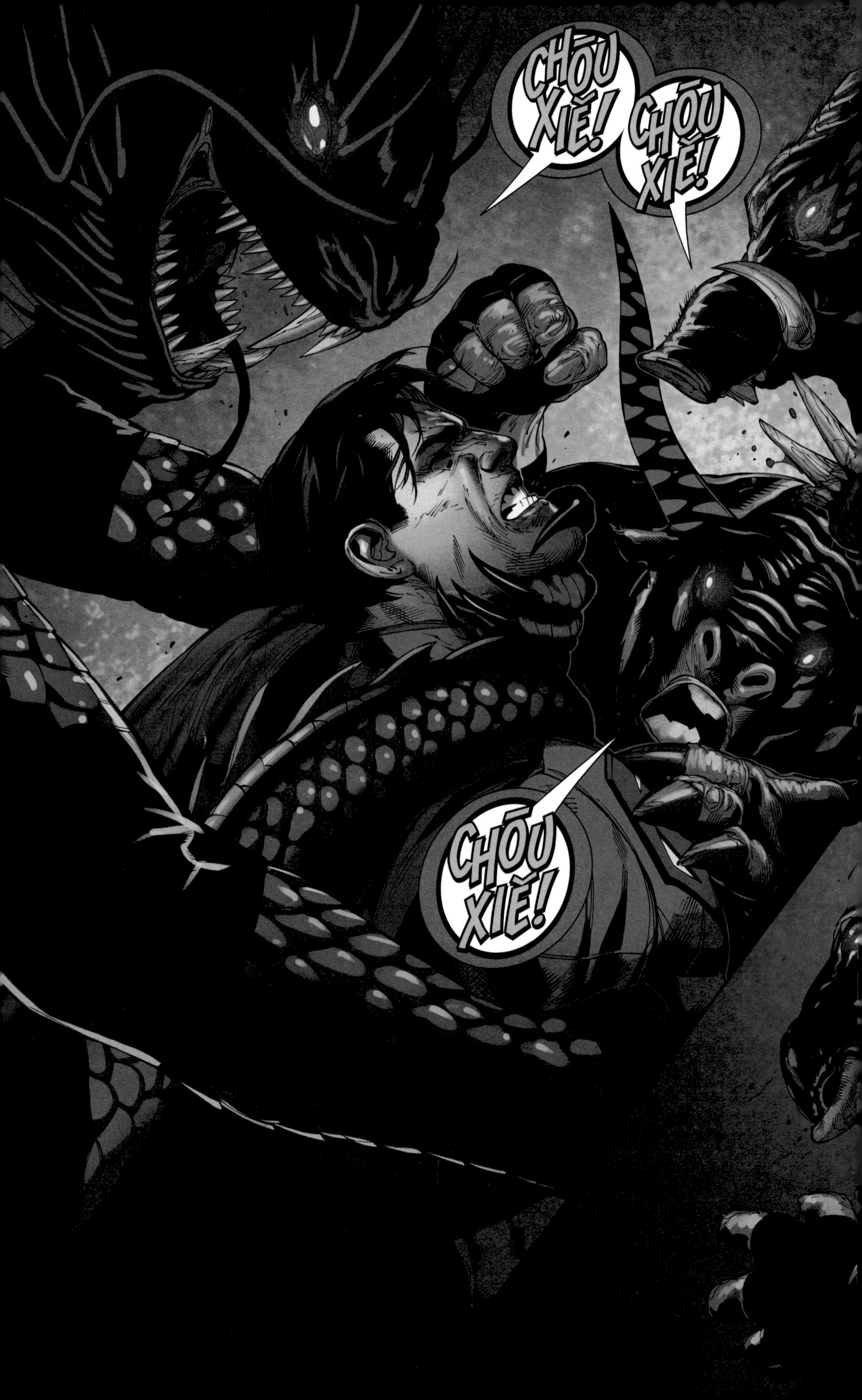
CHŌU XIĚ!
CHŌU XIĚ!
CHŌU XIĚ!

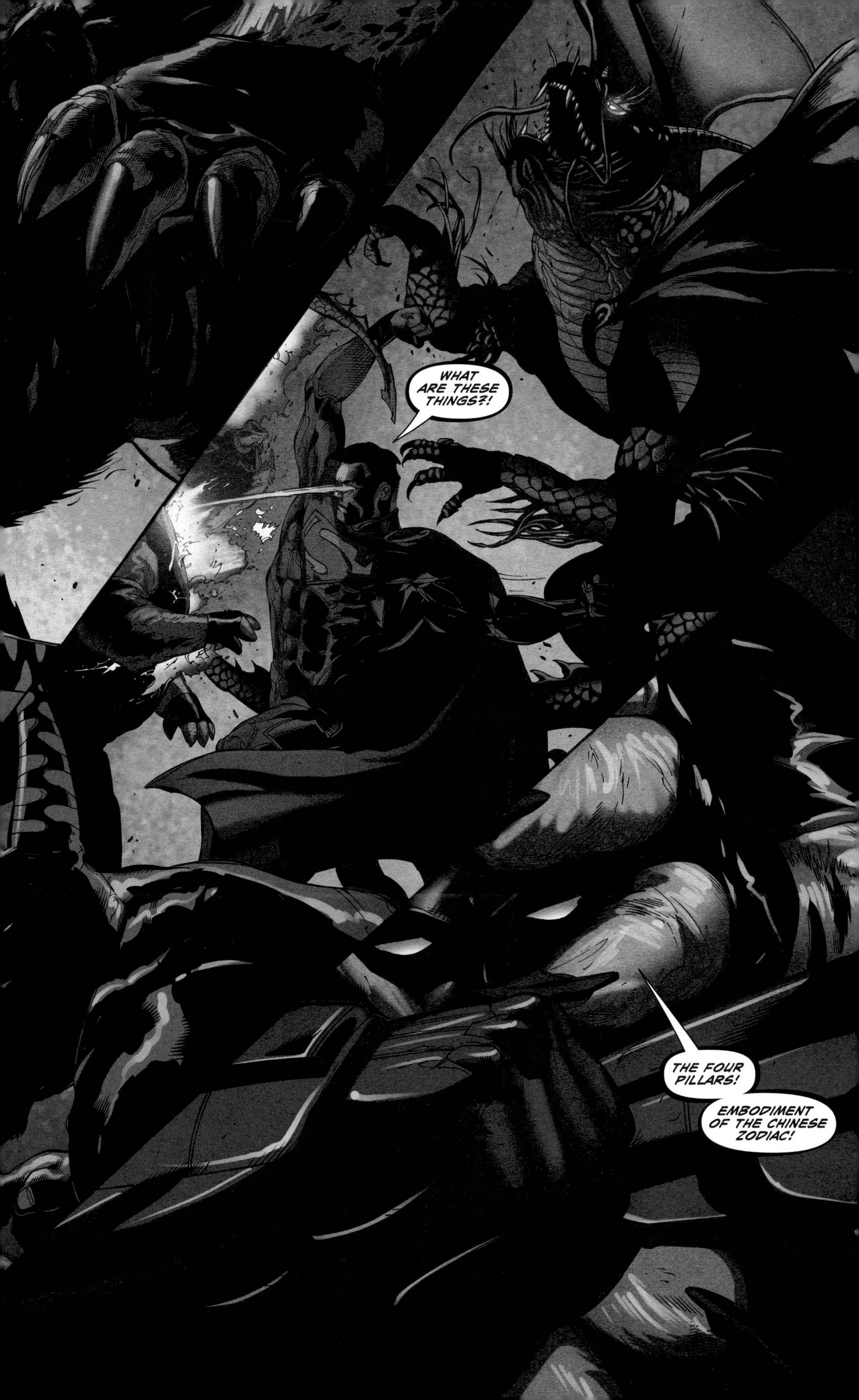
WHAT ARE THESE THINGS?!
THE FOUR PILLARS!
EMBODIMENT OF THE CHINESE ZODIAC!

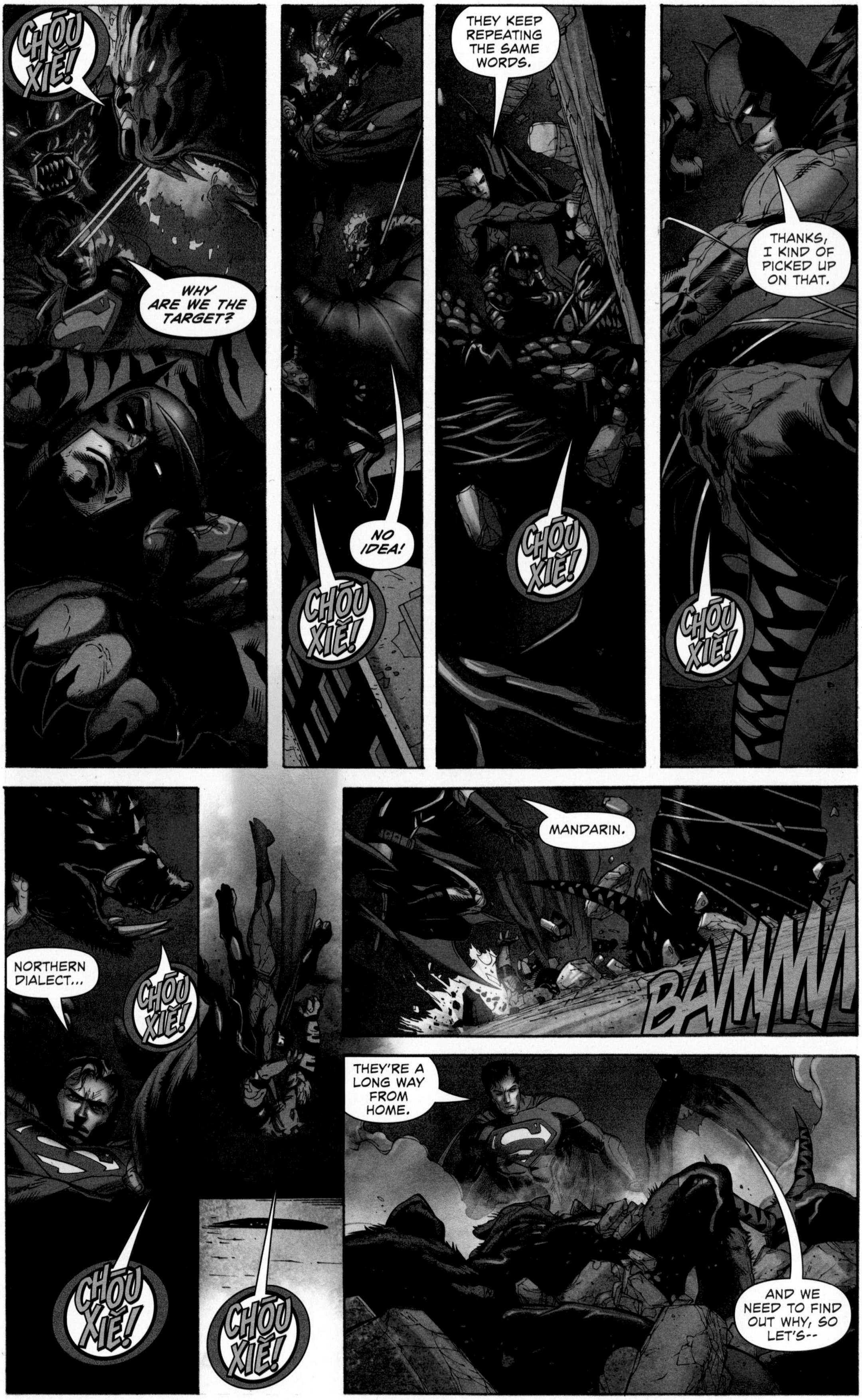
CHŌU XIĚ!
WHY ARE WE THE TARGET?
NO IDEA!
CHŌU XIĚ!
THEY KEEP REPEATING THE SAME WORDS.
CHŌU XIĚ!
THANKS, I KIND OF PICKED UP ON THAT.
CHŌU XIĚ!
NORTHERN DIALECT...
CHŌU XIĚ!
CHŌU XIĚ!
CHŌU XIĚ!
MANDARIN.
BAMMM
THEY'RE A LONG WAY FROM HOME.
AND WE NEED TO FIND OUT WHY, SO LET'S--

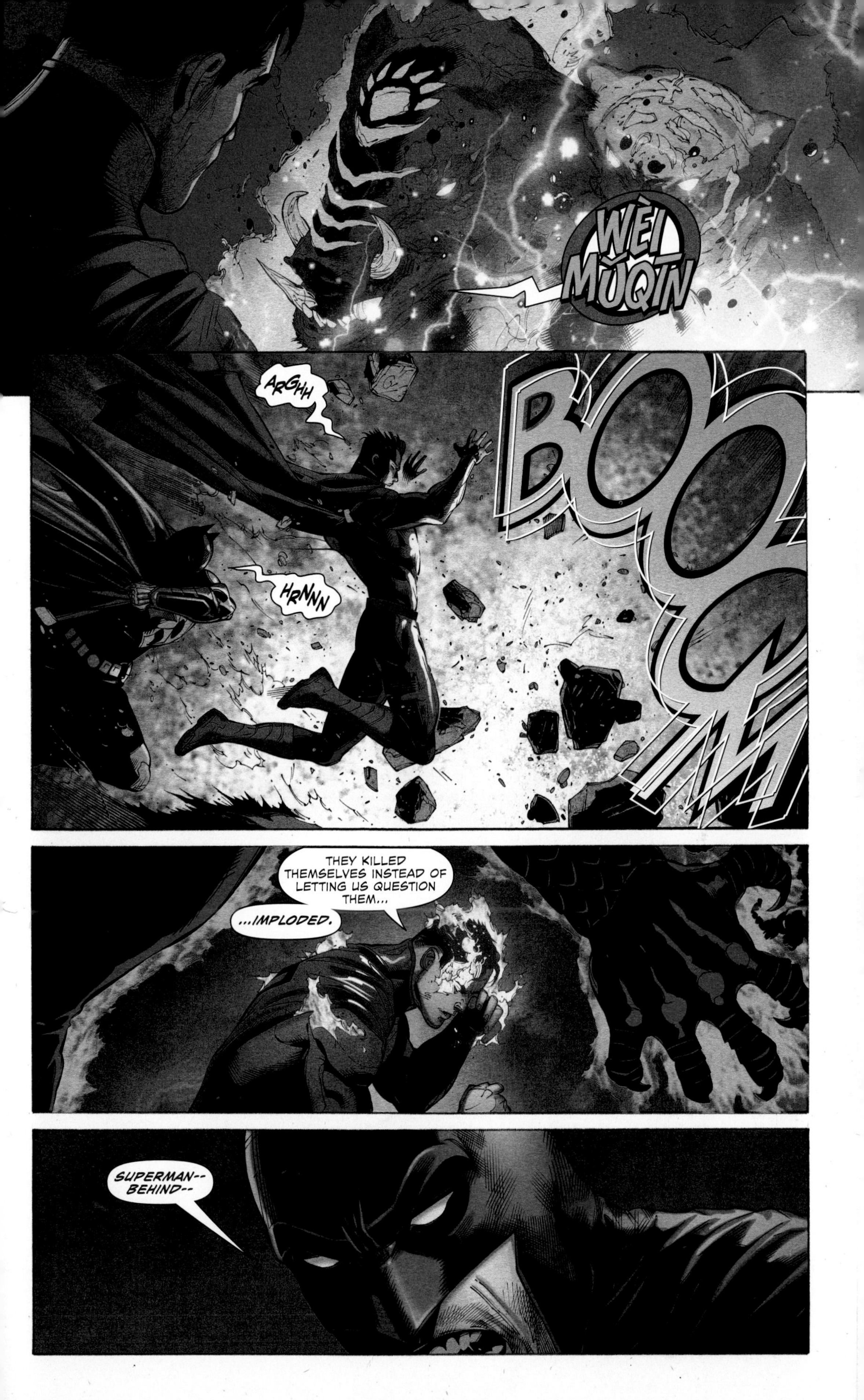
WÈI MÙQIN
ARGHH
HRNNN
BOOM
THEY KILLED THEMSELVES INSTEAD OF LETTING US QUESTION THEM...
...IMPLODED.
SUPERMAN-- BEHIND--

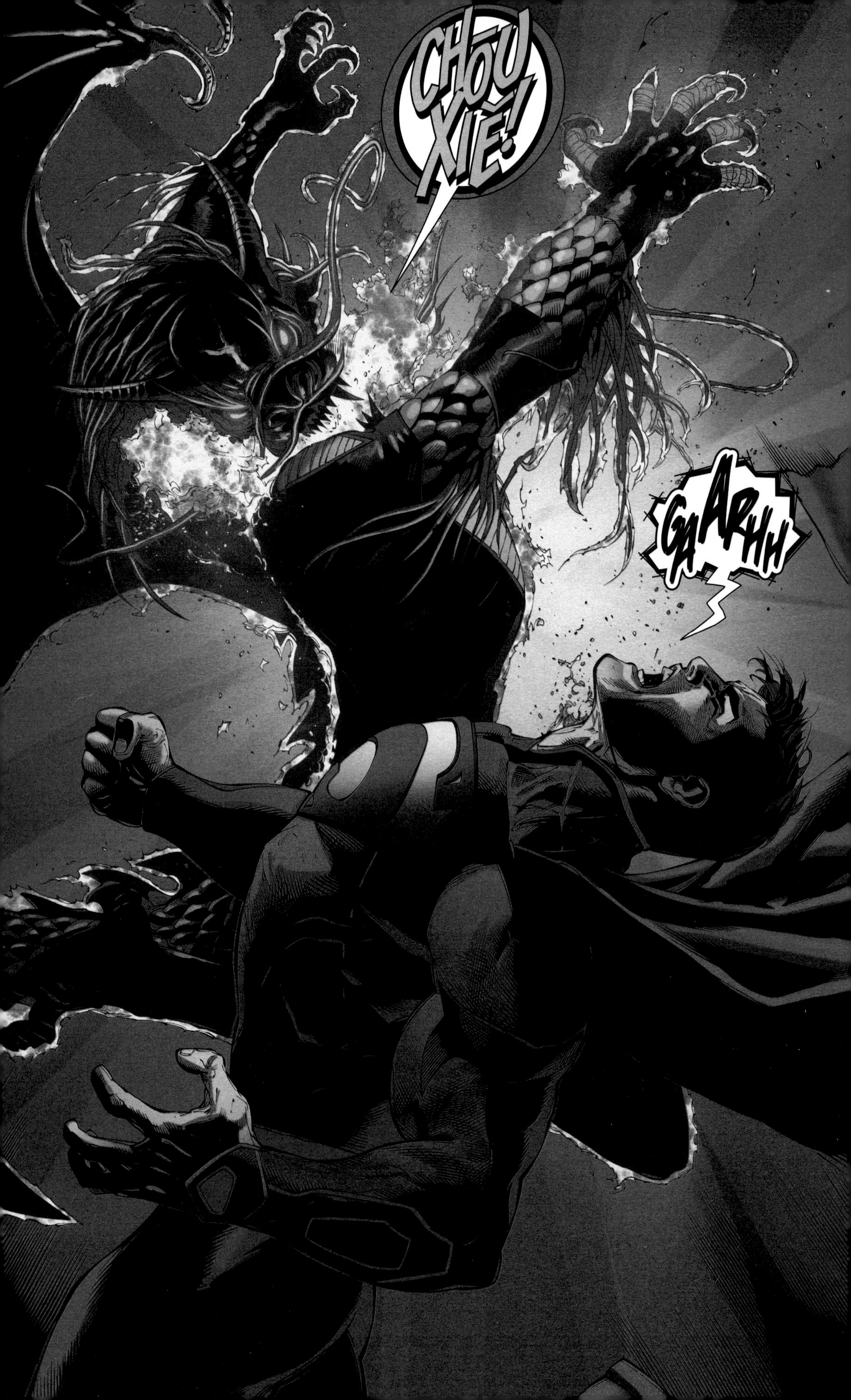
CHŌU XIĚ!
GAARHH

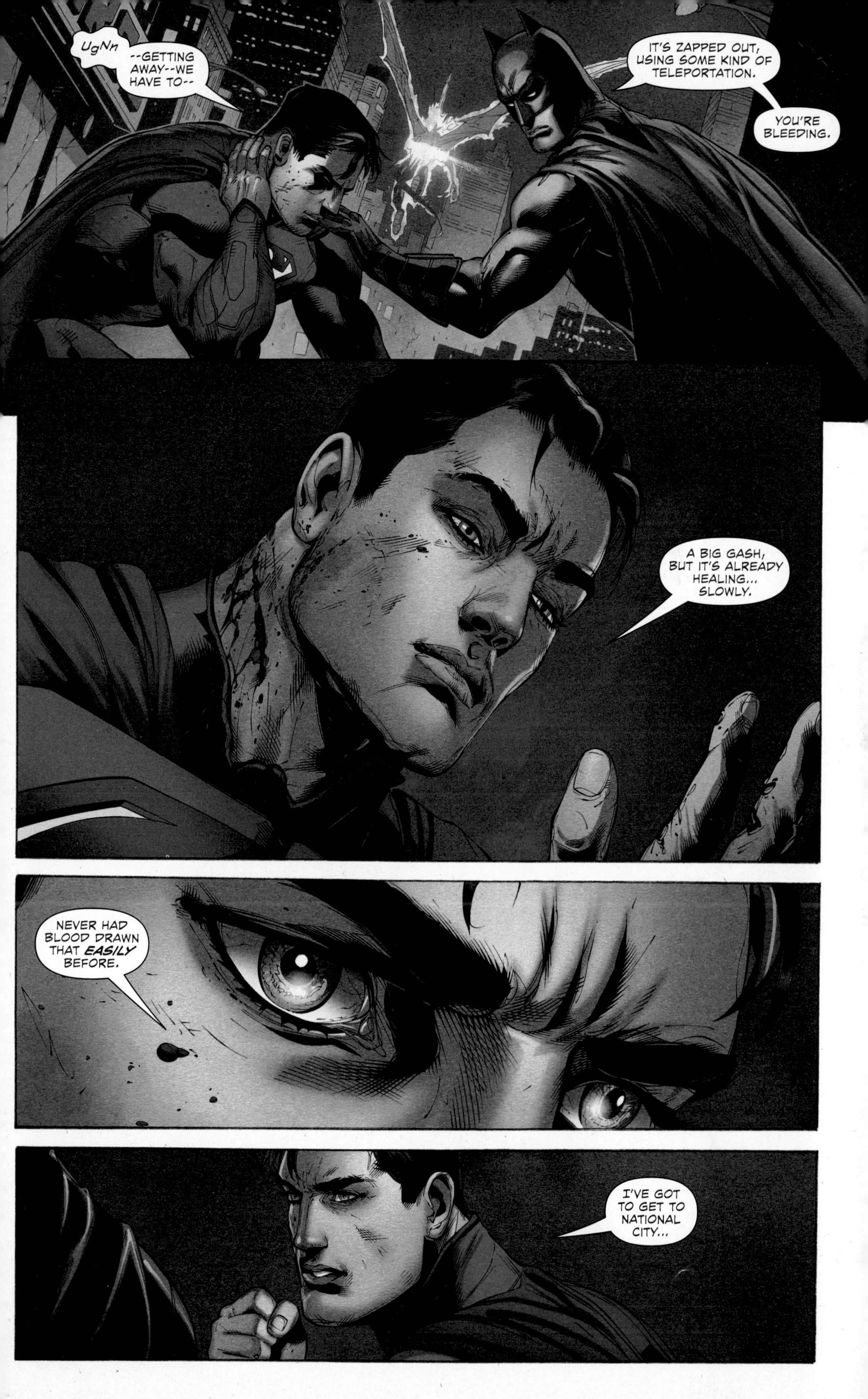
UgNn
--GETTING AWAY--WE HAVE TO--
IT'S ZAPPED OUT, USING SOME KIND OF TELEPORTATION.
YOU'RE BLEEDING.
A BIG GASH, BUT IT'S ALREADY HEALING... SLOWLY.
NEVER HAD BLOOD DRAWN THAT EASILY BEFORE.
I'VE GOT TO GET TO NATIONAL CITY...

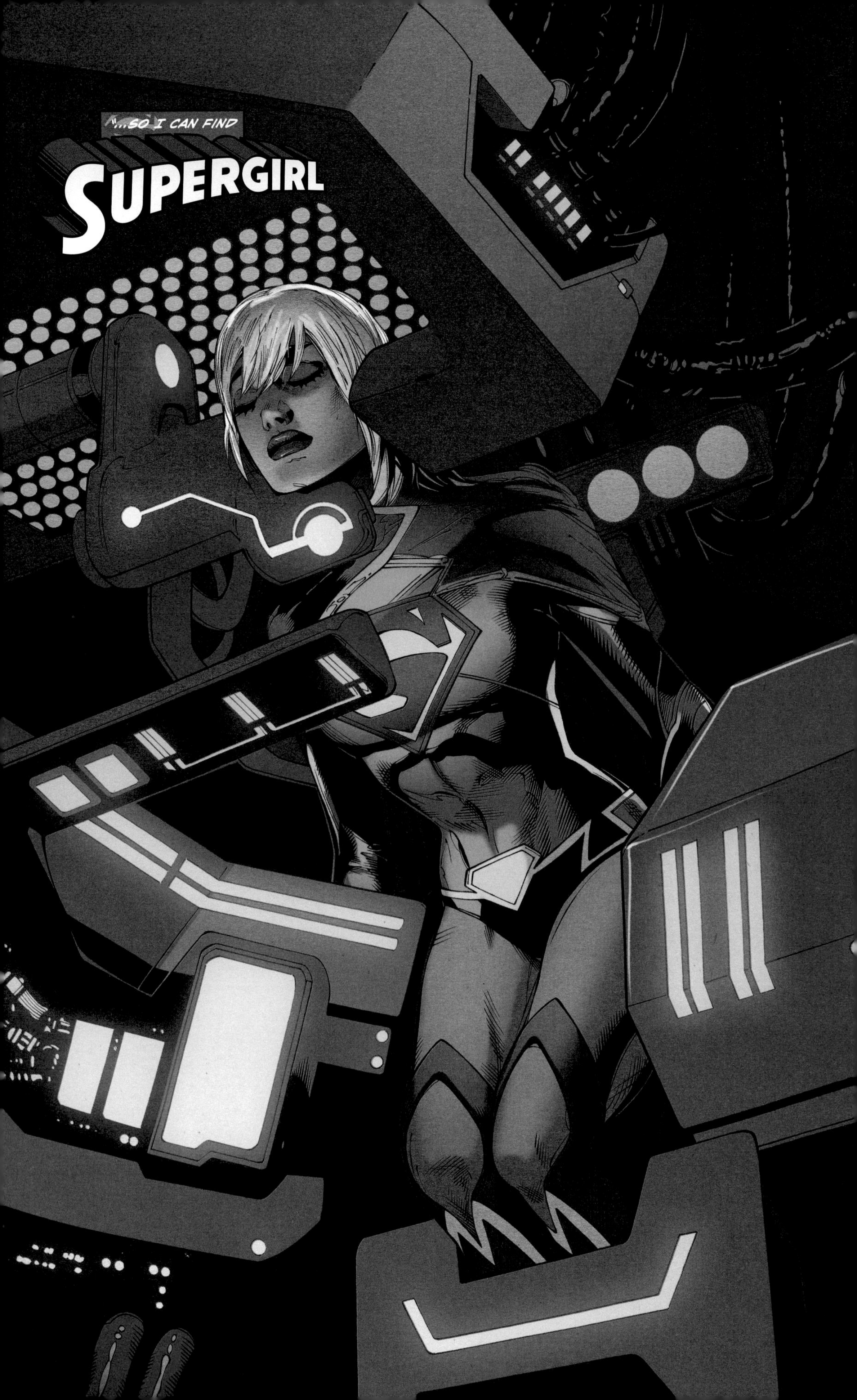
"...SO I CAN FIND
SUPERGIRL

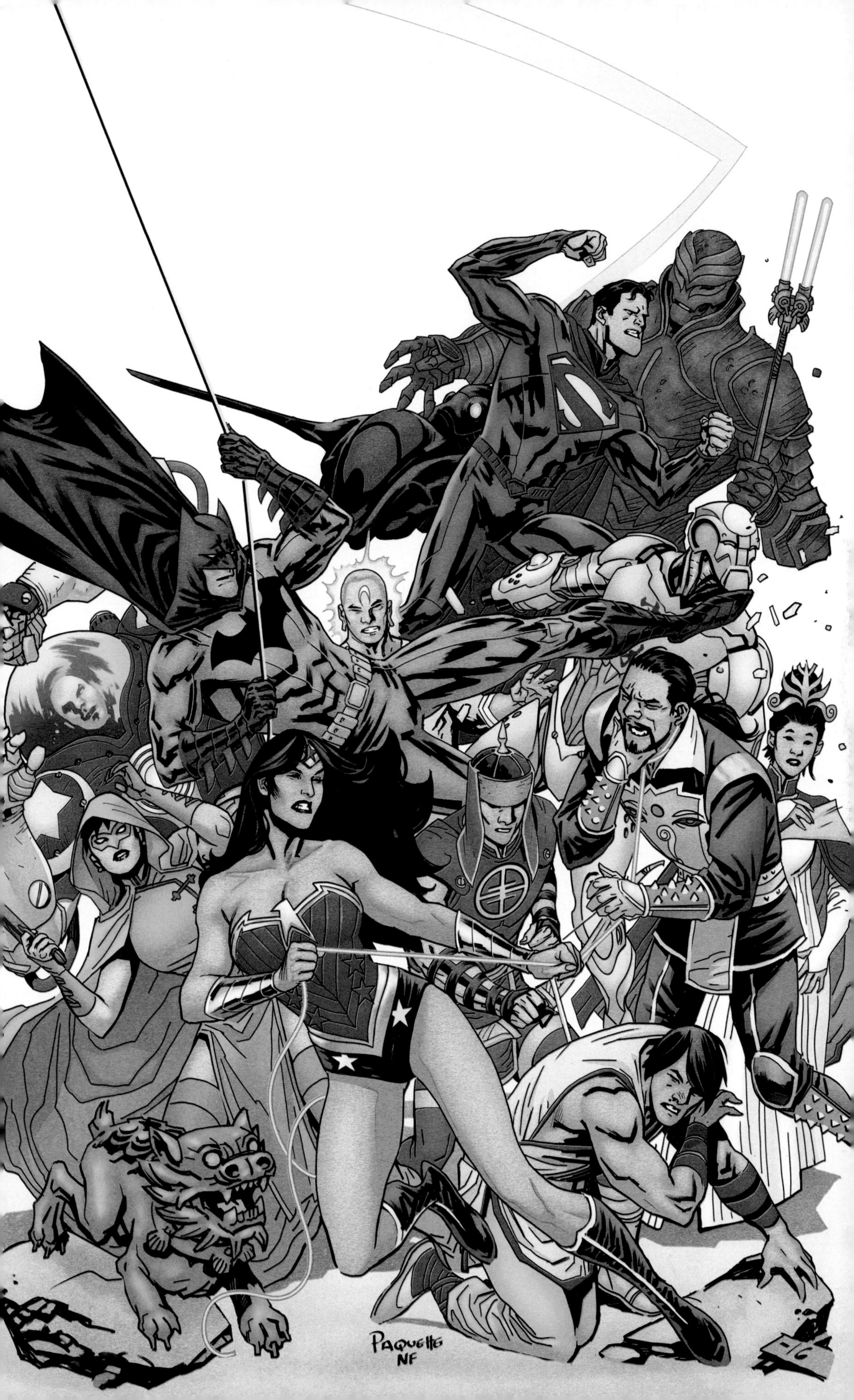
PAQUETTE
NF

Previously,
in ACTION COMICS #51
and SUPERMAN/WONDER WOMAN #28...

Shocked to find Supergirl voluntarily imprisoned in a secret D.E.O. laboratory, Superman takes Kara to the Fortress of Solitude where she will take on the mantle of Earth's sole Kryptonian protector. They are tracked there by a heartbroken Wonder Woman, who has come to hear about Clark's condition directly.

Meanwhile, the unstable Superman imposter attempts to go to work at the *Daily Planet*, causing havoc when he's unable to control his temper or the scorching energy emanating from his body. Steve Trevor and A.R.G.U.S. are able to contain this false Superman, but only after three security guards are left dead in his wake.

Back at A.R.G.U.S. headquarters, Clark, Diana and Steve work to discover the connection between Superman and his impersonator. They realize his powers are similar to the solar flare energy the Man of Steel used to defeat Ulysses, but not before the imposter manifests a solar flare strong enough to allow him to break out of his containment cell...

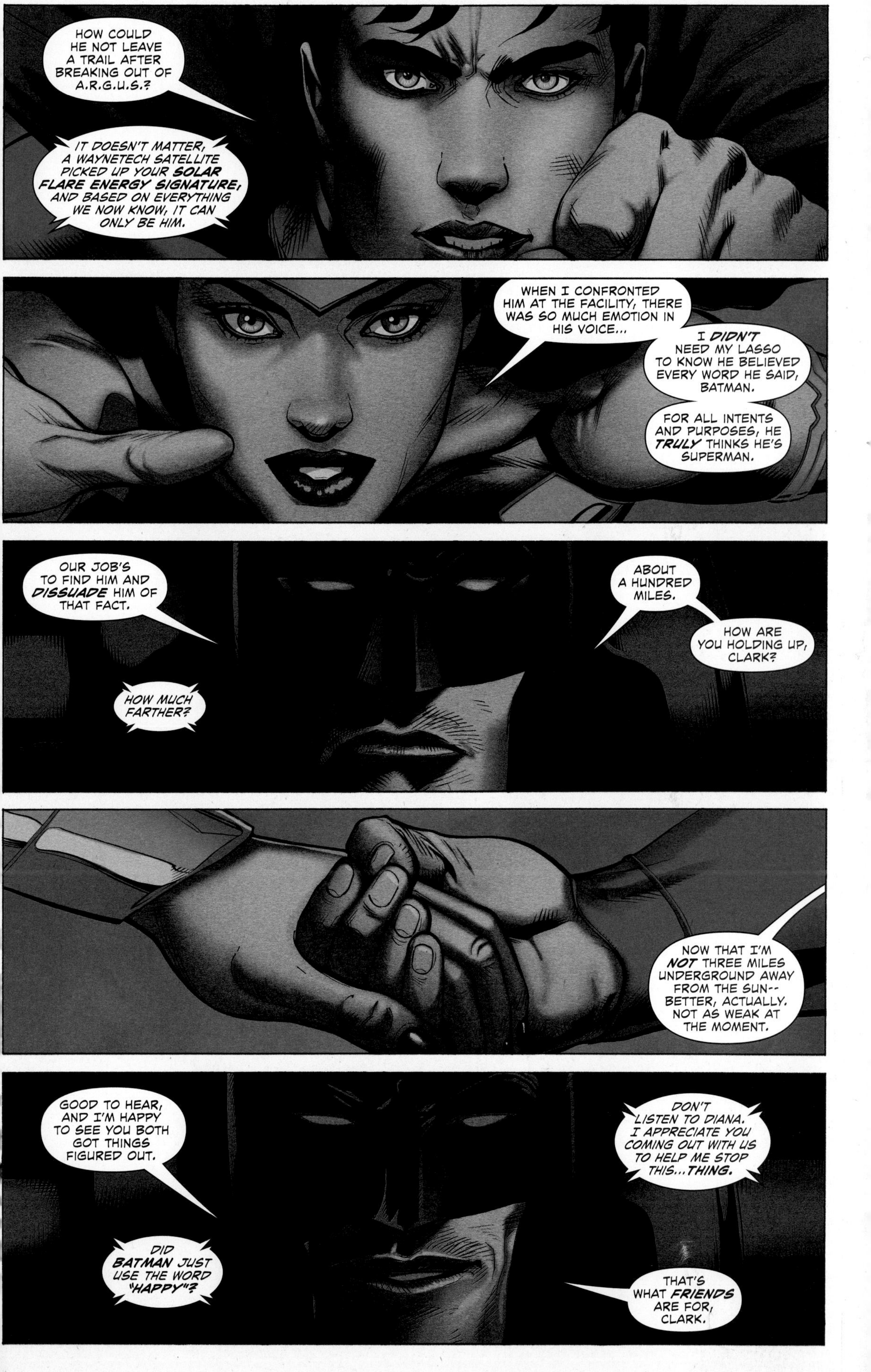
HOW COULD HE NOT LEAVE A TRAIL AFTER BREAKING OUT OF A.R.G.U.S.?
IT DOESN'T MATTER, A WAYNETECH SATELLITE PICKED UP YOUR SOLAR FLARE ENERGY SIGNATURE, AND BASED ON EVERYTHING WE NOW KNOW, IT CAN ONLY BE HIM.
WHEN I CONFRONTED HIM AT THE FACILITY, THERE WAS SO MUCH EMOTION IN HIS VOICE...
I DIDN'T NEED MY LASSO TO KNOW HE BELIEVED EVERY WORD HE SAID, BATMAN.
FOR ALL INTENTS AND PURPOSES, HE TRULY THINKS HE'S SUPERMAN.
OUR JOB'S TO FIND HIM AND DISSUADE HIM OF THAT FACT.
HOW MUCH FARTHER?
ABOUT A HUNDRED MILES.
HOW ARE YOU HOLDING UP, CLARK?
NOW THAT I'M NOT THREE MILES UNDERGROUND AWAY FROM THE SUN-- BETTER, ACTUALLY. NOT AS WEAK AT THE MOMENT.
GOOD TO HEAR, AND I'M HAPPY TO SEE YOU BOTH GOT THINGS FIGURED OUT.
DID BATMAN JUST USE THE WORD "HAPPY"?
DON'T LISTEN TO DIANA. I APPRECIATE YOU COMING OUT WITH US TO HELP ME STOP THIS...THING.
THAT'S WHAT FRIENDS ARE FOR, CLARK.

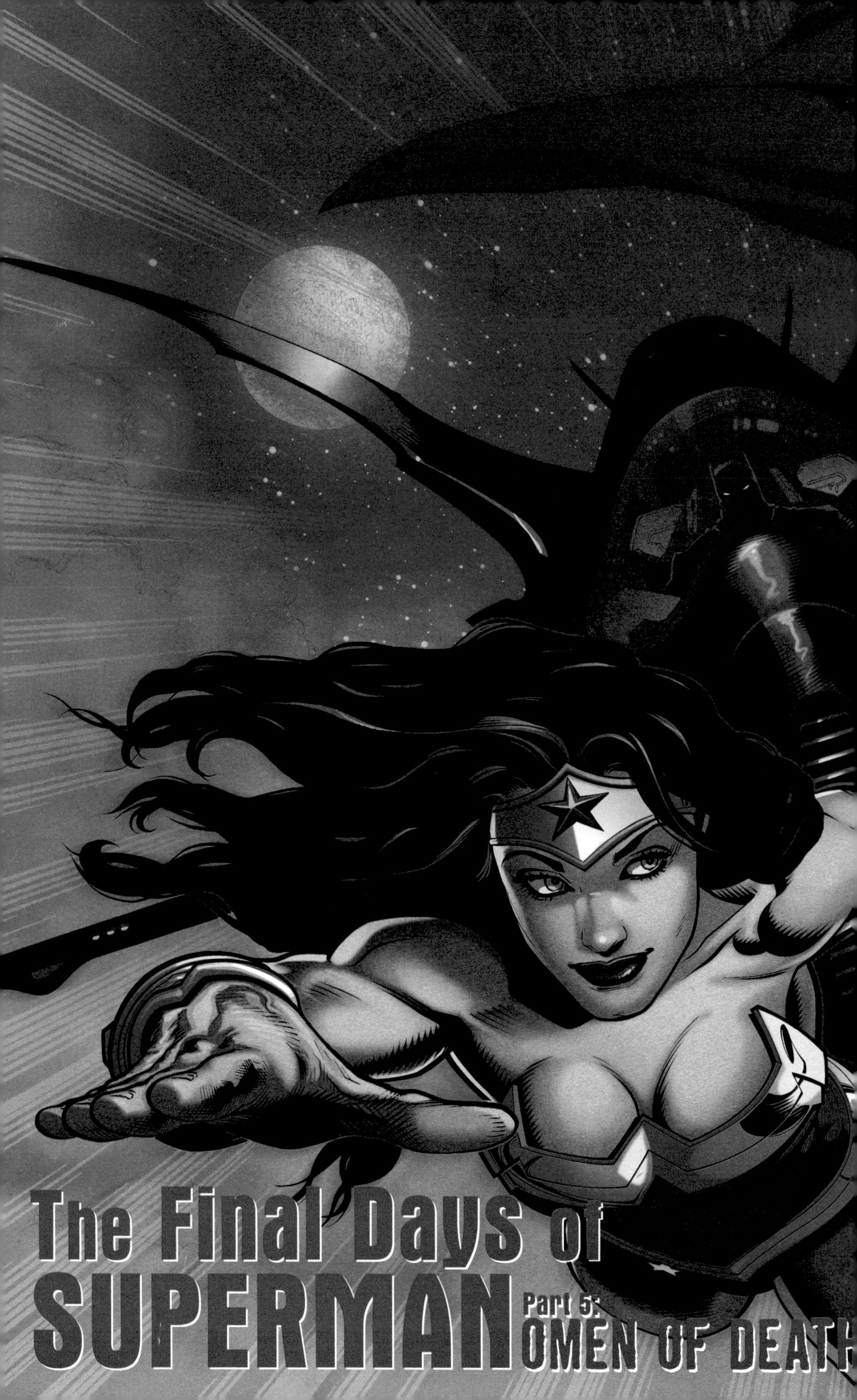
The Final Days of
SUPERMAN
Part 5:
OMEN OF DEATH

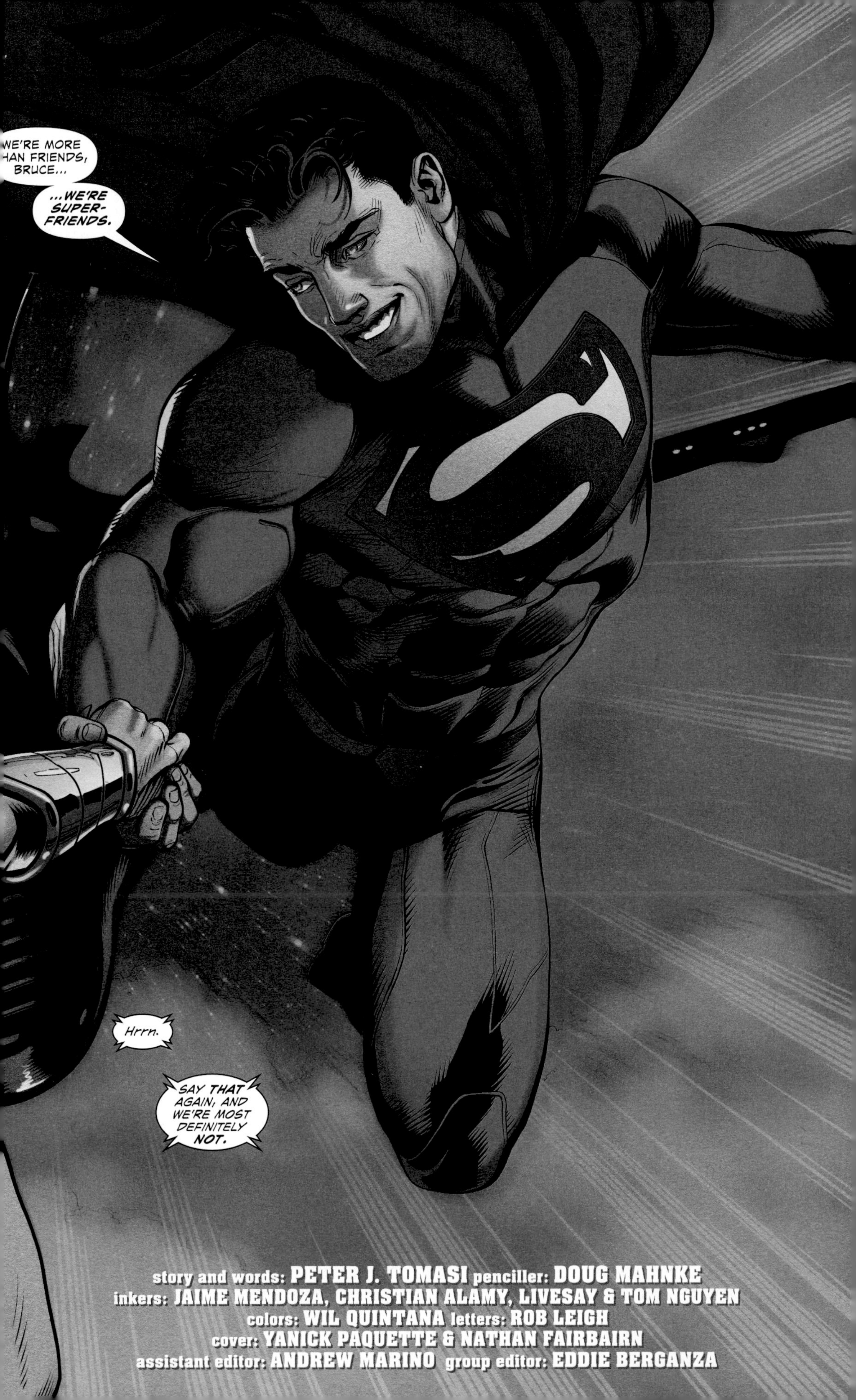
WE'RE MORE HAN FRIENDS, BRUCE...
...WE'RE SUPER-FRIENDS.
Hrrn.
SAY THAT AGAIN, AND WE'RE MOST DEFINITELY NOT.

story and words: PETER J. TOMASI penciller: DOUG MAHNKE
inkers: JAIME MENDOZA, CHRISTIAN ALAMY, LIVESAY & TOM NGUYEN
colors: WIL QUINTANA letters: ROB LEIGH
cover: YANICK PAQUETTE & NATHAN FAIRBAIRN
assistant editor: ANDREW MARINO group editor: EDDIE BERGANZA

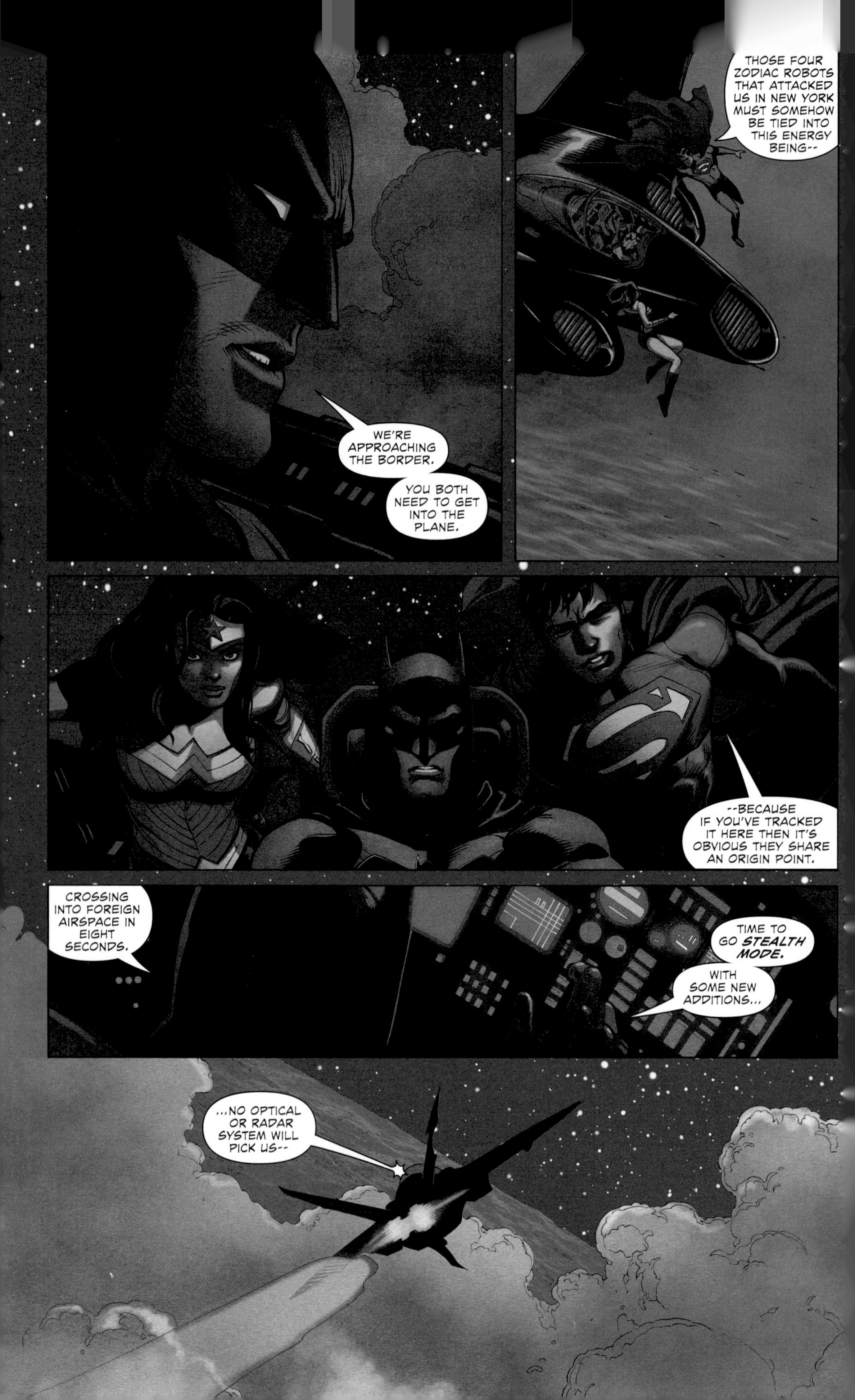
WE'RE APPROACHING THE BORDER.
YOU BOTH NEED TO GET INTO THE PLANE.
THOSE FOUR ZODIAC ROBOTS THAT ATTACKED US IN NEW YORK MUST SOMEHOW BE TIED INTO THIS ENERGY BEING--
--BECAUSE IF YOU'VE TRACKED IT HERE THEN IT'S OBVIOUS THEY SHARE AN ORIGIN POINT.
CROSSING INTO FOREIGN AIRSPACE IN EIGHT SECONDS.
TIME TO GO STEALTH MODE.
WITH SOME NEW ADDITIONS...
...NO OPTICAL OR RADAR SYSTEM WILL PICK US--

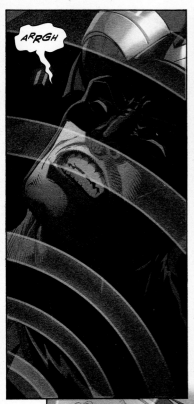

ARRGH

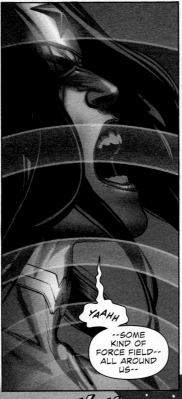

YAAHH

--SOME KIND OF FORCE FIELD-- ALL AROUND US--

NRGGH

--I HEAR SOMETHING-- HIGH-RANGE VOCAL DISTORTION--

WMMMMMM

--PLANE'S BEING PUSHED DOWN-- --CAN'T EJECT--

FRAAAH

KOOM

WE'RE NOT GOING TO HAVE TO LOOK FAR TO FIND WHO DID THIS.

HELLO...

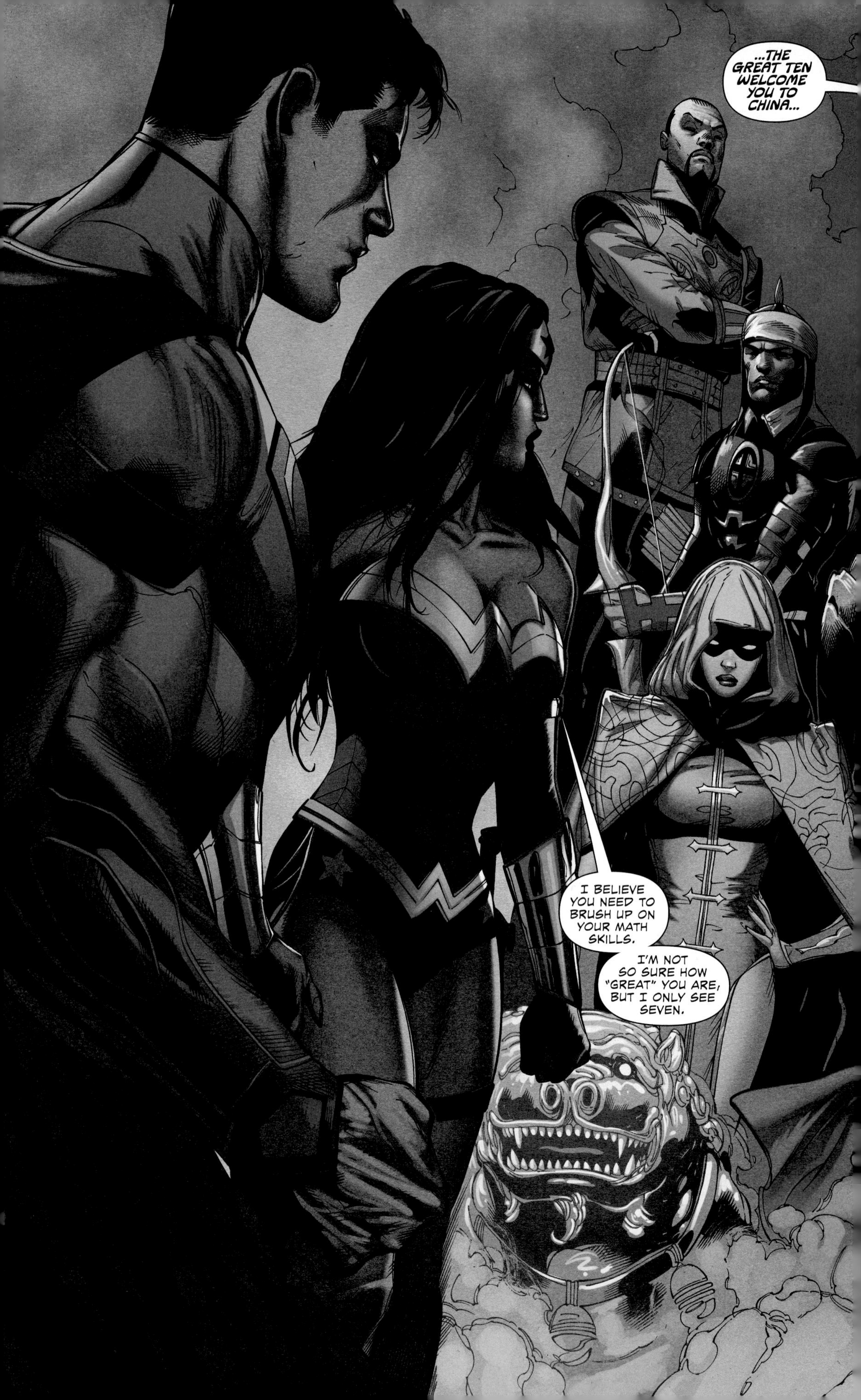
...THE GREAT TEN WELCOME YOU TO CHINA...
I BELIEVE YOU NEED TO BRUSH UP ON YOUR MATH SKILLS.
I'M NOT SO SURE HOW "GREAT" YOU ARE, BUT I ONLY SEE SEVEN.

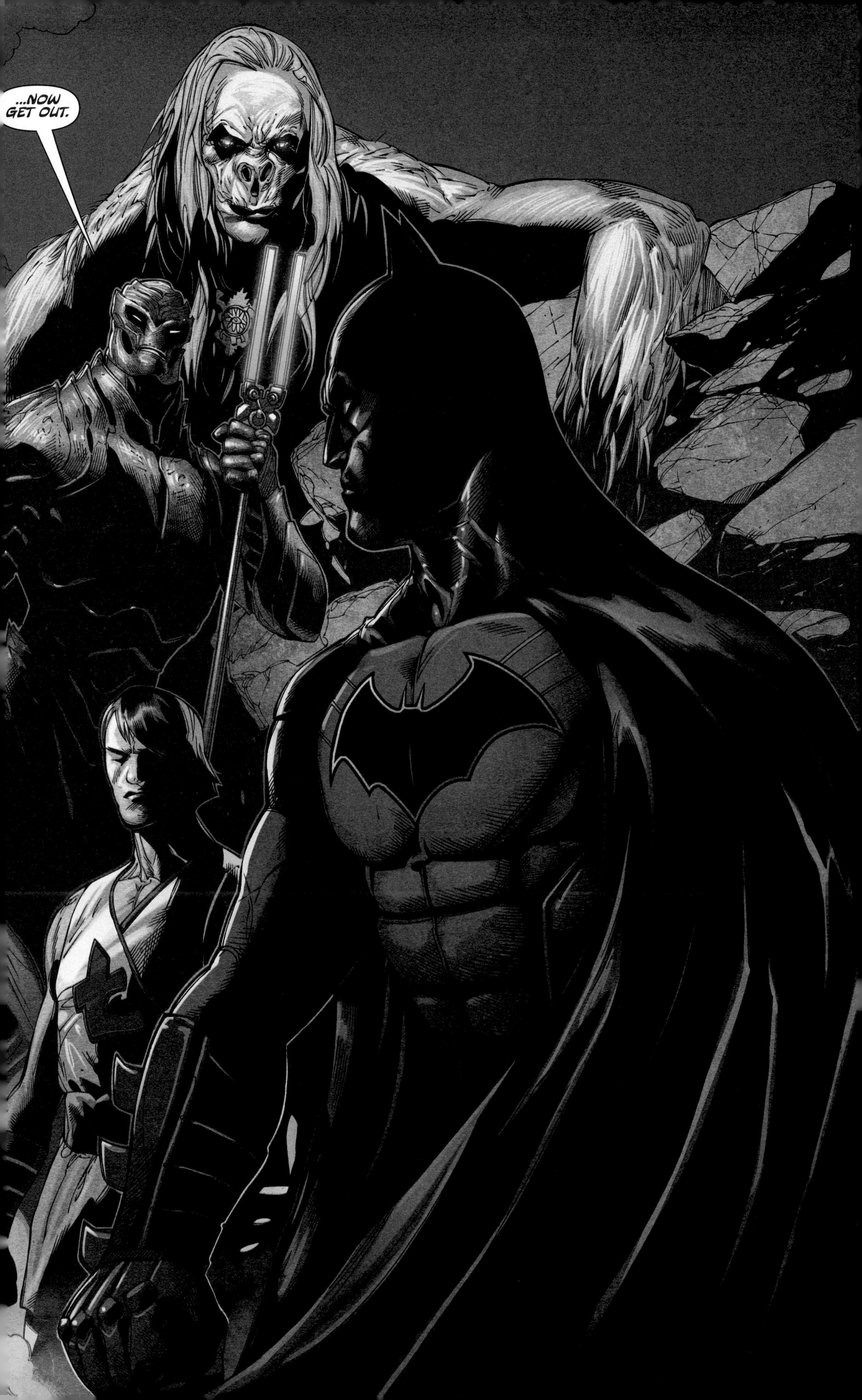
...NOW GET OUT.

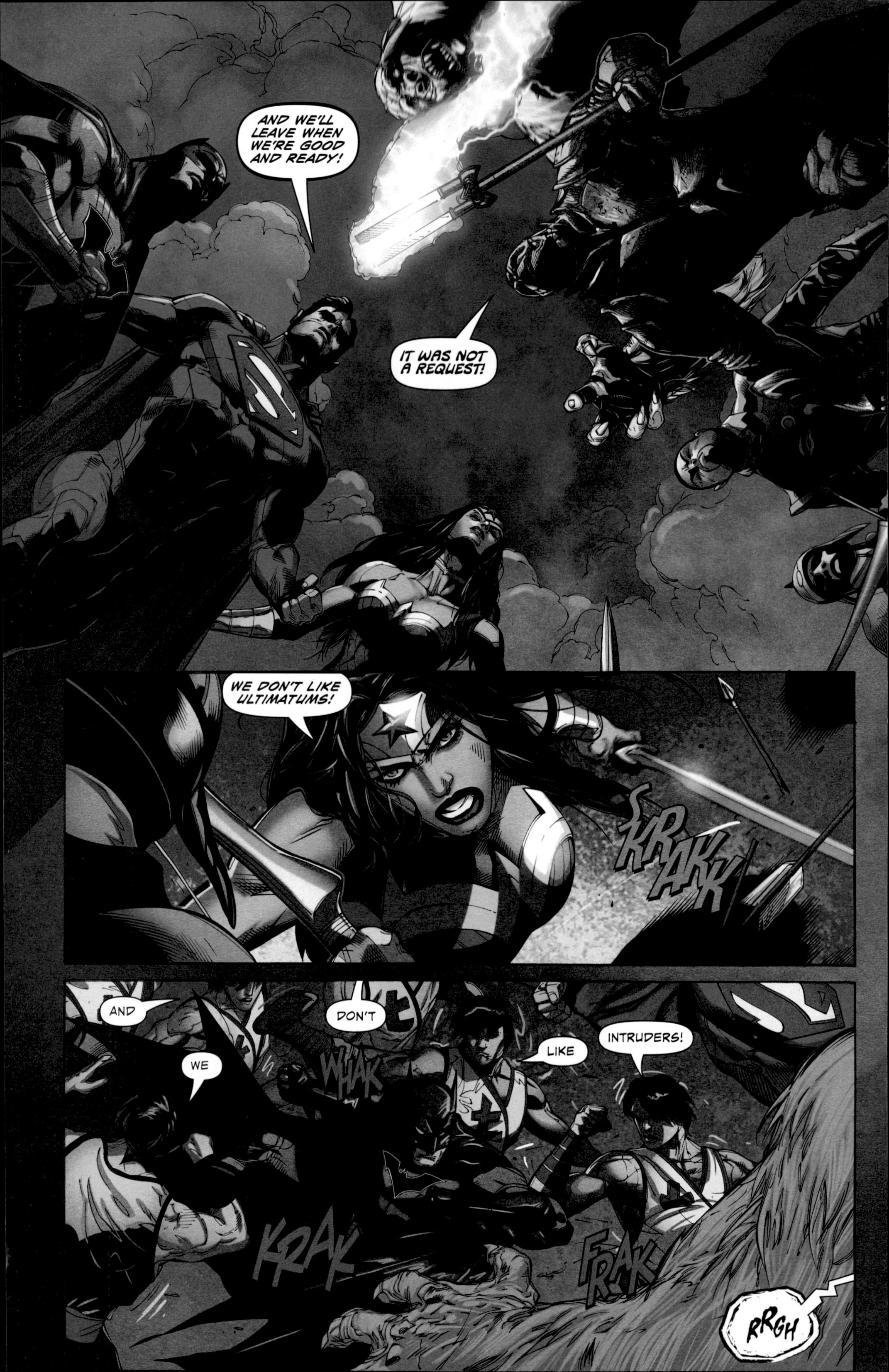
AND WE'LL LEAVE WHEN WE'RE GOOD AND READY!
IT WAS NOT A REQUEST!
WE DON'T LIKE ULTIMATUMS!
KRAKK
AND
WE
DON'T
WHAK
LIKE
INTRUDERS!
KRAK
FRAK
RRGH

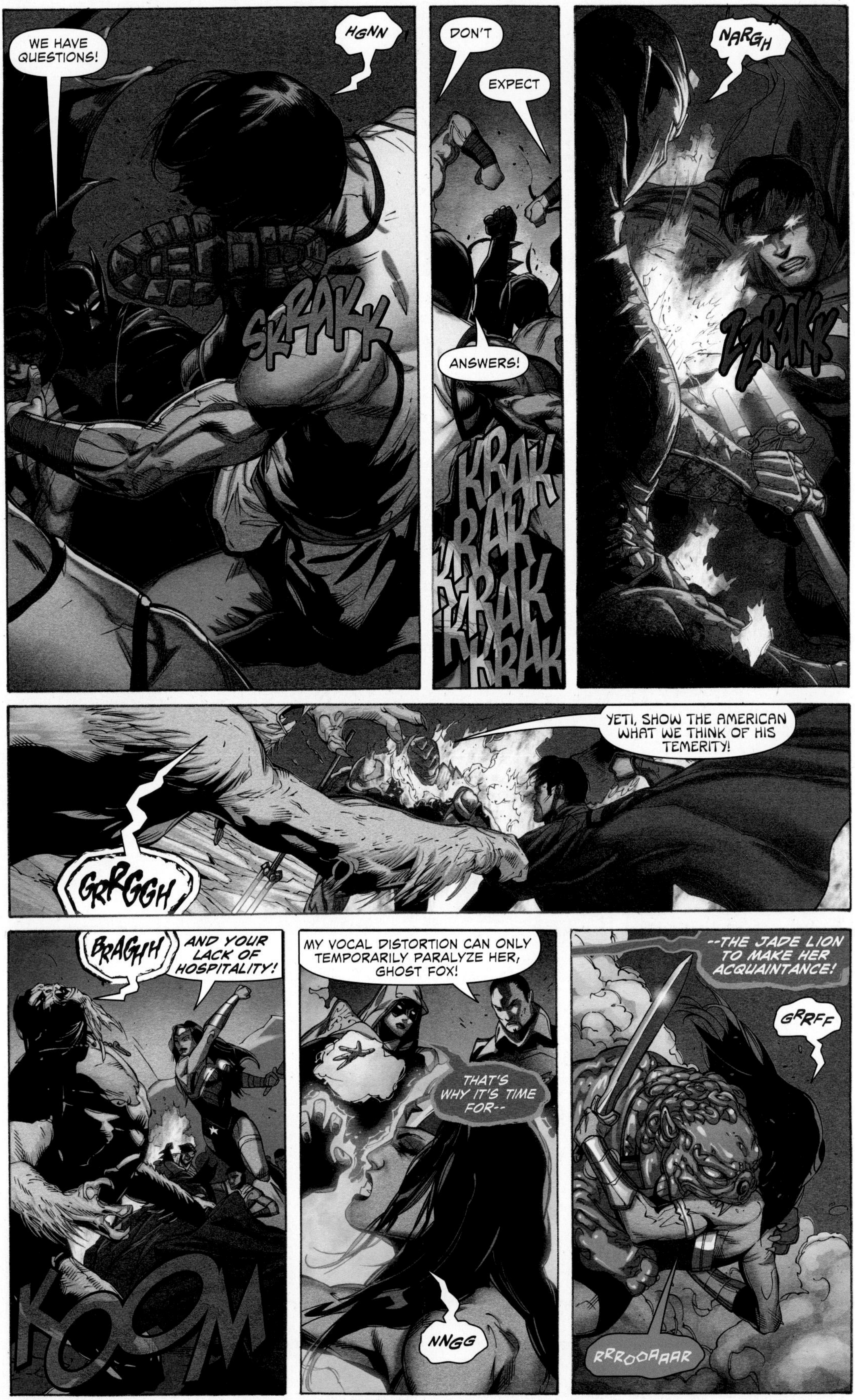

WE HAVE QUESTIONS!
HGNN
SKRAKK
DON'T
EXPECT
ANSWERS!
KRAK
RAK
KRAK
KRAK
KRAK
NARGH
ZZRAKK
YETI, SHOW THE AMERICAN WHAT WE THINK OF HIS TEMERITY!
GRRGGH
BRAGHH
AND YOUR LACK OF HOSPITALITY!
KOOM
MY VOCAL DISTORTION CAN ONLY TEMPORARILY PARALYZE HER, GHOST FOX!
THAT'S WHY IT'S TIME FOR--
NNGG
--THE JADE LION TO MAKE HER ACQUAINTANCE!
GRRFF
RRROOAAAAR

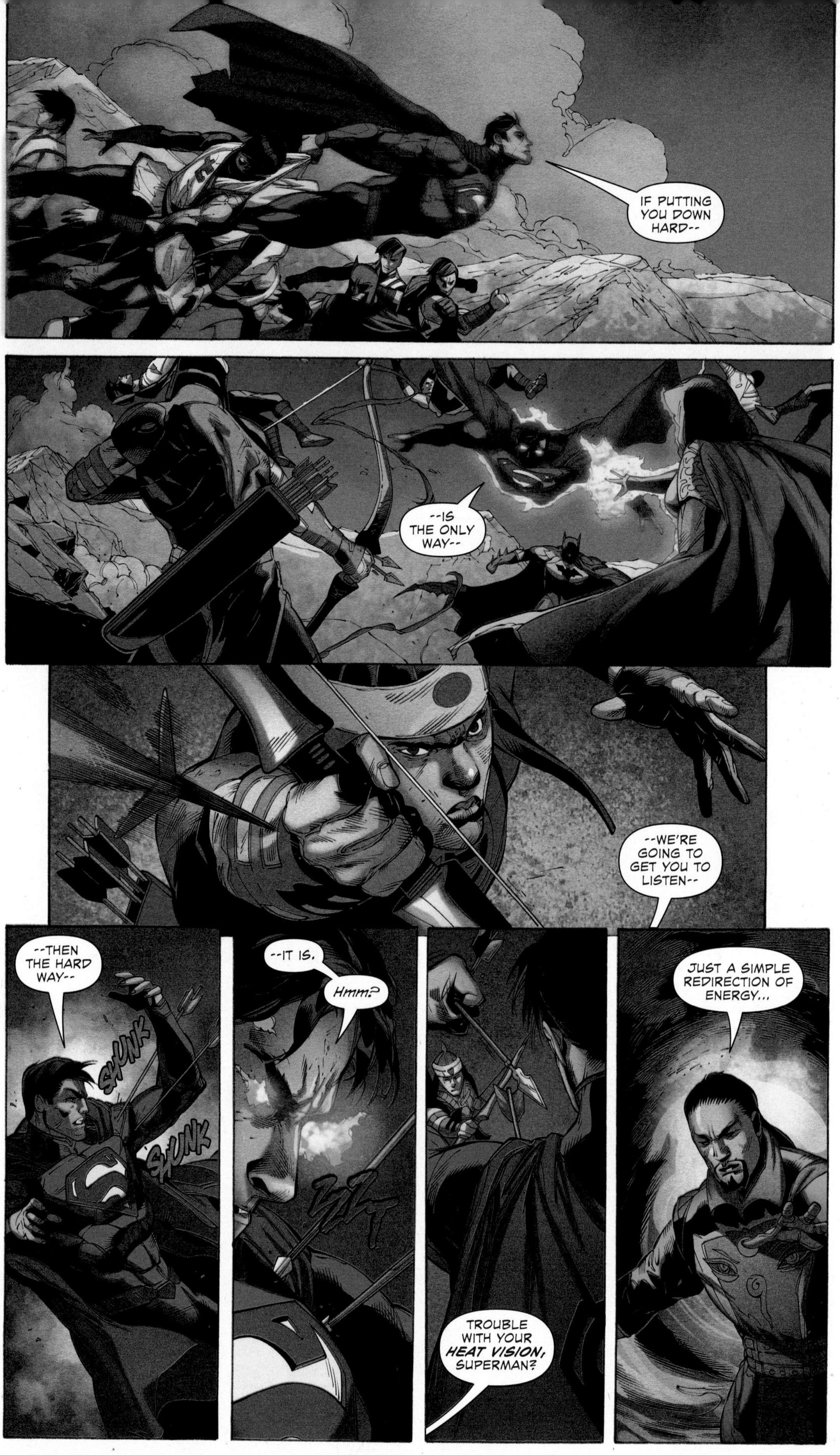
IF PUTTING YOU DOWN HARD--
--IS THE ONLY WAY--
--WE'RE GOING TO GET YOU TO LISTEN--
--THEN THE HARD WAY--
SHUNK
SHUNK
--IT IS.
Hmm?
TROUBLE WITH YOUR HEAT VISION, SUPERMAN?
JUST A SIMPLE REDIRECTION OF ENERGY...

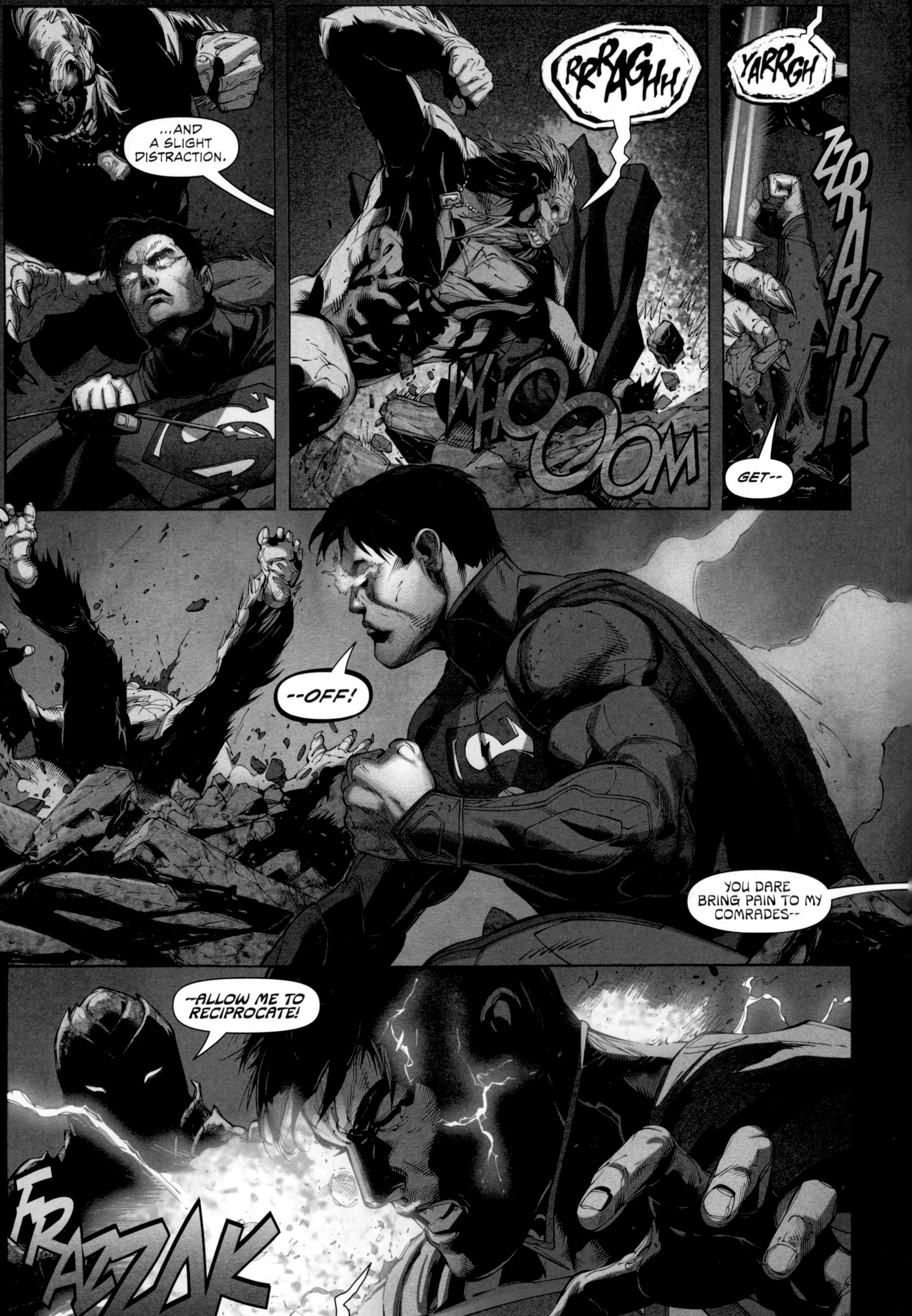
...AND A SLIGHT DISTRACTION.
RRRAGHH
WHOOOOM
YARRGH
ZRAKKK
GET--
--OFF!
YOU DARE BRING PAIN TO MY COMRADES--
--ALLOW ME TO RECIPROCATE!
FRAZZAK
NARRGH

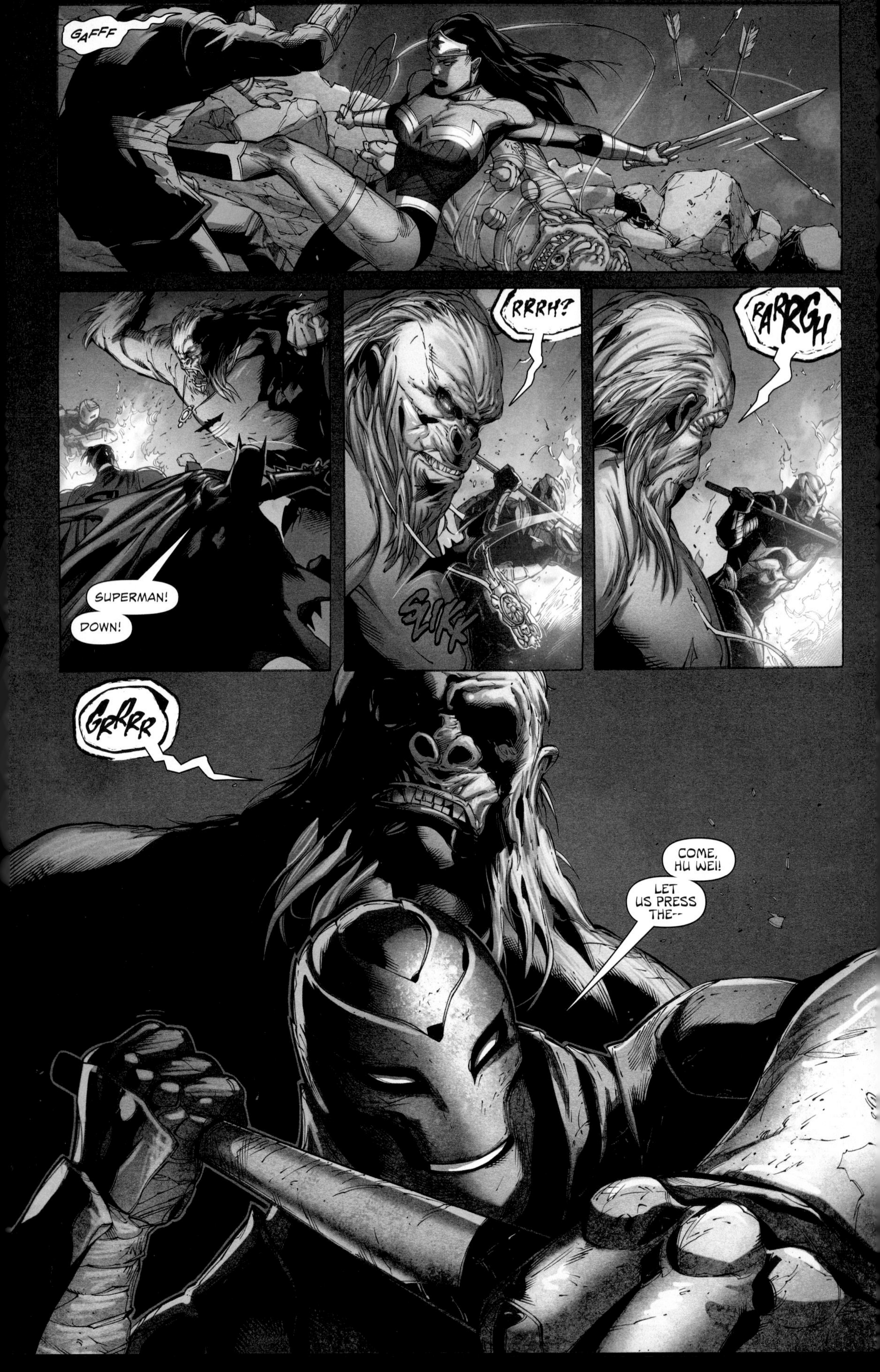
GAFFF
SUPERMAN!
DOWN!
RRRH?
SLIK
RARRGH
GRRRR
COME, HU WEI!
LET US PRESS THE--

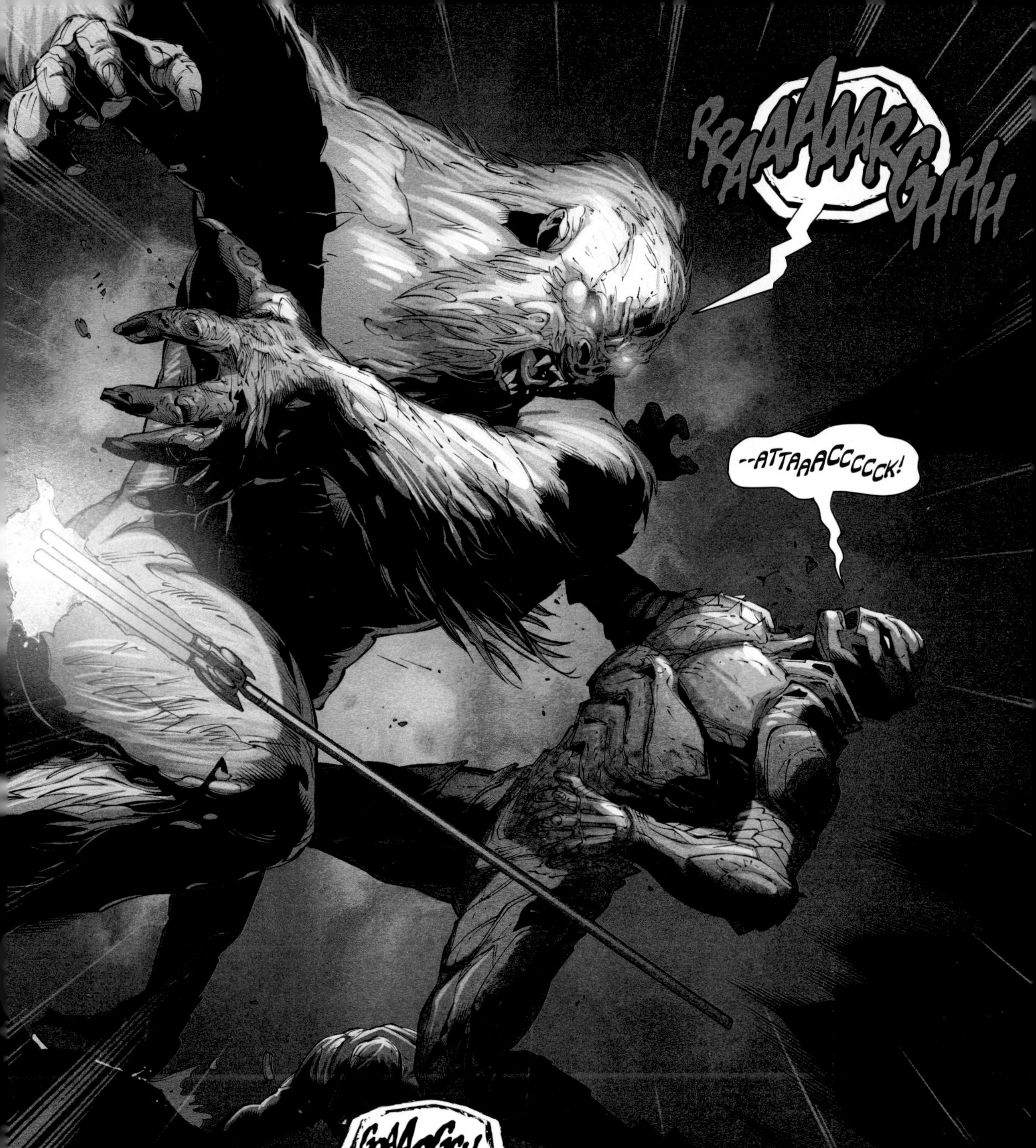
RRAAAAARGHHH
--ATTAAACCCCCK!

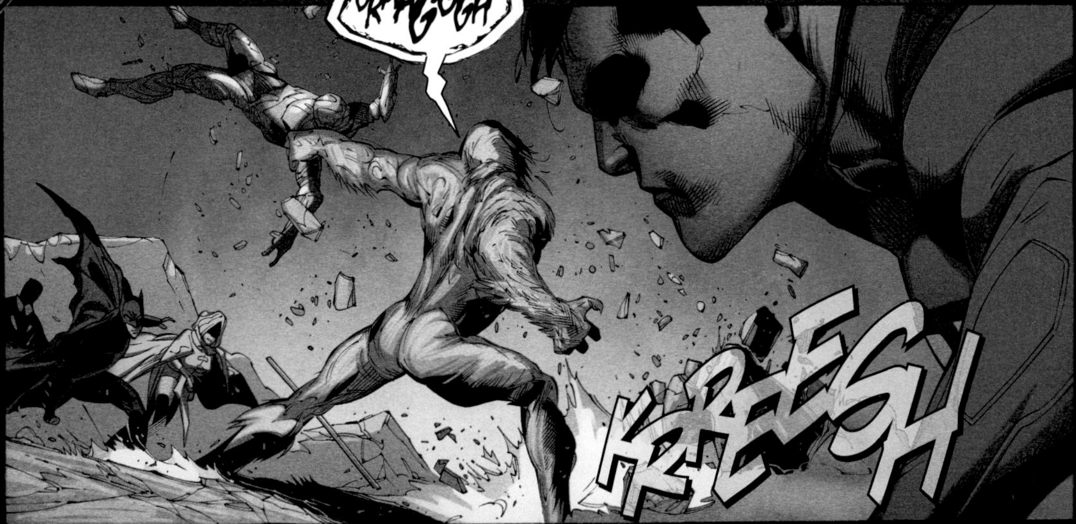
GRAAGGGH
KREESH

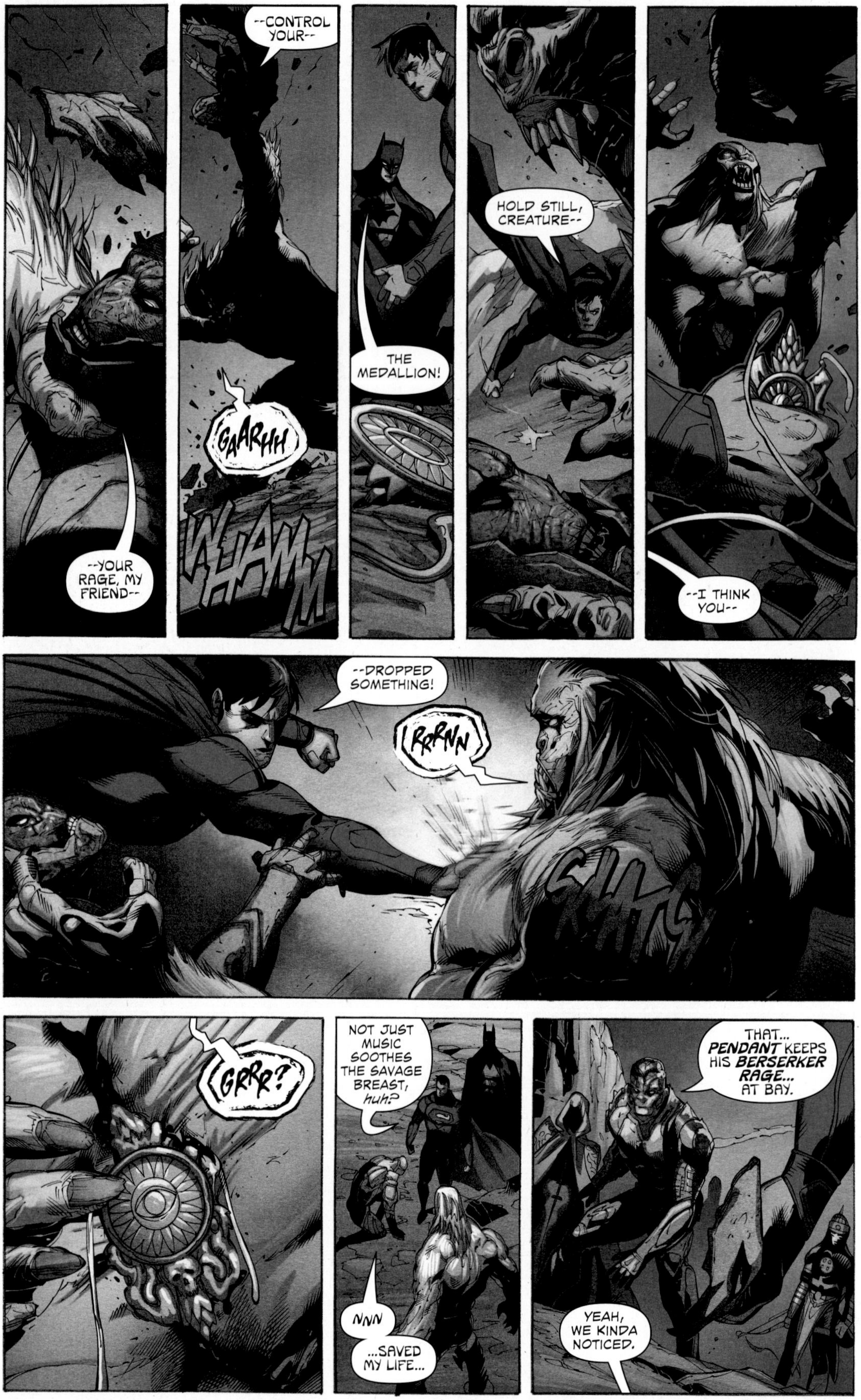
--YOUR RAGE, MY FRIEND--
--CONTROL YOUR--
GAARHH
WHAMM
THE MEDALLION!
HOLD STILL, CREATURE--
--I THINK YOU--
--DROPPED SOMETHING!
RRRNN
GRRR?
NOT JUST MUSIC SOOTHES THE SAVAGE BREAST, huh?
NNN
...SAVED MY LIFE...
THAT... PENDANT KEEPS HIS BERSERKER RAGE... AT BAY.
YEAH, WE KINDA NOTICED.

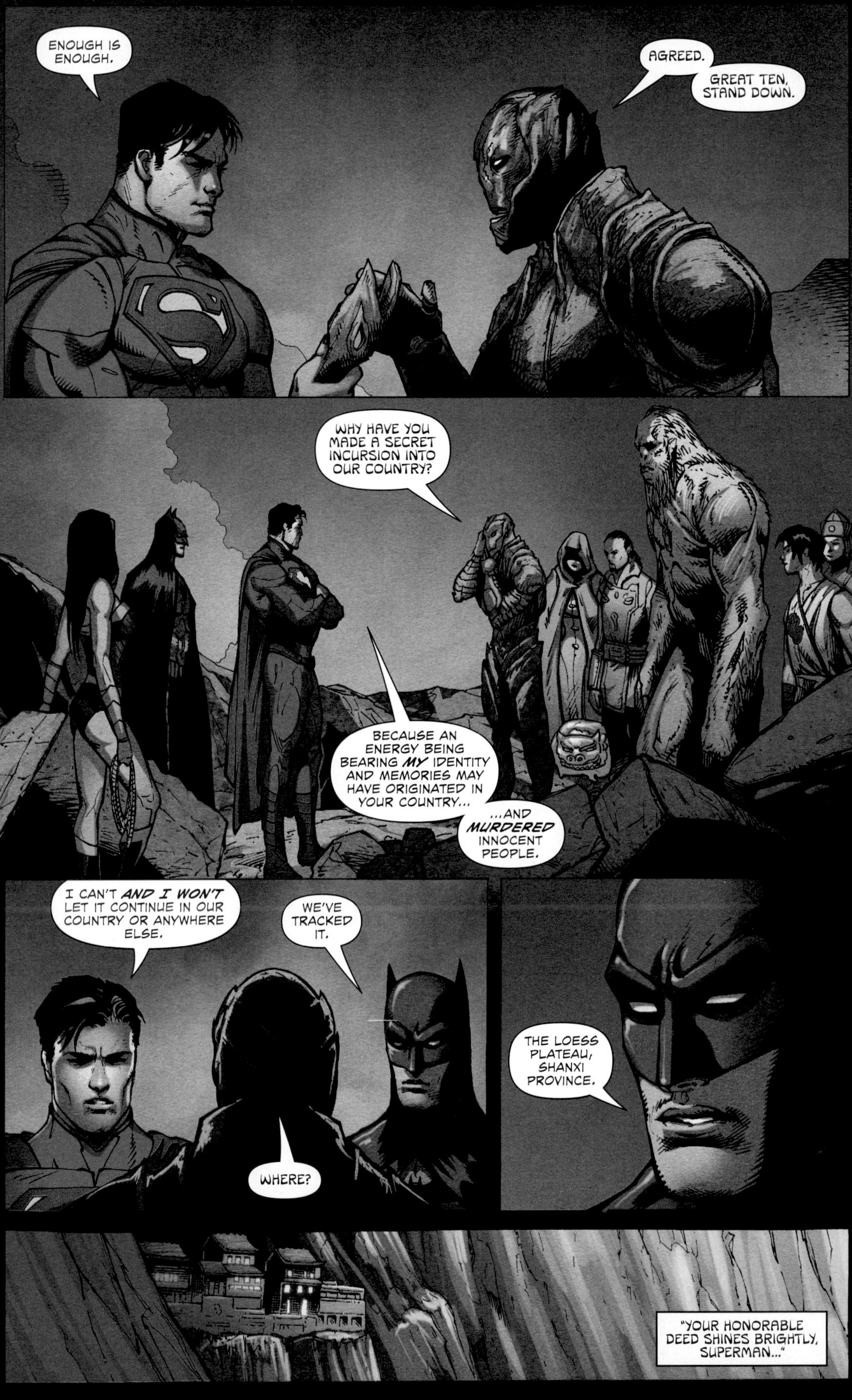
ENOUGH IS ENOUGH.
AGREED.
GREAT TEN, STAND DOWN.
WHY HAVE YOU MADE A SECRET INCURSION INTO OUR COUNTRY?
BECAUSE AN ENERGY BEING BEARING MY IDENTITY AND MEMORIES MAY HAVE ORIGINATED IN YOUR COUNTRY...
...AND MURDERED INNOCENT PEOPLE.
I CAN'T AND I WON'T LET IT CONTINUE IN OUR COUNTRY OR ANYWHERE ELSE.
WE'VE TRACKED IT.
WHERE?
THE LOESS PLATEAU, SHANXI PROVINCE.
"YOUR HONORABLE DEED SHINES BRIGHTLY, SUPERMAN..."

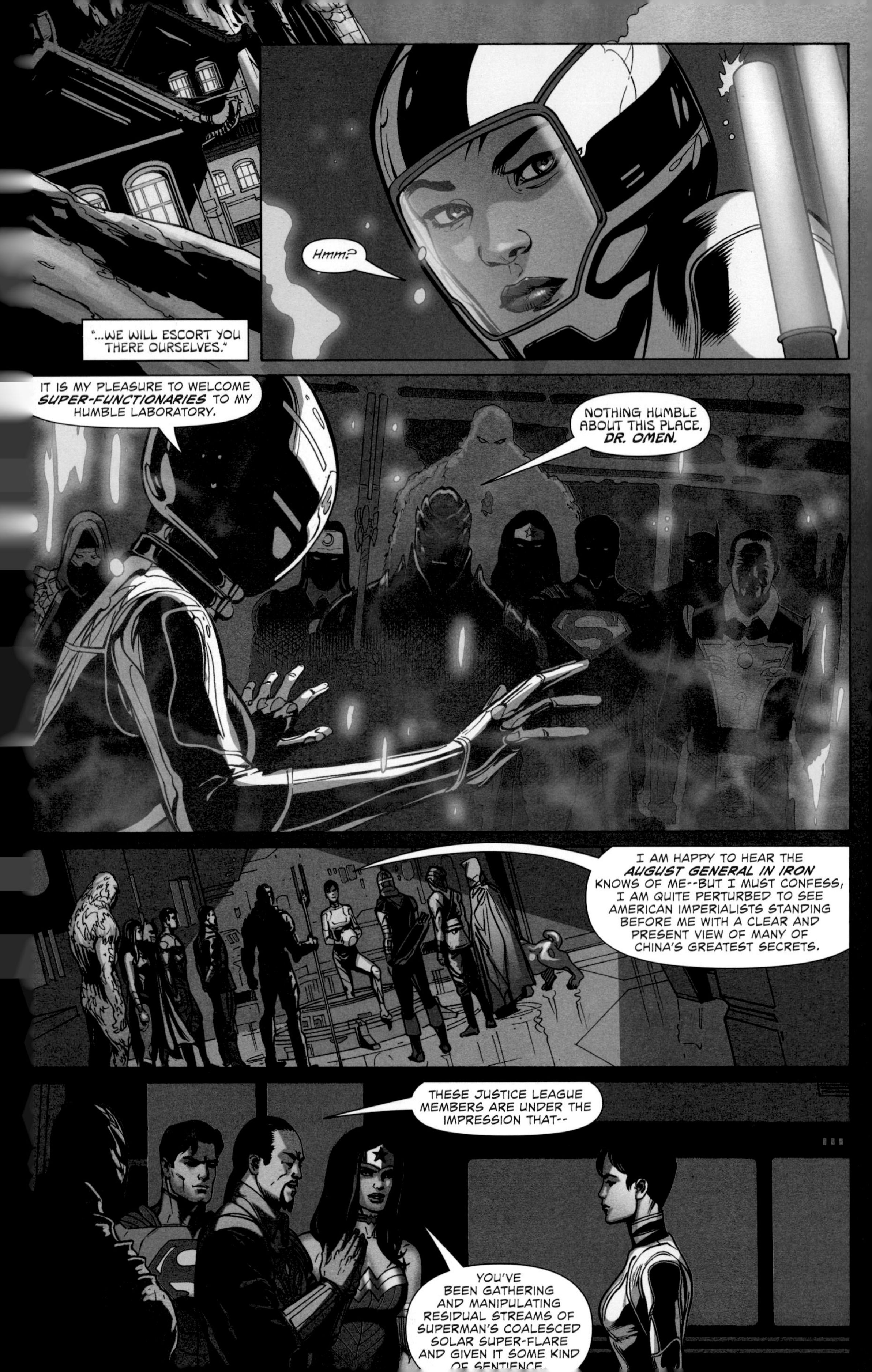
Hmm?
"...WE WILL ESCORT YOU THERE OURSELVES."
IT IS MY PLEASURE TO WELCOME *SUPER-FUNCTIONARIES* TO MY HUMBLE LABORATORY.
NOTHING HUMBLE ABOUT THIS PLACE, *DR. OMEN.*
I AM HAPPY TO HEAR THE *AUGUST GENERAL IN IRON* KNOWS OF ME--BUT I MUST CONFESS, I AM QUITE PERTURBED TO SEE AMERICAN IMPERIALISTS STANDING BEFORE ME WITH A CLEAR AND PRESENT VIEW OF MANY OF CHINA'S GREATEST SECRETS.
THESE JUSTICE LEAGUE MEMBERS ARE UNDER THE IMPRESSION THAT--
YOU'VE BEEN GATHERING AND MANIPULATING RESIDUAL STREAMS OF SUPERMAN'S COALESCED SOLAR SUPER-FLARE AND GIVEN IT SOME KIND OF SENTIENCE.

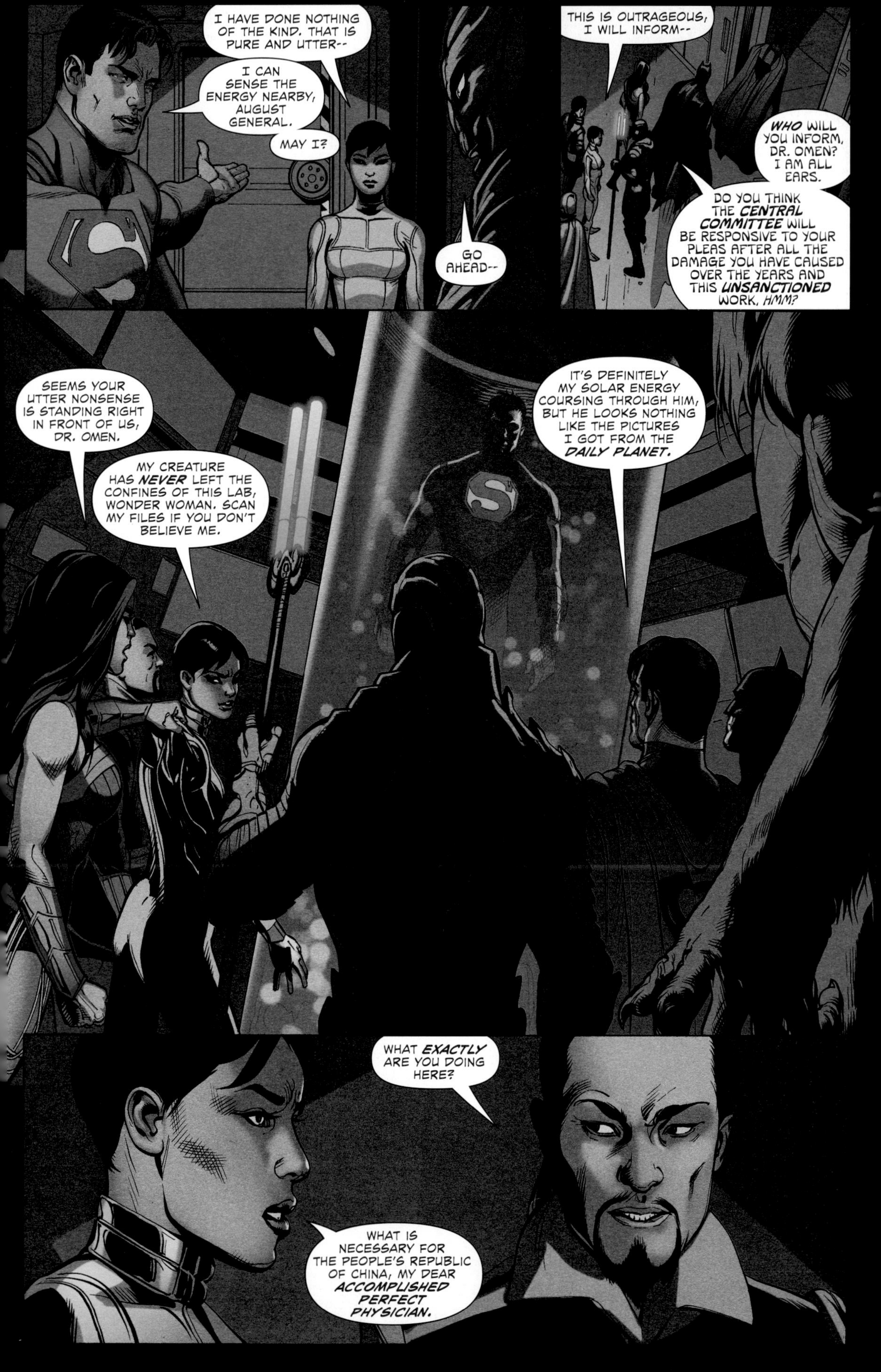
I HAVE DONE NOTHING OF THE KIND. THAT IS PURE AND UTTER--
I CAN SENSE THE ENERGY NEARBY, AUGUST GENERAL.
MAY I?
GO AHEAD--
THIS IS OUTRAGEOUS, I WILL INFORM--
WHO WILL YOU INFORM, DR. OMEN? I AM ALL EARS.
DO YOU THINK THE CENTRAL COMMITTEE WILL BE RESPONSIVE TO YOUR PLEAS AFTER ALL THE DAMAGE YOU HAVE CAUSED OVER THE YEARS AND THIS UNSANCTIONED WORK, HMM?
SEEMS YOUR UTTER NONSENSE IS STANDING RIGHT IN FRONT OF US, DR. OMEN.
MY CREATURE HAS NEVER LEFT THE CONFINES OF THIS LAB, WONDER WOMAN. SCAN MY FILES IF YOU DON'T BELIEVE ME.
IT'S DEFINITELY MY SOLAR ENERGY COURSING THROUGH HIM, BUT HE LOOKS NOTHING LIKE THE PICTURES I GOT FROM THE DAILY PLANET.
WHAT EXACTLY ARE YOU DOING HERE?
WHAT IS NECESSARY FOR THE PEOPLE'S REPUBLIC OF CHINA, MY DEAR ACCOMPLISHED PERFECT PHYSICIAN.

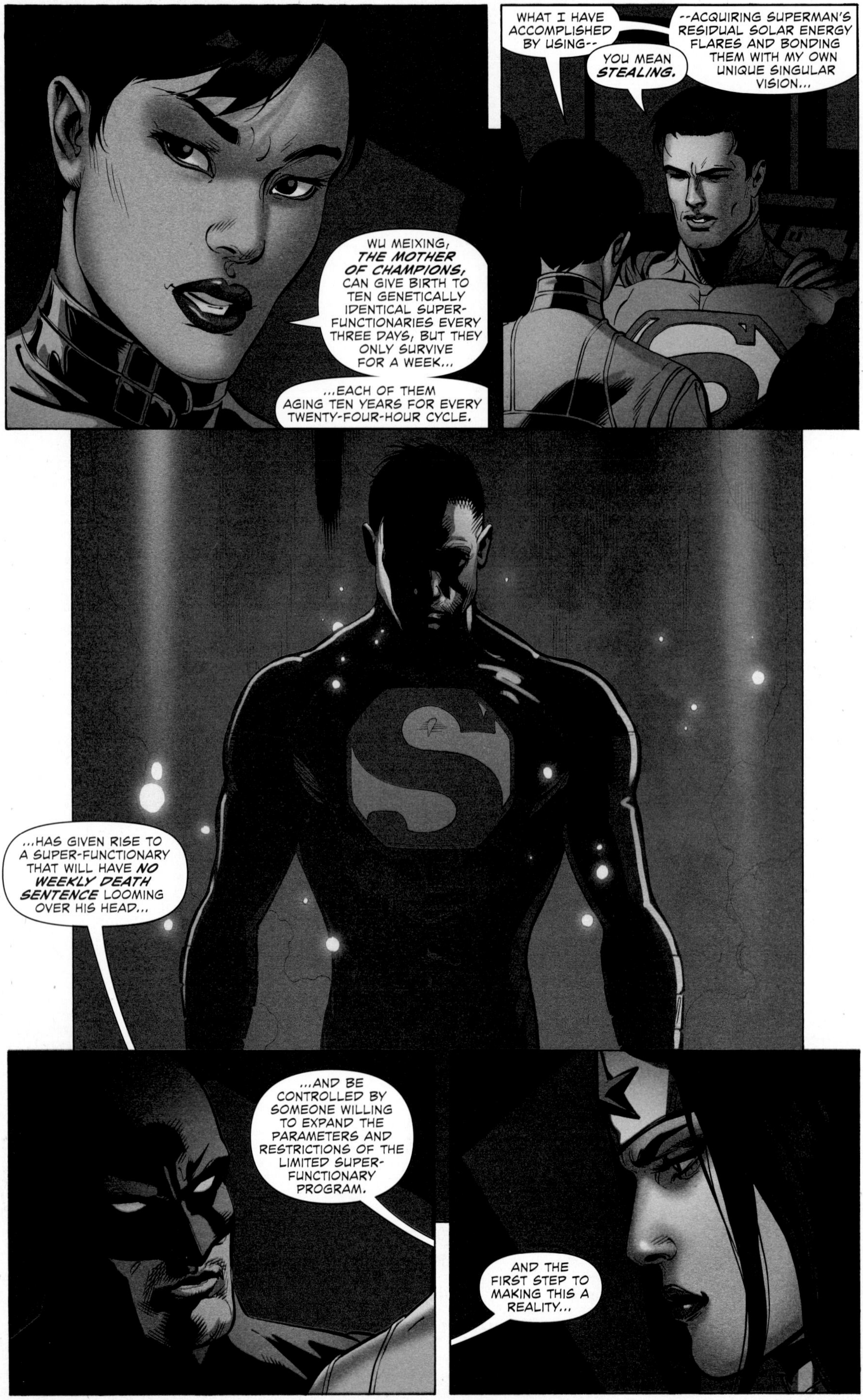
WU MEIXING, ***THE MOTHER OF CHAMPIONS,*** CAN GIVE BIRTH TO TEN GENETICALLY IDENTICAL SUPER-FUNCTIONARIES EVERY THREE DAYS, BUT THEY ONLY SURVIVE FOR A WEEK...
...EACH OF THEM AGING TEN YEARS FOR EVERY TWENTY-FOUR-HOUR CYCLE.
WHAT I HAVE ACCOMPLISHED BY USING--
YOU MEAN ***STEALING.***
--ACQUIRING SUPERMAN'S RESIDUAL SOLAR ENERGY FLARES AND BONDING THEM WITH MY OWN UNIQUE SINGULAR VISION...
...HAS GIVEN RISE TO A SUPER-FUNCTIONARY THAT WILL HAVE ***NO WEEKLY DEATH SENTENCE*** LOOMING OVER HIS HEAD...
...AND BE CONTROLLED BY SOMEONE WILLING TO EXPAND THE PARAMETERS AND RESTRICTIONS OF THE LIMITED SUPER-FUNCTIONARY PROGRAM.
AND THE FIRST STEP TO MAKING THIS A REALITY...

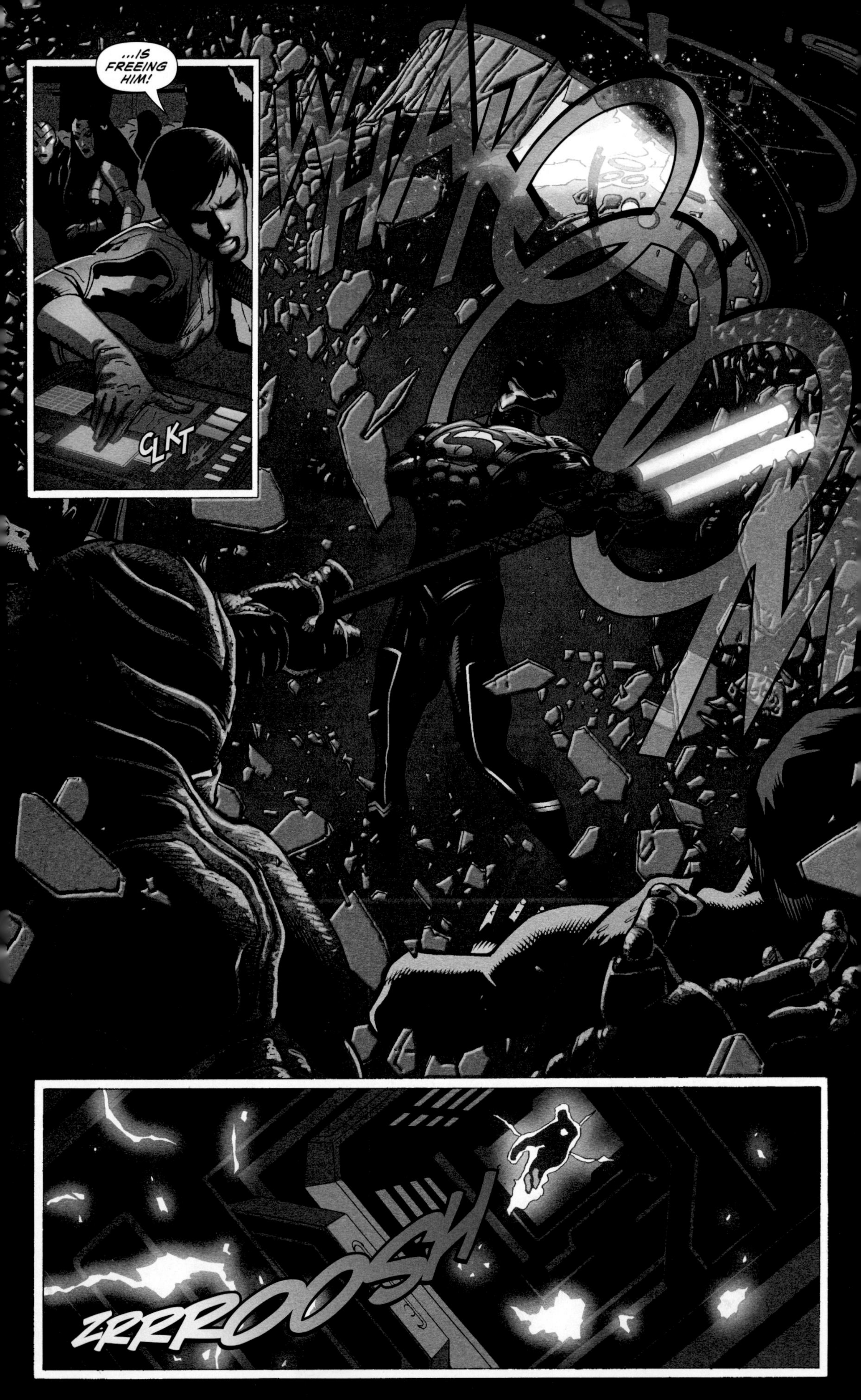
...IS FREEING HIM!
CLKT
ZRRROOSH

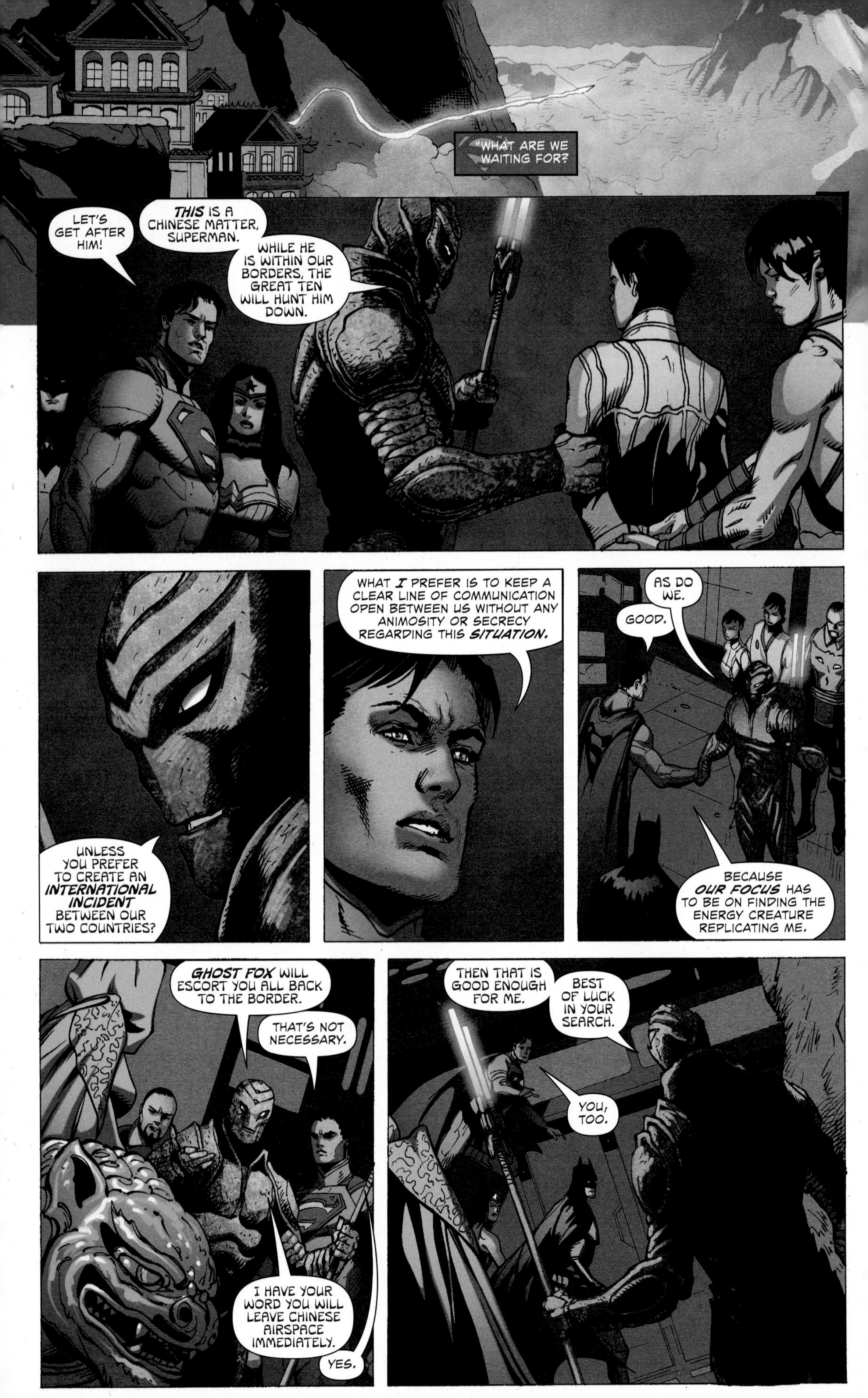
"WHAT ARE WE WAITING FOR?
LET'S GET AFTER HIM!
THIS IS A CHINESE MATTER, SUPERMAN.
WHILE HE IS WITHIN OUR BORDERS, THE GREAT TEN WILL HUNT HIM DOWN.
UNLESS YOU PREFER TO CREATE AN INTERNATIONAL INCIDENT BETWEEN OUR TWO COUNTRIES?
WHAT I PREFER IS TO KEEP A CLEAR LINE OF COMMUNICATION OPEN BETWEEN US WITHOUT ANY ANIMOSITY OR SECRECY REGARDING THIS SITUATION.
AS DO WE.
GOOD.
BECAUSE OUR FOCUS HAS TO BE ON FINDING THE ENERGY CREATURE REPLICATING ME.
GHOST FOX WILL ESCORT YOU ALL BACK TO THE BORDER.
THAT'S NOT NECESSARY.
I HAVE YOUR WORD YOU WILL LEAVE CHINESE AIRSPACE IMMEDIATELY.
YES.
THEN THAT IS GOOD ENOUGH FOR ME.
BEST OF LUCK IN YOUR SEARCH.
YOU, TOO.

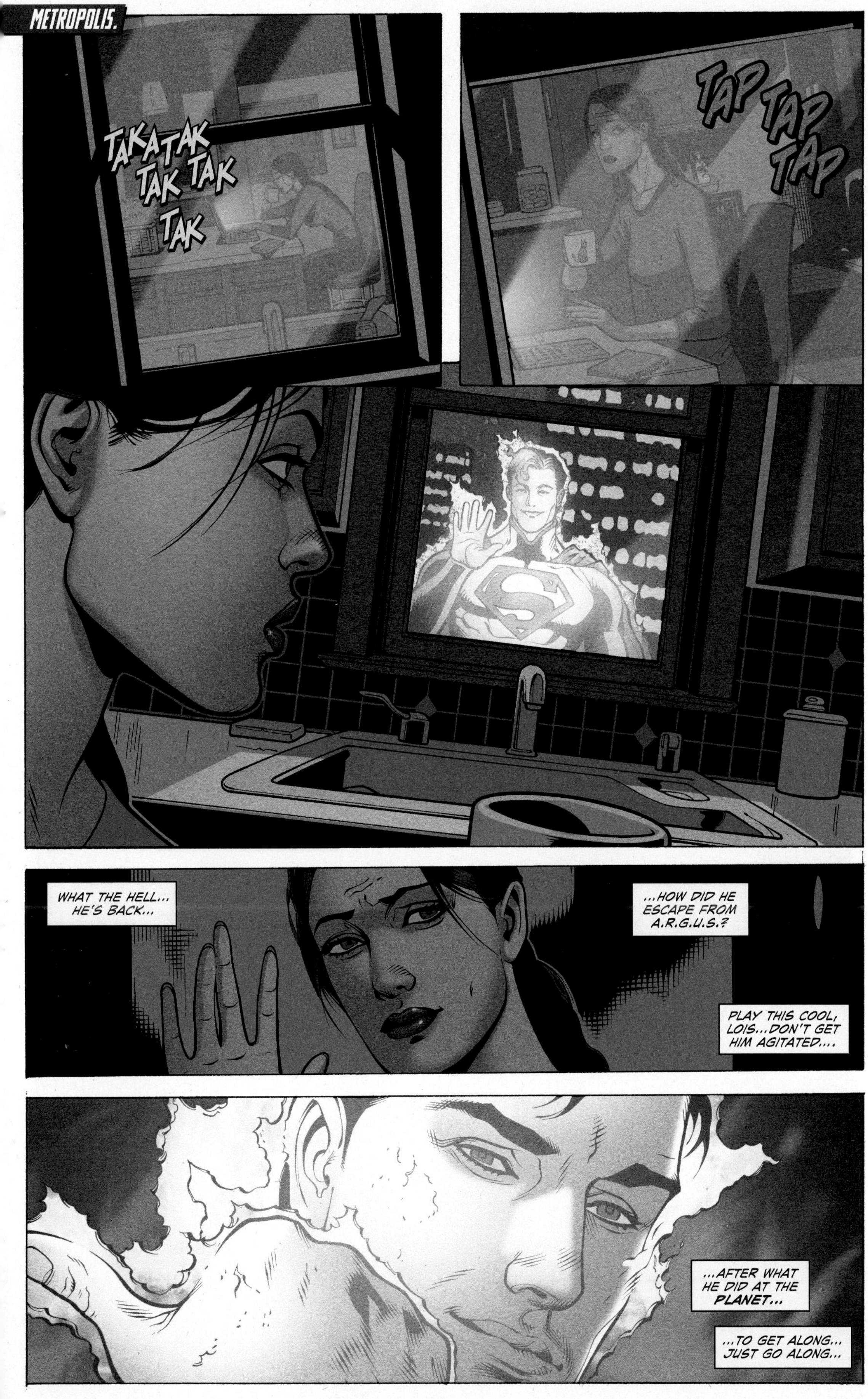
METROPOLIS.
TAKATAK TAK TAK TAK
TAP TAP TAP
WHAT THE HELL... HE'S BACK...
...HOW DID HE ESCAPE FROM A.R.G.U.S.?
PLAY THIS COOL, LOIS...DON'T GET HIM AGITATED....
...AFTER WHAT HE DID AT THE PLANET...
...TO GET ALONG... JUST GO ALONG...

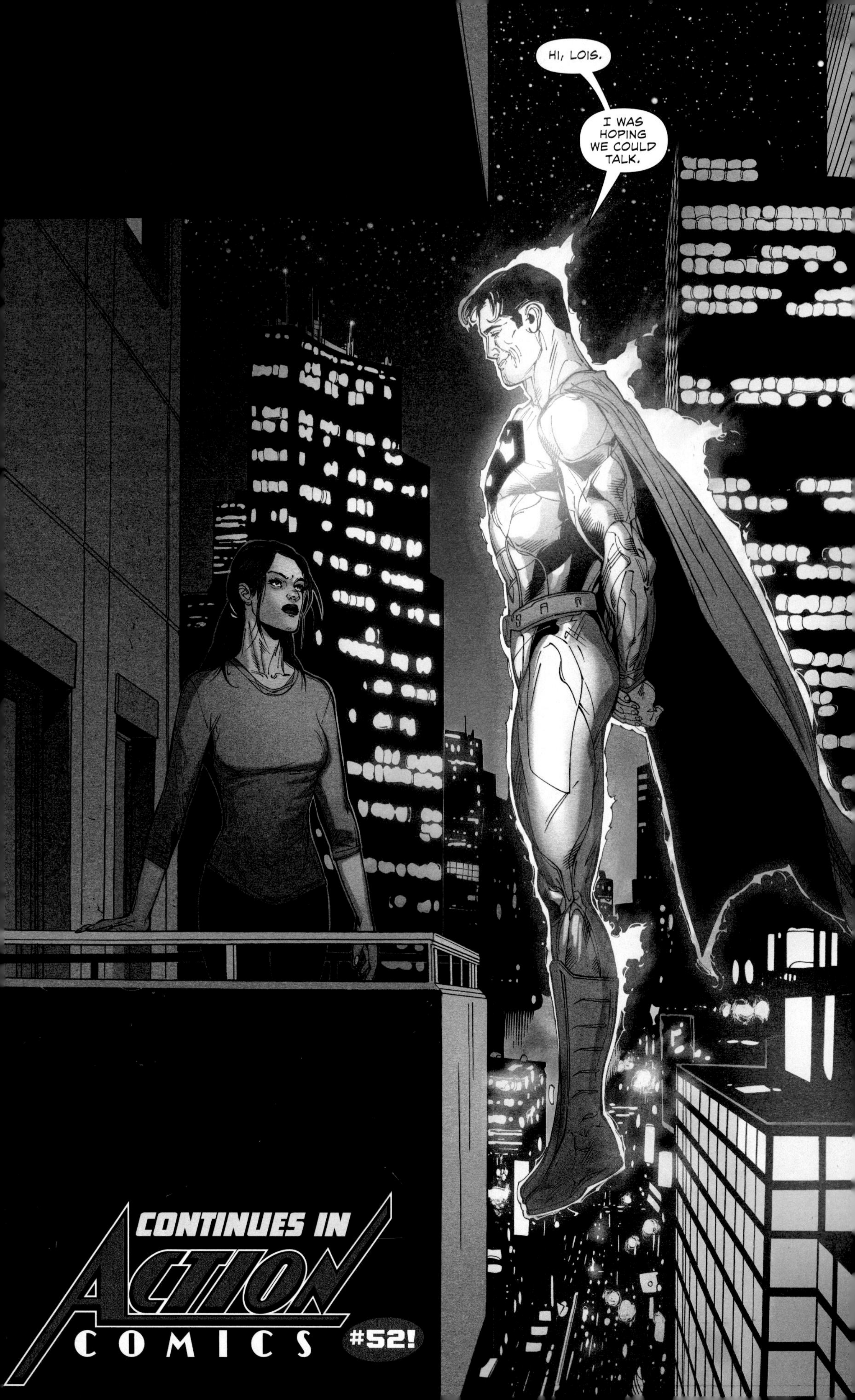
HI, LOIS.
I WAS HOPING WE COULD TALK.
CONTINUES IN ACTION COMICS #52!

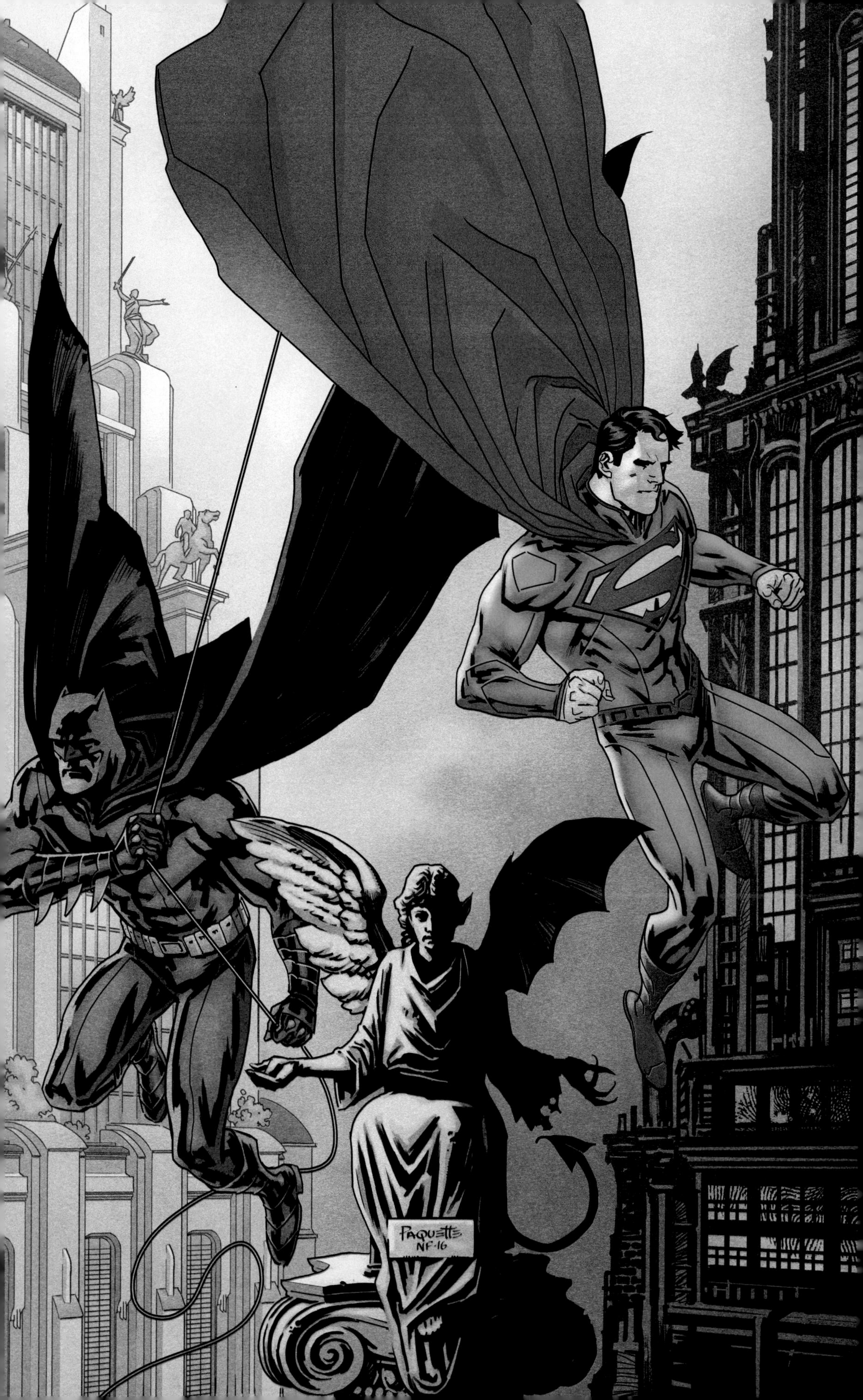
PAQUETTE
NF·16

A note on
BATMAN/SUPERMAN #33, ANNUAL #3 and #34...

These issues were created specifically for inclusion in this collected edition. They take place years before the "Final Days of Superman" story line, which begins in ACTION COMICS #51 and continues in this volume with BATMAN/ SUPERMAN #31.

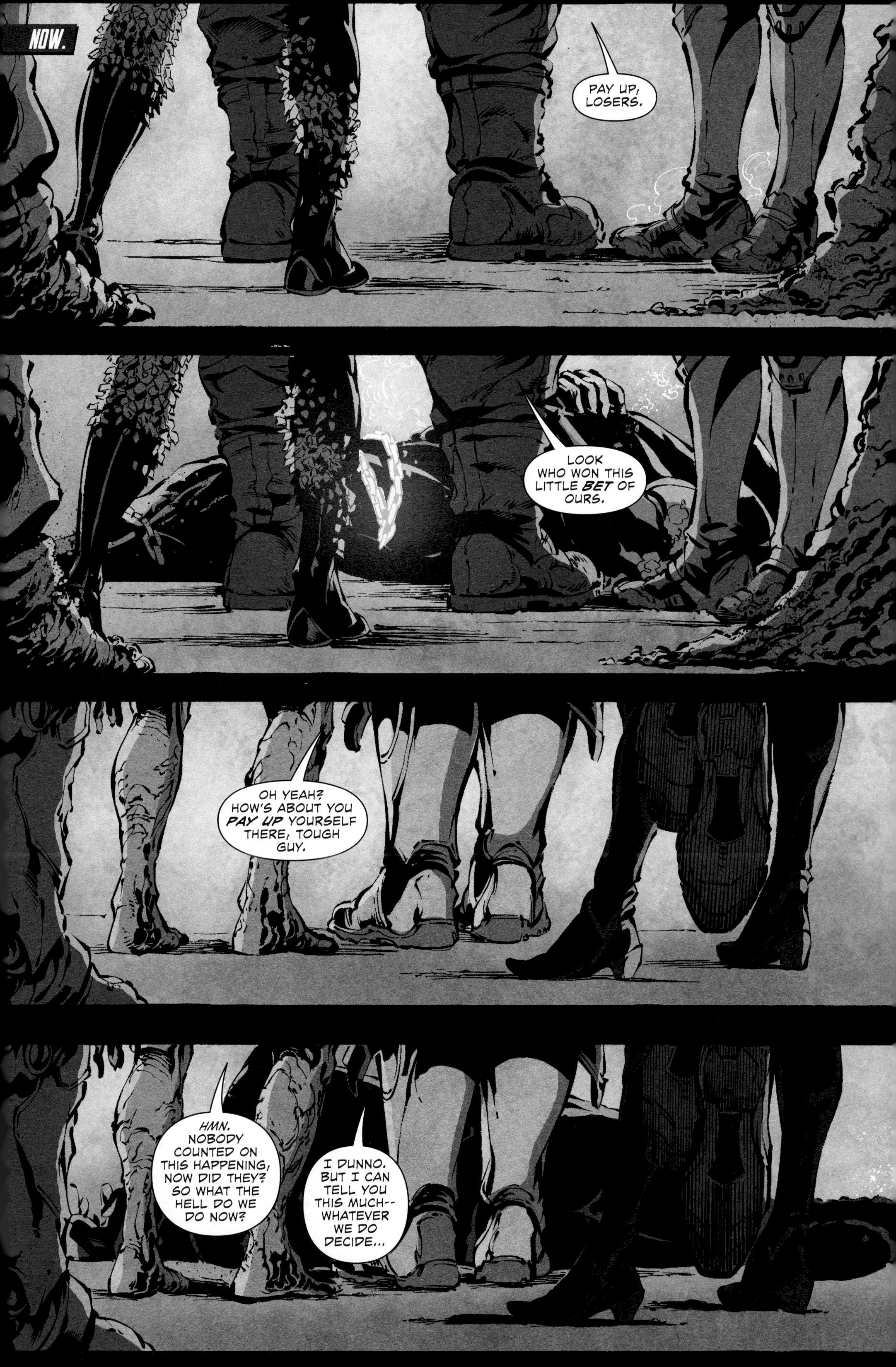
NOW.
PAY UP, LOSERS.
LOOK WHO WON THIS LITTLE BET OF OURS.
OH YEAH? HOW'S ABOUT YOU PAY UP YOURSELF THERE, TOUGH GUY.
HMN. NOBODY COUNTED ON THIS HAPPENING, NOW DID THEY? SO WHAT THE HELL DO WE DO NOW?
I DUNNO. BUT I CAN TELL YOU THIS MUCH-- WHATEVER WE DO DECIDE...

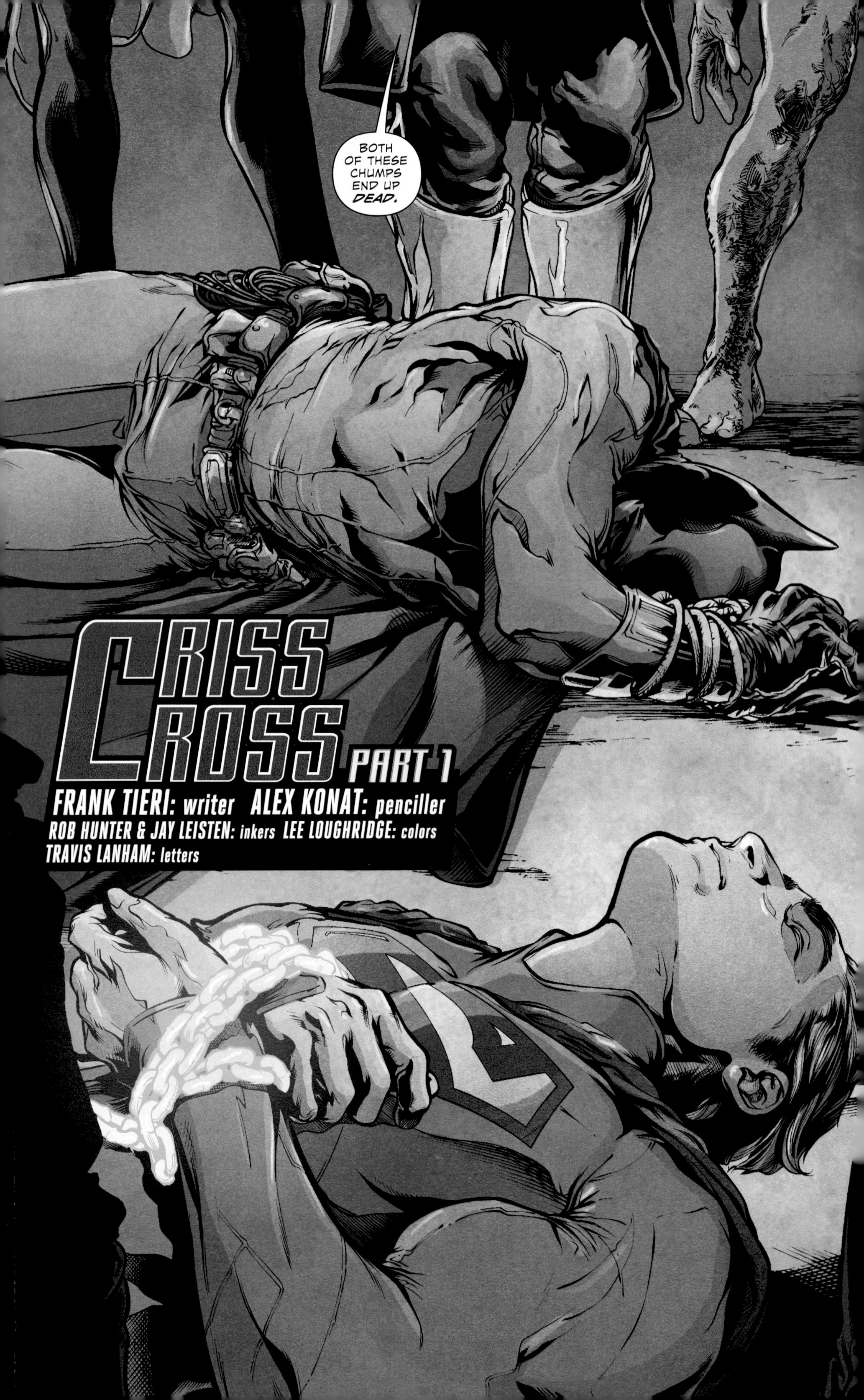
BOTH OF THESE CHUMPS END UP *DEAD.*
CRISS CROSS PART 1
FRANK TIERI: writer ALEX KONAT: penciller
ROB HUNTER & JAY LEISTEN: inkers LEE LOUGHRIDGE: colors
TRAVIS LANHAM: letters

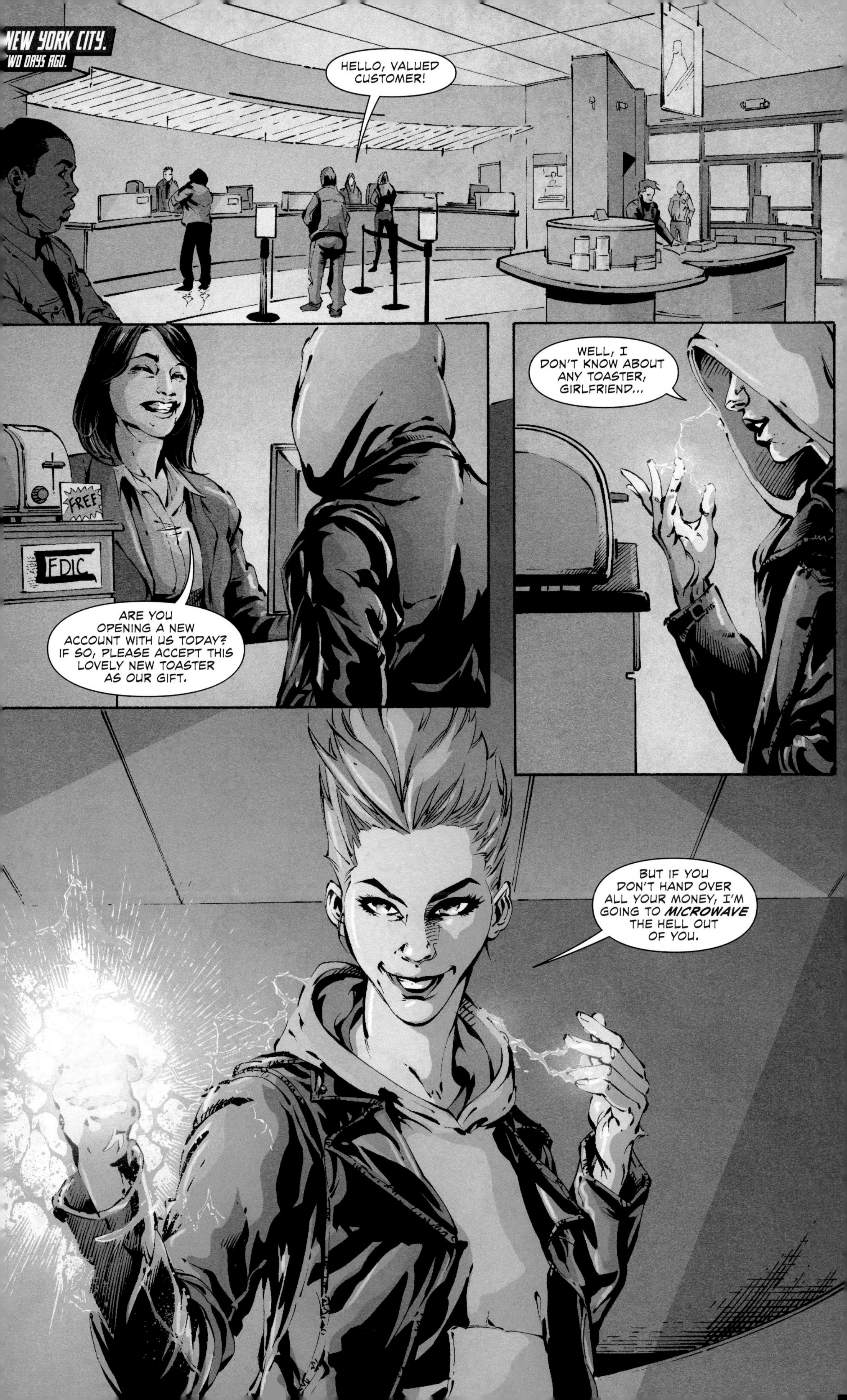
NEW YORK CITY.
WO DAYS AGO.
HELLO, VALUED CUSTOMER!
FREE
FDIC
ARE YOU OPENING A NEW ACCOUNT WITH US TODAY? IF SO, PLEASE ACCEPT THIS LOVELY NEW TOASTER AS OUR GIFT.
WELL, I DON'T KNOW ABOUT ANY TOASTER, GIRLFRIEND...
BUT IF YOU DON'T HAND OVER ALL YOUR MONEY, I'M GOING TO *MICROWAVE* THE HELL OUT OF YOU.

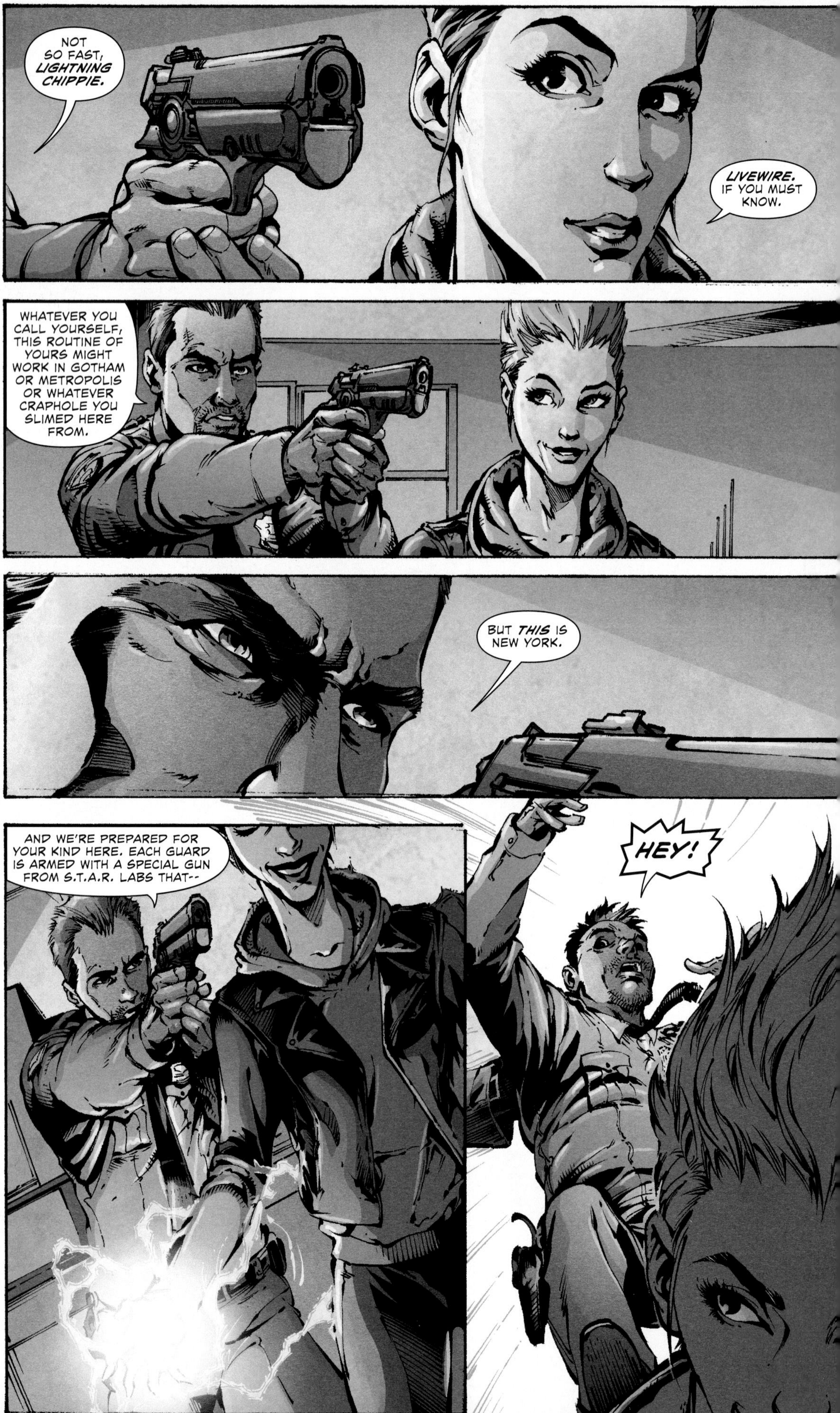
NOT SO FAST, *LIGHTNING CHIPPIE.*
LIVEWIRE. IF YOU MUST KNOW.
WHATEVER YOU CALL YOURSELF, THIS ROUTINE OF YOURS MIGHT WORK IN GOTHAM OR METROPOLIS OR WHATEVER CRAPHOLE YOU SLIMED HERE FROM.
BUT *THIS* IS NEW YORK.
AND WE'RE PREPARED FOR YOUR KIND HERE. EACH GUARD IS ARMED WITH A SPECIAL GUN FROM S.T.A.R. LABS THAT--
HEY!

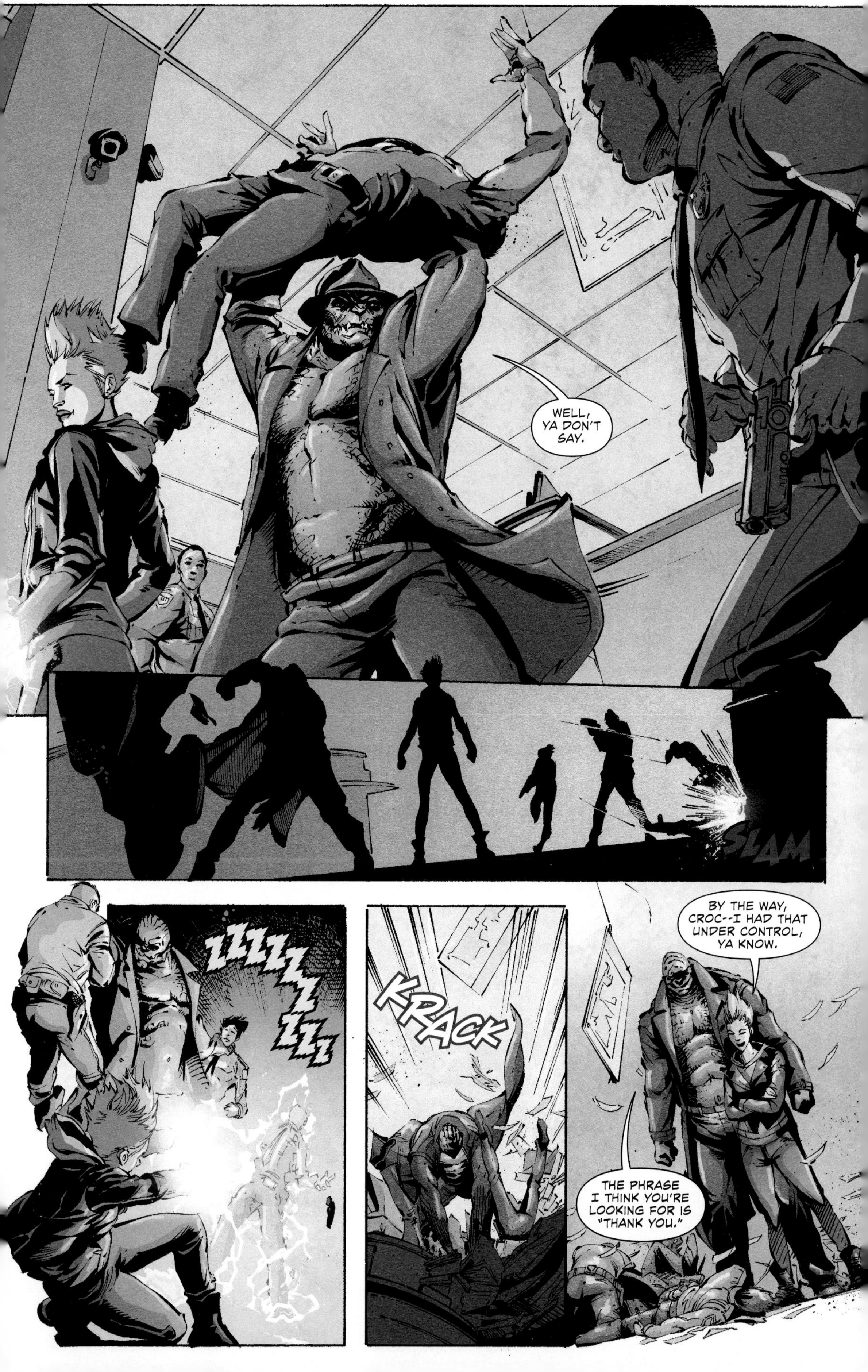
WELL, YA DON'T SAY.
SLAM
ZZZZZZZZZZ
KRACK
BY THE WAY, CROC--I HAD THAT UNDER CONTROL, YA KNOW.
THE PHRASE I THINK YOU'RE LOOKING FOR IS "THANK YOU."

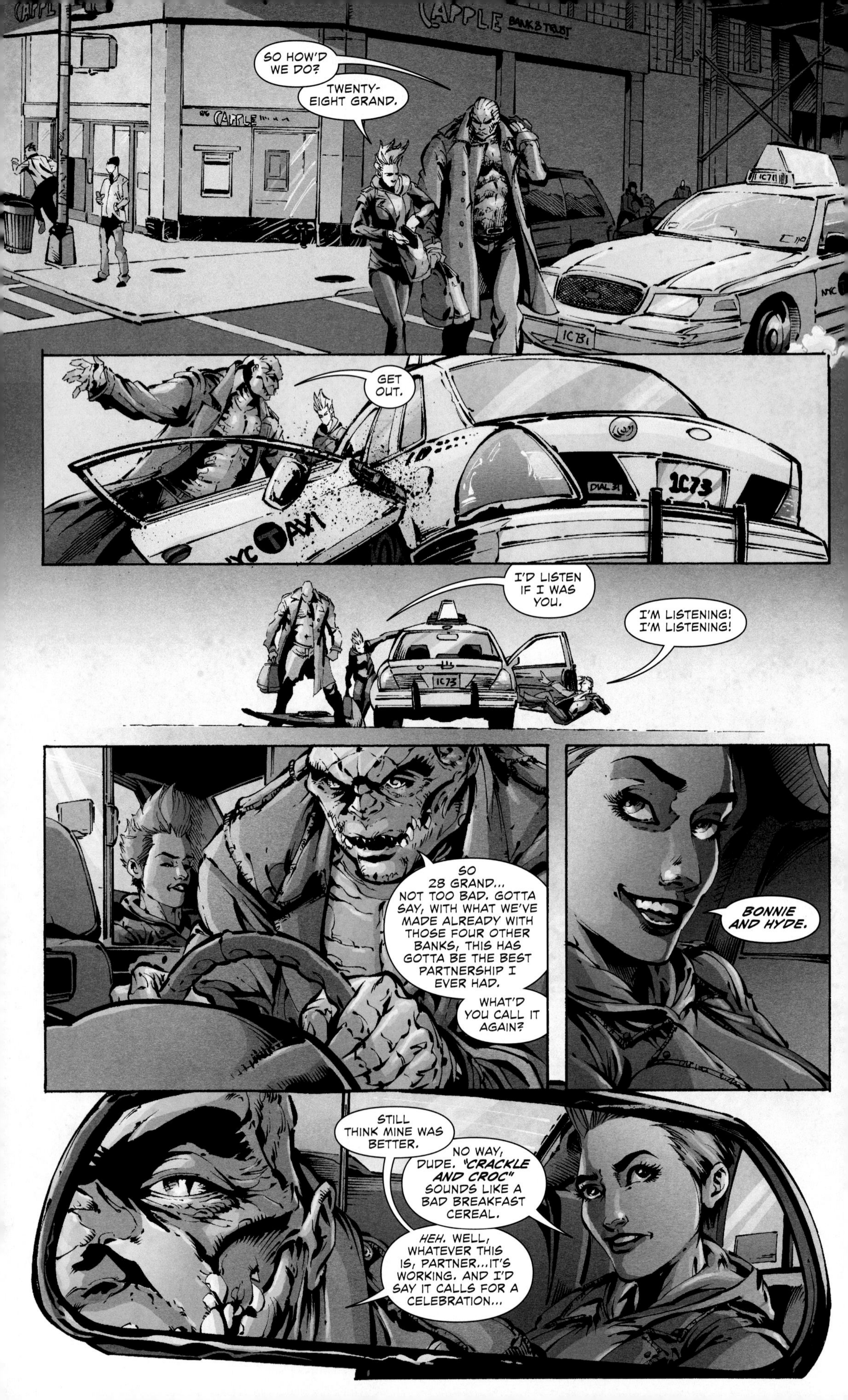
CAPPLE BANK & TRUST
SO HOW'D WE DO?
TWENTY-EIGHT GRAND.
GET OUT.
I'D LISTEN IF I WAS YOU.
I'M LISTENING! I'M LISTENING!
SO 28 GRAND... NOT TOO BAD. GOTTA SAY, WITH WHAT WE'VE MADE ALREADY WITH THOSE FOUR OTHER BANKS, THIS HAS GOTTA BE THE BEST PARTNERSHIP I EVER HAD.
WHAT'D YOU CALL IT AGAIN?
BONNIE AND HYDE.
STILL THINK MINE WAS BETTER.
NO WAY, DUDE. "CRACKLE AND CROC" SOUNDS LIKE A BAD BREAKFAST CEREAL.
HEH. WELL, WHATEVER THIS IS, PARTNER...IT'S WORKING. AND I'D SAY IT CALLS FOR A CELEBRATION...

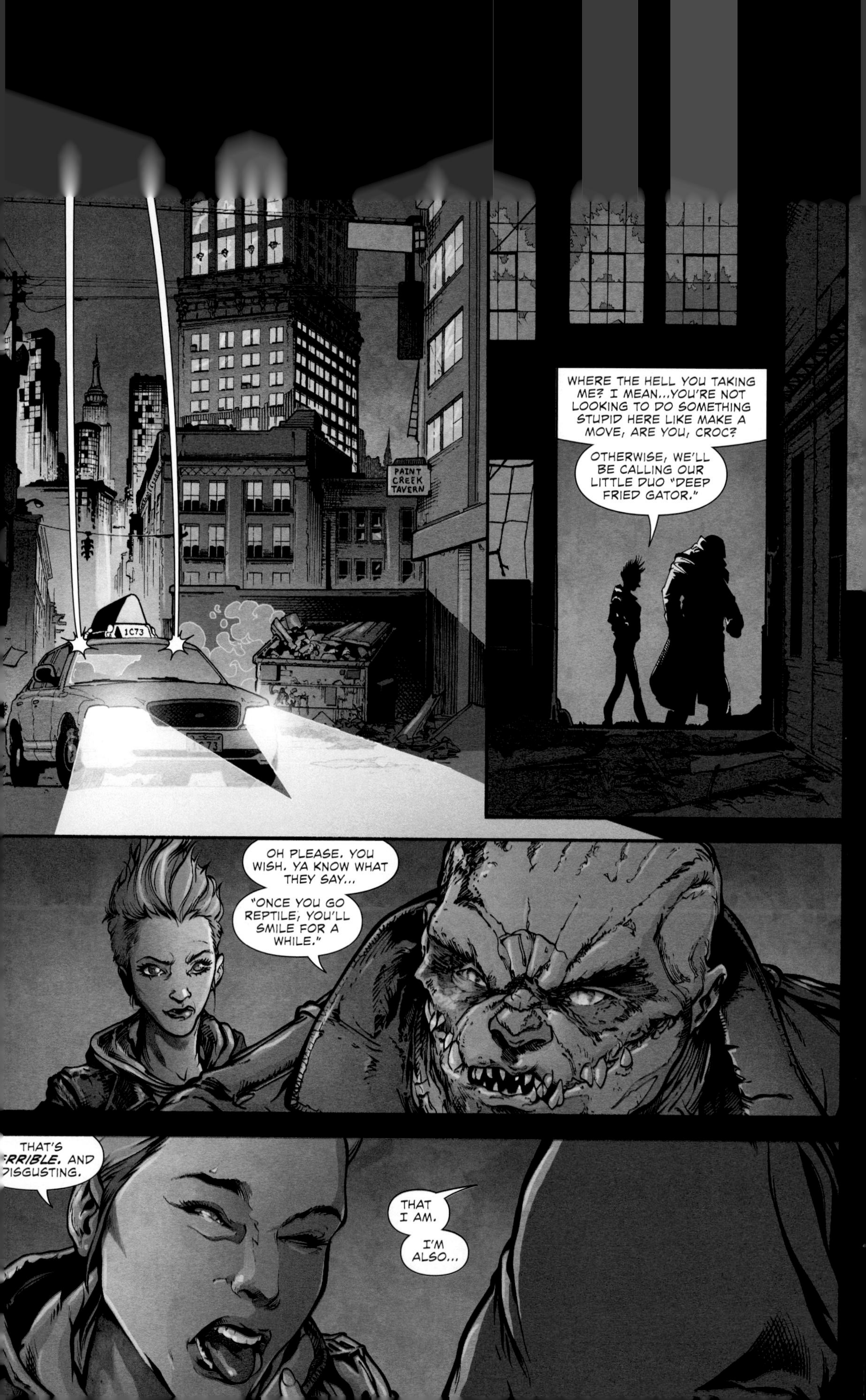
1C73
PAINT CREEK TAVERN
WHERE THE HELL YOU TAKING ME? I MEAN...YOU'RE NOT LOOKING TO DO SOMETHING STUPID HERE LIKE MAKE A MOVE, ARE YOU, CROC?
OTHERWISE, WE'LL BE CALLING OUR LITTLE DUO "DEEP FRIED GATOR."
OH PLEASE. YOU WISH. YA KNOW WHAT THEY SAY...
"ONCE YOU GO REPTILE, YOU'LL SMILE FOR A WHILE."
THAT'S RRIBLE. AND DISGUSTING.
THAT I AM.
I'M ALSO...

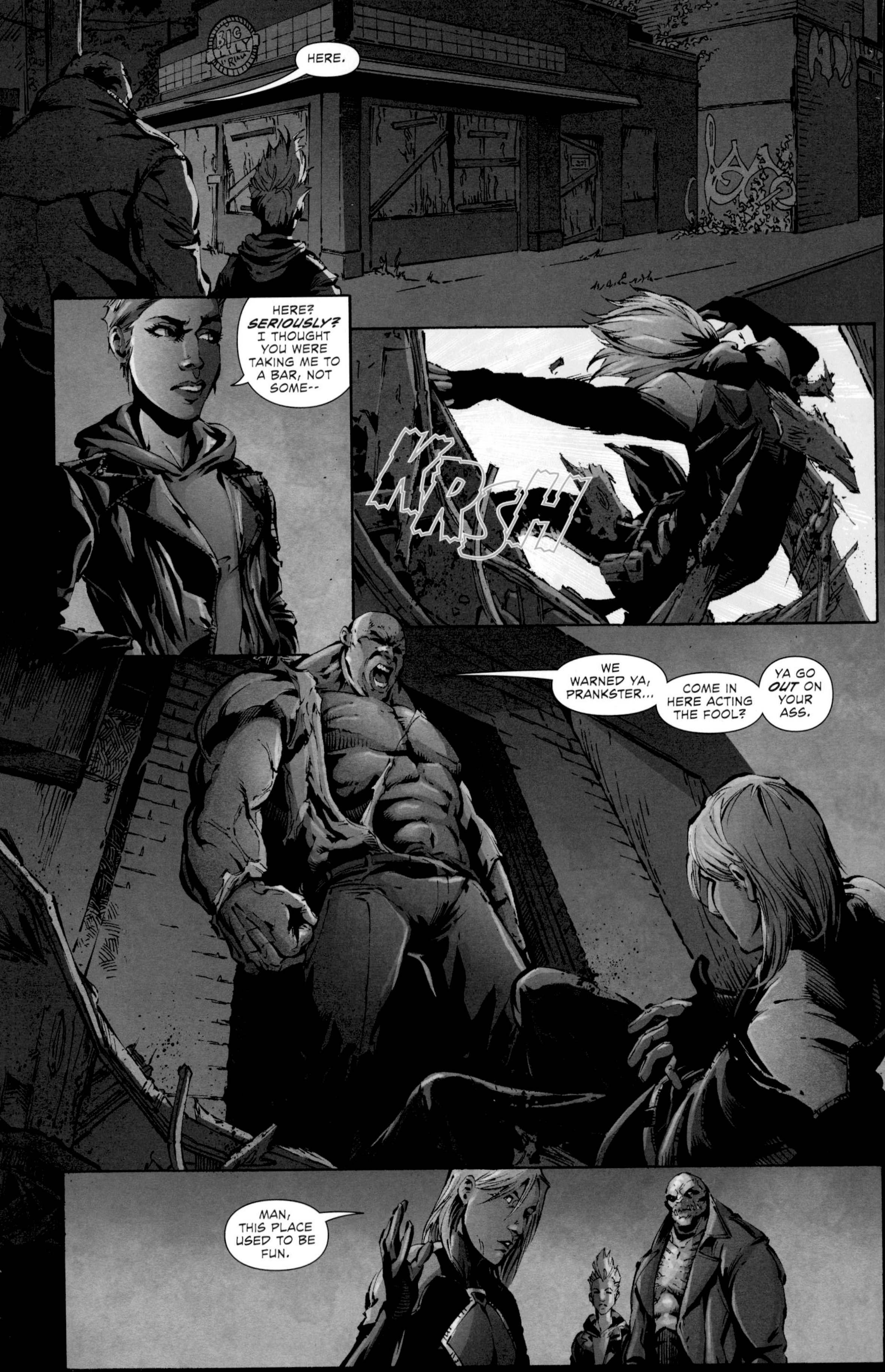
HERE.
HERE? SERIOUSLY? I THOUGHT YOU WERE TAKING ME TO A BAR, NOT SOME--
KRSH
WE WARNED YA, PRANKSTER...
COME IN HERE ACTING THE FOOL?
YA GO OUT ON YOUR ASS.
MAN, THIS PLACE USED TO BE FUN.

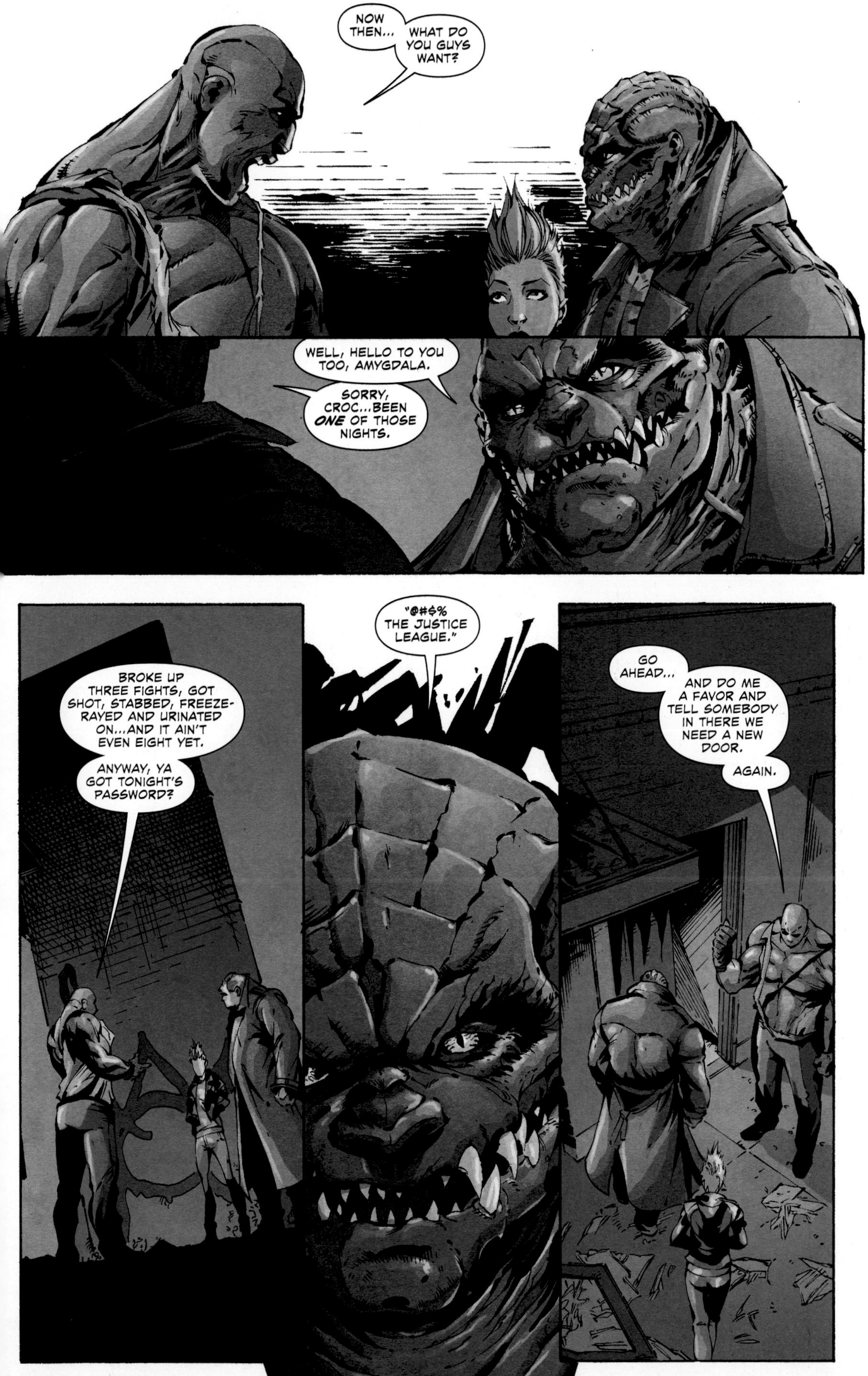
NOW THEN...
WHAT DO YOU GUYS WANT?
WELL, HELLO TO YOU TOO, AMYGDALA.
SORRY, CROC...BEEN ONE OF THOSE NIGHTS.
BROKE UP THREE FIGHTS, GOT SHOT, STABBED, FREEZE-RAYED AND URINATED ON...AND IT AIN'T EVEN EIGHT YET.
ANYWAY, YA GOT TONIGHT'S PASSWORD?
"@#$% THE JUSTICE LEAGUE."
GO AHEAD...
AND DO ME A FAVOR AND TELL SOMEBODY IN THERE WE NEED A NEW DOOR.
AGAIN.

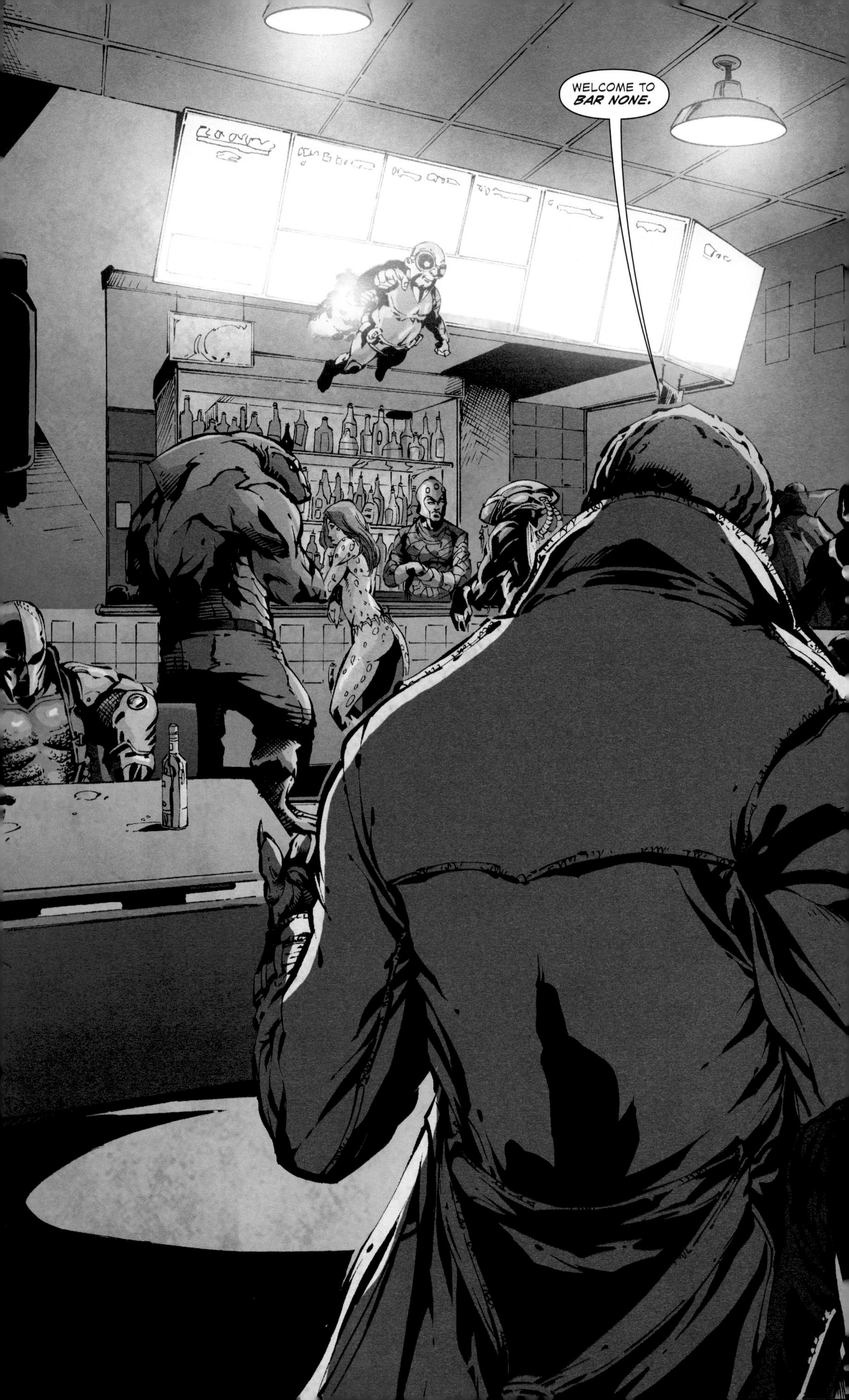
WELCOME TO BAR NONE.

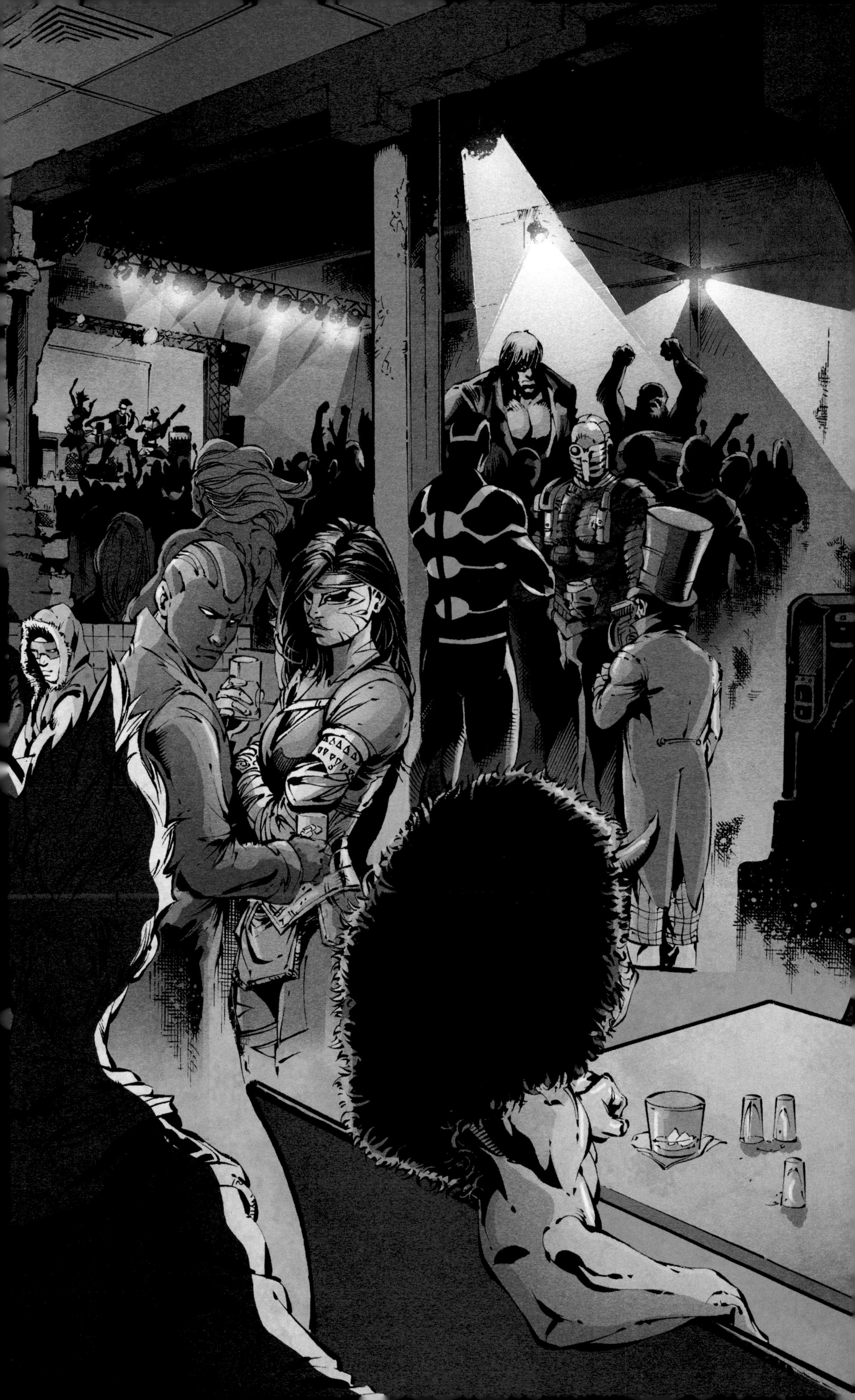

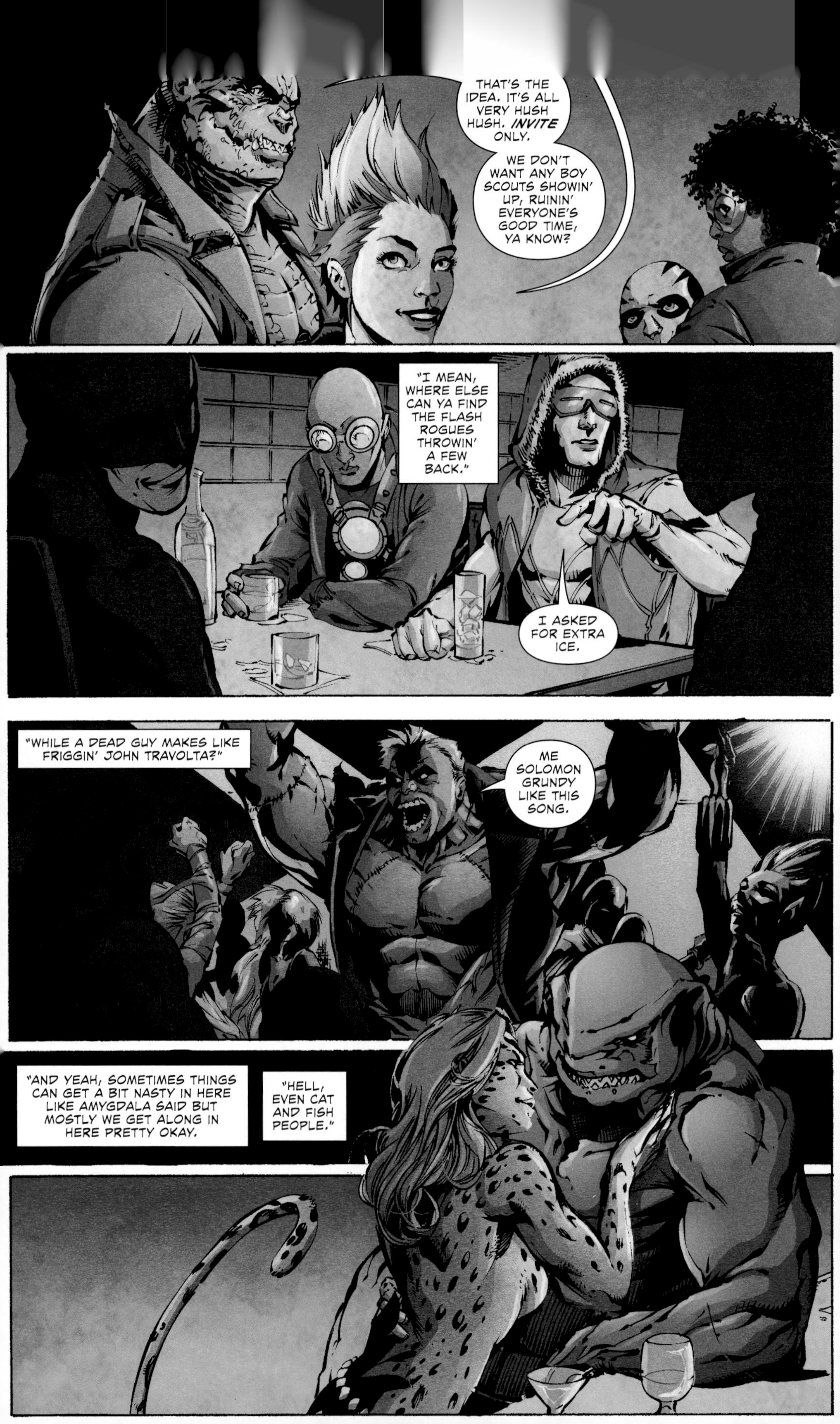
THAT'S THE IDEA. IT'S ALL VERY HUSH HUSH. *INVITE* ONLY.
WE DON'T WANT ANY BOY SCOUTS SHOWIN' UP, RUININ' EVERYONE'S GOOD TIME, YA KNOW?
"I MEAN, WHERE ELSE CAN YA FIND THE FLASH ROGUES THROWIN' A FEW BACK."
I ASKED FOR EXTRA ICE.
"WHILE A DEAD GUY MAKES LIKE FRIGGIN' JOHN TRAVOLTA?"
ME SOLOMON GRUNDY LIKE THIS SONG.
"AND YEAH, SOMETIMES THINGS CAN GET A BIT NASTY IN HERE LIKE AMYGDALA SAID BUT MOSTLY WE GET ALONG IN HERE PRETTY OKAY.
"HELL, EVEN CAT AND FISH PEOPLE."

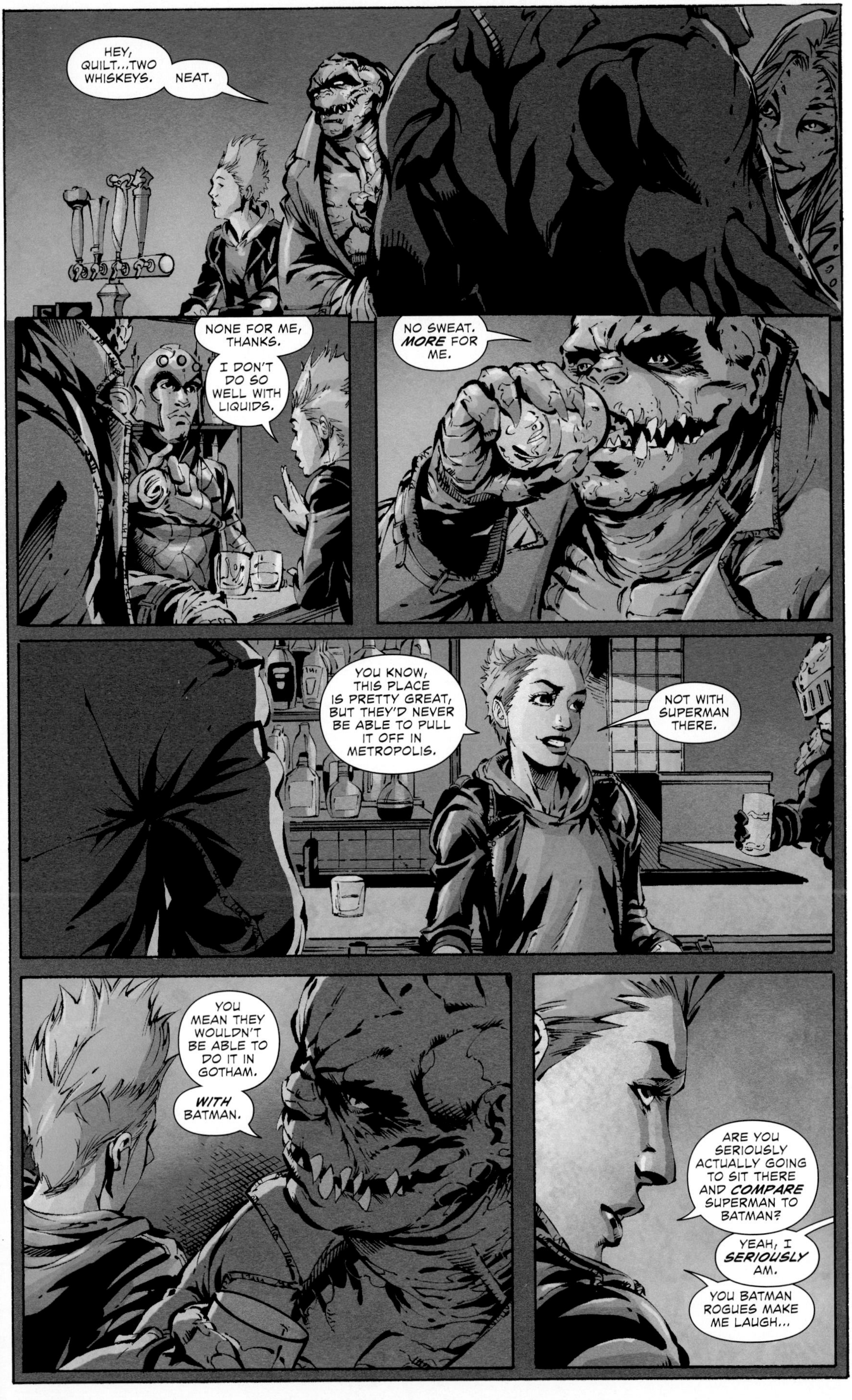
HEY, QUILT...TWO WHISKEYS.
NEAT.
NONE FOR ME, THANKS.
I DON'T DO SO WELL WITH LIQUIDS.
NO SWEAT. MORE FOR ME.
YOU KNOW, THIS PLACE IS PRETTY GREAT, BUT THEY'D NEVER BE ABLE TO PULL IT OFF IN METROPOLIS.
NOT WITH SUPERMAN THERE.
YOU MEAN THEY WOULDN'T BE ABLE TO DO IT IN GOTHAM.
WITH BATMAN.
ARE YOU SERIOUSLY ACTUALLY GOING TO SIT THERE AND COMPARE SUPERMAN TO BATMAN?
YEAH, I SERIOUSLY AM.
YOU BATMAN ROGUES MAKE ME LAUGH...

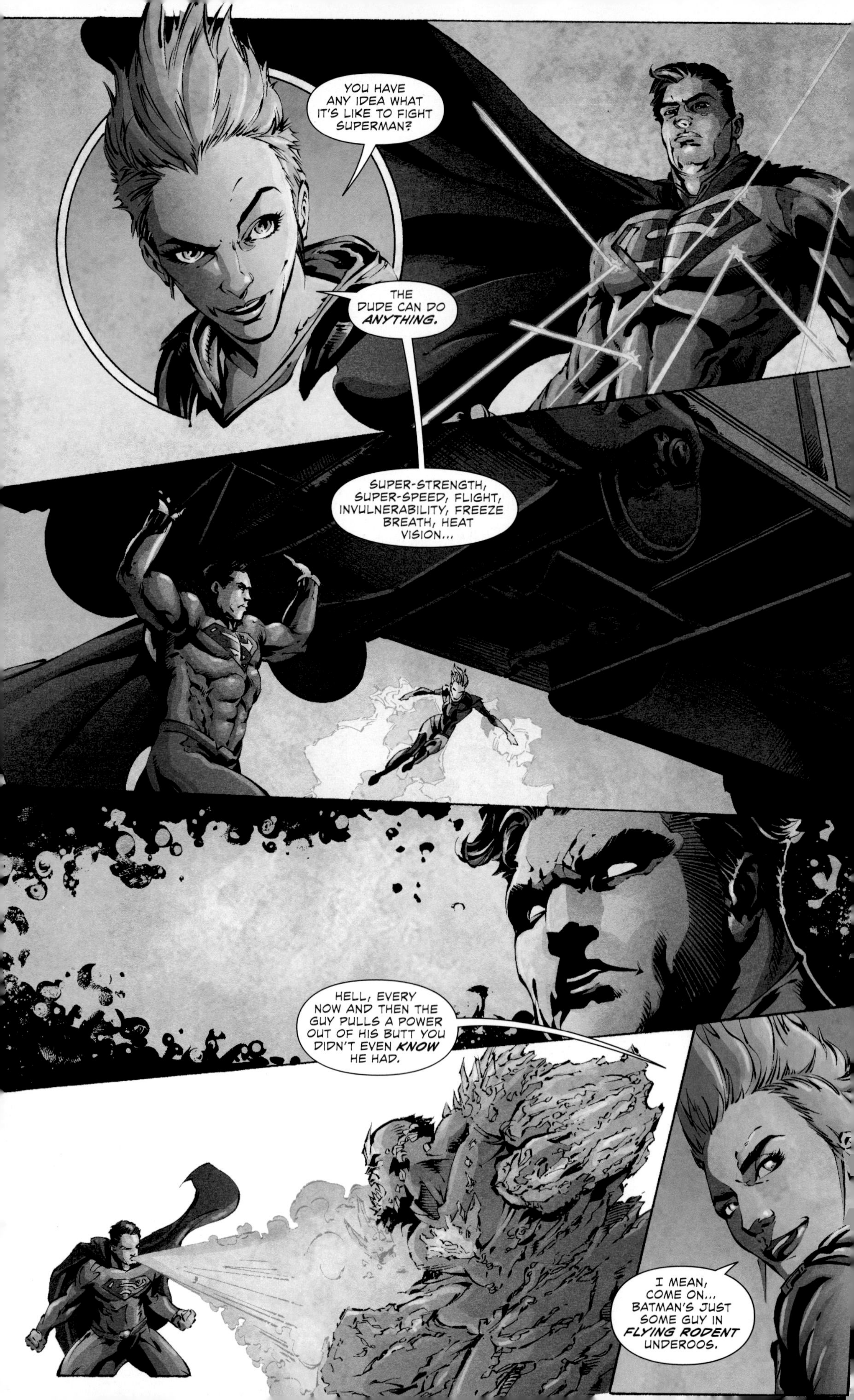
YOU HAVE ANY IDEA WHAT IT'S LIKE TO FIGHT SUPERMAN?
THE DUDE CAN DO *ANYTHING.*
SUPER-STRENGTH, SUPER-SPEED, FLIGHT, INVULNERABILITY, FREEZE BREATH, HEAT VISION...
HELL, EVERY NOW AND THEN THE GUY PULLS A POWER OUT OF HIS BUTT YOU DIDN'T EVEN *KNOW* HE HAD.
I MEAN, COME ON... BATMAN'S JUST SOME GUY IN *FLYING RODENT* UNDEROOS.

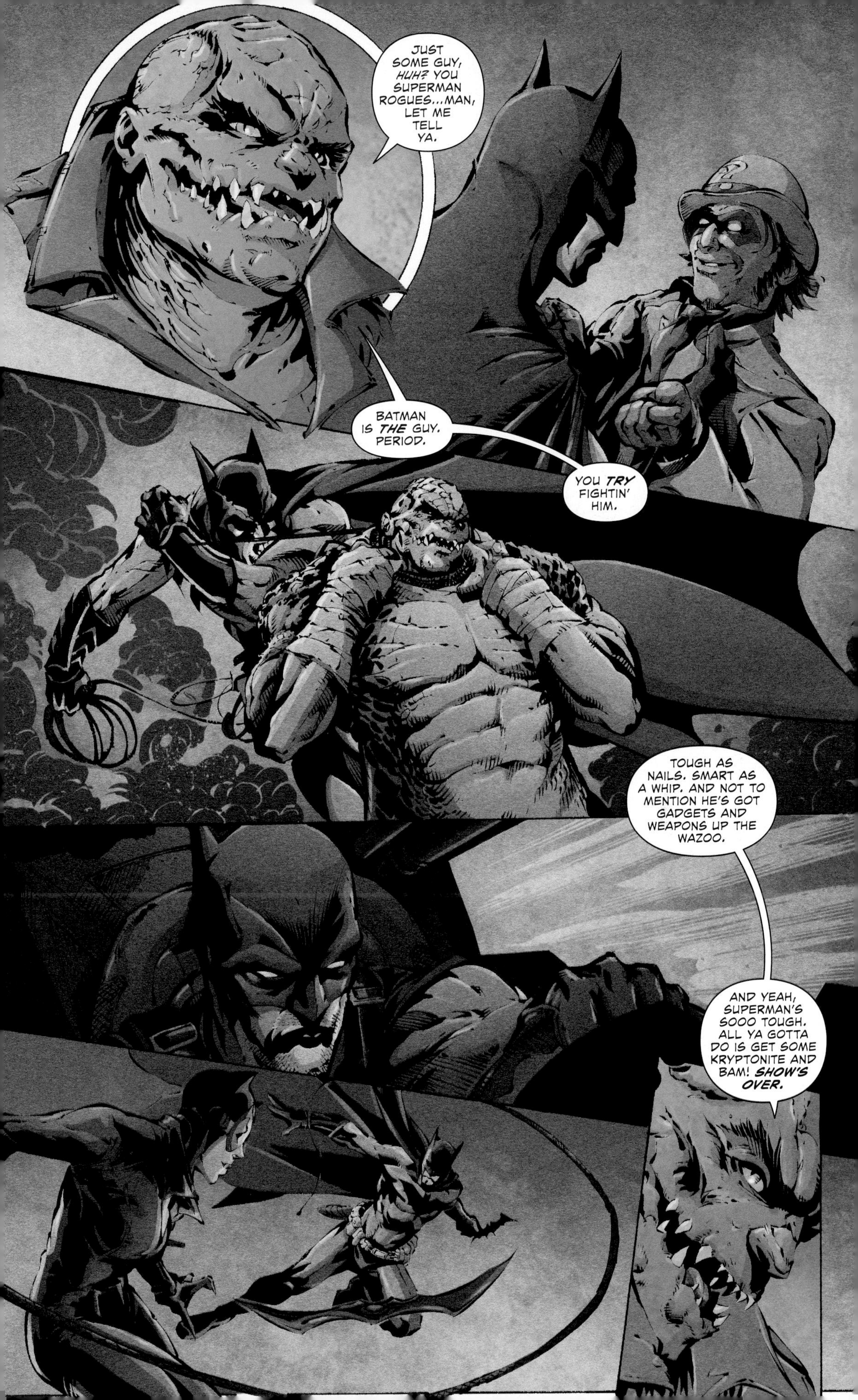
JUST SOME GUY, *HUH?* YOU SUPERMAN ROGUES...MAN, LET ME TELL YA.
BATMAN IS ***THE*** GUY. PERIOD.
YOU ***TRY*** FIGHTIN' HIM.
TOUGH AS NAILS. SMART AS A WHIP. AND NOT TO MENTION HE'S GOT GADGETS AND WEAPONS UP THE WAZOO.
AND YEAH, SUPERMAN'S SOOO TOUGH. ALL YA GOTTA DO IS GET SOME KRYPTONITE AND BAM! ***SHOW'S OVER.***

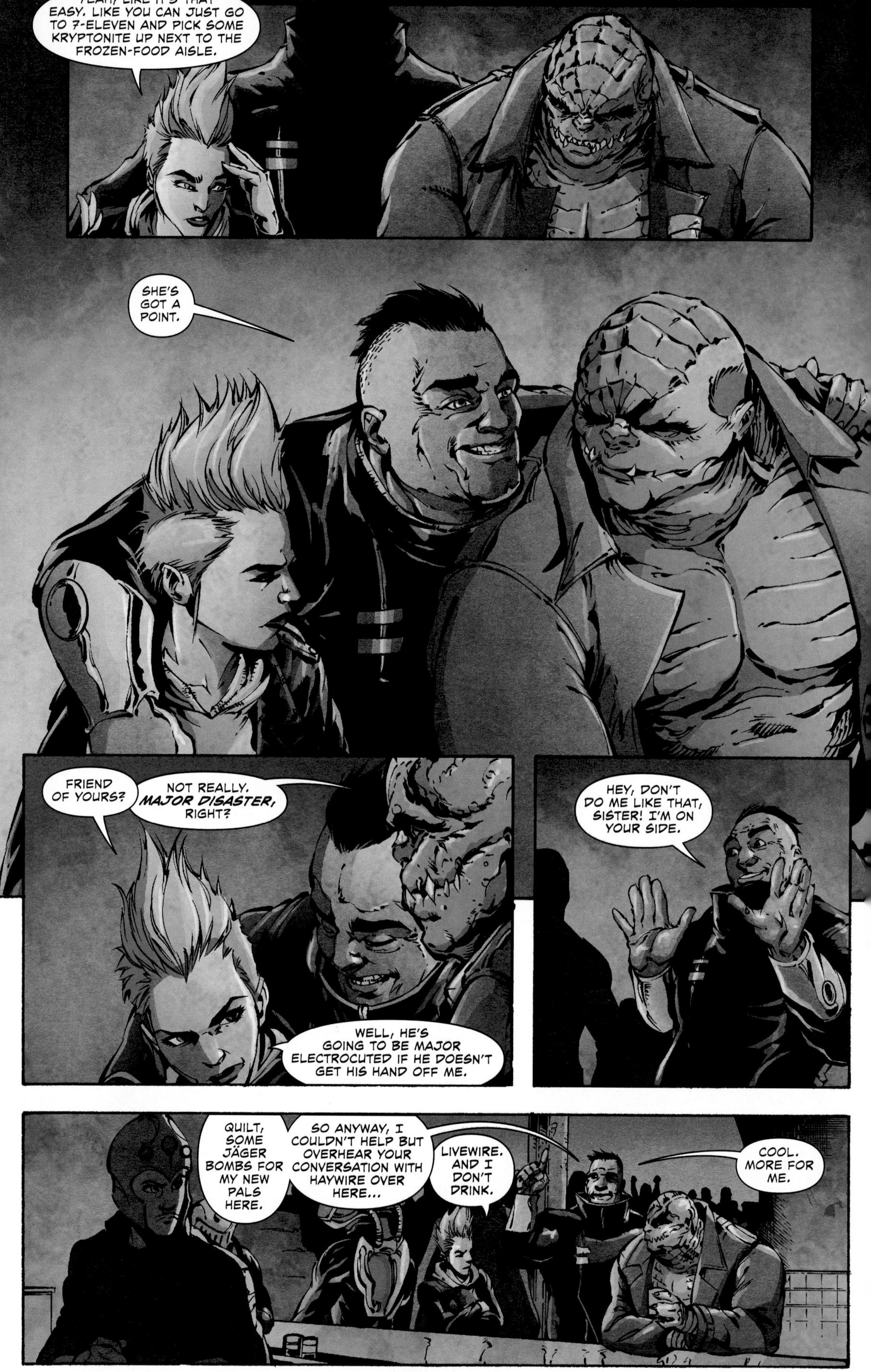
YEAH, LIKE IT'S THAT EASY. LIKE YOU CAN JUST GO TO 7-ELEVEN AND PICK SOME KRYPTONITE UP NEXT TO THE FROZEN-FOOD AISLE.
SHE'S GOT A POINT.
FRIEND OF YOURS?
NOT REALLY. ***MAJOR DISASTER,*** RIGHT?
WELL, HE'S GOING TO BE MAJOR ELECTROCUTED IF HE DOESN'T GET HIS HAND OFF ME.
HEY, DON'T DO ME LIKE THAT, SISTER! I'M ON YOUR SIDE.
QUILT, SOME JÄGER BOMBS FOR MY NEW PALS HERE.
SO ANYWAY, I COULDN'T HELP BUT OVERHEAR YOUR CONVERSATION WITH HAYWIRE OVER HERE...
LIVEWIRE. AND I DON'T DRINK.
COOL. MORE FOR ME.

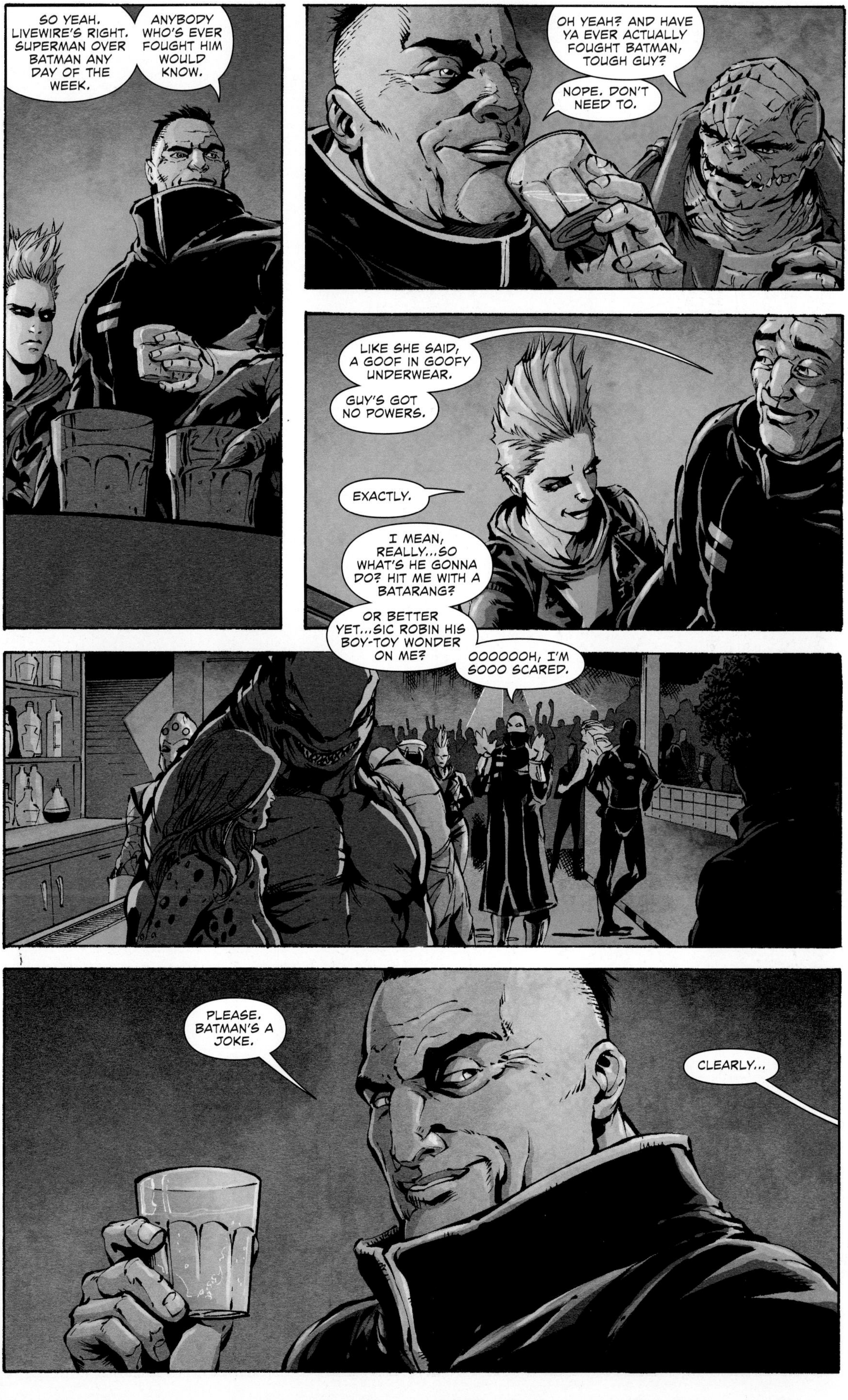
SO YEAH. LIVEWIRE'S RIGHT. SUPERMAN OVER BATMAN ANY DAY OF THE WEEK.
ANYBODY WHO'S EVER FOUGHT HIM WOULD KNOW.
OH YEAH? AND HAVE YA EVER ACTUALLY FOUGHT BATMAN, TOUGH GUY?
NOPE. DON'T NEED TO.
LIKE SHE SAID, A GOOF IN GOOFY UNDERWEAR.
GUY'S GOT NO POWERS.
EXACTLY.
I MEAN, REALLY...SO WHAT'S HE GONNA DO? HIT ME WITH A BATARANG?
OR BETTER YET...SIC ROBIN HIS BOY-TOY WONDER ON ME?
OOOOOOH, I'M SOOO SCARED.
PLEASE. BATMAN'S A JOKE.
CLEARLY...

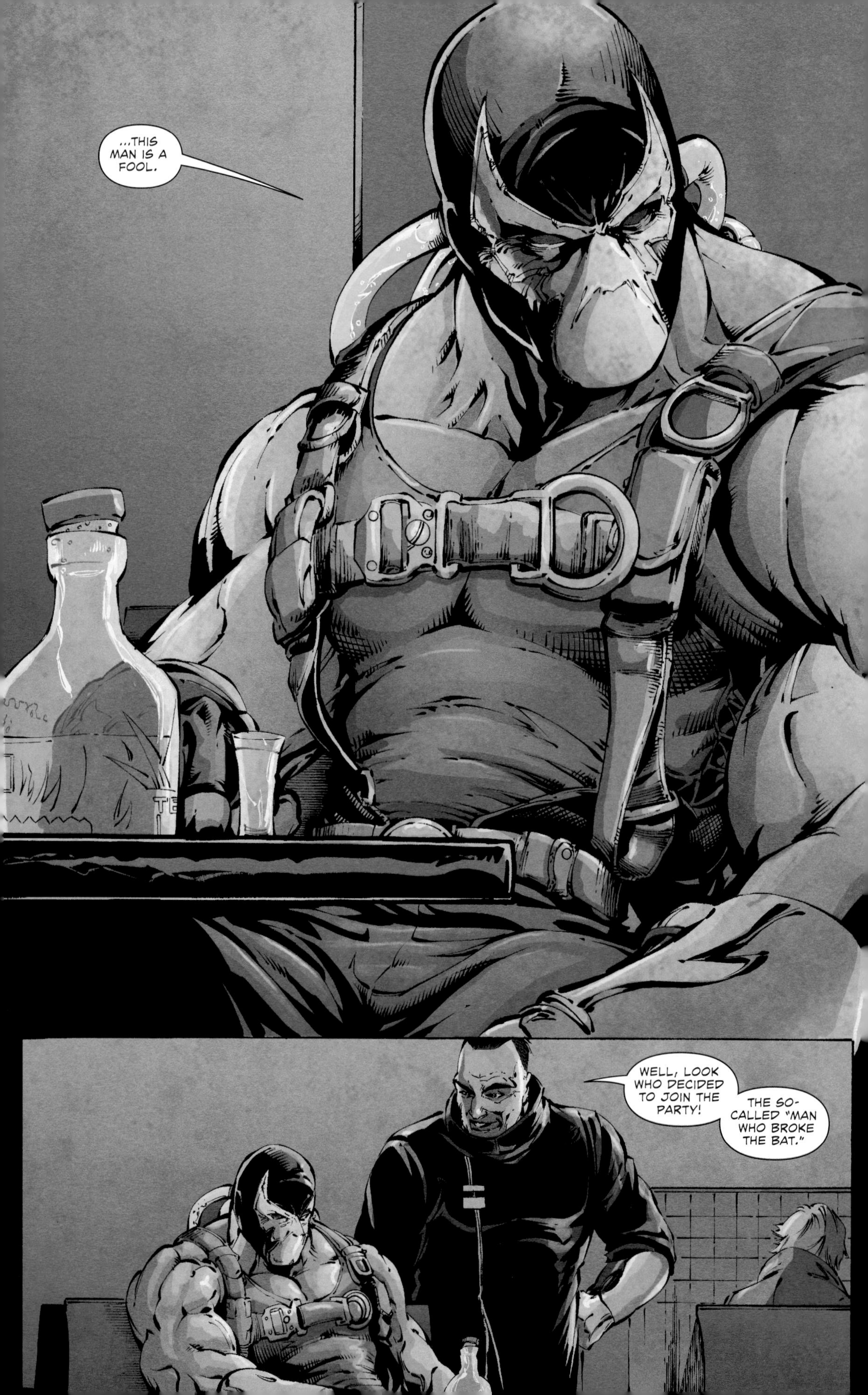
...THIS MAN IS A FOOL.
WELL, LOOK WHO DECIDED TO JOIN THE PARTY!
THE SO-CALLED "MAN WHO BROKE THE BAT."

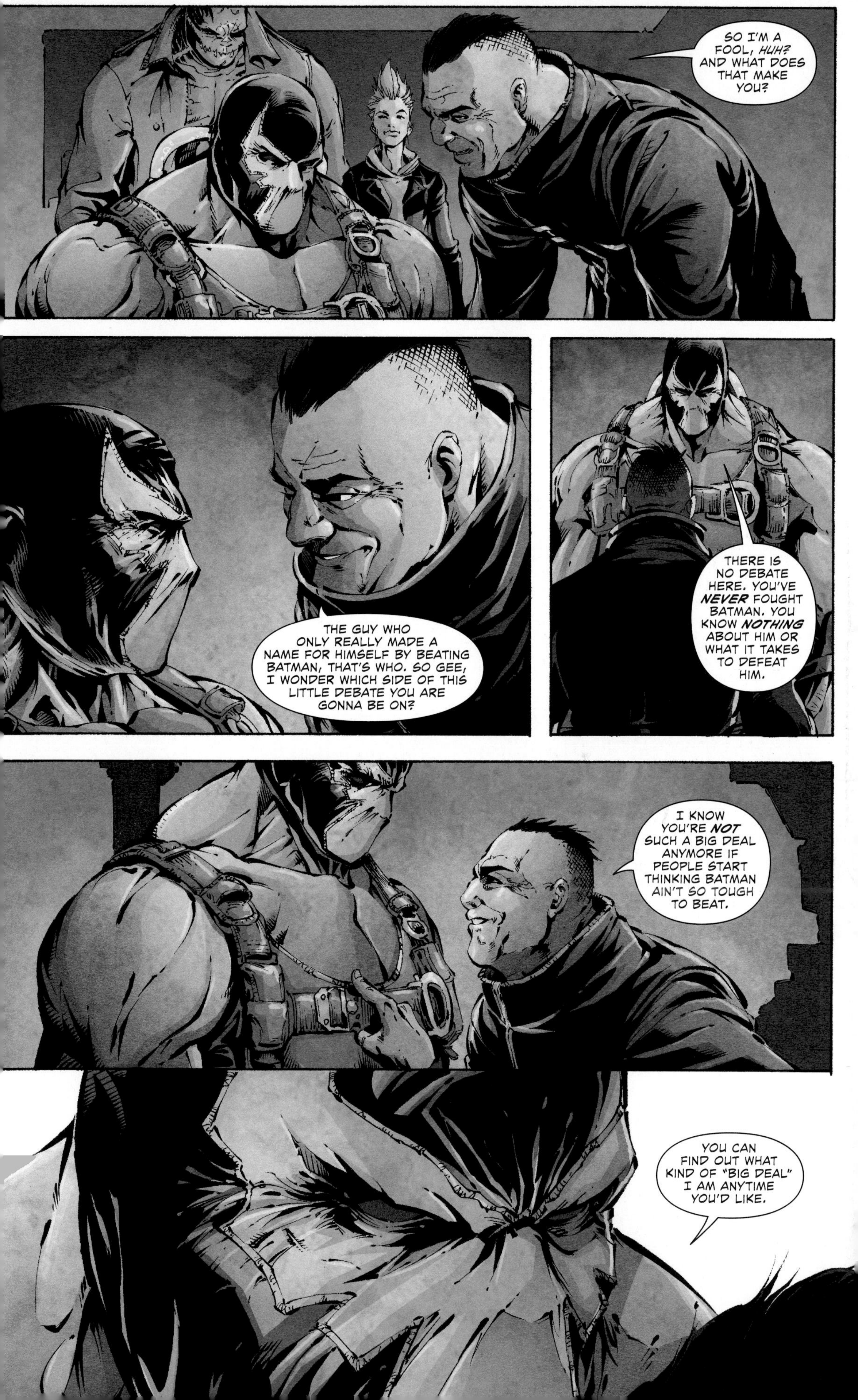
SO I'M A FOOL, *HUH?* AND WHAT DOES THAT MAKE YOU?
THE GUY WHO ONLY REALLY MADE A NAME FOR HIMSELF BY BEATING BATMAN, THAT'S WHO. SO GEE, I WONDER WHICH SIDE OF THIS LITTLE DEBATE YOU ARE GONNA BE ON?
THERE IS NO DEBATE HERE. YOU'VE ***NEVER*** FOUGHT BATMAN. YOU KNOW ***NOTHING*** ABOUT HIM OR WHAT IT TAKES TO DEFEAT HIM.
I KNOW YOU'RE ***NOT*** SUCH A BIG DEAL ANYMORE IF PEOPLE START THINKING BATMAN AIN'T SO TOUGH TO BEAT.
YOU CAN FIND OUT WHAT KIND OF "BIG DEAL" I AM ANYTIME YOU'D LIKE.

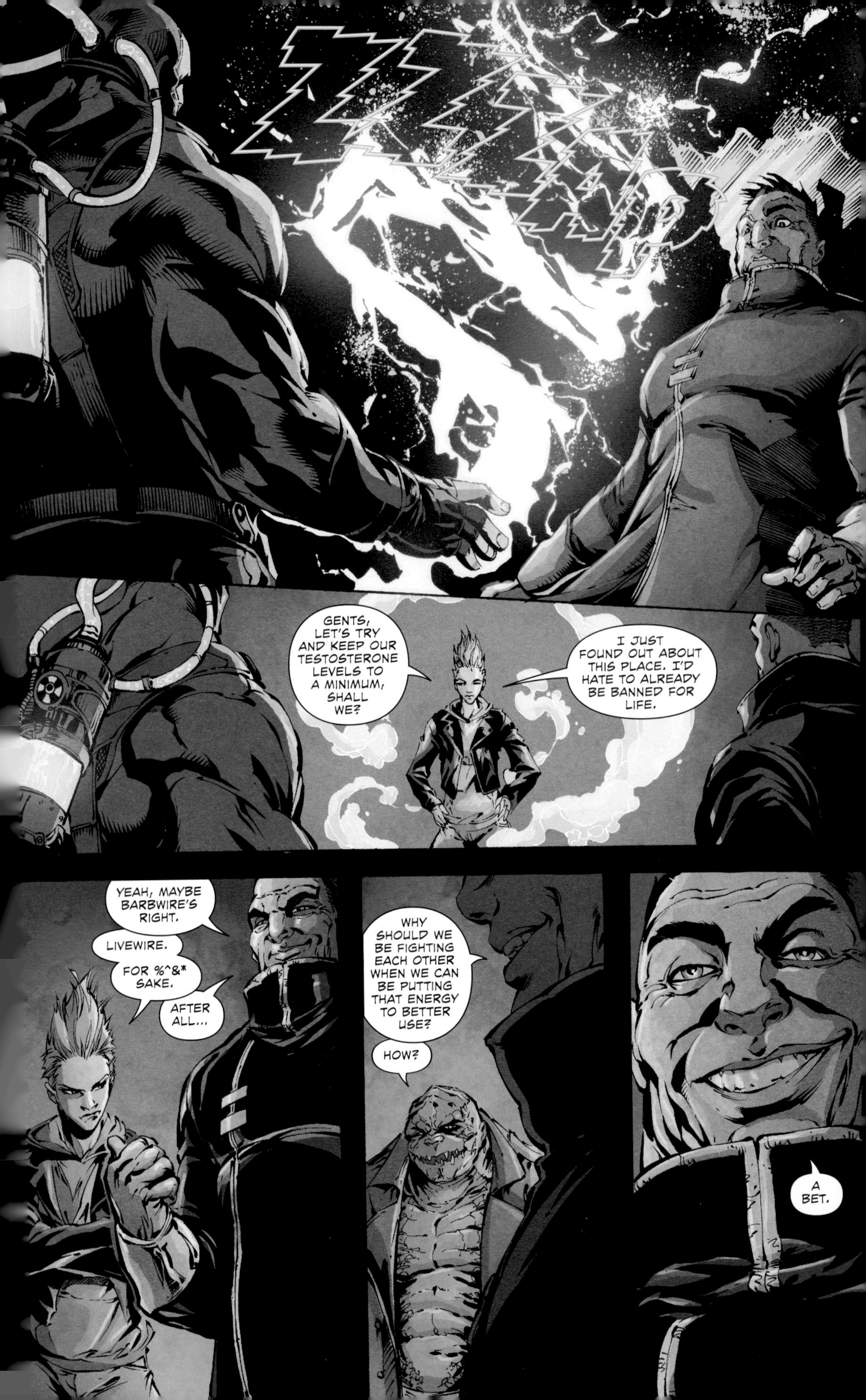
GENTS, LET'S TRY AND KEEP OUR TESTOSTERONE LEVELS TO A MINIMUM, SHALL WE?
I JUST FOUND OUT ABOUT THIS PLACE. I'D HATE TO ALREADY BE BANNED FOR LIFE.
YEAH, MAYBE BARBWIRE'S RIGHT.
LIVEWIRE.
FOR %^&* SAKE.
AFTER ALL...
WHY SHOULD WE BE FIGHTING EACH OTHER WHEN WE CAN BE PUTTING THAT ENERGY TO BETTER USE?
HOW?
A BET.

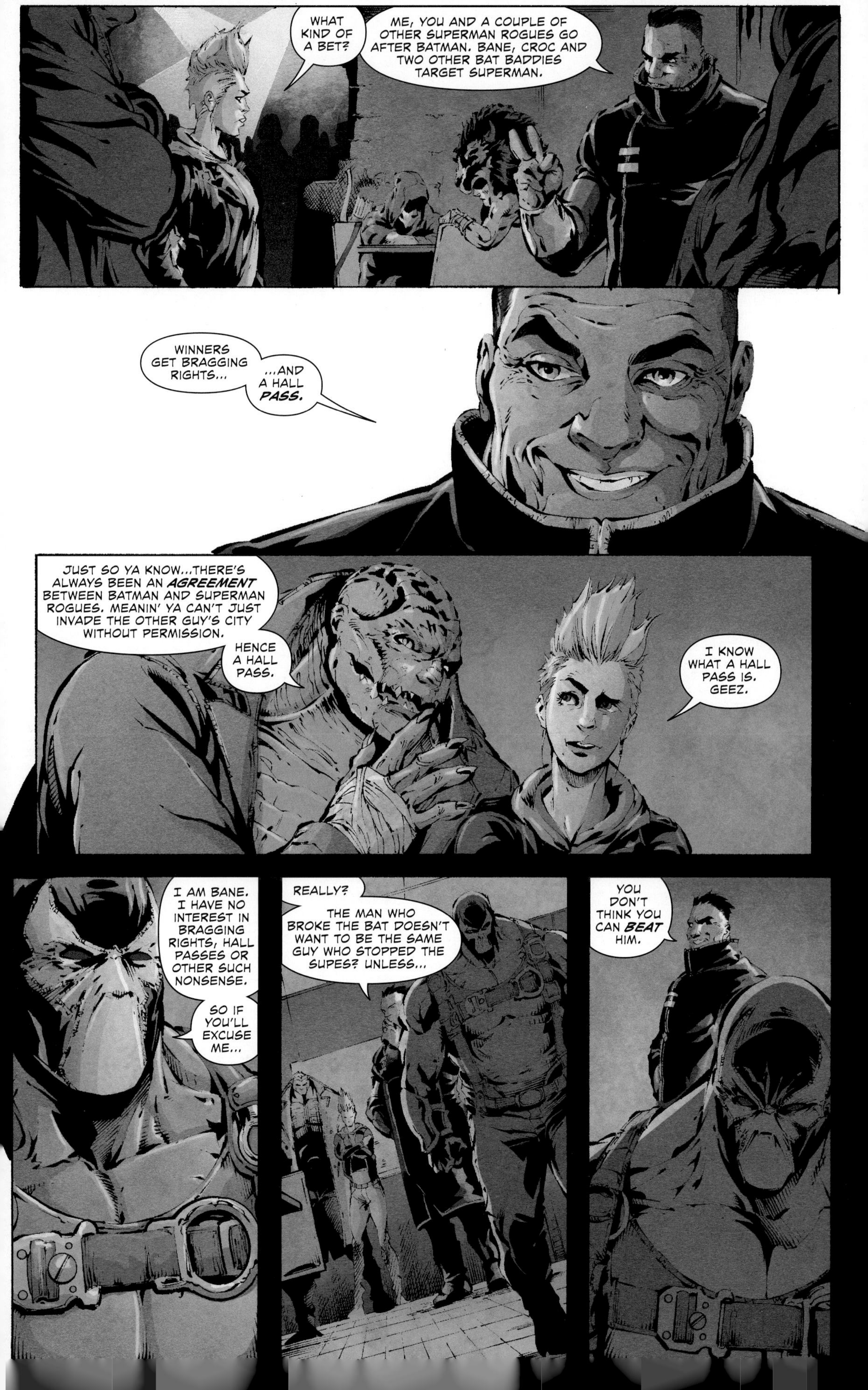
WHAT KIND OF A BET?
ME, YOU AND A COUPLE OF OTHER SUPERMAN ROGUES GO AFTER BATMAN. BANE, CROC AND TWO OTHER BAT BADDIES TARGET SUPERMAN.
WINNERS GET BRAGGING RIGHTS...
...AND A HALL PASS.
JUST SO YA KNOW...THERE'S ALWAYS BEEN AN AGREEMENT BETWEEN BATMAN AND SUPERMAN ROGUES. MEANIN' YA CAN'T JUST INVADE THE OTHER GUY'S CITY WITHOUT PERMISSION.
HENCE A HALL PASS.
I KNOW WHAT A HALL PASS IS. GEEZ.
I AM BANE. I HAVE NO INTEREST IN BRAGGING RIGHTS, HALL PASSES OR OTHER SUCH NONSENSE.
SO IF YOU'LL EXCUSE ME...
REALLY?
THE MAN WHO BROKE THE BAT DOESN'T WANT TO BE THE SAME GUY WHO STOPPED THE SUPES? UNLESS...
YOU DON'T THINK YOU CAN BEAT HIM.

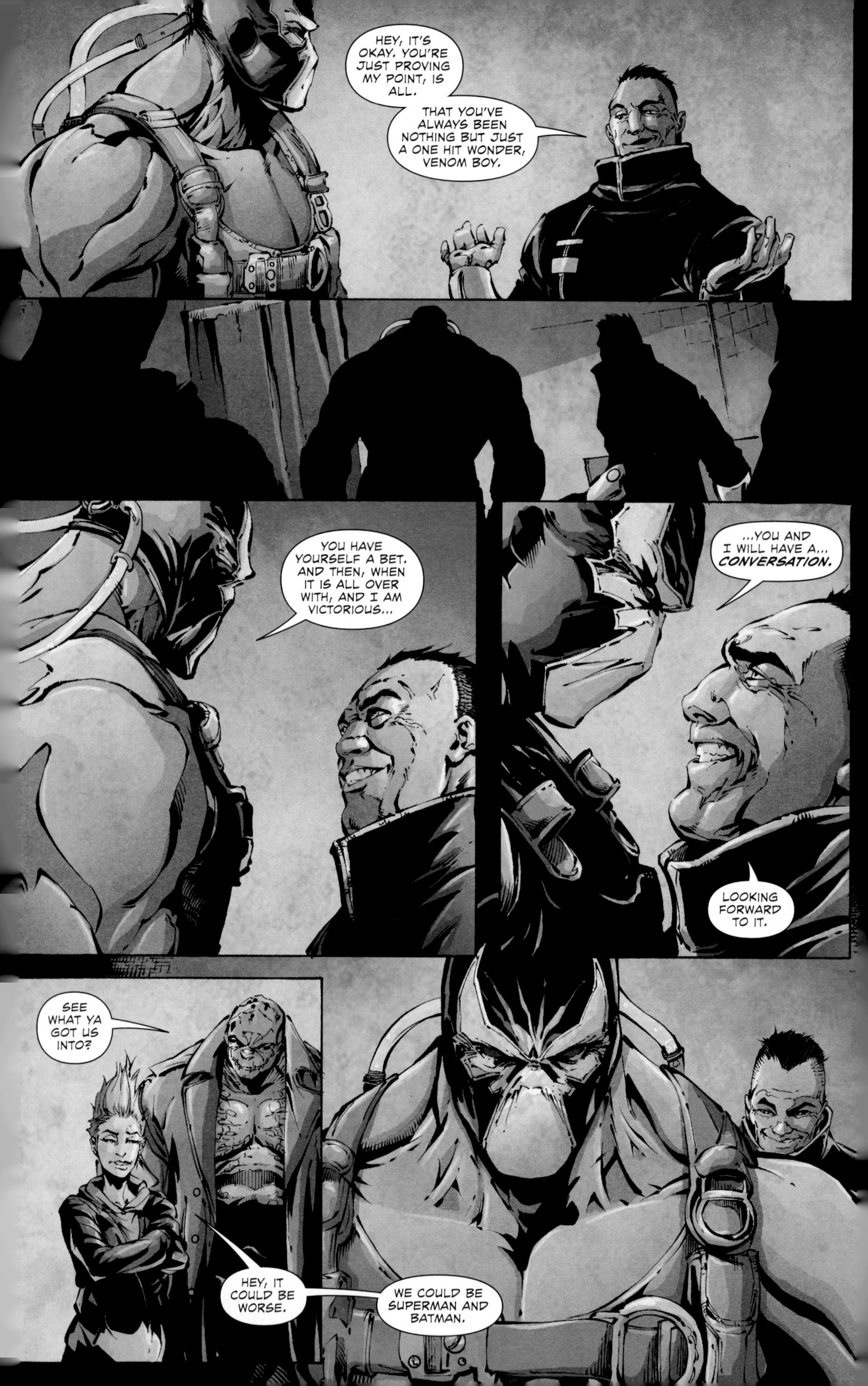
HEY, IT'S OKAY. YOU'RE JUST PROVING MY POINT, IS ALL.
THAT YOU'VE ALWAYS BEEN NOTHING BUT JUST A ONE HIT WONDER, VENOM BOY.
YOU HAVE YOURSELF A BET. AND THEN, WHEN IT IS ALL OVER WITH, AND I AM VICTORIOUS...
...YOU AND I WILL HAVE A... CONVERSATION.
LOOKING FORWARD TO IT.
SEE WHAT YA GOT US INTO?
HEY, IT COULD BE WORSE.
WE COULD BE SUPERMAN AND BATMAN.

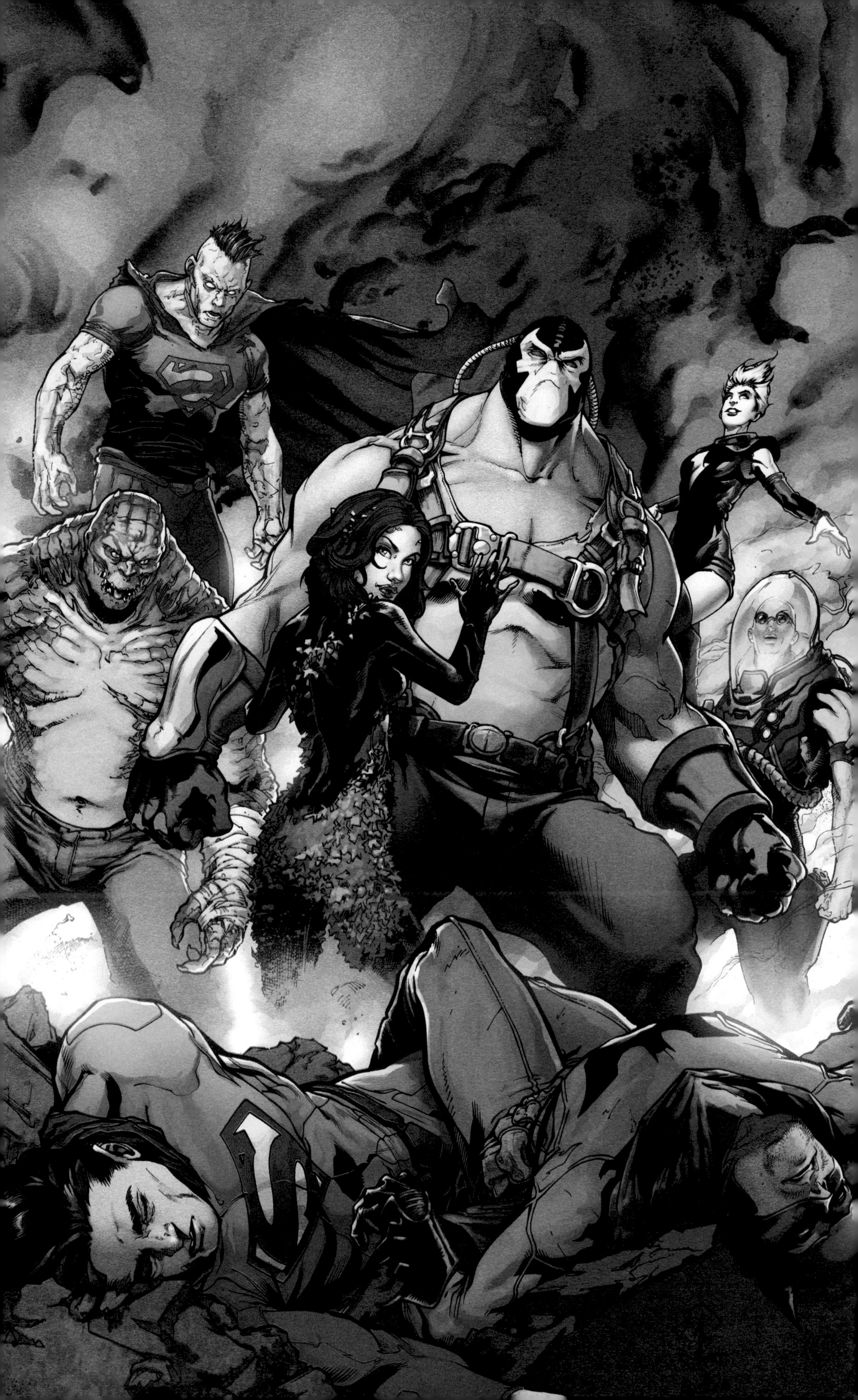

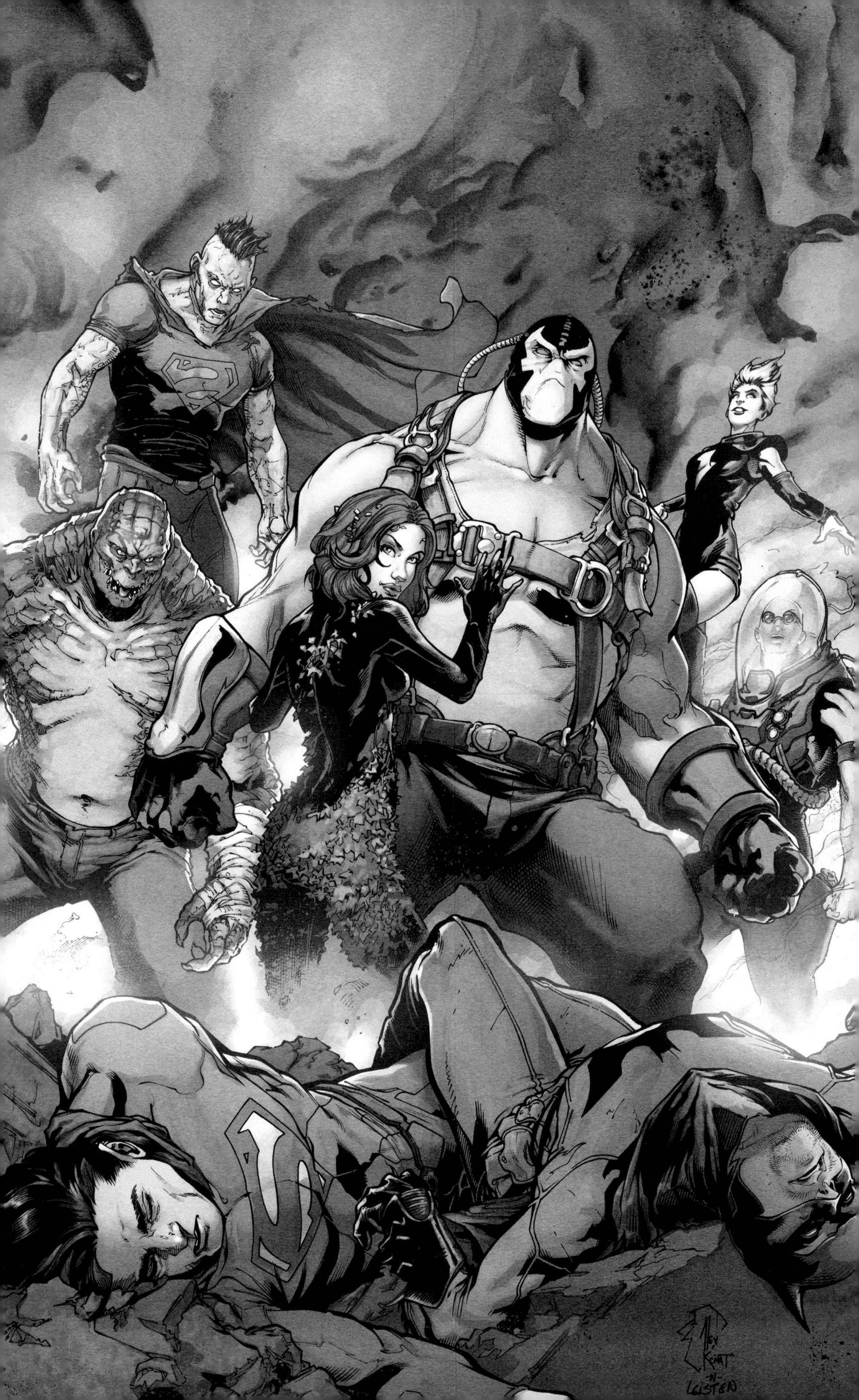

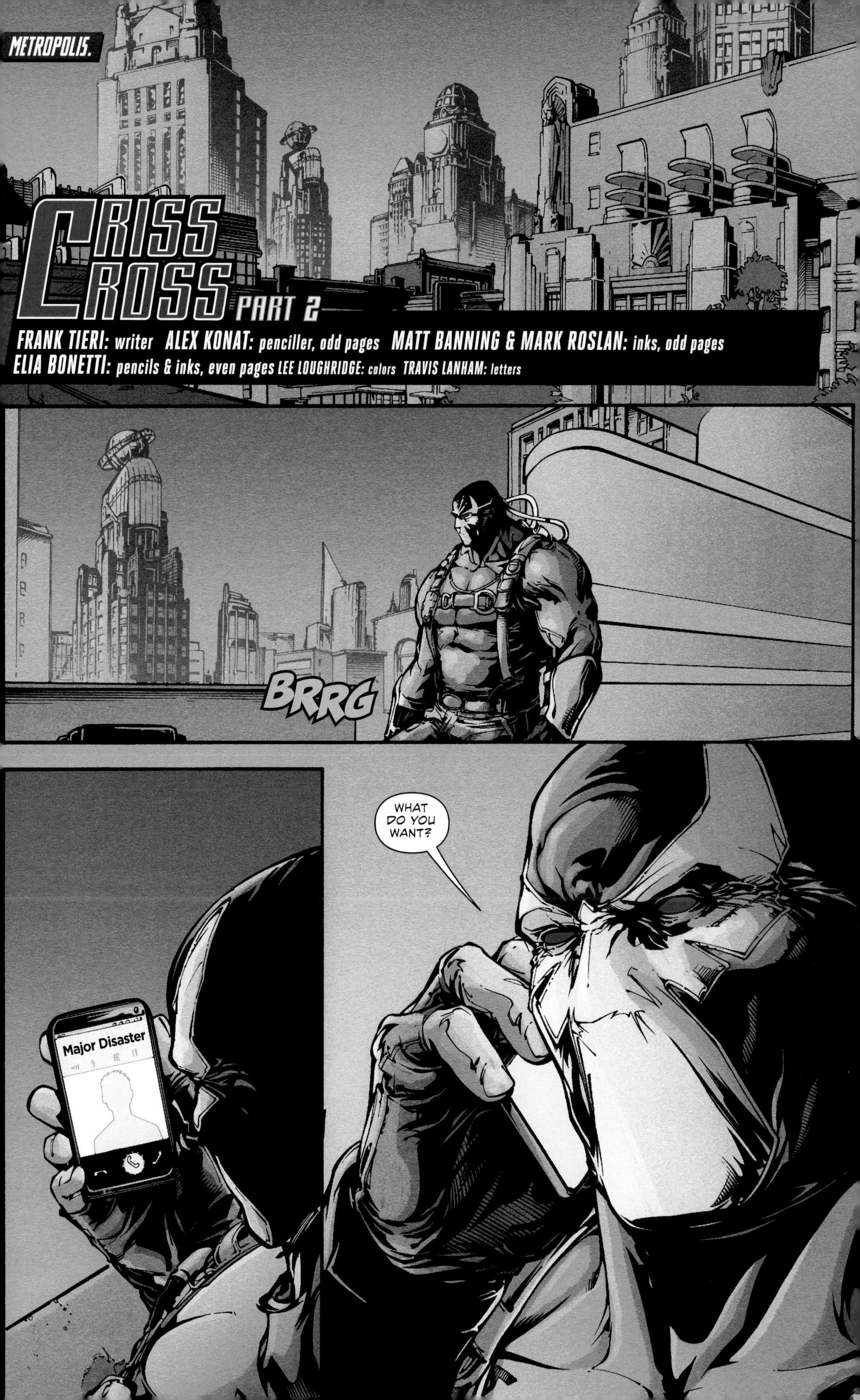

METROPOLIS.
CRISS CROSS PART 2
FRANK TIERI: writer ALEX KONAT: penciller, odd pages MATT BANNING & MARK ROSLAN: inks, odd pages
ELIA BONETTI: pencils & inks, even pages LEE LOUGHRIDGE: colors TRAVIS LANHAM: letters
BRRG
Major Disaster
WHAT DO YOU WANT?

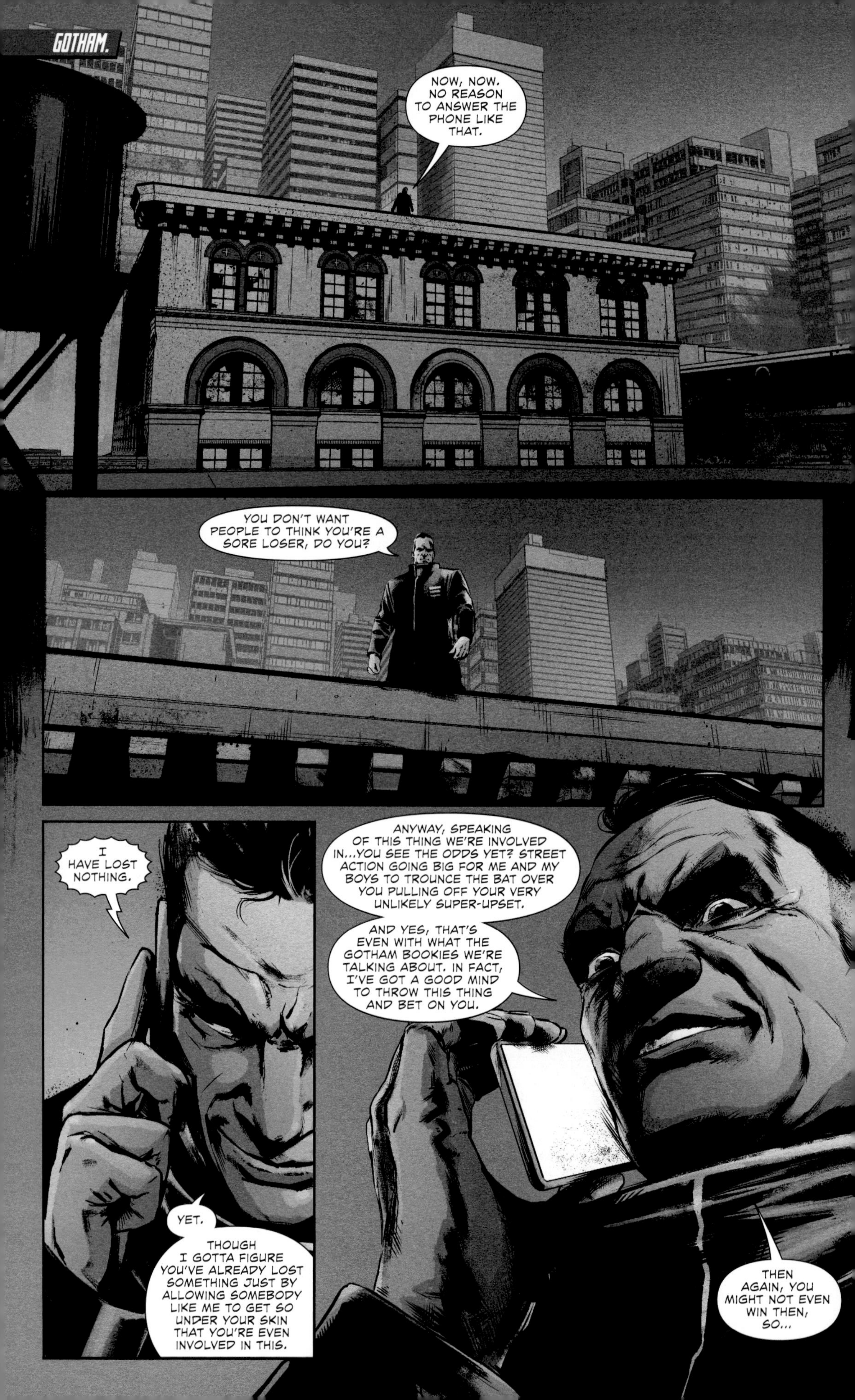
GOTHAM.
NOW, NOW. NO REASON TO ANSWER THE PHONE LIKE THAT.
YOU DON'T WANT PEOPLE TO THINK YOU'RE A SORE LOSER, DO YOU?
I HAVE LOST NOTHING.
ANYWAY, SPEAKING OF THIS THING WE'RE INVOLVED IN...YOU SEE THE ODDS YET? STREET ACTION GOING BIG FOR ME AND MY BOYS TO TROUNCE THE BAT OVER YOU PULLING OFF YOUR VERY UNLIKELY SUPER-UPSET.
AND YES, THAT'S EVEN WITH WHAT THE GOTHAM BOOKIES WE'RE TALKING ABOUT. IN FACT, I'VE GOT A GOOD MIND TO THROW THIS THING AND BET ON YOU.
YET.
THOUGH I GOTTA FIGURE YOU'VE ALREADY LOST SOMETHING JUST BY ALLOWING SOMEBODY LIKE ME TO GET SO UNDER YOUR SKIN THAT YOU'RE EVEN INVOLVED IN THIS.
THEN AGAIN, YOU MIGHT NOT EVEN WIN THEN, SO...

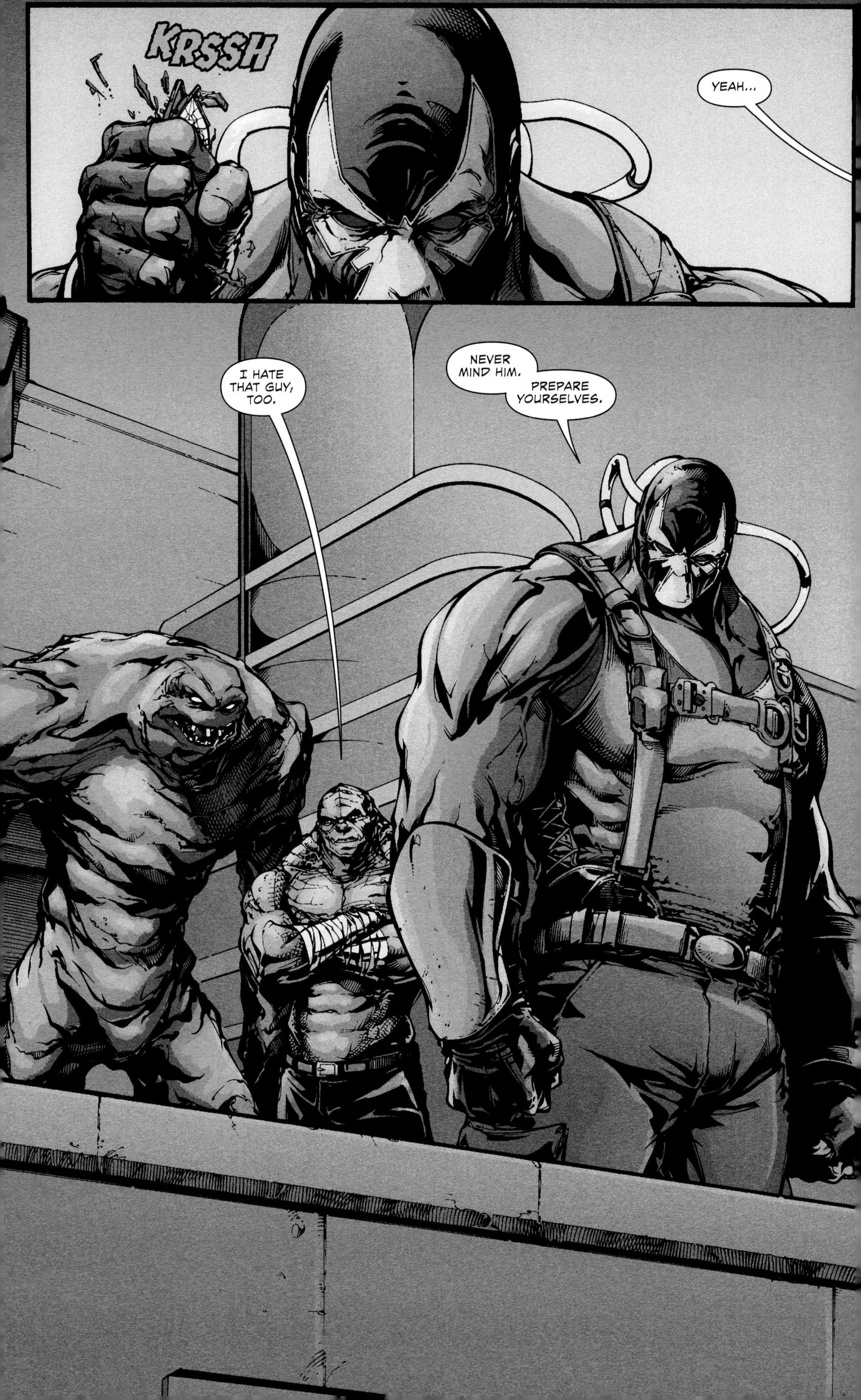
KRSSH
YEAH...
I HATE THAT GUY, TOO.
NEVER MIND HIM.
PREPARE YOURSELVES.

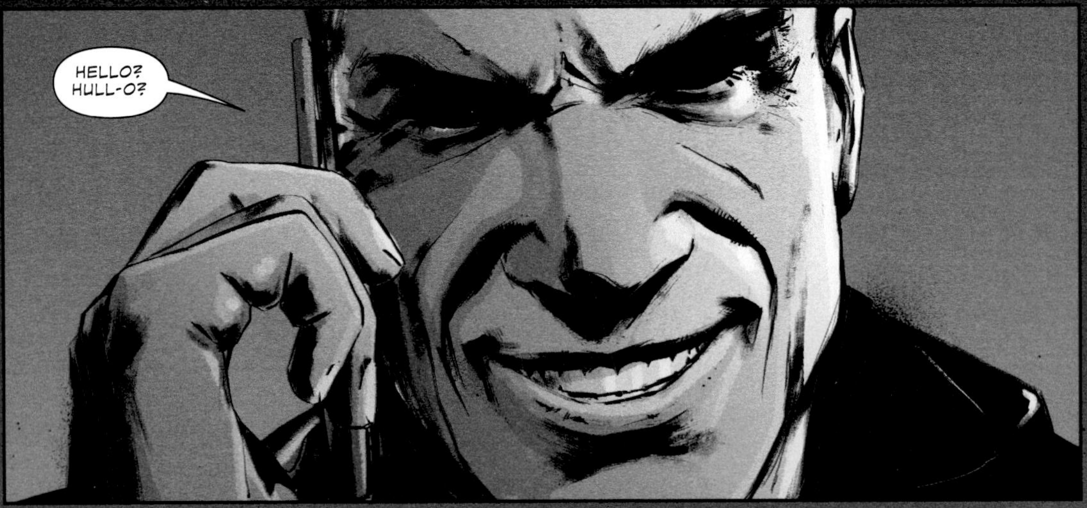
HELLO? HULL-O?

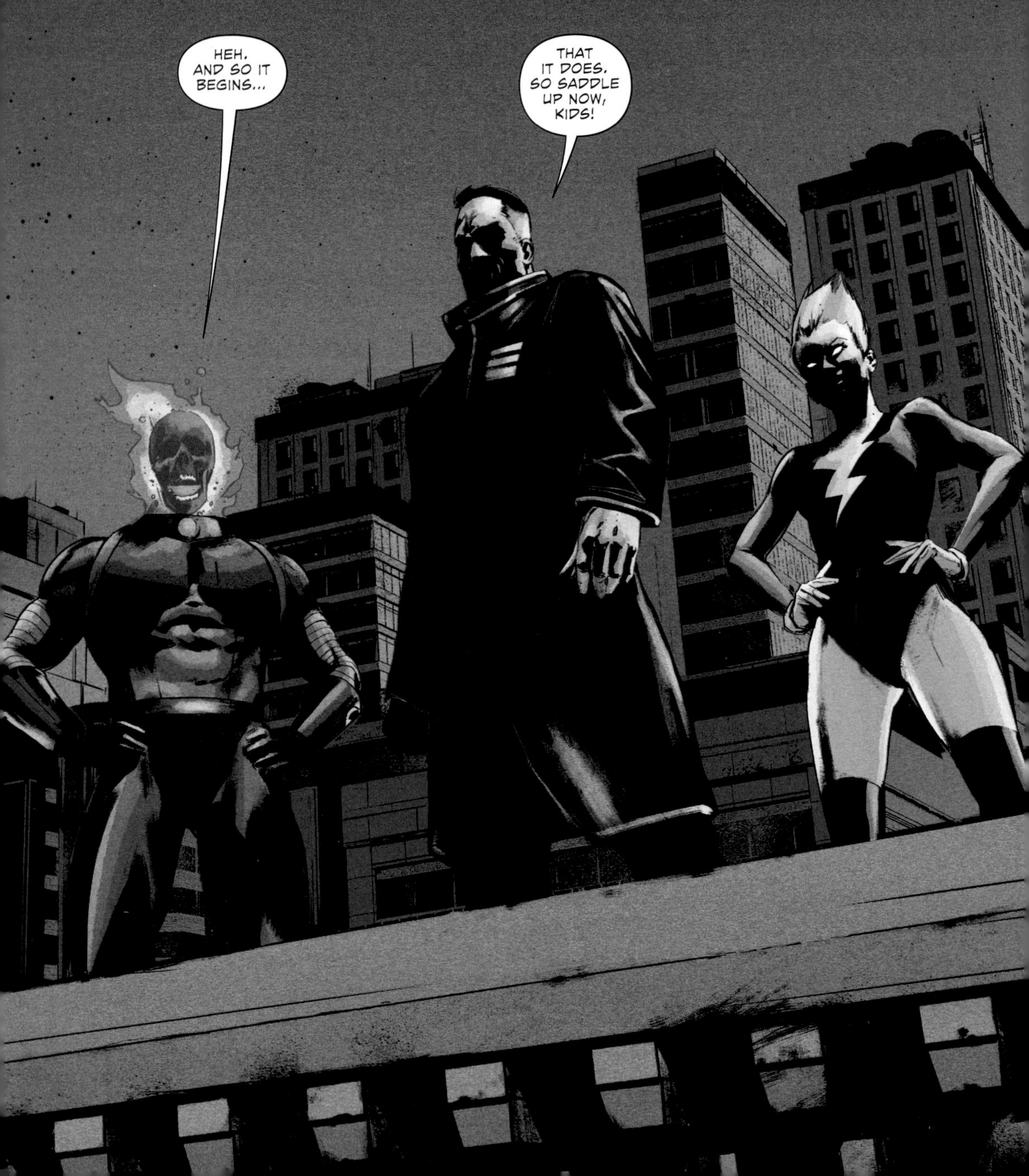
HEH. AND SO IT BEGINS...
THAT IT DOES. SO SADDLE UP NOW, KIDS!

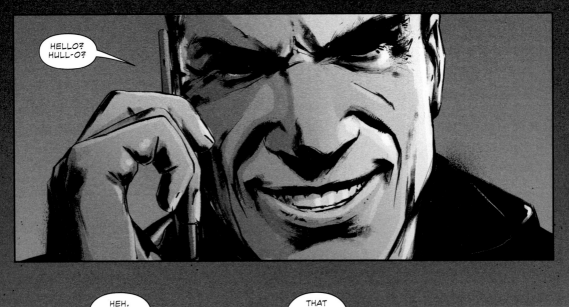

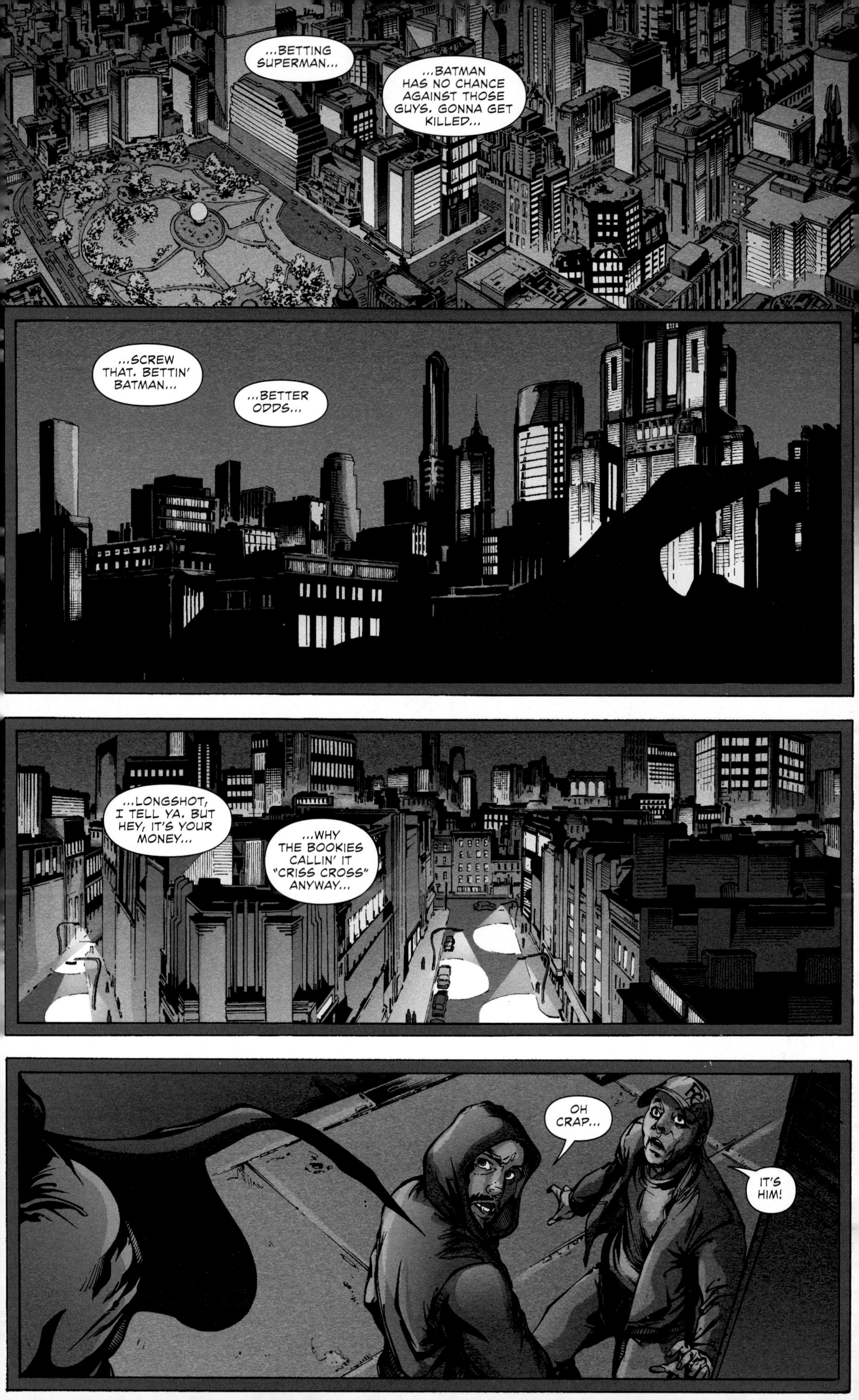
...BETTING SUPERMAN...
...BATMAN HAS NO CHANCE AGAINST THOSE GUYS. GONNA GET KILLED...
...SCREW THAT. BETTIN' BATMAN...
...BETTER ODDS...
...LONGSHOT, I TELL YA. BUT HEY, IT'S YOUR MONEY...
...WHY THE BOOKIES CALLIN' IT "CRISS CROSS" ANYWAY...
OH CRAP...
IT'S HIM!

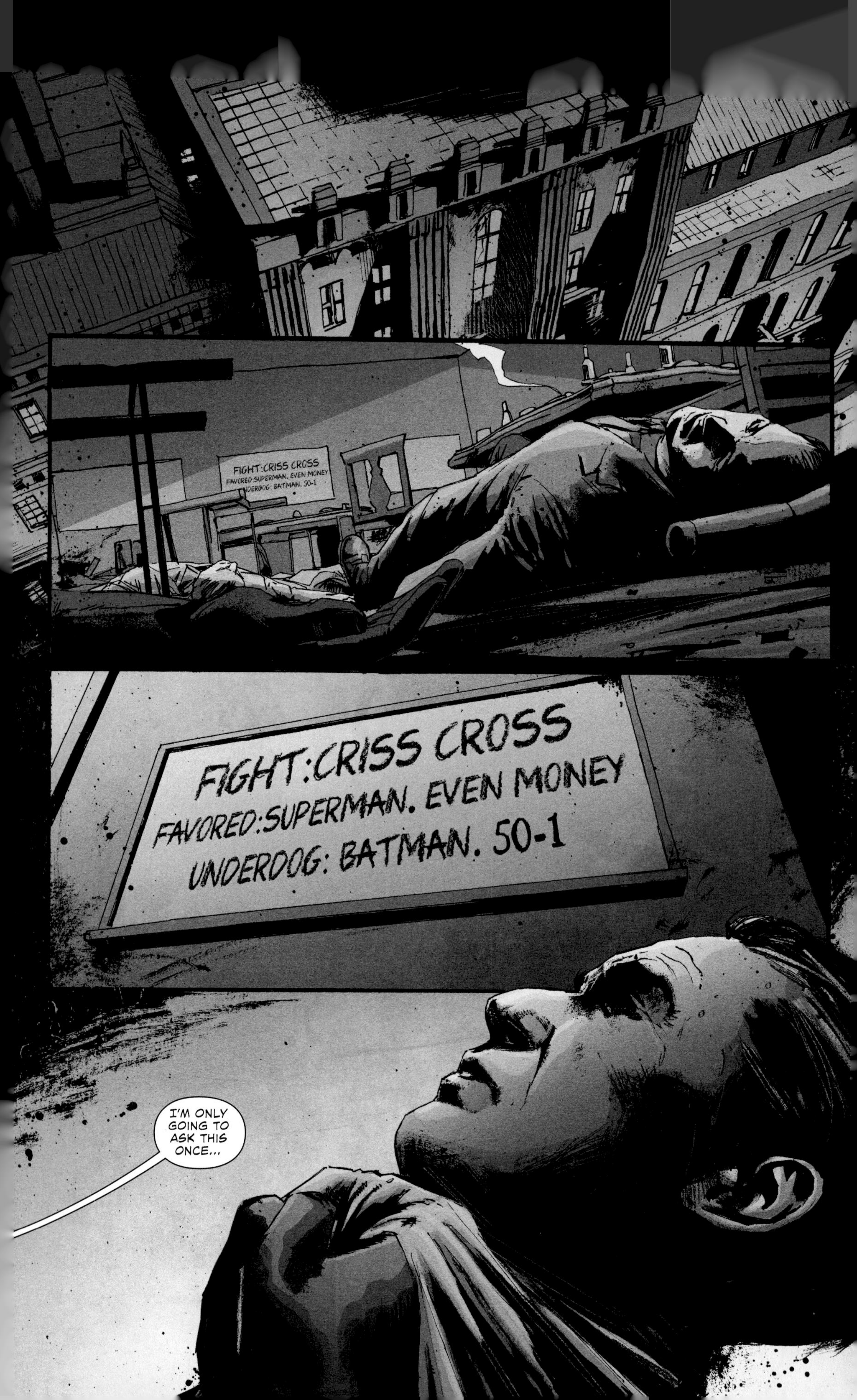
FIGHT: CRISS CROSS
FAVORED: SUPERMAN. EVEN MONEY
UNDERDOG: BATMAN. 50-1
FIGHT: CRISS CROSS
FAVORED: SUPERMAN. EVEN MONEY
UNDERDOG: BATMAN. 50-1
I'M ONLY GOING TO ASK THIS ONCE...

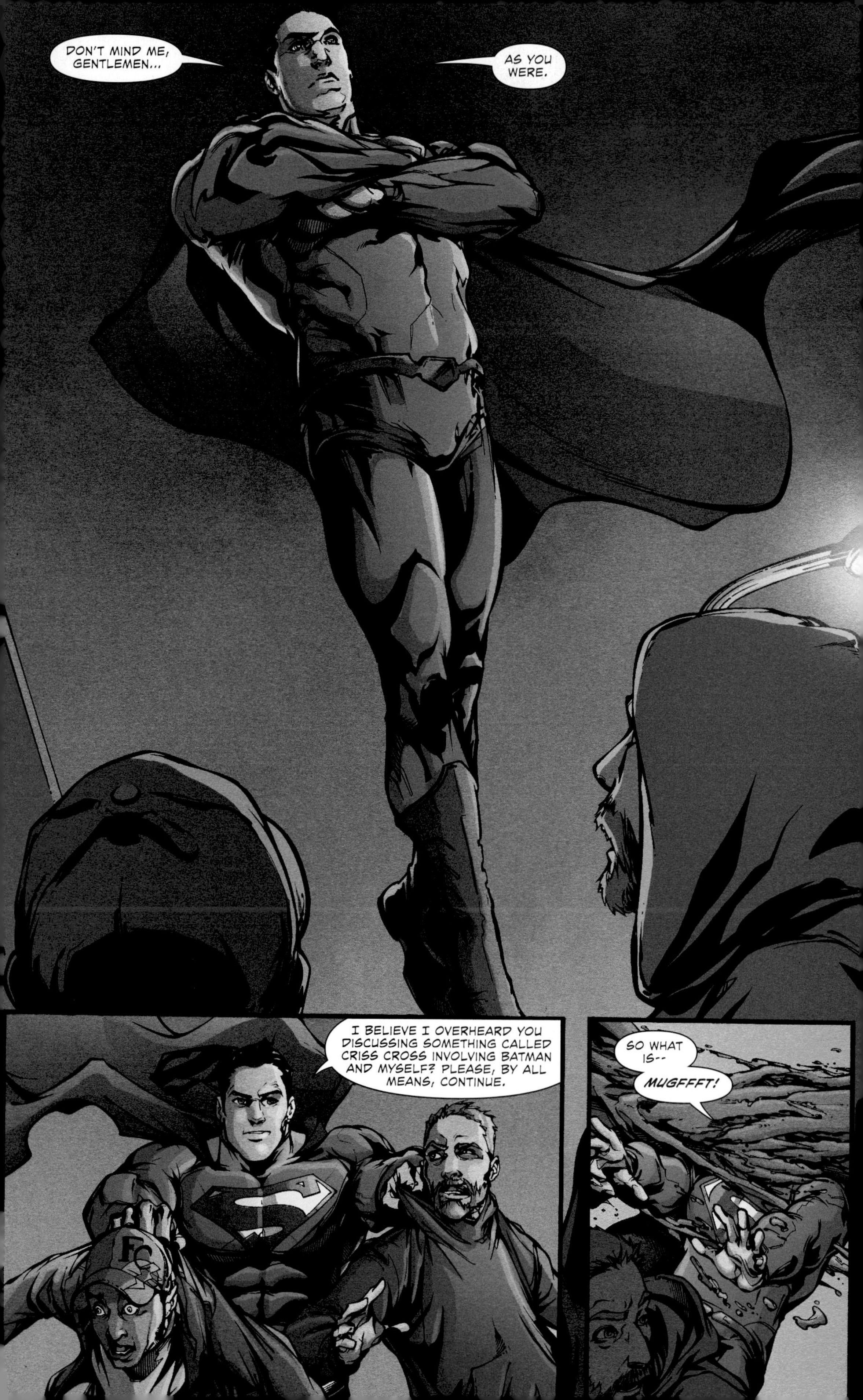
DON'T MIND ME, GENTLEMEN...
AS YOU WERE.
I BELIEVE I OVERHEARD YOU DISCUSSING SOMETHING CALLED CRISS CROSS INVOLVING BATMAN AND MYSELF? PLEASE, BY ALL MEANS, CONTINUE.
SO WHAT IS--
MUGFFFT!

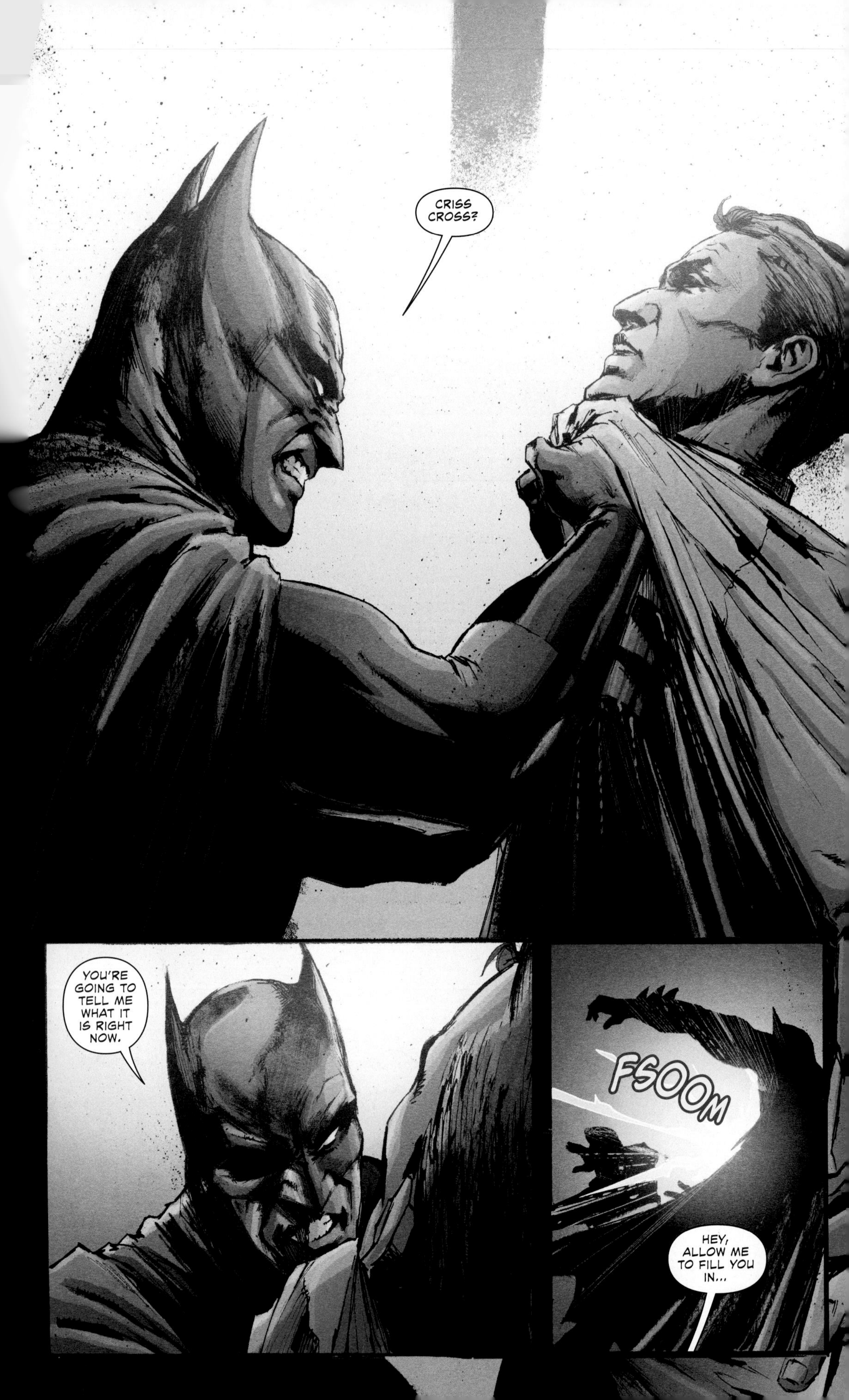
CRISS CROSS?
YOU'RE GOING TO TELL ME WHAT IT IS RIGHT NOW.
FSOOM
HEY, ALLOW ME TO FILL YOU IN...

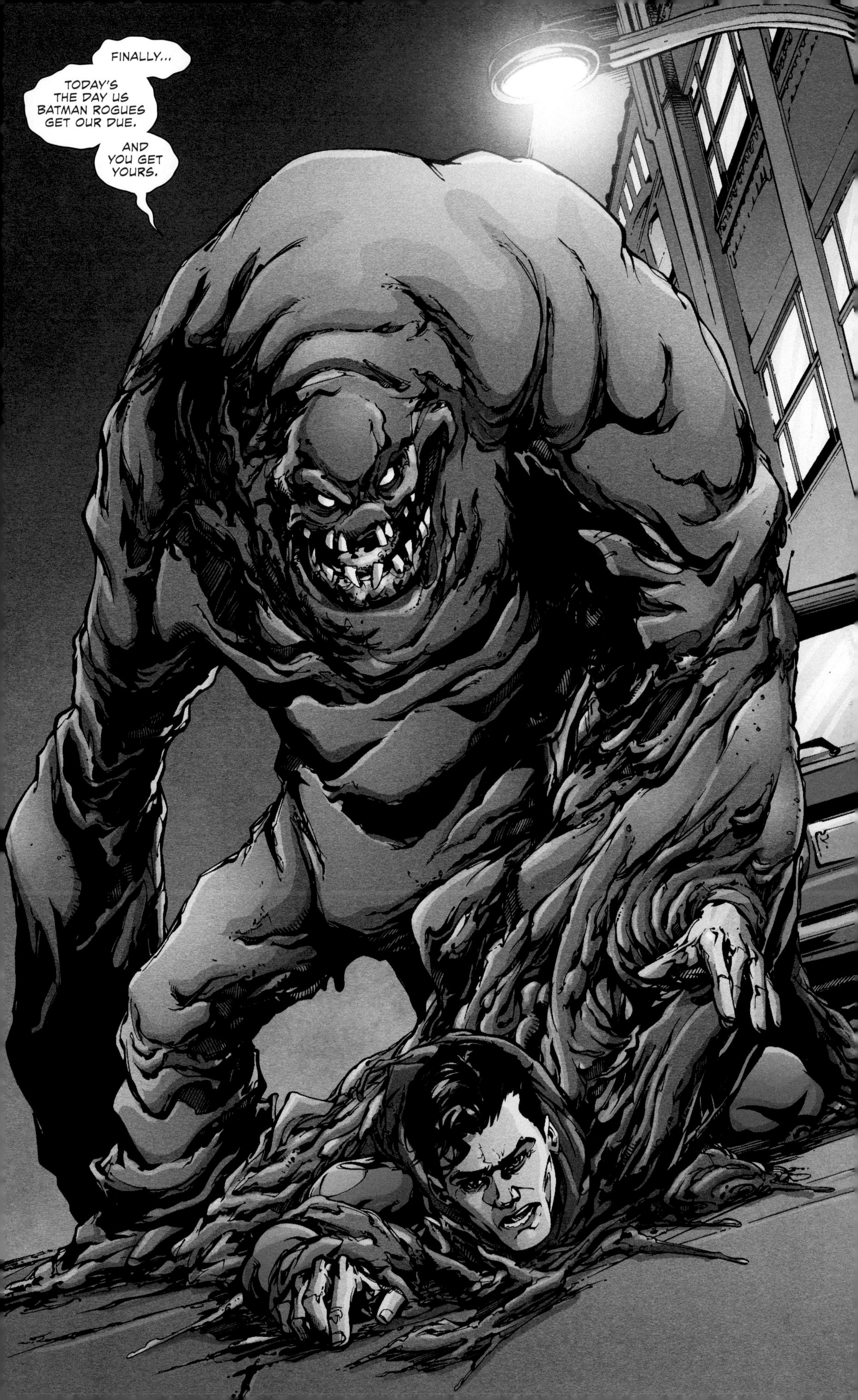
FINALLY...
TODAY'S THE DAY US BATMAN ROGUES GET OUR DUE.
AND YOU GET YOURS.

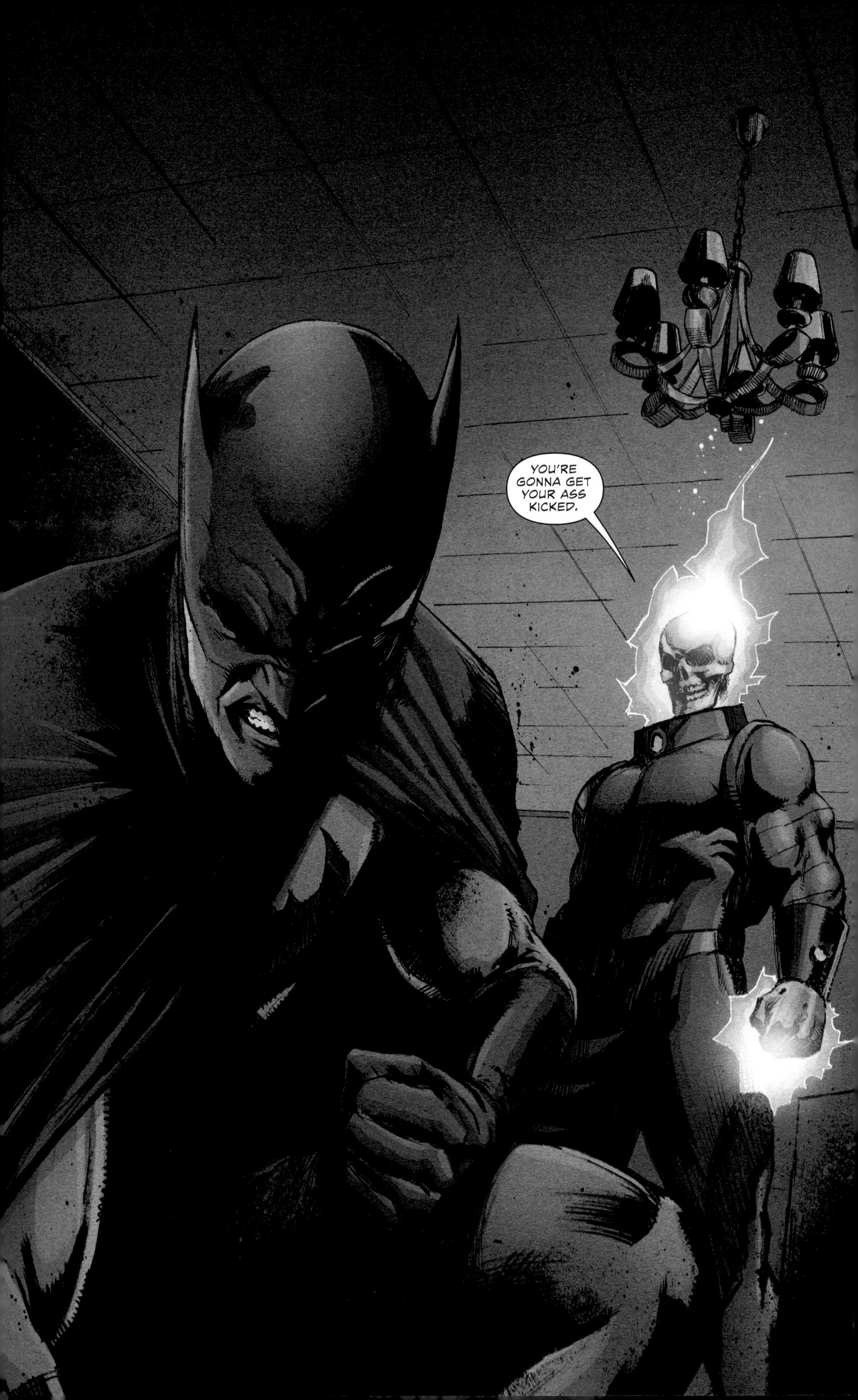
YOU'RE GONNA GET YOUR ASS KICKED.

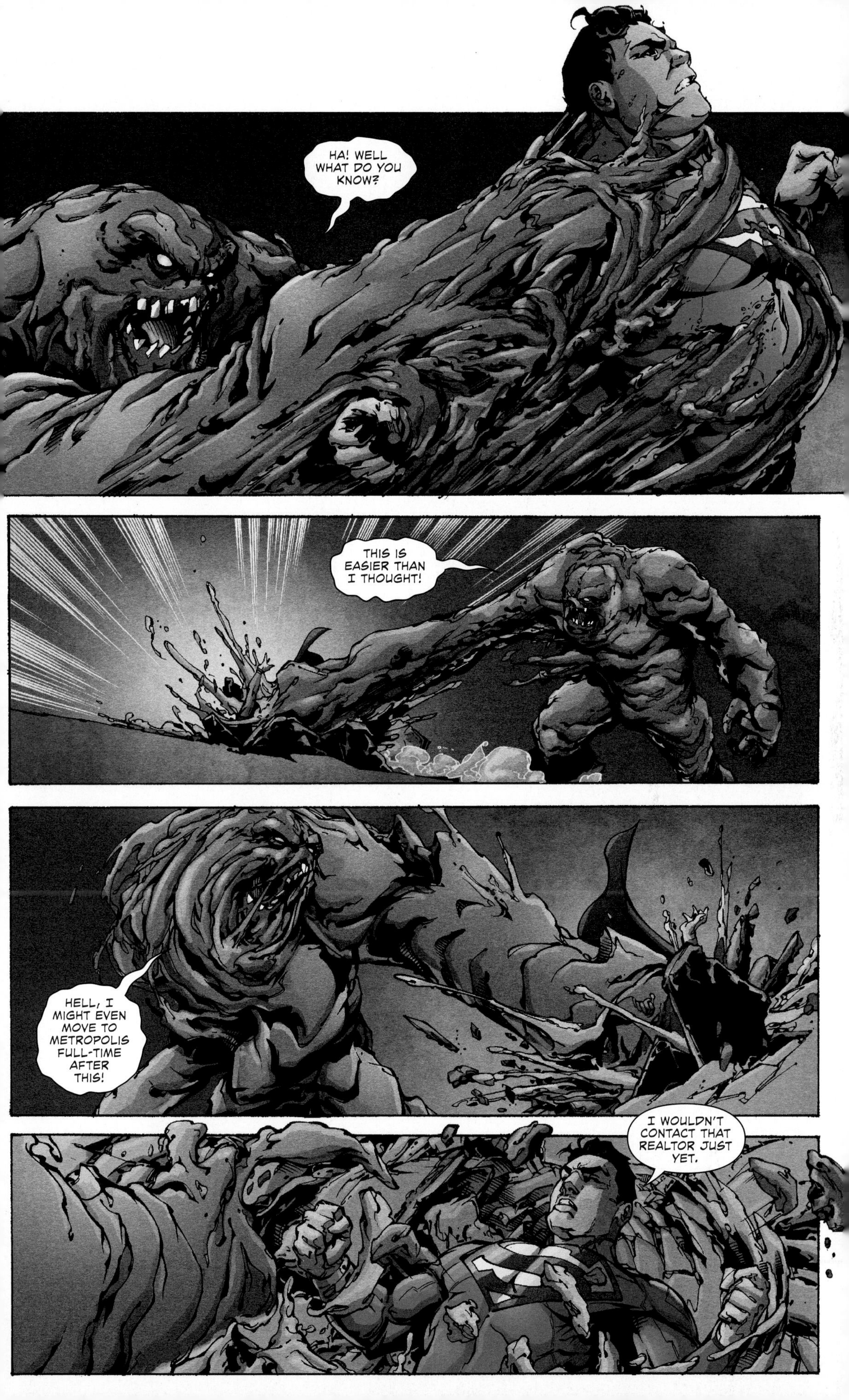
HA! WELL WHAT DO YOU KNOW?
THIS IS EASIER THAN I THOUGHT!
HELL, I MIGHT EVEN MOVE TO METROPOLIS FULL-TIME AFTER THIS!
I WOULDN'T CONTACT THAT REALTOR JUST YET.

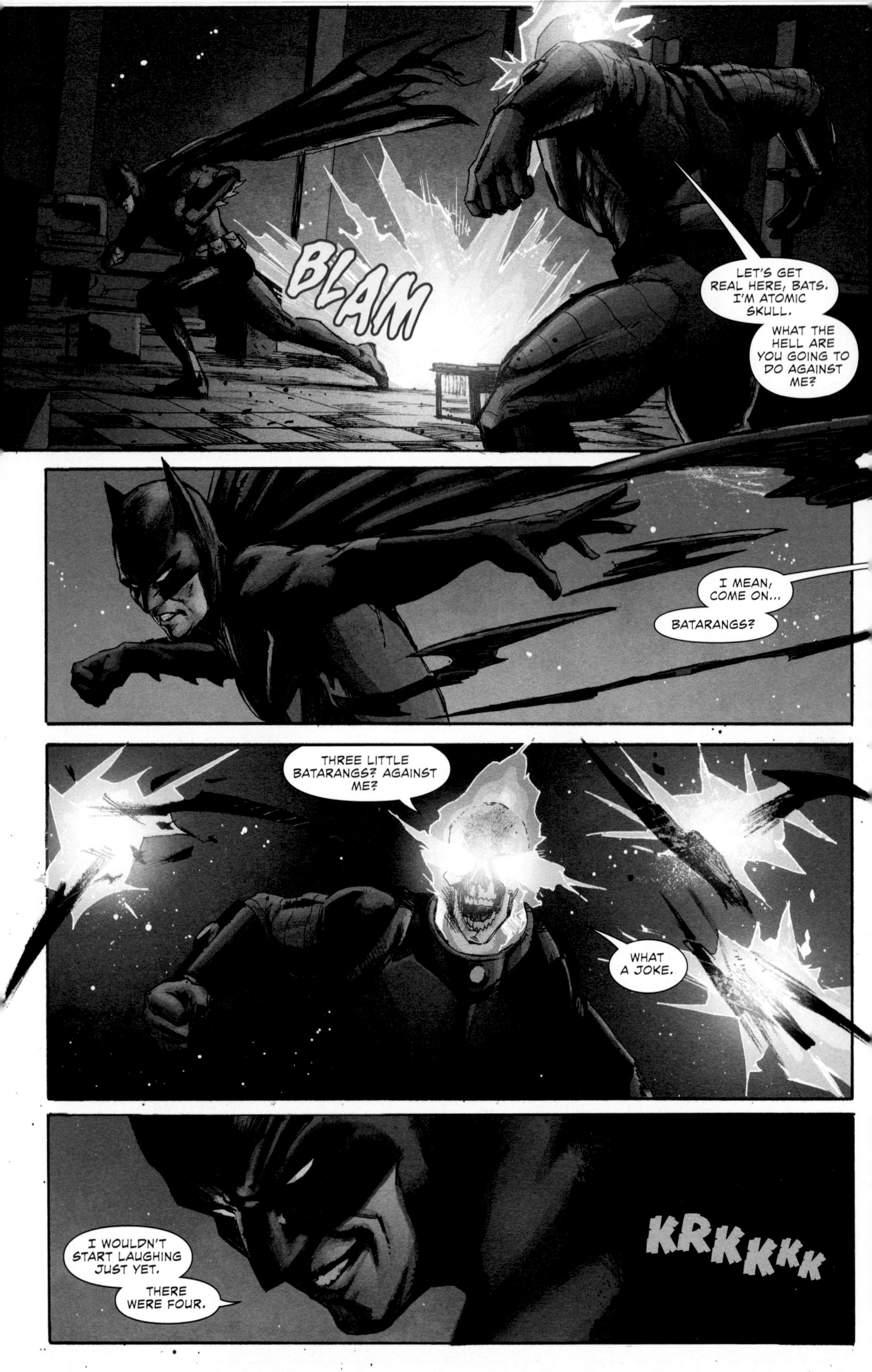
BLAM
LET'S GET REAL HERE, BATS. I'M ATOMIC SKULL.
WHAT THE HELL ARE YOU GOING TO DO AGAINST ME?
I MEAN, COME ON...
BATARANGS?
THREE LITTLE BATARANGS? AGAINST ME?
WHAT A JOKE.
KRKKKK
I WOULDN'T START LAUGHING JUST YET.
THERE WERE FOUR.

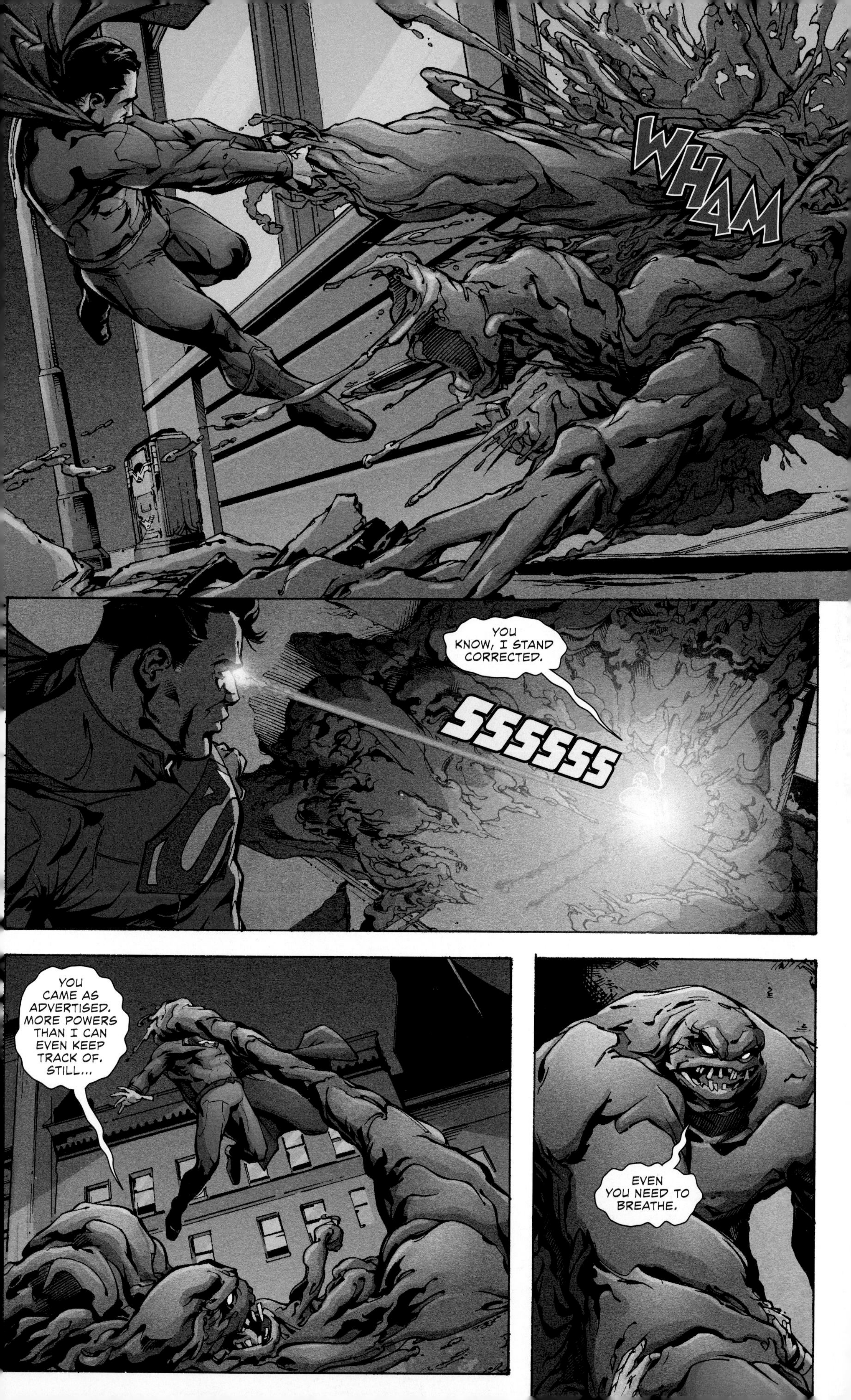
WHAM
YOU KNOW, I STAND CORRECTED.
SSSSSS
YOU CAME AS ADVERTISED. MORE POWERS THAN I CAN EVEN KEEP TRACK OF. STILL...
EVEN YOU NEED TO BREATHE.

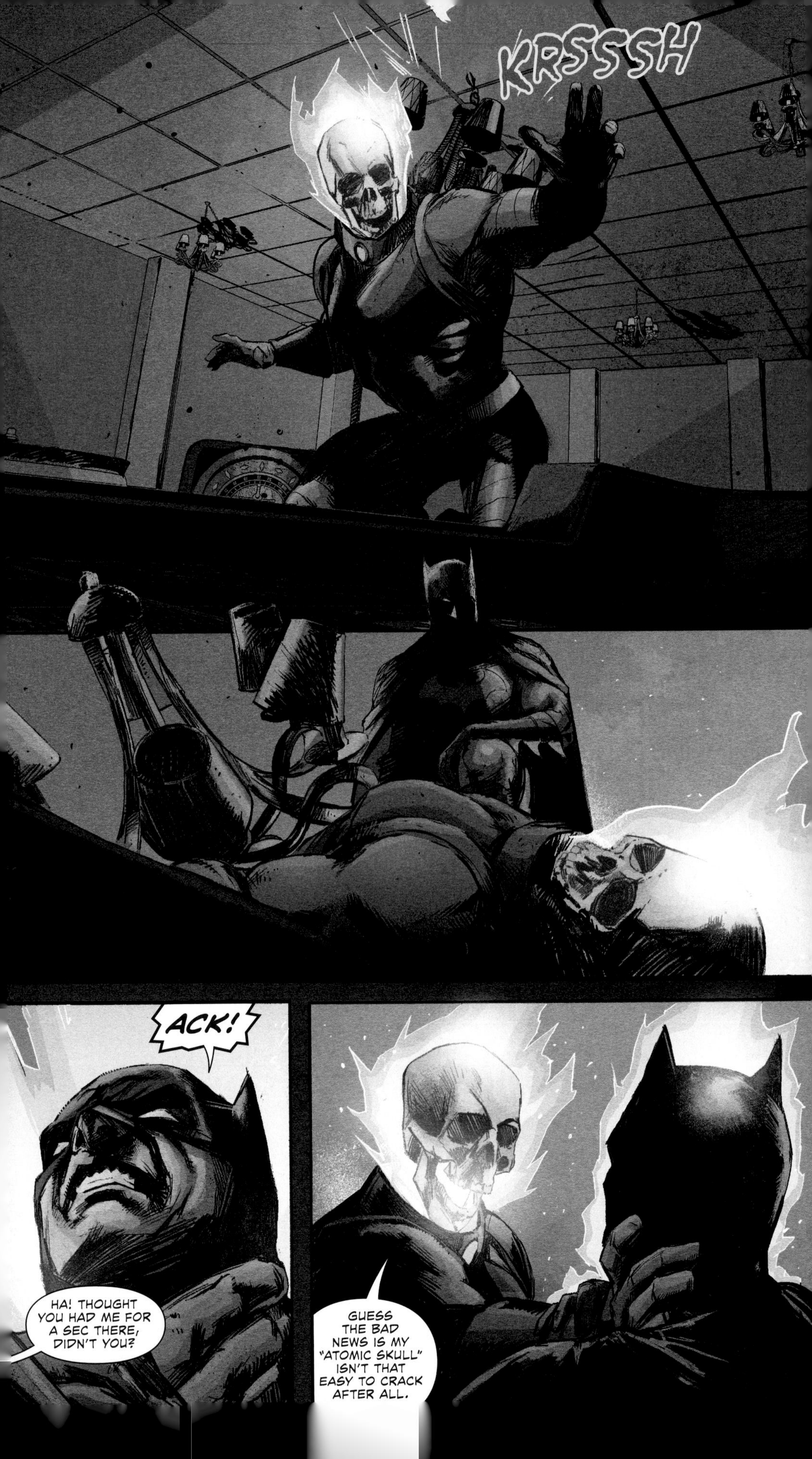
KRSSSH
ACK!
HA! THOUGHT YOU HAD ME FOR A SEC THERE, DIDN'T YOU?
GUESS THE BAD NEWS IS MY "ATOMIC SKULL" ISN'T THAT EASY TO CRACK AFTER ALL.

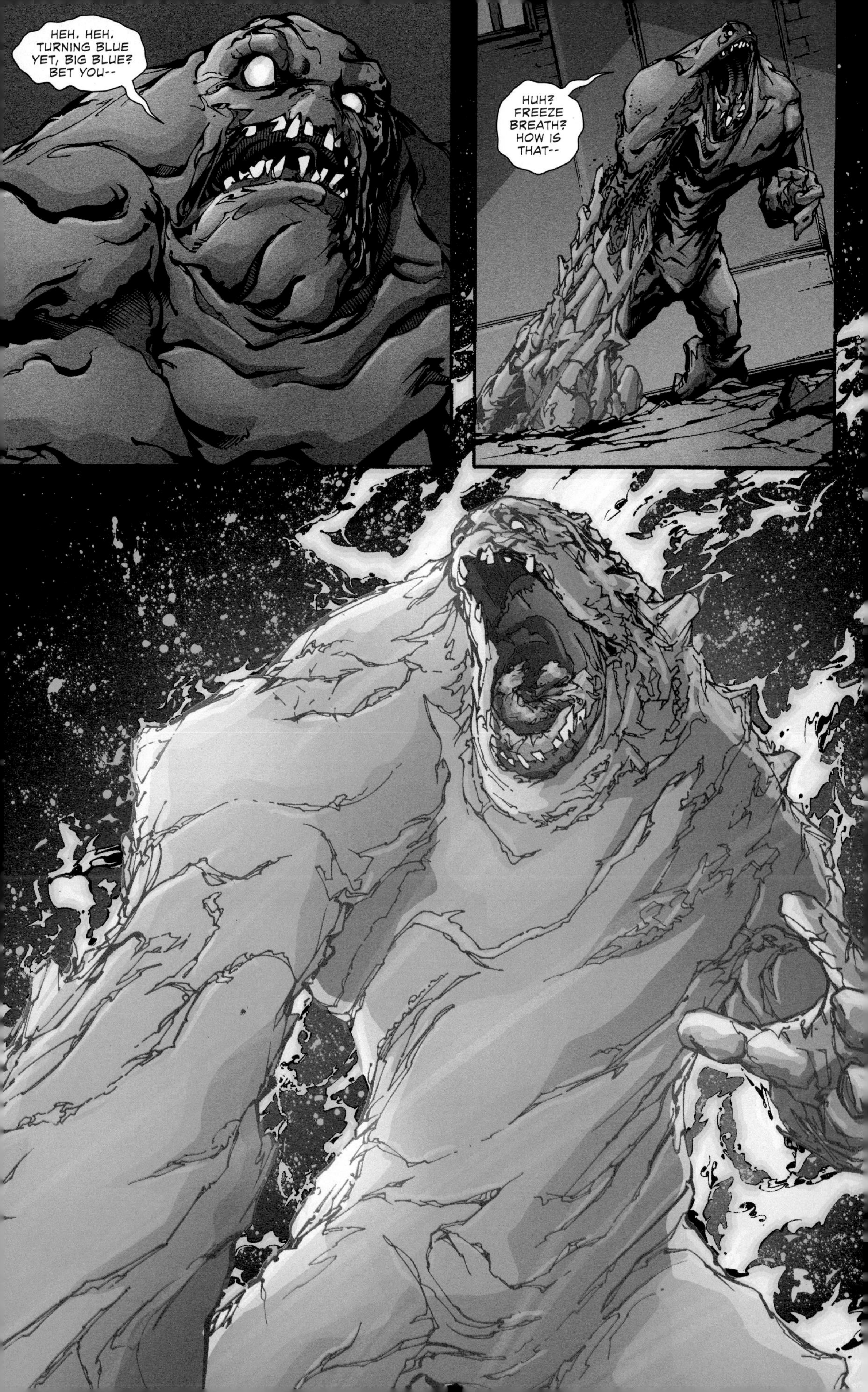
HEH. HEH. TURNING BLUE YET, BIG BLUE? BET YOU--
HUH? FREEZE BREATH? HOW IS THAT--

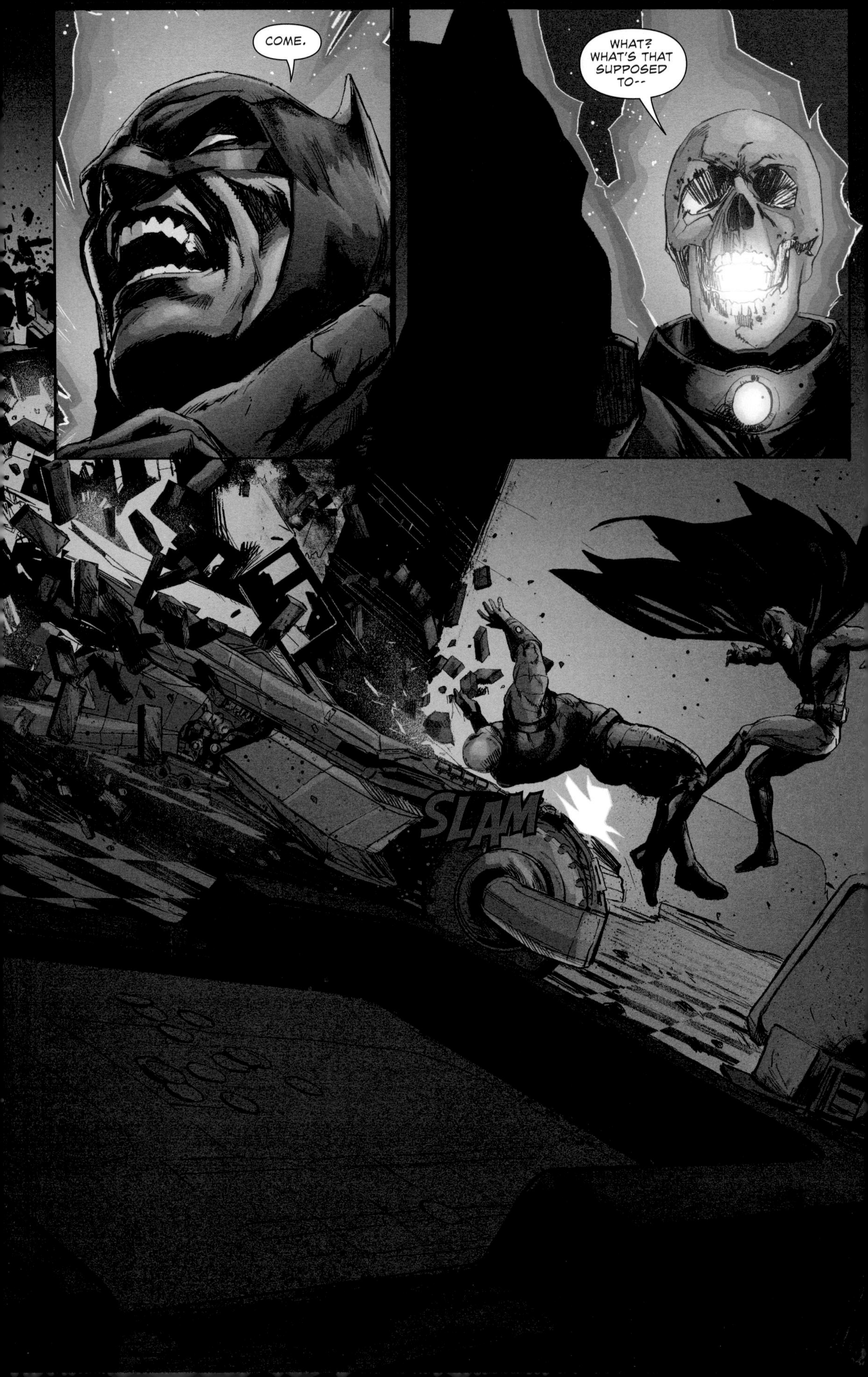
COME.
WHAT? WHAT'S THAT SUPPOSED TO--
SLAM

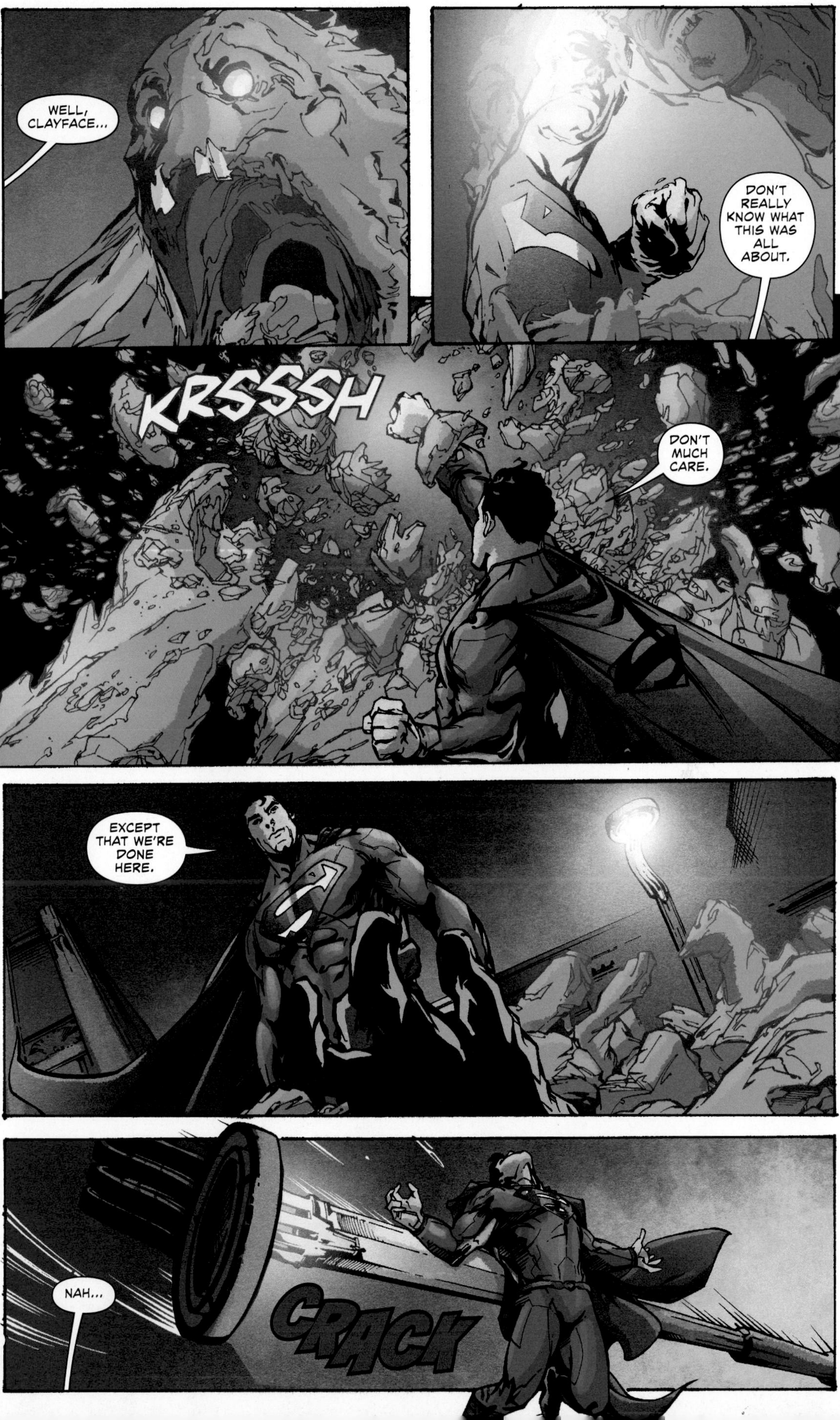
WELL, CLAYFACE...
DON'T REALLY KNOW WHAT THIS WAS ALL ABOUT.
KRSSSH
DON'T MUCH CARE.
EXCEPT THAT WE'RE DONE HERE.
NAH...
CRACK

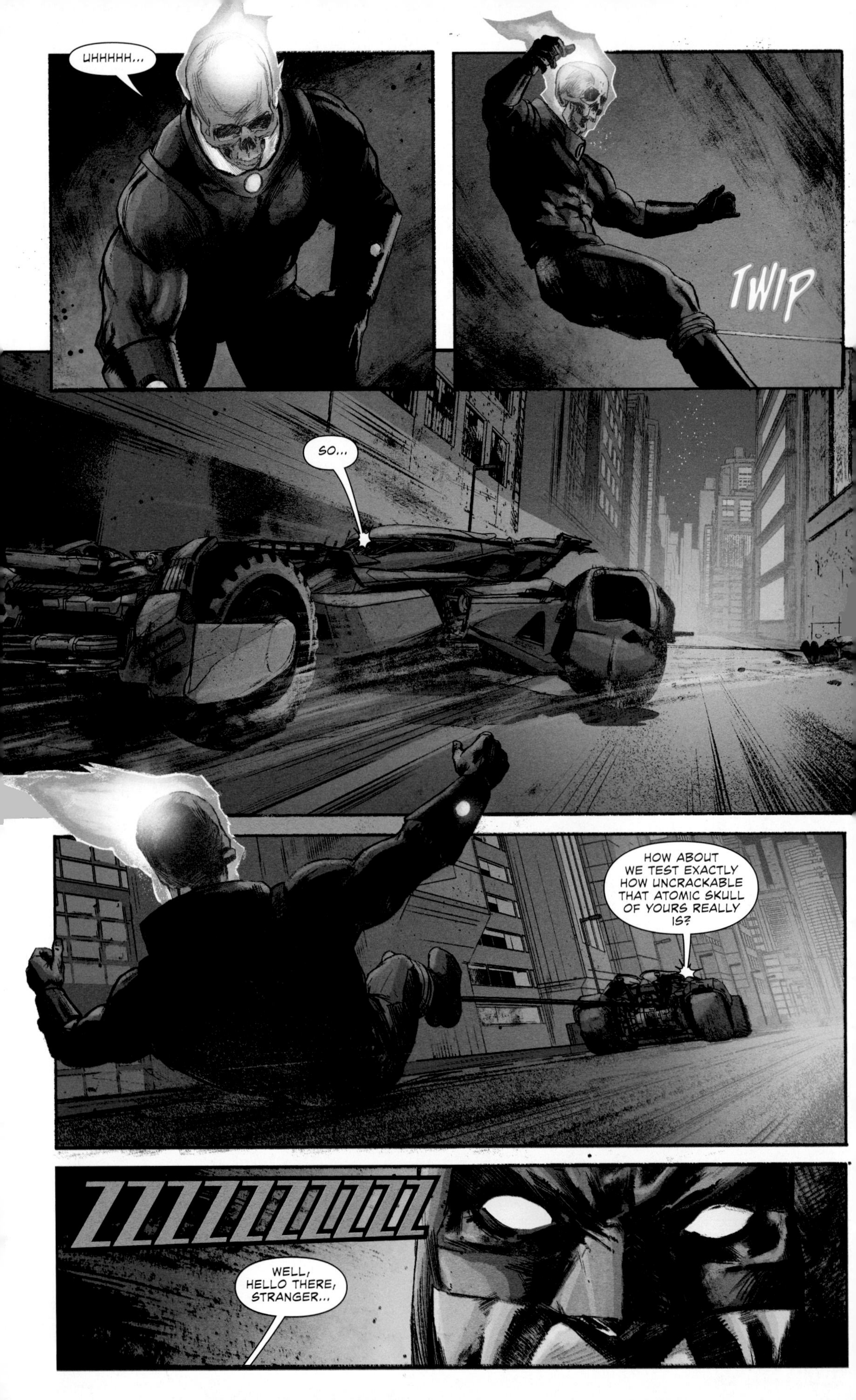
UHHHHH...
TWIP
SO...
HOW ABOUT WE TEST EXACTLY HOW UNCRACKABLE THAT ATOMIC SKULL OF YOURS REALLY IS?
ZZZZZZZZZZZZ
WELL, HELLO THERE, STRANGER...

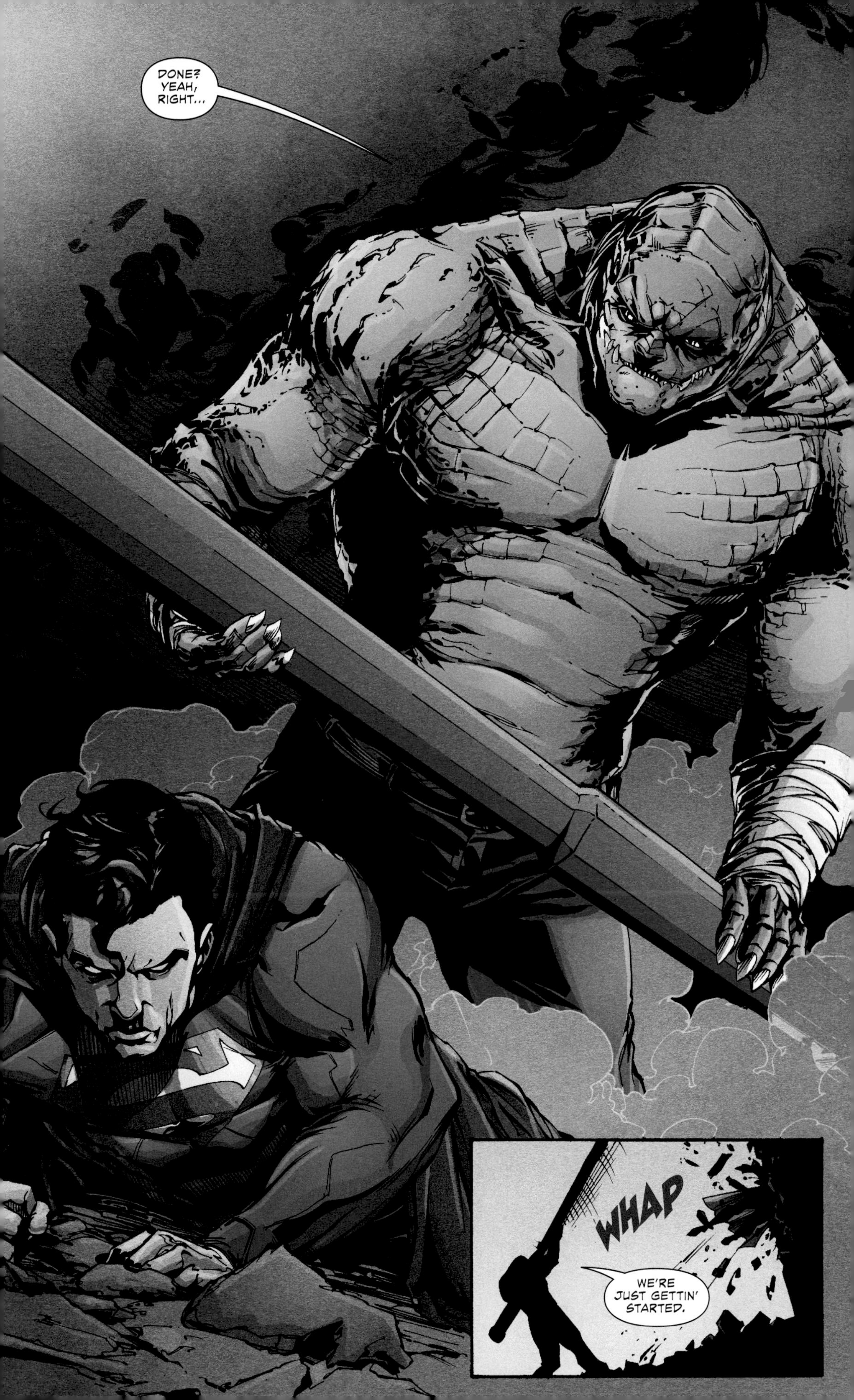
DONE? YEAH, RIGHT...
WHAP
WE'RE JUST GETTIN' STARTED.

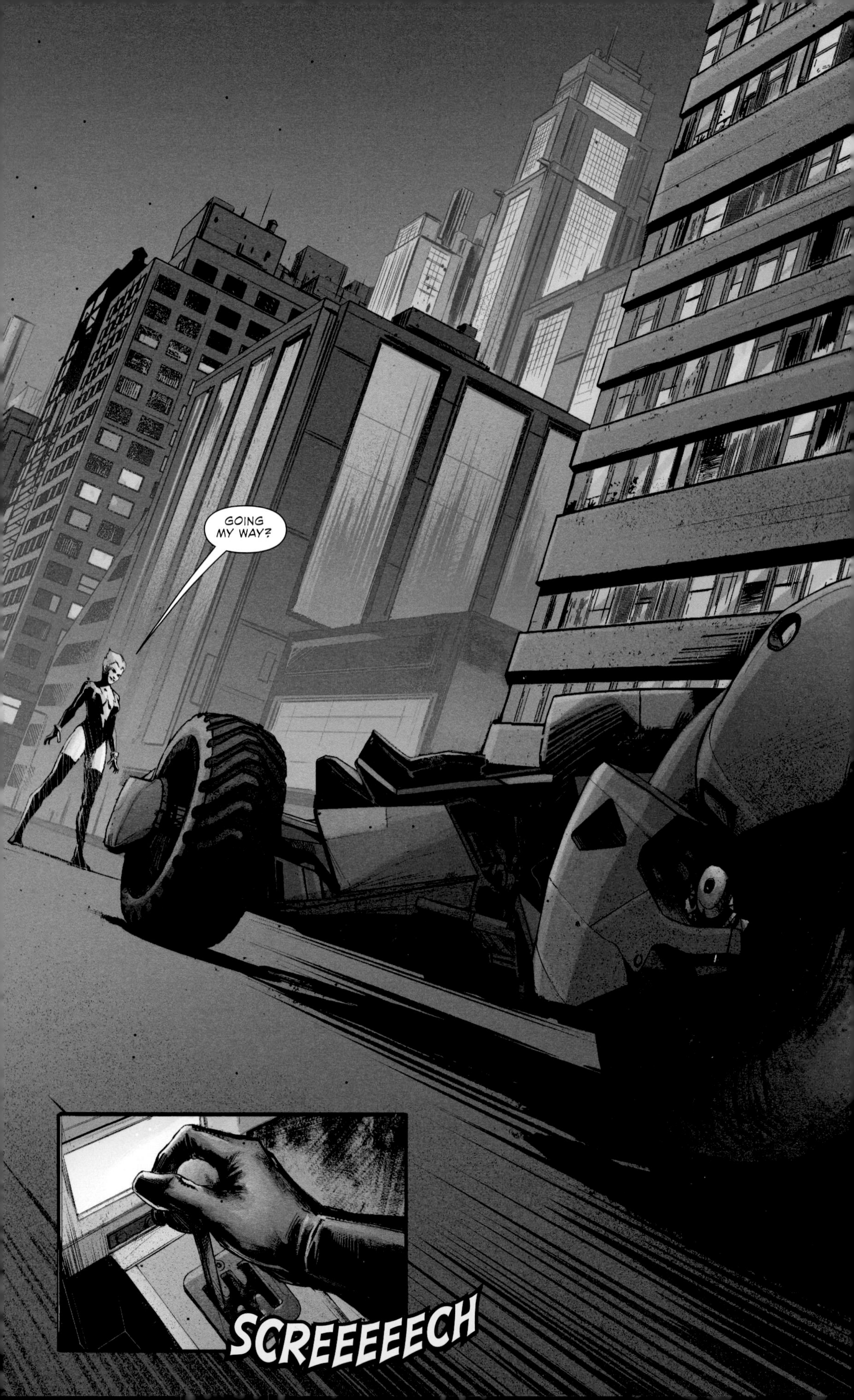
GOING MY WAY?
SCREEEEEECH

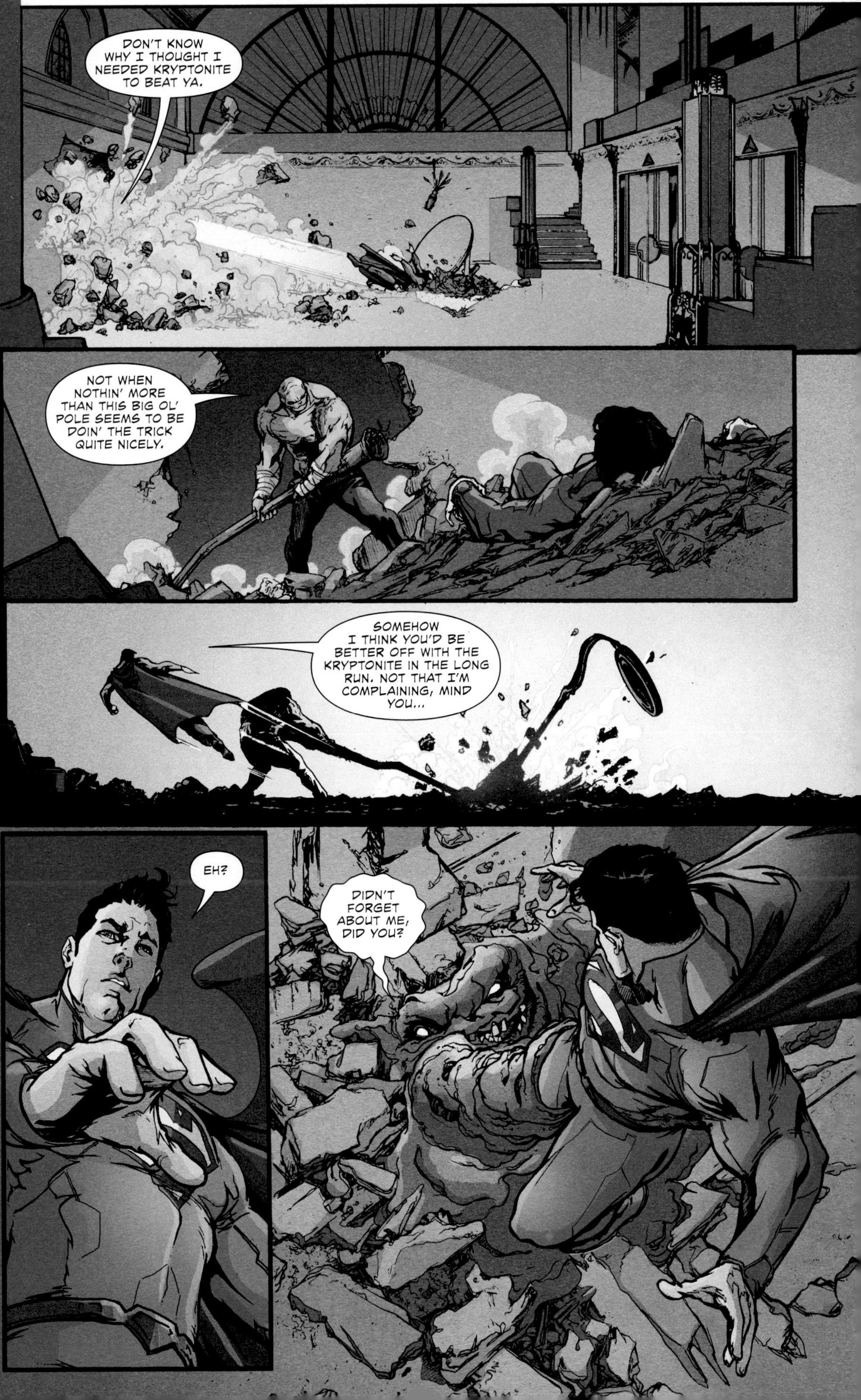
DON'T KNOW WHY I THOUGHT I NEEDED KRYPTONITE TO BEAT YA.
NOT WHEN NOTHIN' MORE THAN THIS BIG OL' POLE SEEMS TO BE DOIN' THE TRICK QUITE NICELY.
SOMEHOW I THINK YOU'D BE BETTER OFF WITH THE KRYPTONITE IN THE LONG RUN. NOT THAT I'M COMPLAINING, MIND YOU...
EH?
DIDN'T FORGET ABOUT ME, DID YOU?

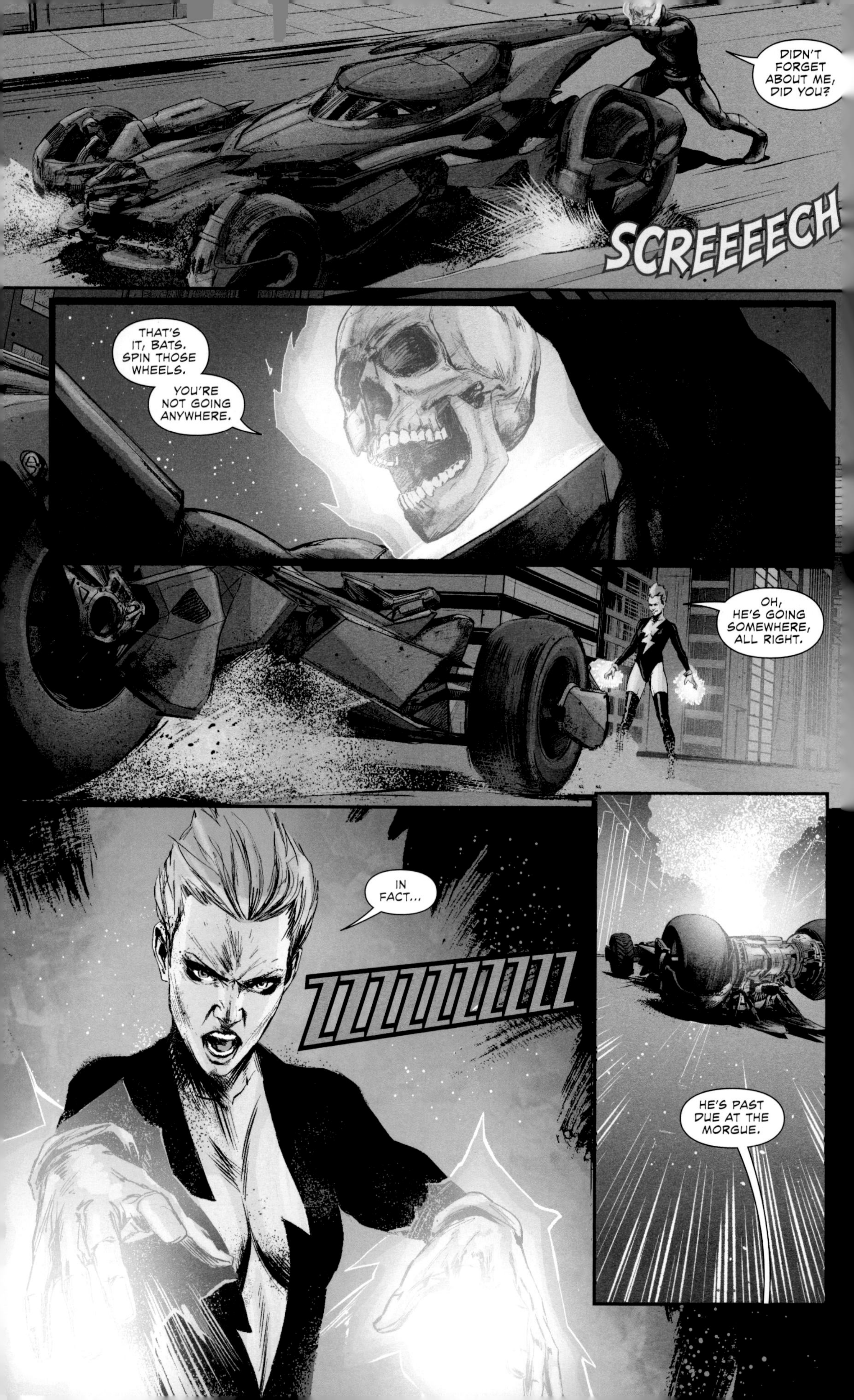

DIDN'T FORGET ABOUT ME, DID YOU?
SCREEEECH
THAT'S IT, BATS. SPIN THOSE WHEELS.
YOU'RE NOT GOING ANYWHERE.
OH, HE'S GOING SOMEWHERE, ALL RIGHT.
IN FACT...
ZZZZZZZZZZZZ
HE'S PAST DUE AT THE MORGUE.

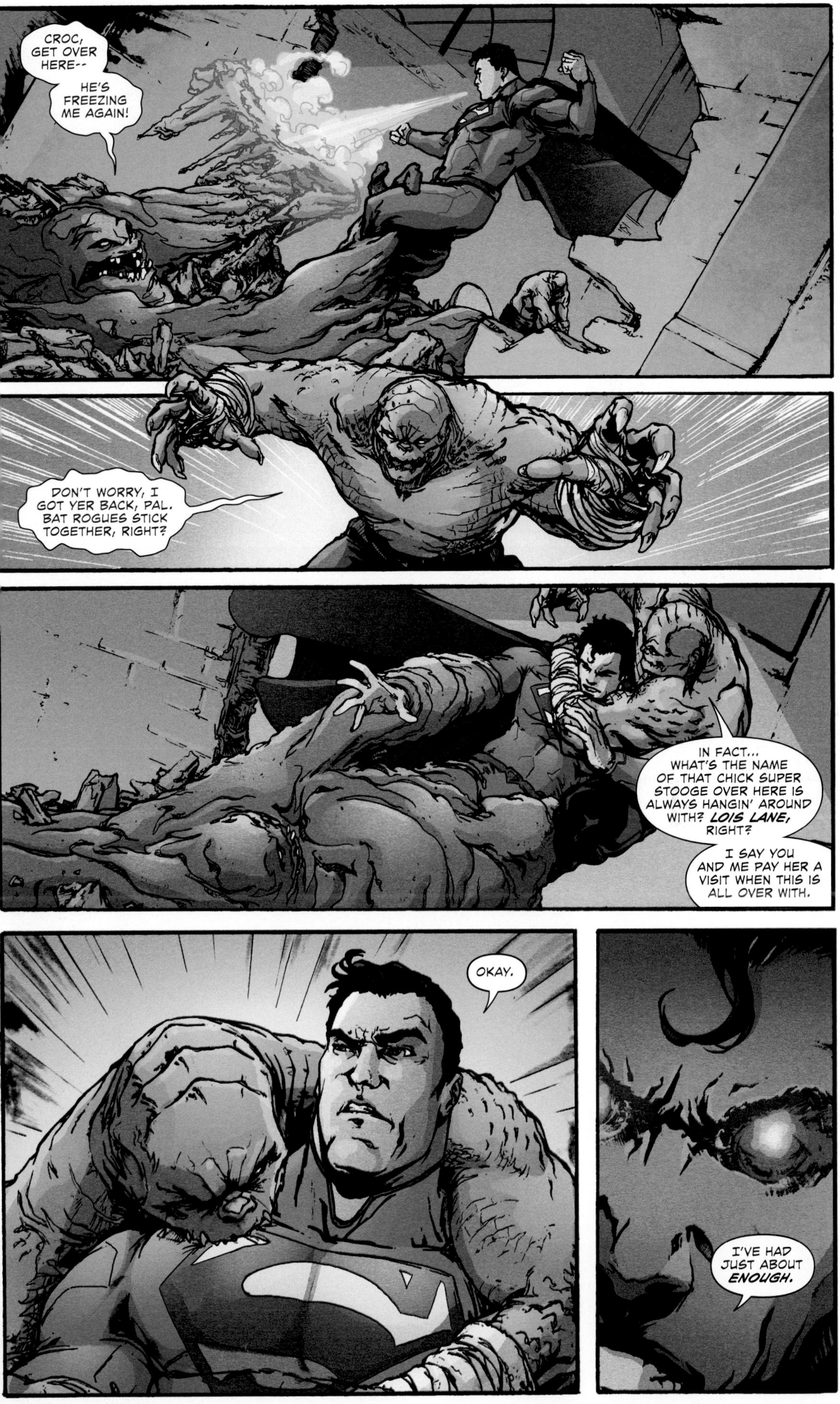
CROC, GET OVER HERE--
HE'S FREEZING ME AGAIN!
DON'T WORRY, I GOT YER BACK, PAL. BAT ROGUES STICK TOGETHER, RIGHT?
IN FACT... WHAT'S THE NAME OF THAT CHICK SUPER STOOGE OVER HERE IS ALWAYS HANGIN' AROUND WITH? *LOIS LANE,* RIGHT?
I SAY YOU AND ME PAY HER A VISIT WHEN THIS IS ALL OVER WITH.
OKAY.
I'VE HAD JUST ABOUT *ENOUGH.*

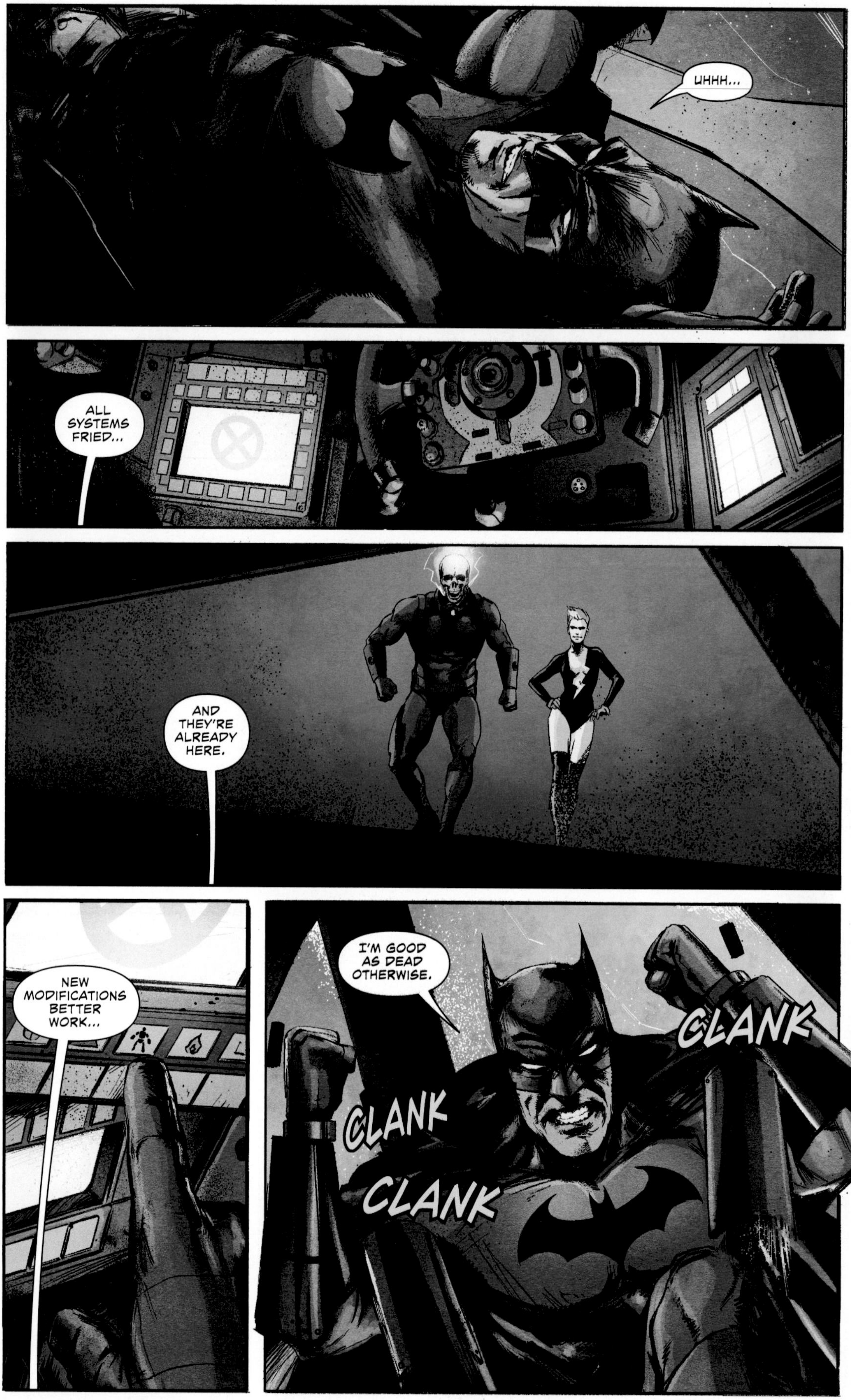
UHHH...
ALL SYSTEMS FRIED...
AND THEY'RE ALREADY HERE.
NEW MODIFICATIONS BETTER WORK...
I'M GOOD AS DEAD OTHERWISE.
CLANK
CLANK
CLANK

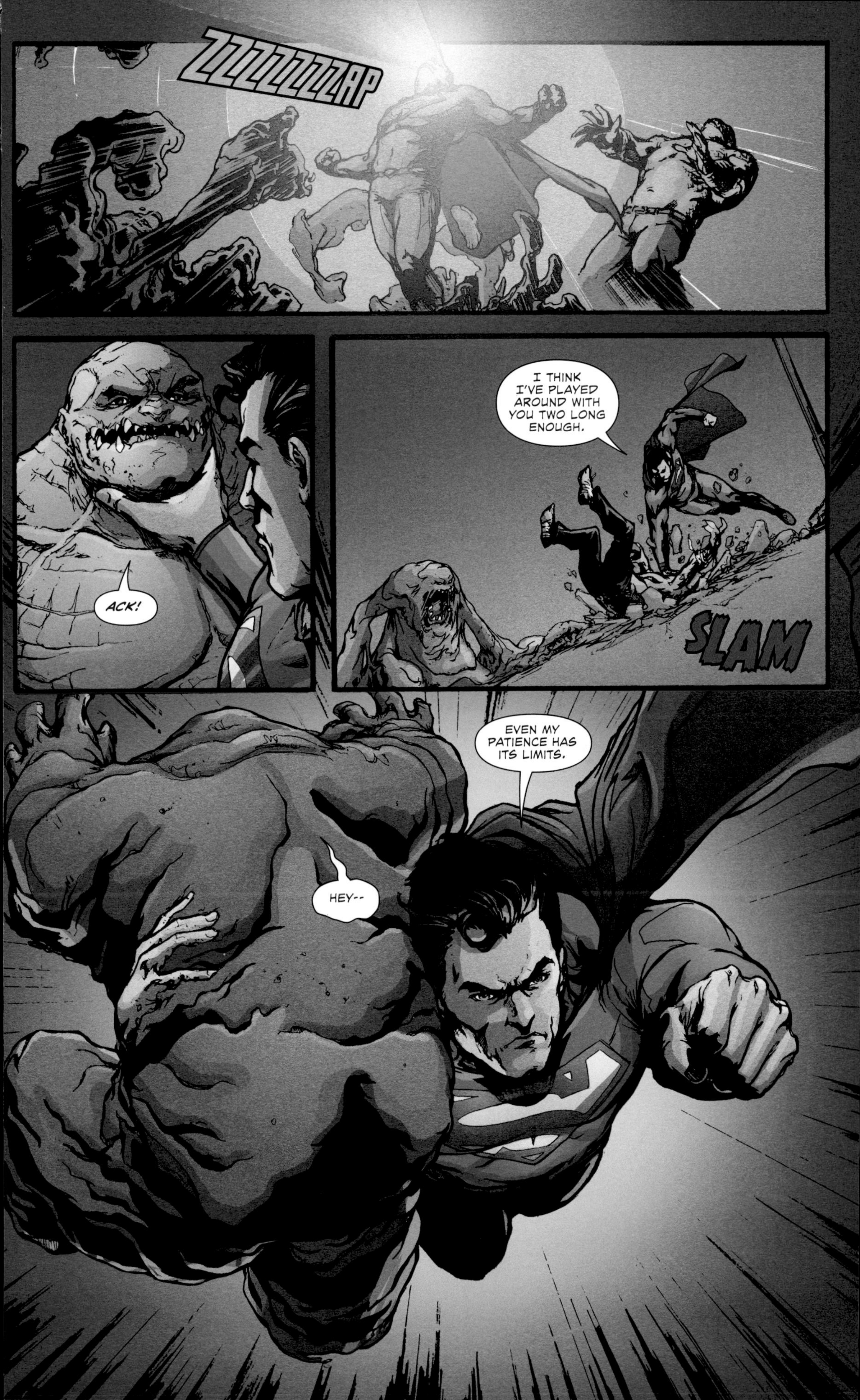
ZZZZZZZZAP
ACK!
I THINK I'VE PLAYED AROUND WITH YOU TWO LONG ENOUGH.
SLAM
EVEN MY PATIENCE HAS ITS LIMITS.
HEY--

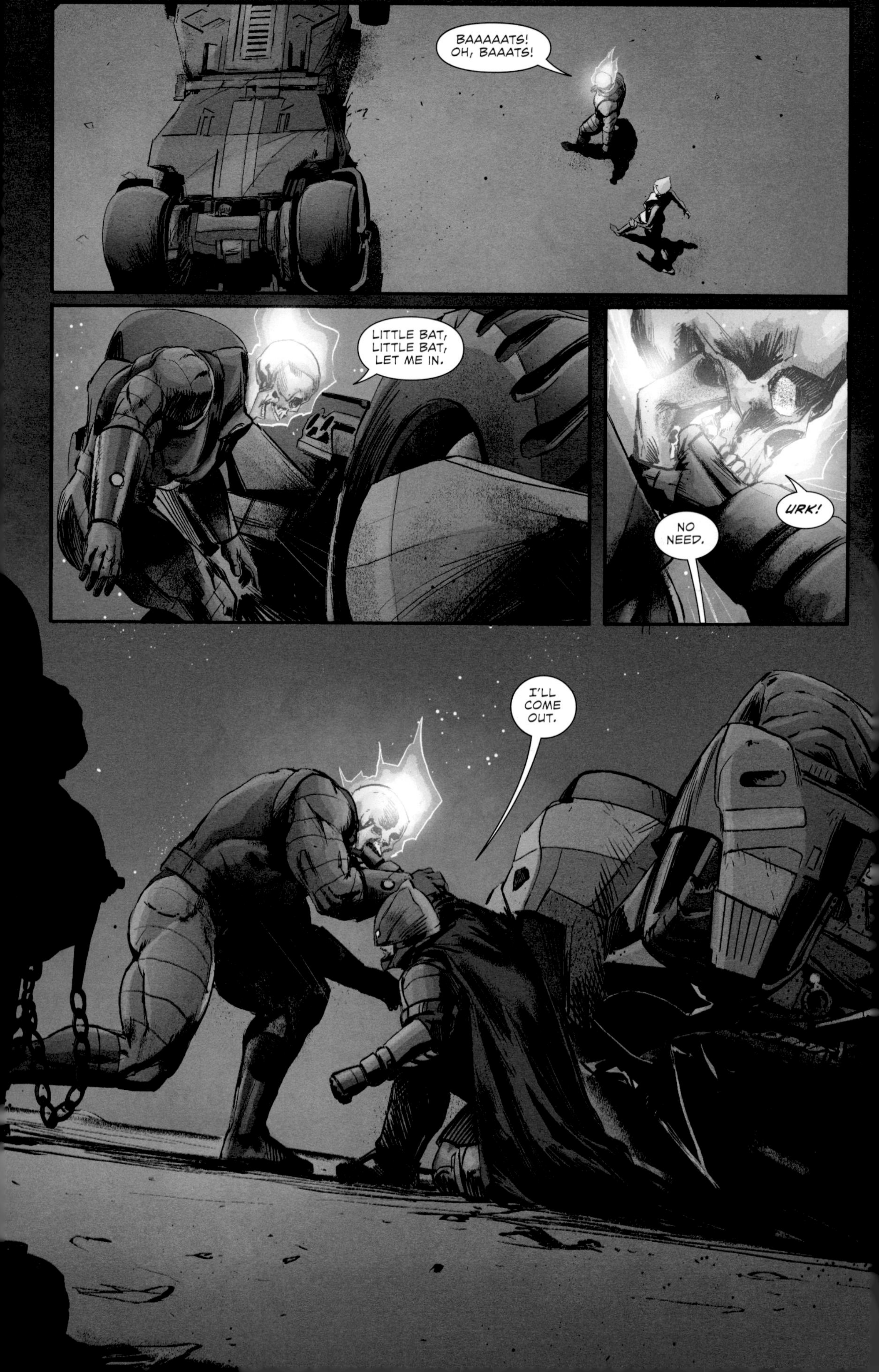
BAAAAATS! OH, BAAATS!
LITTLE BAT, LITTLE BAT, LET ME IN.
URK!
NO NEED.
I'LL COME OUT.

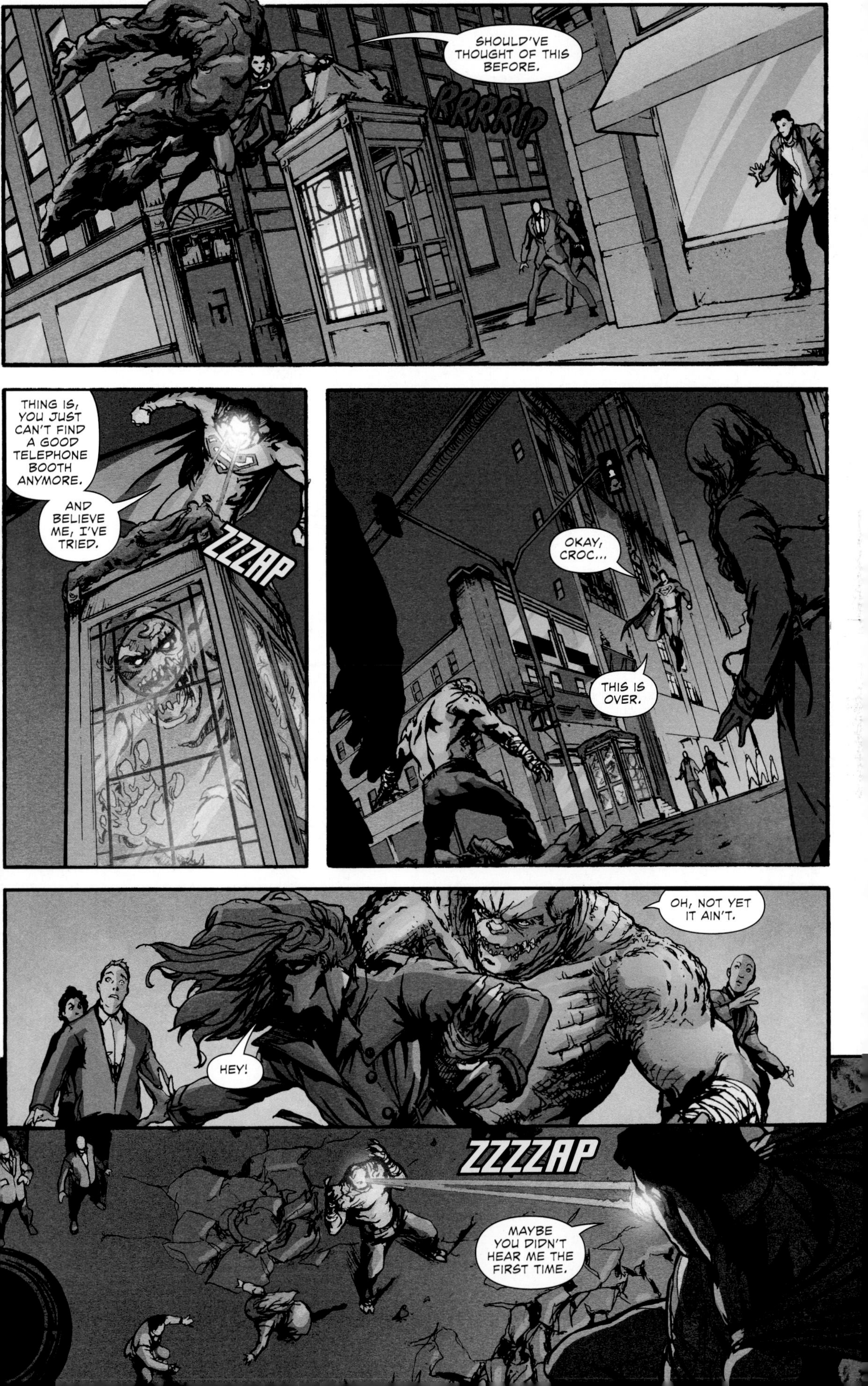
SHOULD'VE THOUGHT OF THIS BEFORE.
RRRRIP
THING IS, YOU JUST CAN'T FIND A GOOD TELEPHONE BOOTH ANYMORE.
AND BELIEVE ME, I'VE TRIED.
ZZZAP
OKAY, CROC...
THIS IS OVER.
OH, NOT YET IT AIN'T.
HEY!
ZZZZAP
MAYBE YOU DIDN'T HEAR ME THE FIRST TIME.

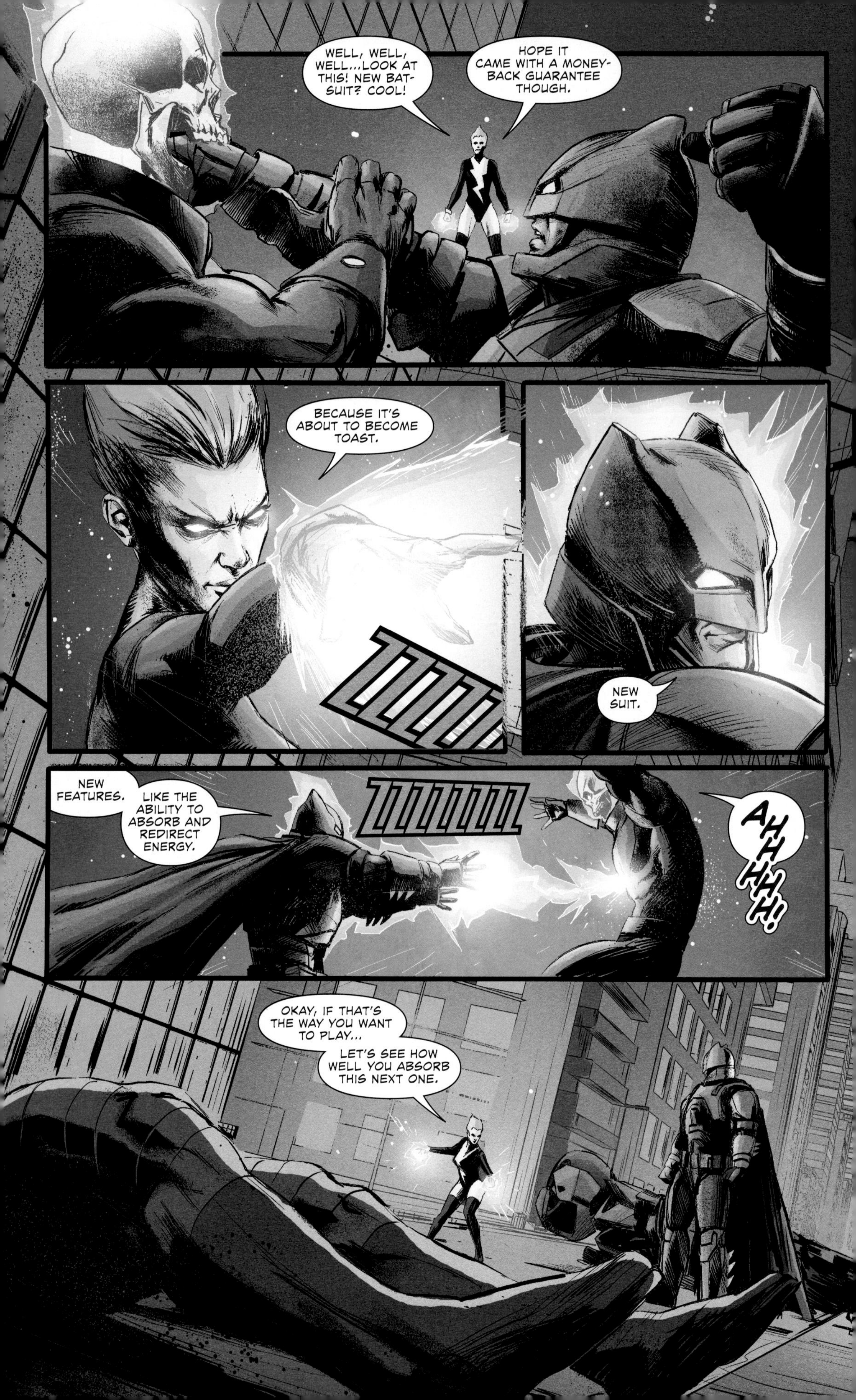
WELL, WELL, WELL...LOOK AT THIS! NEW BAT-SUIT? COOL!
HOPE IT CAME WITH A MONEY-BACK GUARANTEE THOUGH.
BECAUSE IT'S ABOUT TO BECOME TOAST.
ZZZZZ
NEW SUIT.
NEW FEATURES.
LIKE THE ABILITY TO ABSORB AND REDIRECT ENERGY.
ZZZZZZZZZ
AHHHHH!
OKAY, IF THAT'S THE WAY YOU WANT TO PLAY...
LET'S SEE HOW WELL YOU ABSORB THIS NEXT ONE.

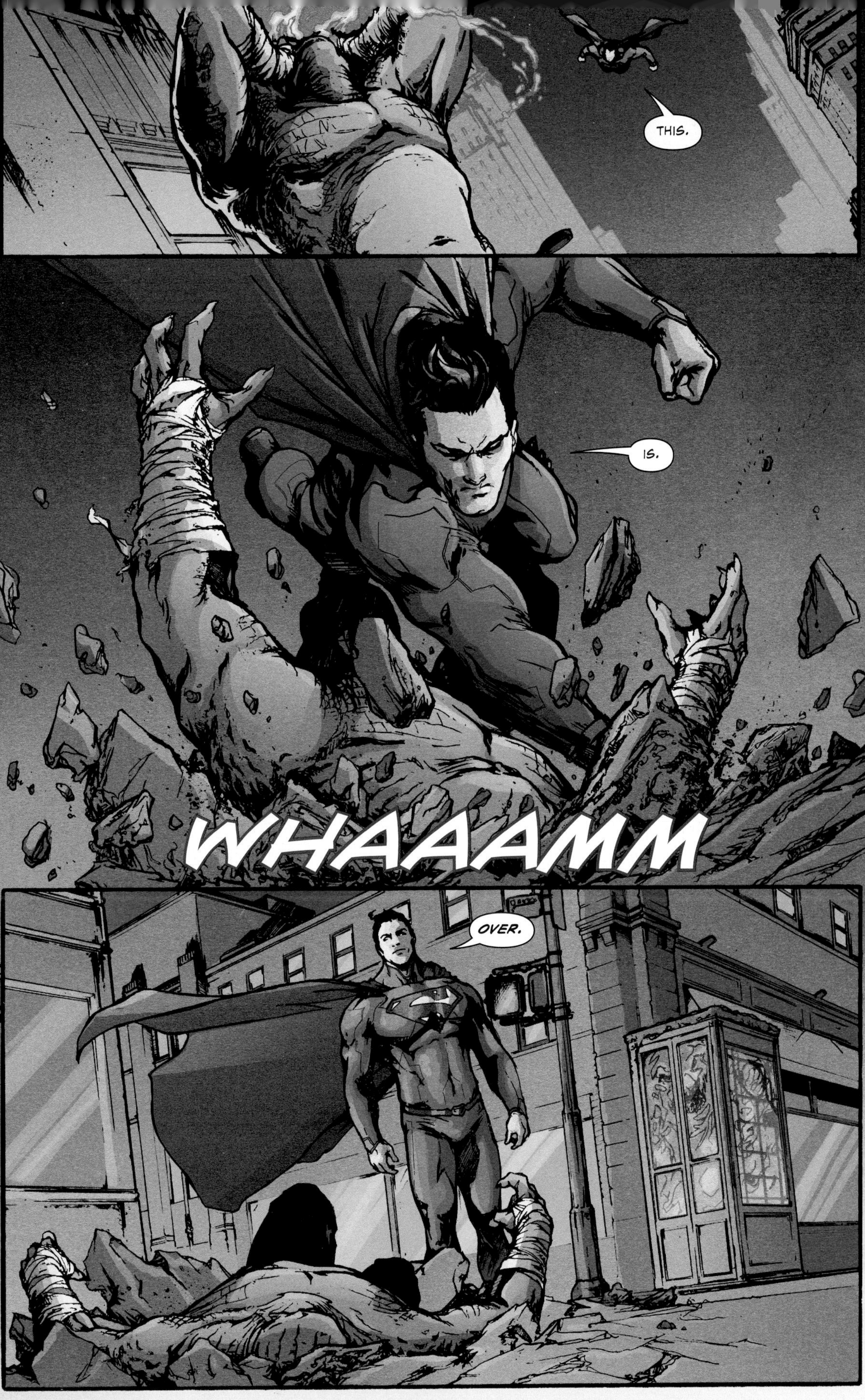
THIS.
IS.
WHAAAAMM
OVER.

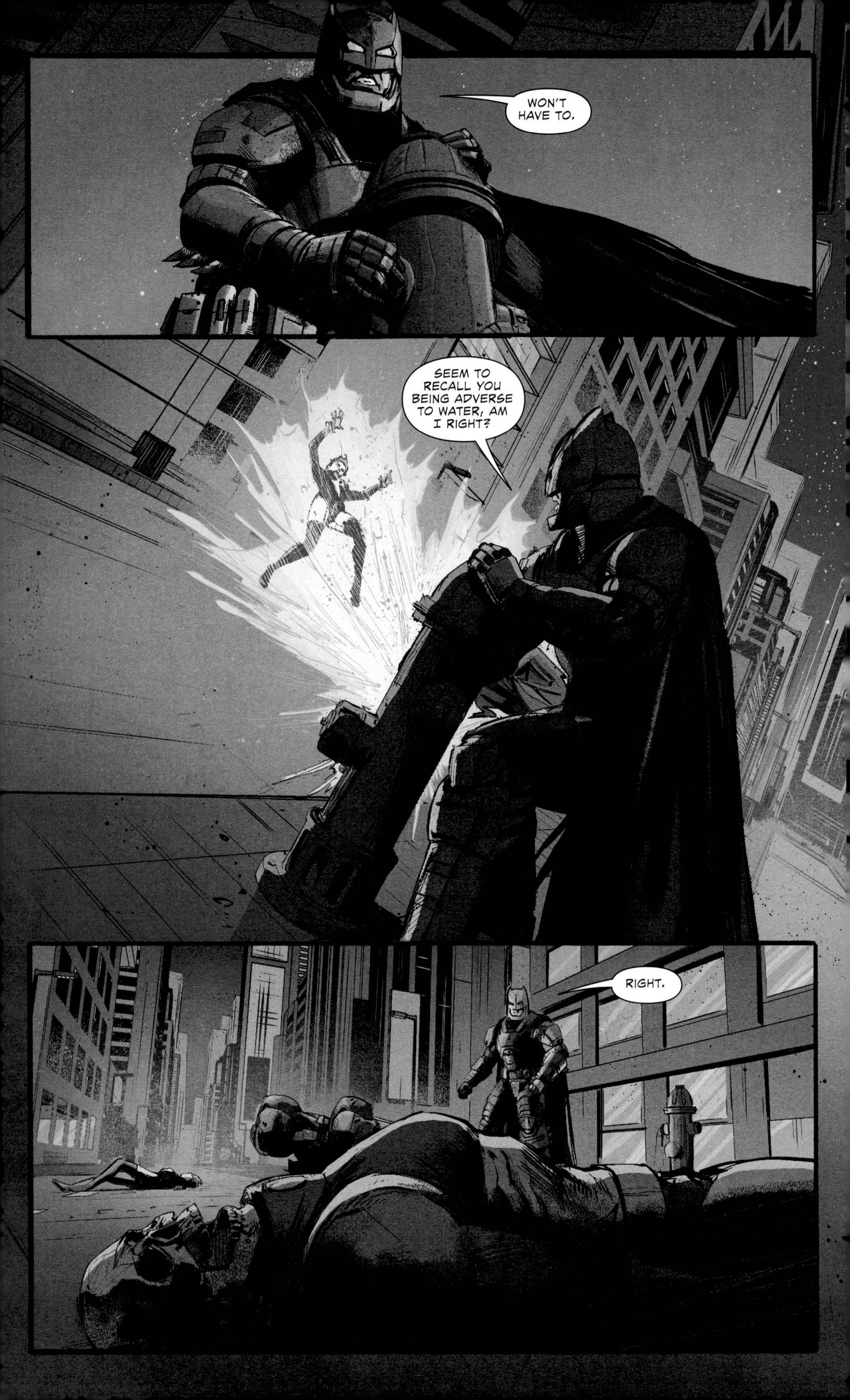
WON'T HAVE TO.
SEEM TO RECALL YOU BEING ADVERSE TO WATER, AM I RIGHT?
RIGHT.

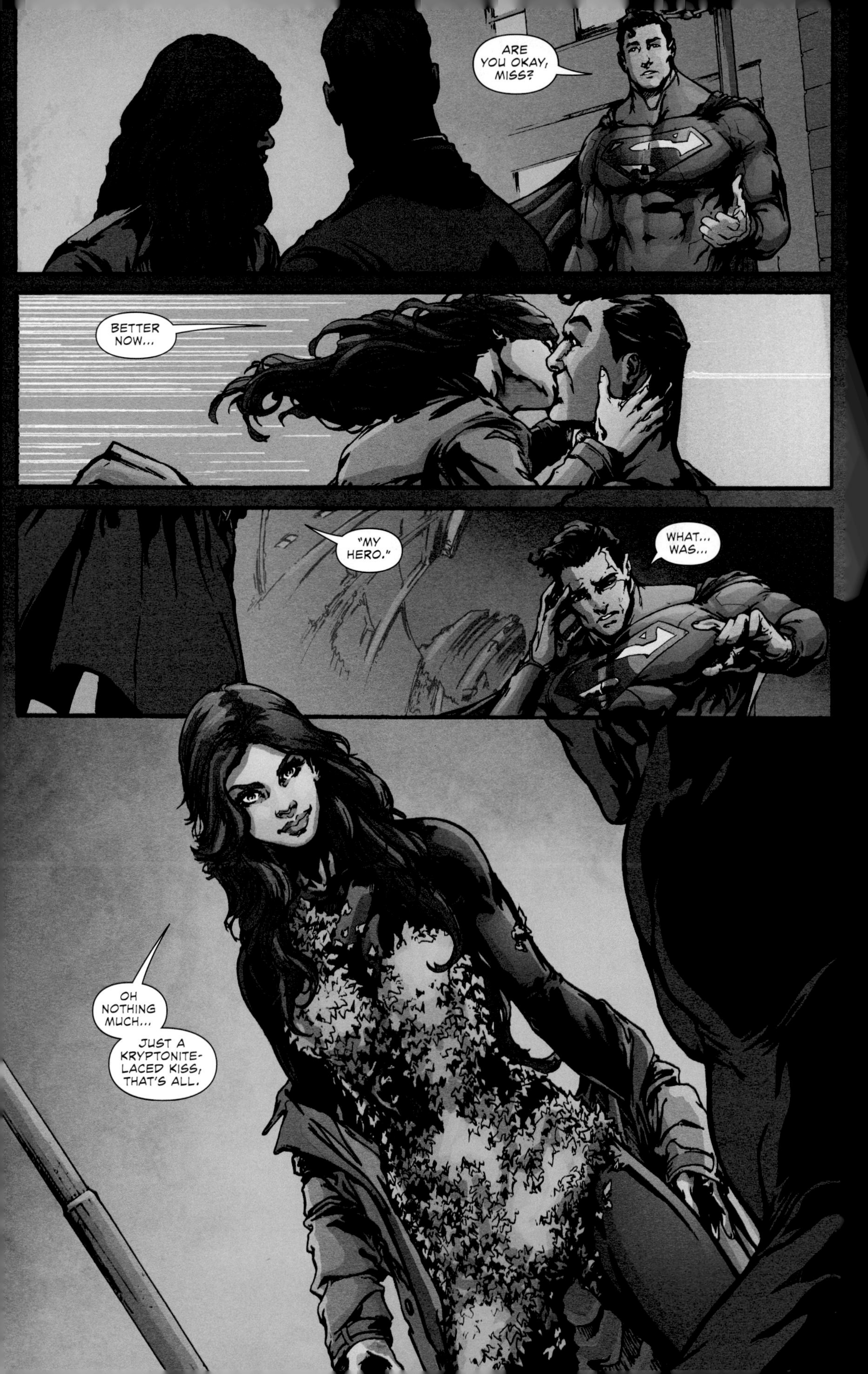
ARE YOU OKAY, MISS?
BETTER NOW...
"MY HERO."
WHAT... WAS...
OH NOTHING MUCH...
JUST A KRYPTONITE-LACED KISS, THAT'S ALL.

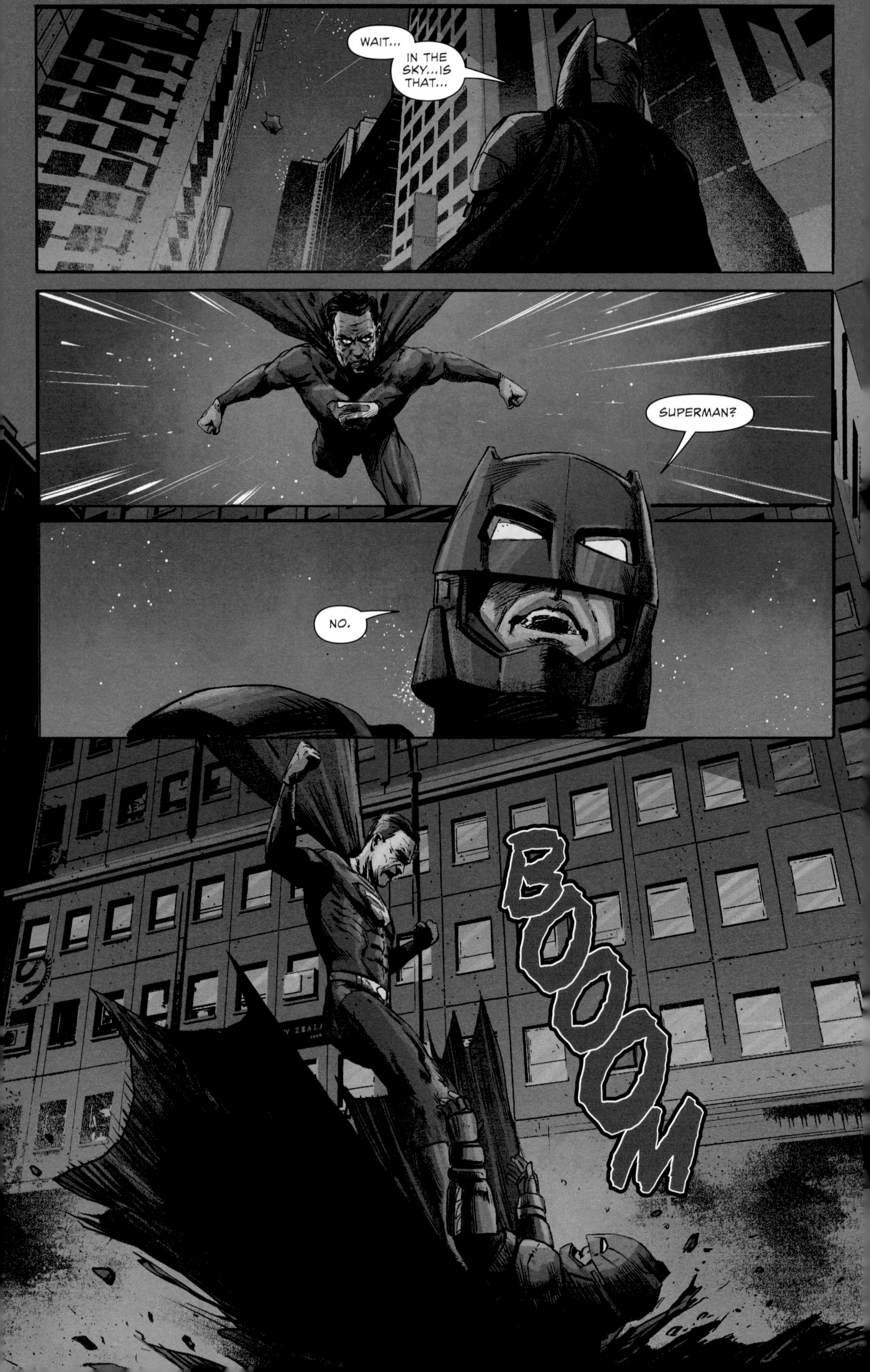
WAIT...
IN THE SKY...IS THAT...
SUPERMAN?
NO.
BOOOOM

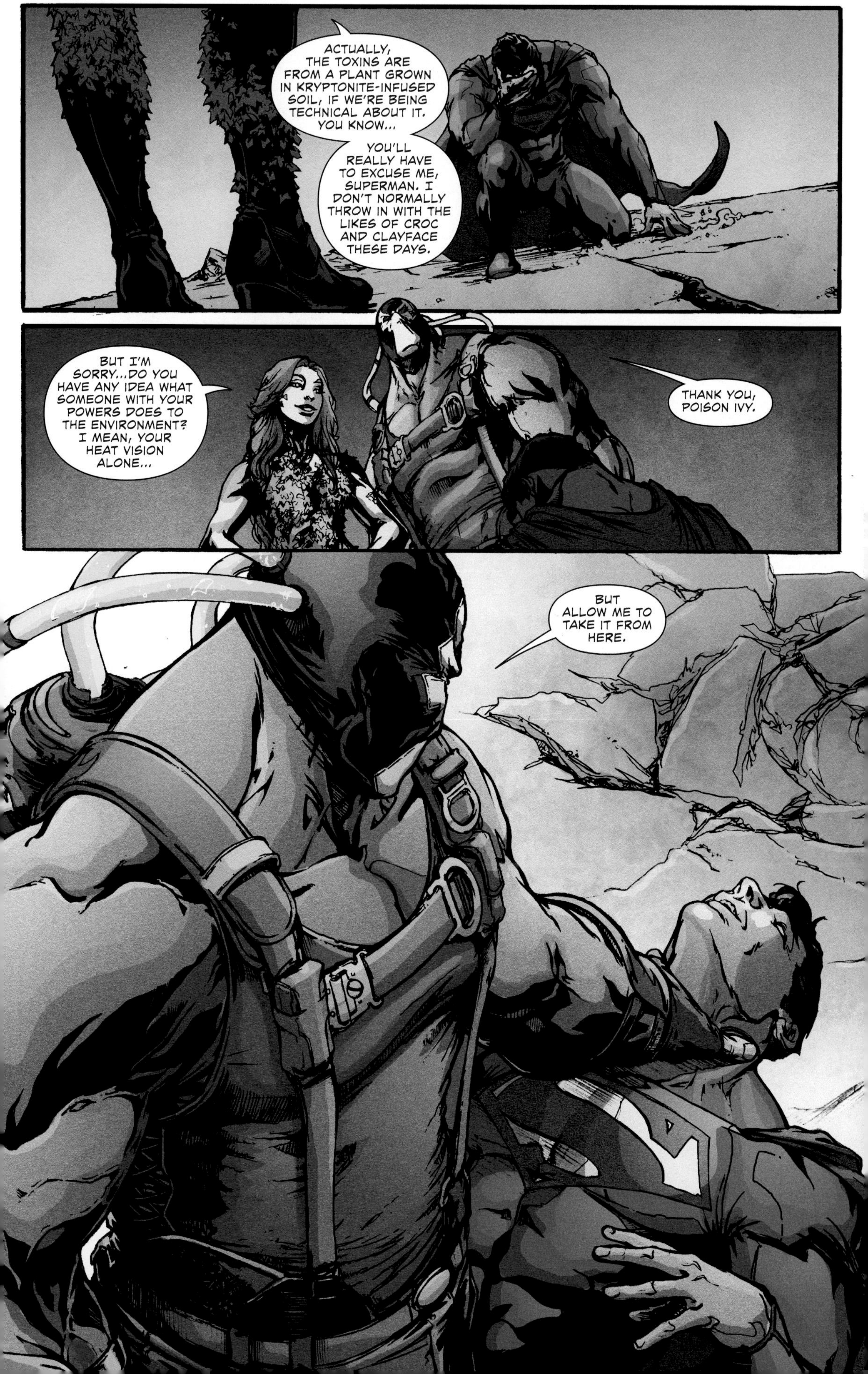
ACTUALLY, THE TOXINS ARE FROM A PLANT GROWN IN KRYPTONITE-INFUSED SOIL, IF WE'RE BEING TECHNICAL ABOUT IT. YOU KNOW...
YOU'LL REALLY HAVE TO EXCUSE ME, SUPERMAN. I DON'T NORMALLY THROW IN WITH THE LIKES OF CROC AND CLAYFACE THESE DAYS.
BUT I'M SORRY...DO YOU HAVE ANY IDEA WHAT SOMEONE WITH YOUR POWERS DOES TO THE ENVIRONMENT? I MEAN, YOUR HEAT VISION ALONE...
THANK YOU, POISON IVY.
BUT ALLOW ME TO TAKE IT FROM HERE.

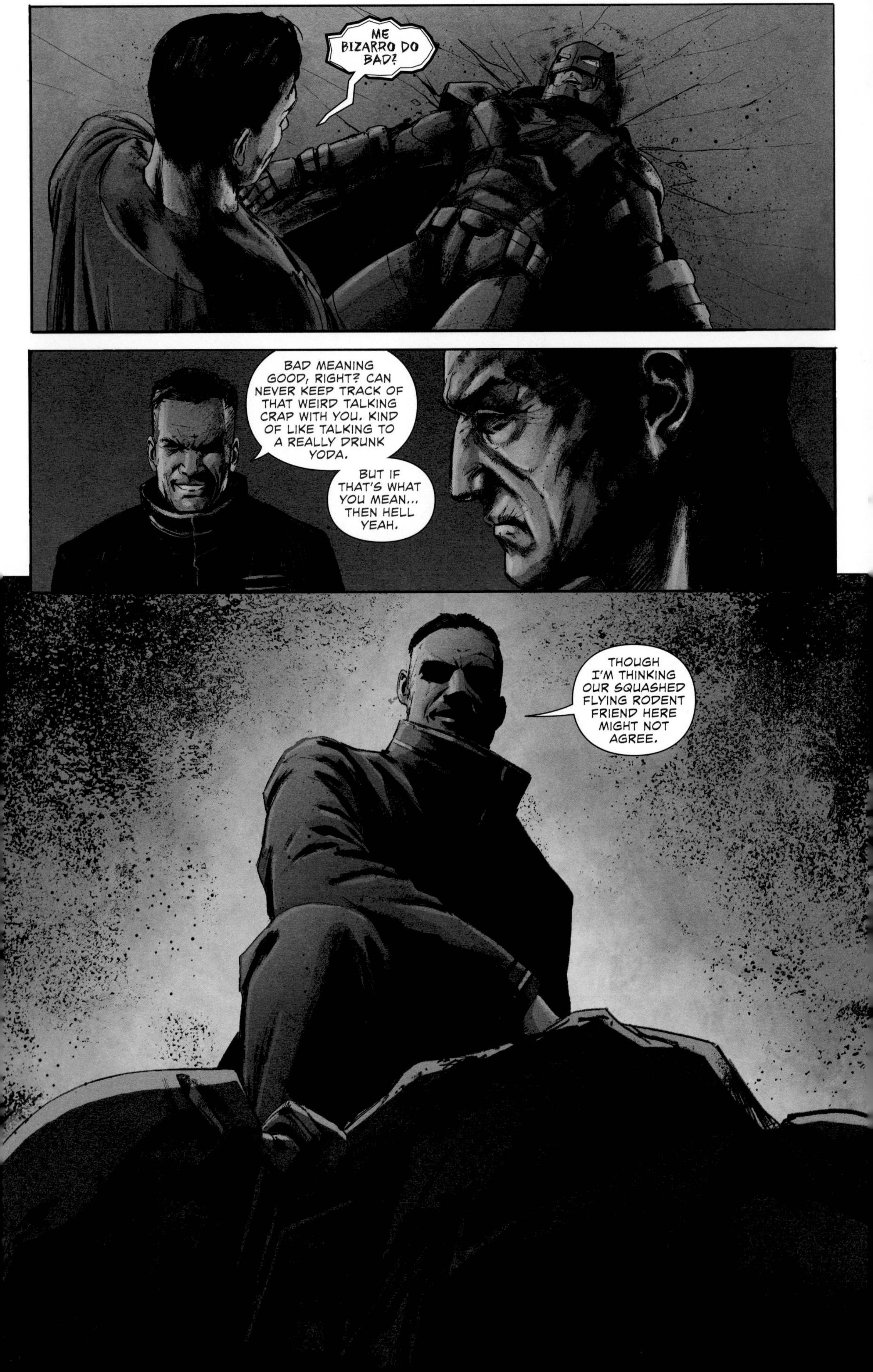
ME BIZARRO DO BAD?
BAD MEANING GOOD, RIGHT? CAN NEVER KEEP TRACK OF THAT WEIRD TALKING CRAP WITH YOU. KIND OF LIKE TALKING TO A REALLY DRUNK YODA.
BUT IF THAT'S WHAT YOU MEAN... THEN HELL YEAH.
THOUGH I'M THINKING OUR SQUASHED FLYING RODENT FRIEND HERE MIGHT NOT AGREE.

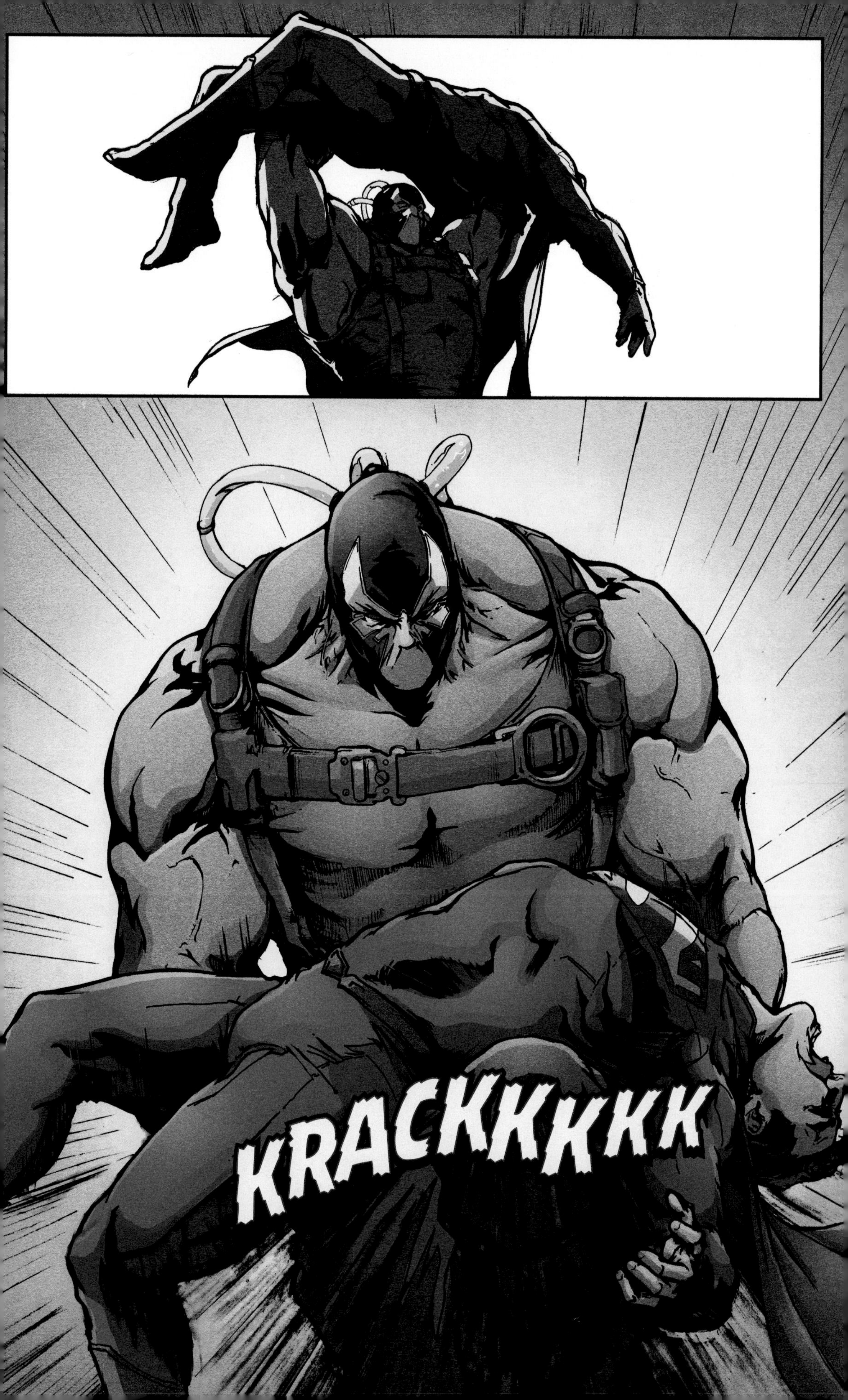
KRACKKKKKK

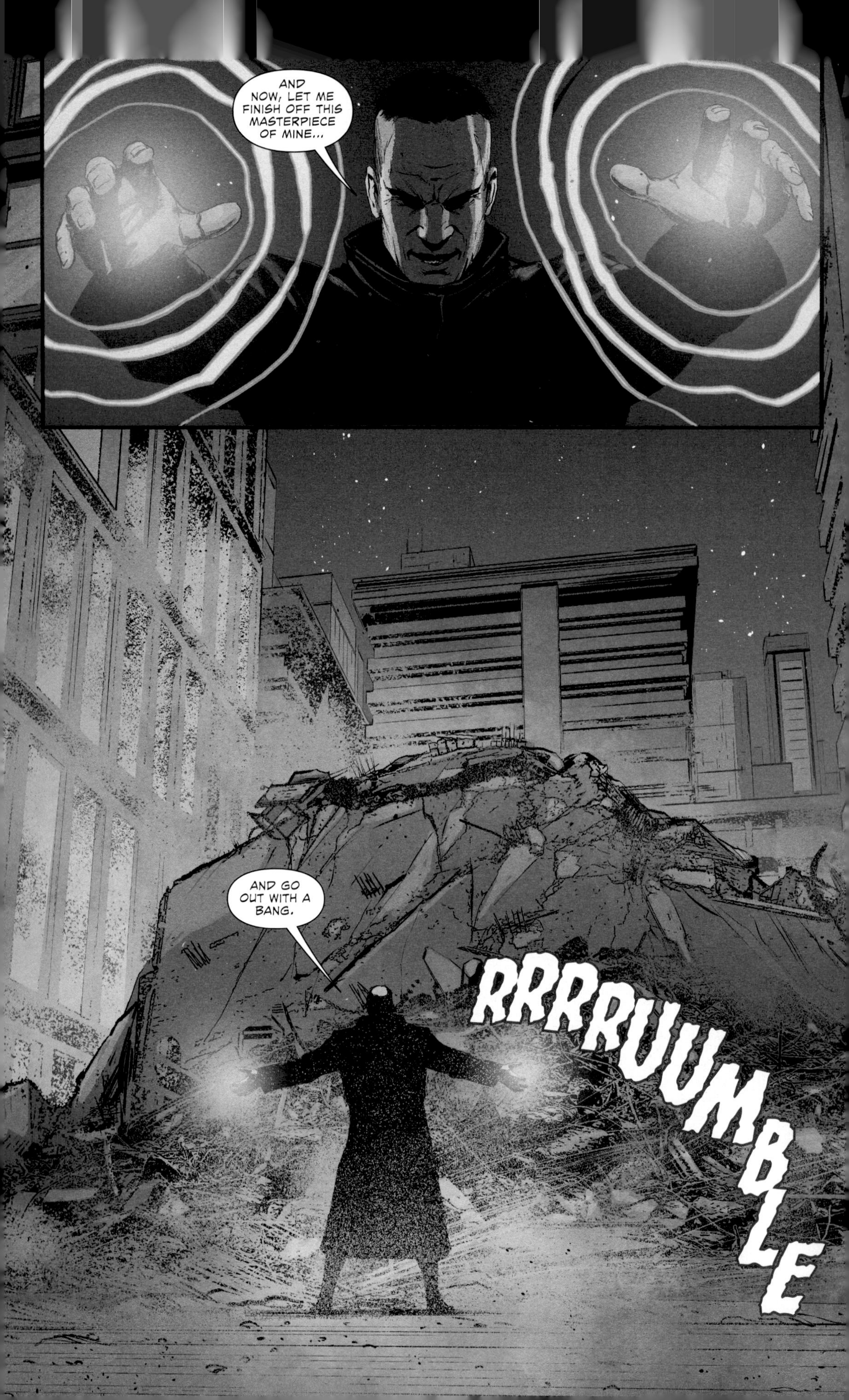
AND NOW, LET ME FINISH OFF THIS MASTERPIECE OF MINE...
AND GO OUT WITH A BANG.
RRRRUUMBLE

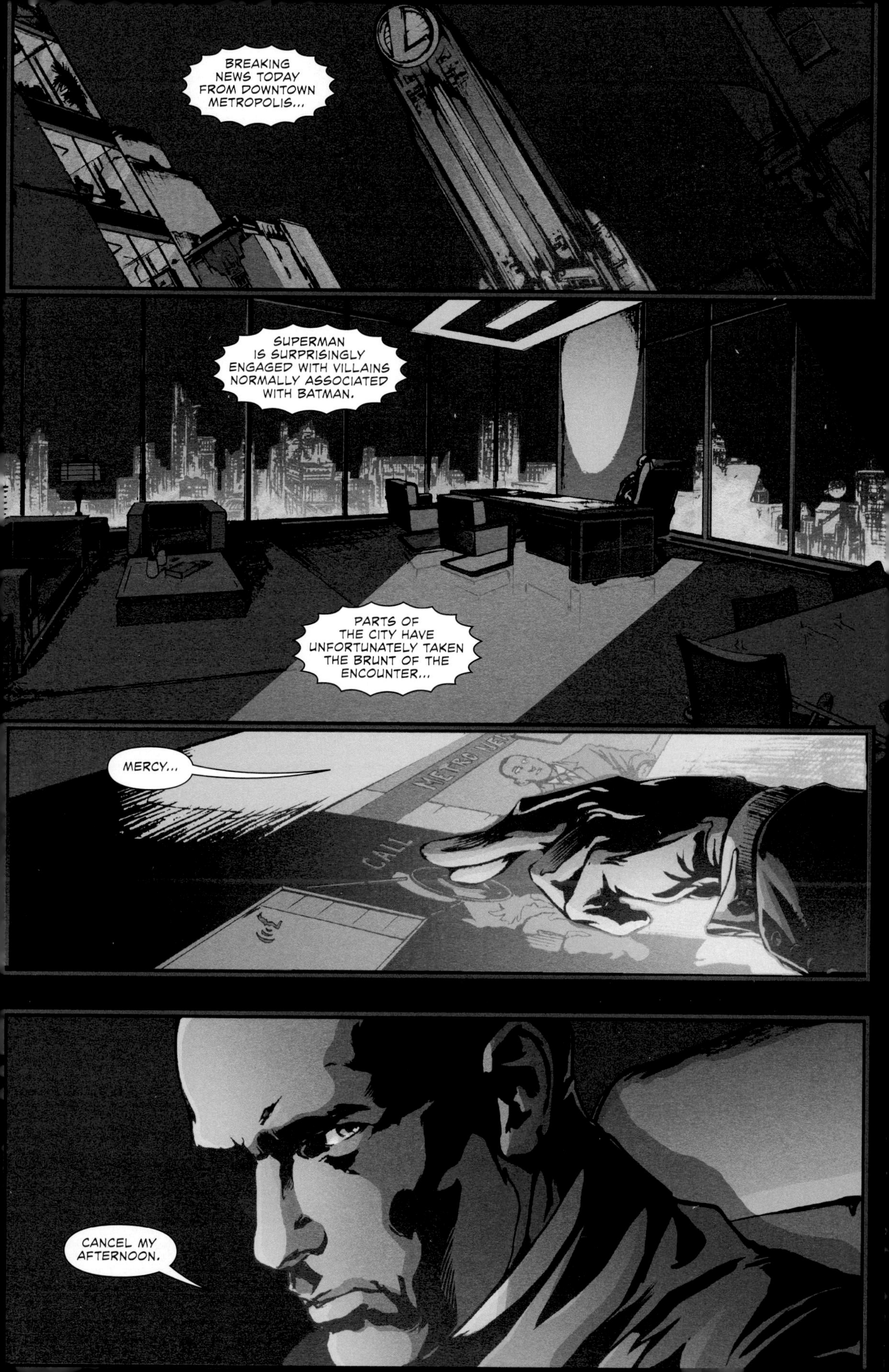
BREAKING NEWS TODAY FROM DOWNTOWN METROPOLIS...
SUPERMAN IS SURPRISINGLY ENGAGED WITH VILLAINS NORMALLY ASSOCIATED WITH BATMAN.
PARTS OF THE CITY HAVE UNFORTUNATELY TAKEN THE BRUNT OF THE ENCOUNTER...
MERCY...
CALL
CANCEL MY AFTERNOON.

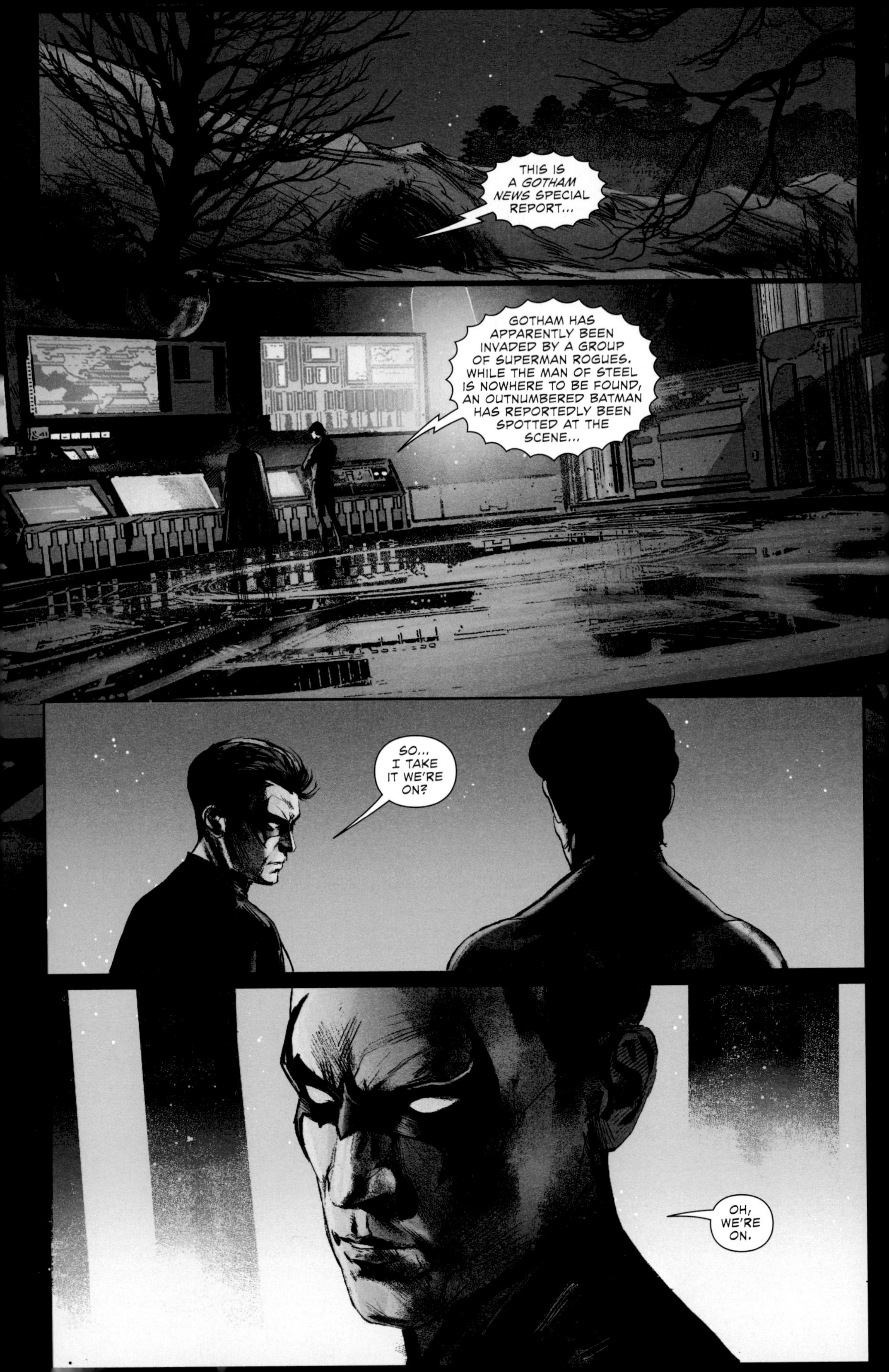
THIS IS A *GOTHAM NEWS* SPECIAL REPORT...
GOTHAM HAS APPARENTLY BEEN INVADED BY A GROUP OF SUPERMAN ROGUES. WHILE THE MAN OF STEEL IS NOWHERE TO BE FOUND, AN OUTNUMBERED BATMAN HAS REPORTEDLY BEEN SPOTTED AT THE SCENE...
SO... I TAKE IT WE'RE ON?
OH, WE'RE ON.

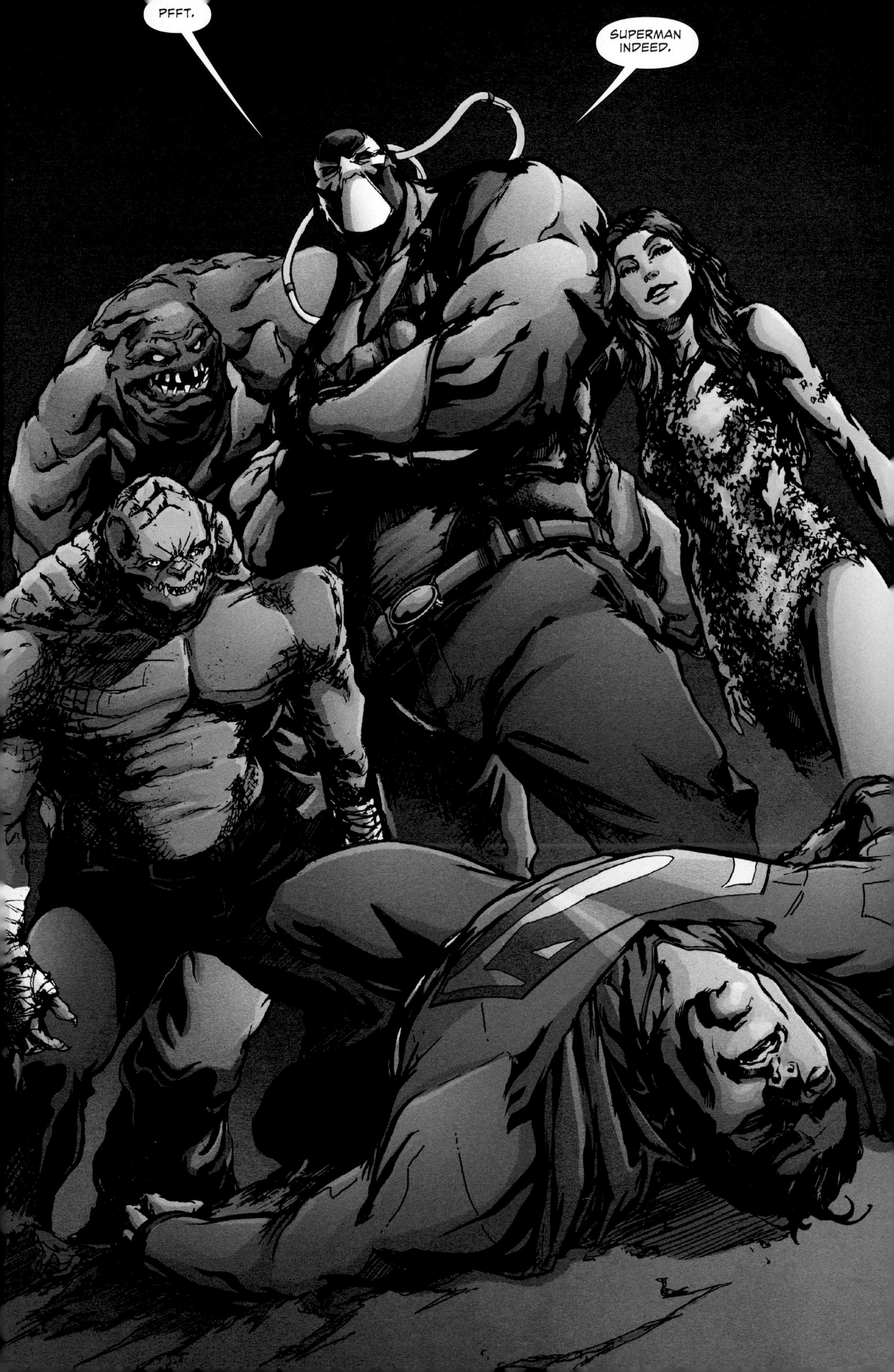
PFFT.
SUPERMAN INDEED.

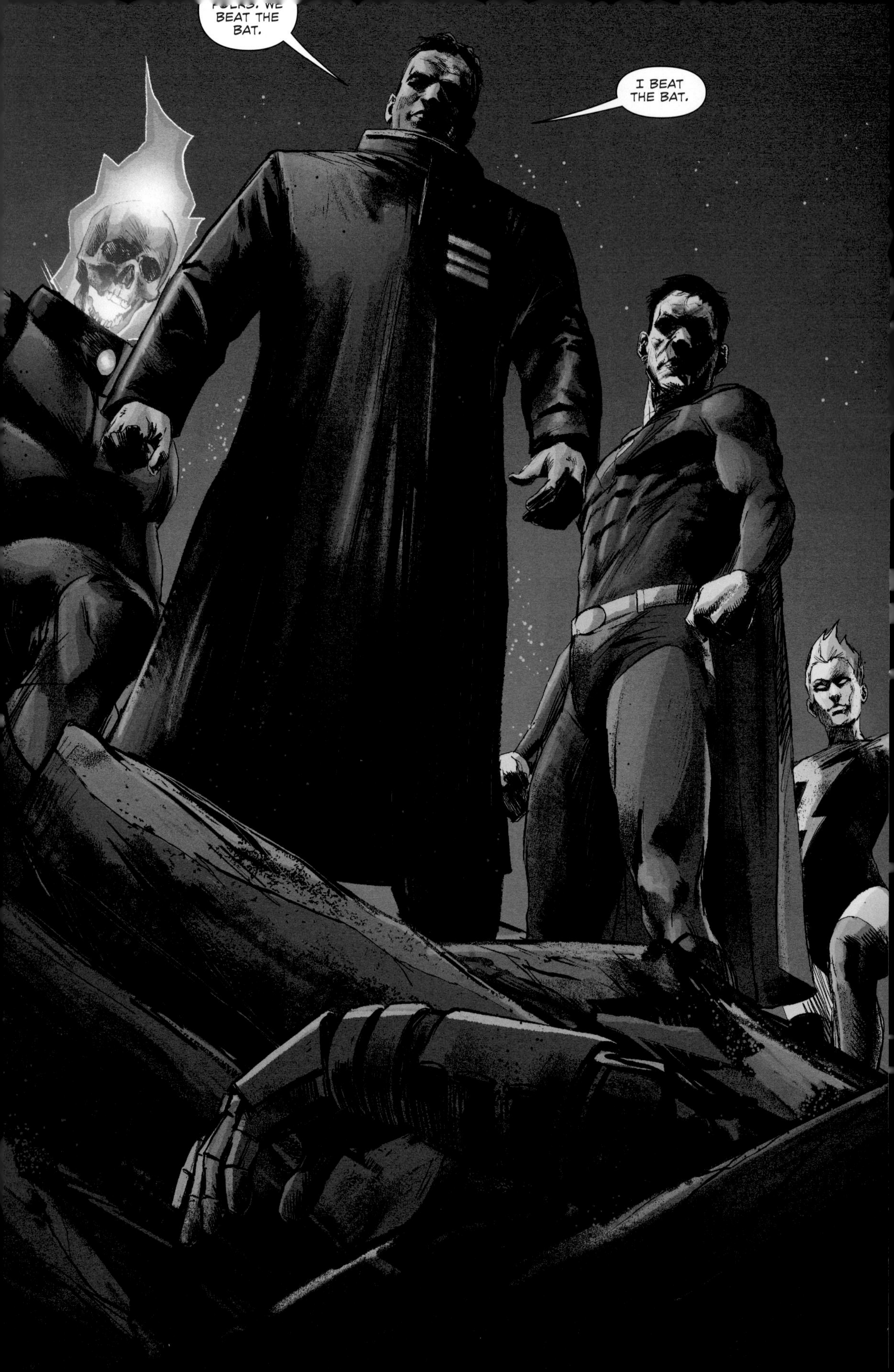
BEAT THE BAT.
I BEAT THE BAT.

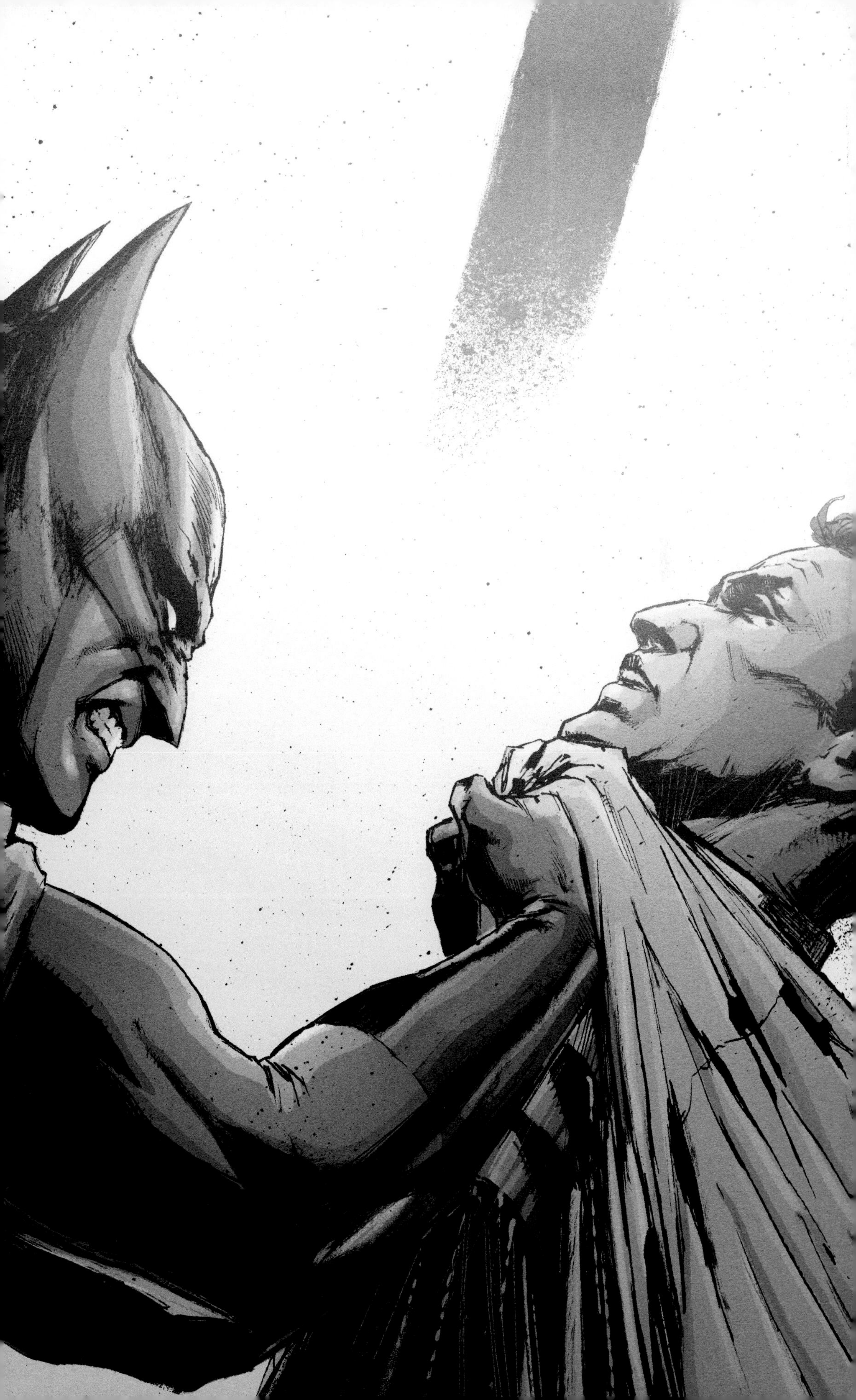

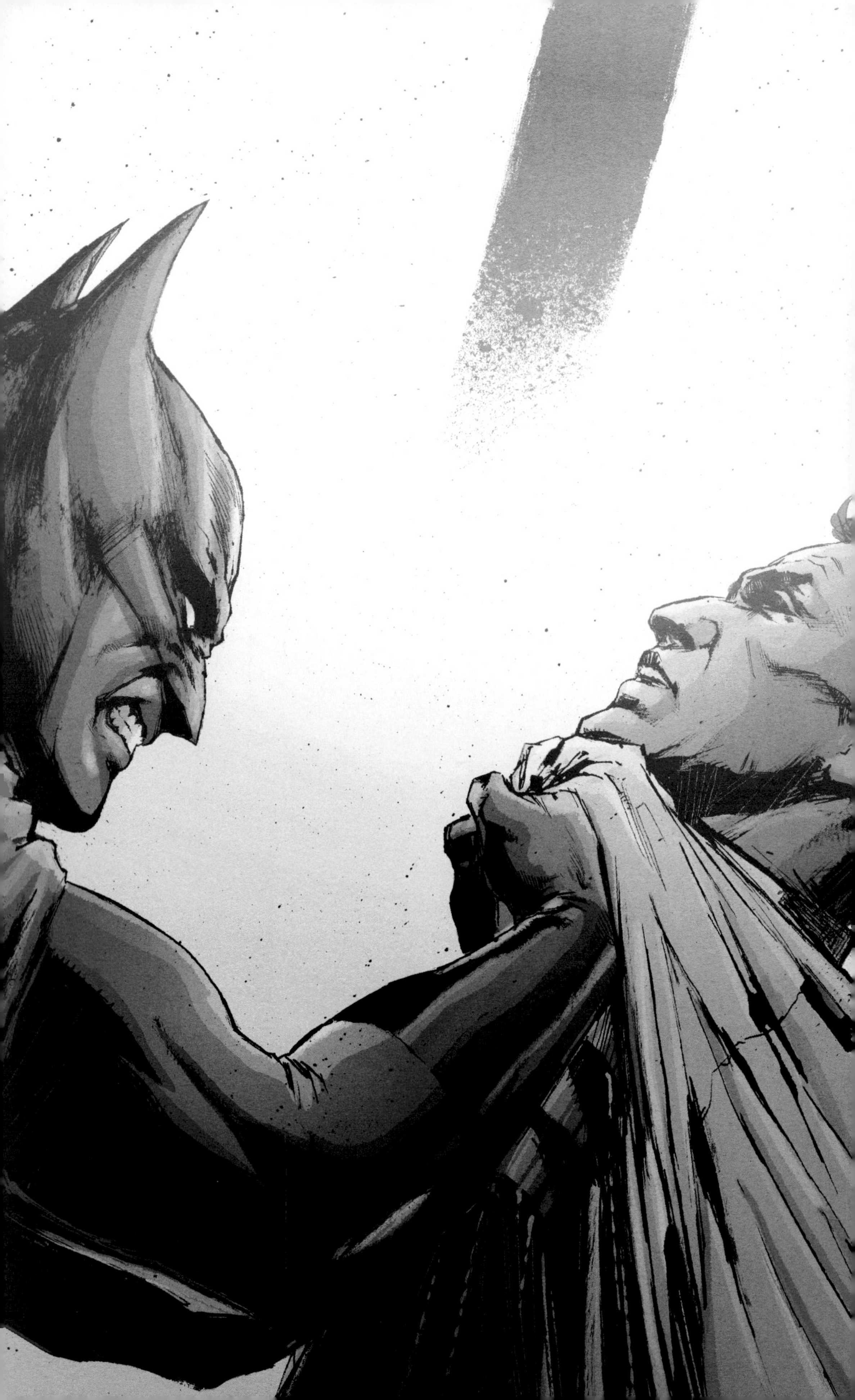

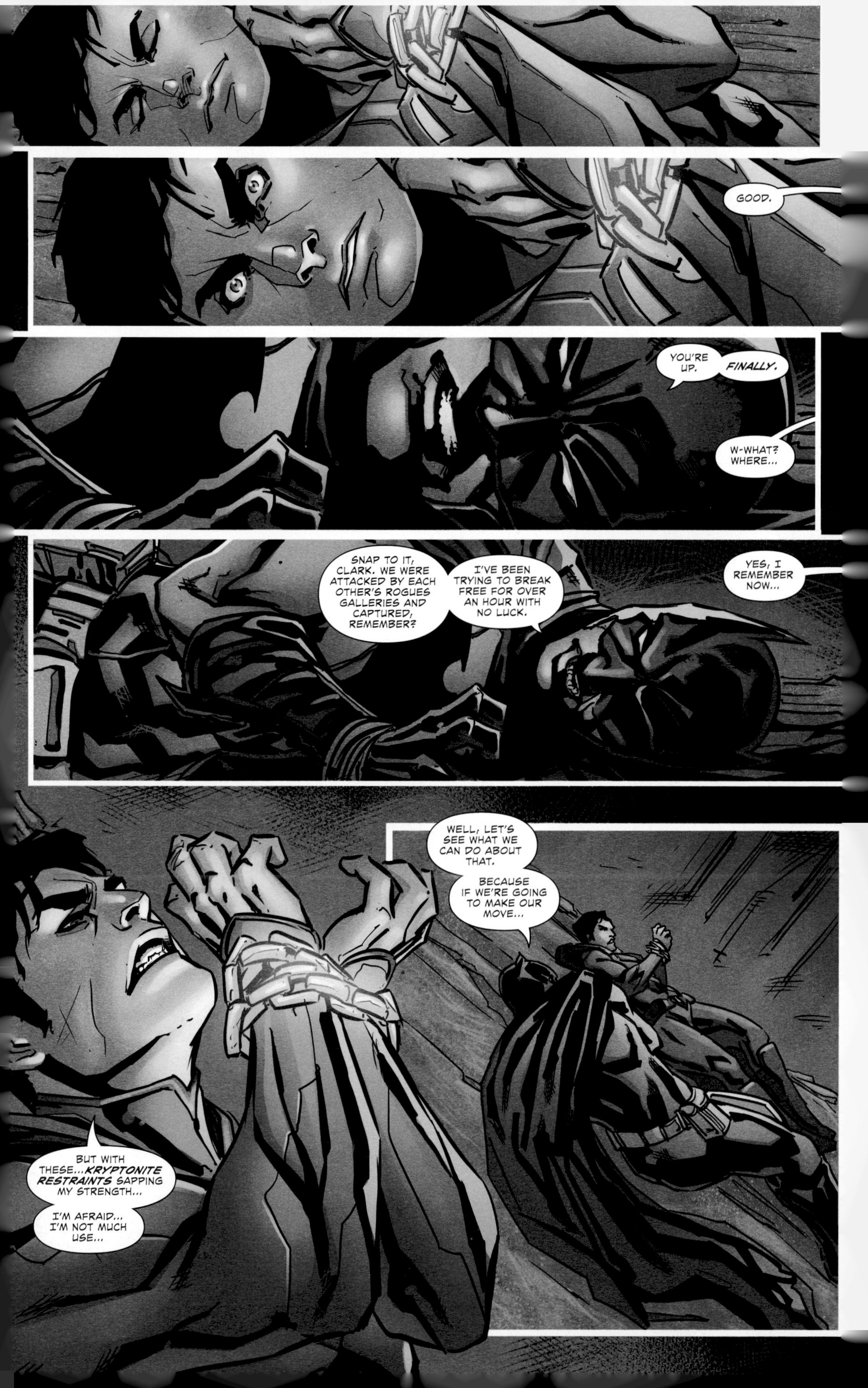
GOOD.
YOU'RE UP. *FINALLY.*
W-WHAT? WHERE...
SNAP TO IT, CLARK. WE WERE ATTACKED BY EACH OTHER'S ROGUES GALLERIES AND CAPTURED, REMEMBER?
I'VE BEEN TRYING TO BREAK FREE FOR OVER AN HOUR WITH NO LUCK.
YES, I REMEMBER NOW...
WELL, LET'S SEE WHAT WE CAN DO ABOUT THAT.
BECAUSE IF WE'RE GOING TO MAKE OUR MOVE...
BUT WITH THESE...*KRYPTONITE RESTRAINTS* SAPPING MY STRENGTH...
I'M AFRAID... I'M NOT MUCH USE...

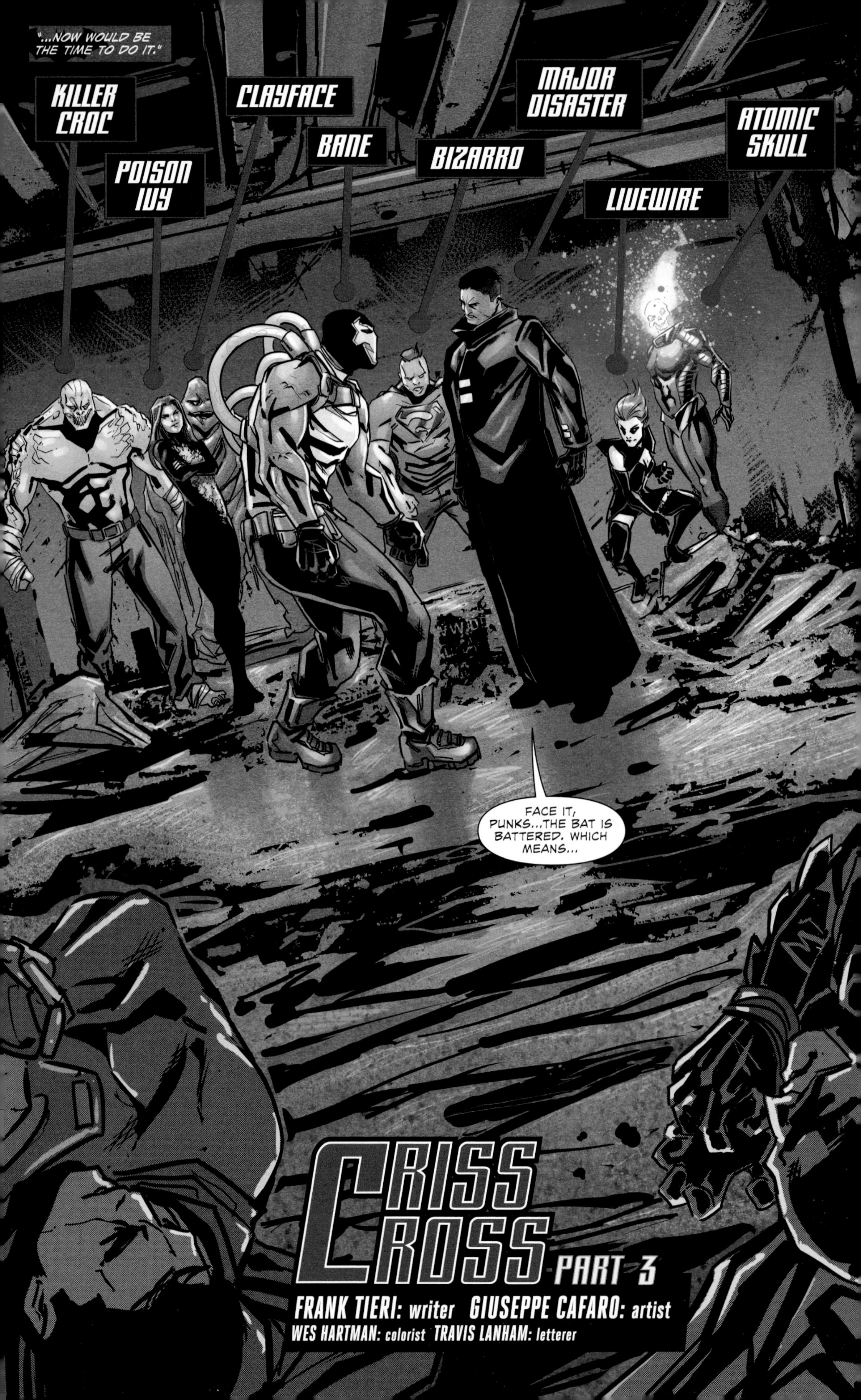
"...NOW WOULD BE THE TIME TO DO IT."
KILLER CROC
POISON IVY
CLAYFACE
BANE
BIZARRO
MAJOR DISASTER
LIVEWIRE
ATOMIC SKULL
FACE IT, PUNKS...THE BAT IS BATTERED. WHICH MEANS...
CRISS CROSS PART 3
FRANK TIERI: writer GIUSEPPE CAFARO: artist
WES HARTMAN: colorist TRAVIS LANHAM: letterer

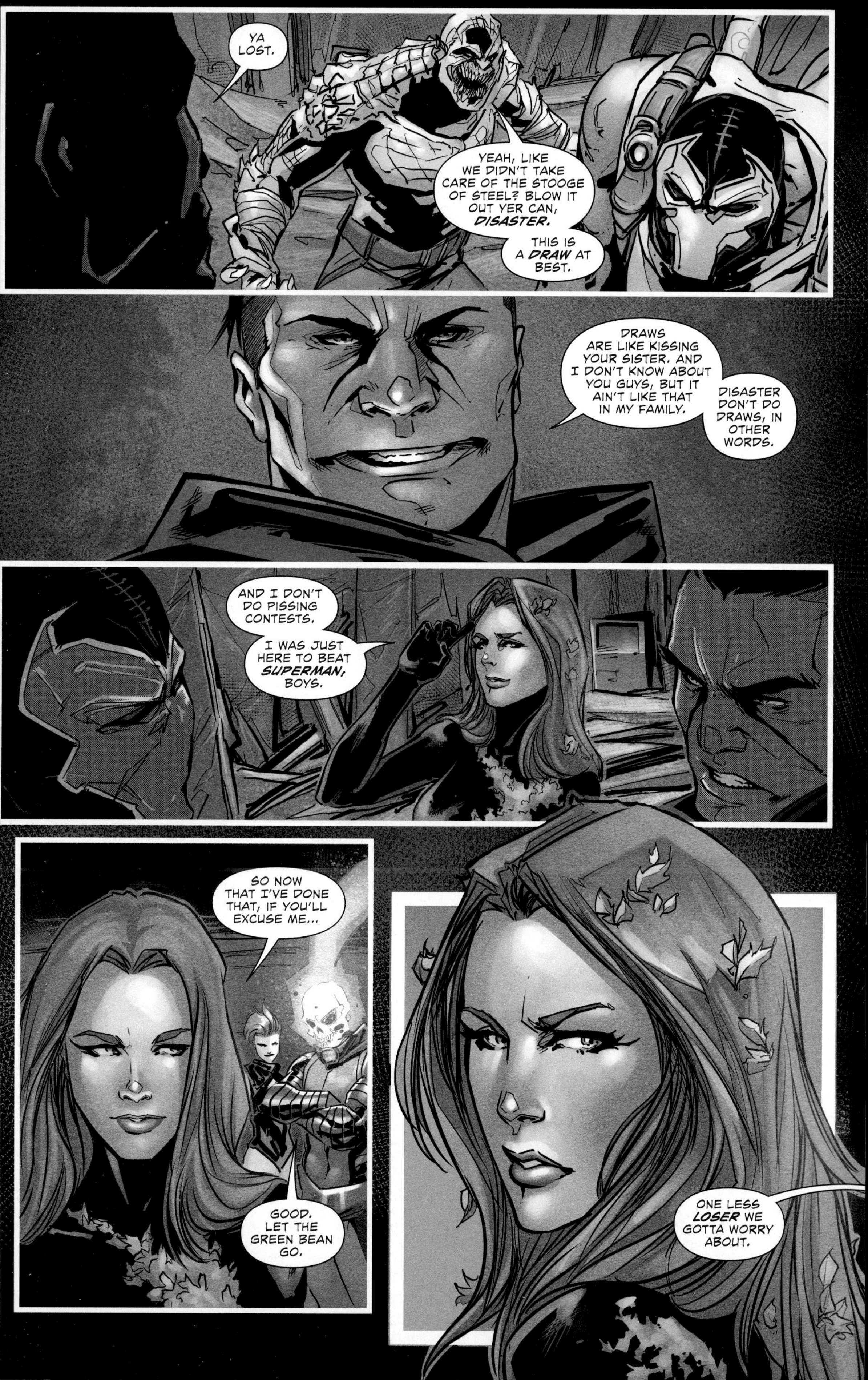
YA LOST.
YEAH, LIKE WE DIDN'T TAKE CARE OF THE STOOGE OF STEEL? BLOW IT OUT YER CAN, DISASTER.
THIS IS A DRAW AT BEST.
DRAWS ARE LIKE KISSING YOUR SISTER. AND I DON'T KNOW ABOUT YOU GUYS, BUT IT AIN'T LIKE THAT IN MY FAMILY.
DISASTER DON'T DO DRAWS, IN OTHER WORDS.
AND I DON'T DO PISSING CONTESTS.
I WAS JUST HERE TO BEAT SUPERMAN, BOYS.
SO NOW THAT I'VE DONE THAT, IF YOU'LL EXCUSE ME...
GOOD. LET THE GREEN BEAN GO.
ONE LESS LOSER WE GOTTA WORRY ABOUT.

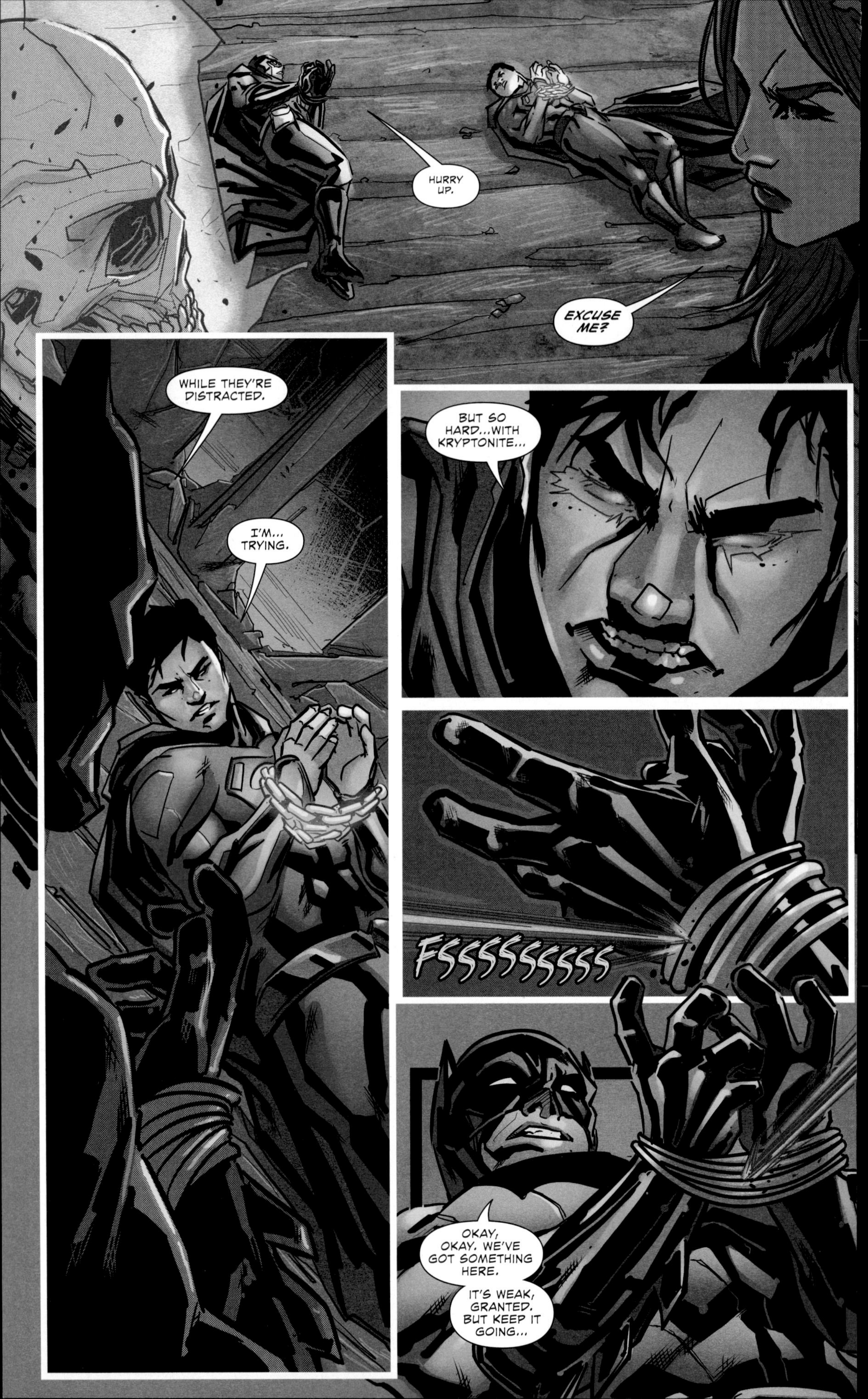
HURRY UP.
EXCUSE ME?
WHILE THEY'RE DISTRACTED.
I'M... TRYING.
BUT SO HARD...WITH KRYPTONITE...
FSSSSSSSSS
OKAY, OKAY. WE'VE GOT SOMETHING HERE.
IT'S WEAK, GRANTED. BUT KEEP IT GOING...

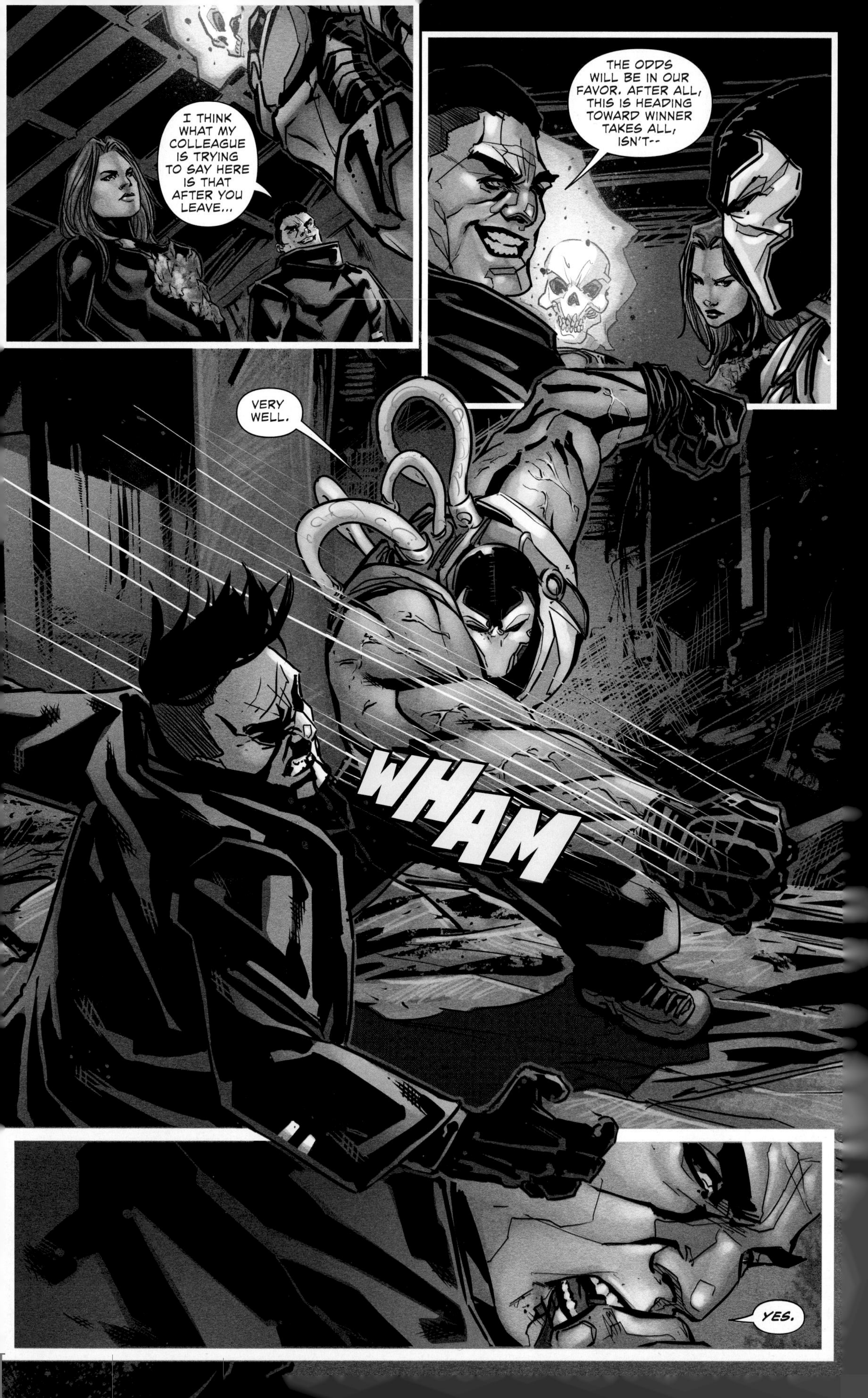
I THINK WHAT MY COLLEAGUE IS TRYING TO SAY HERE IS THAT AFTER YOU LEAVE...
THE ODDS WILL BE IN OUR FAVOR. AFTER ALL, THIS IS HEADING TOWARD WINNER TAKES ALL, ISN'T--
VERY WELL.
WHAM
YES.

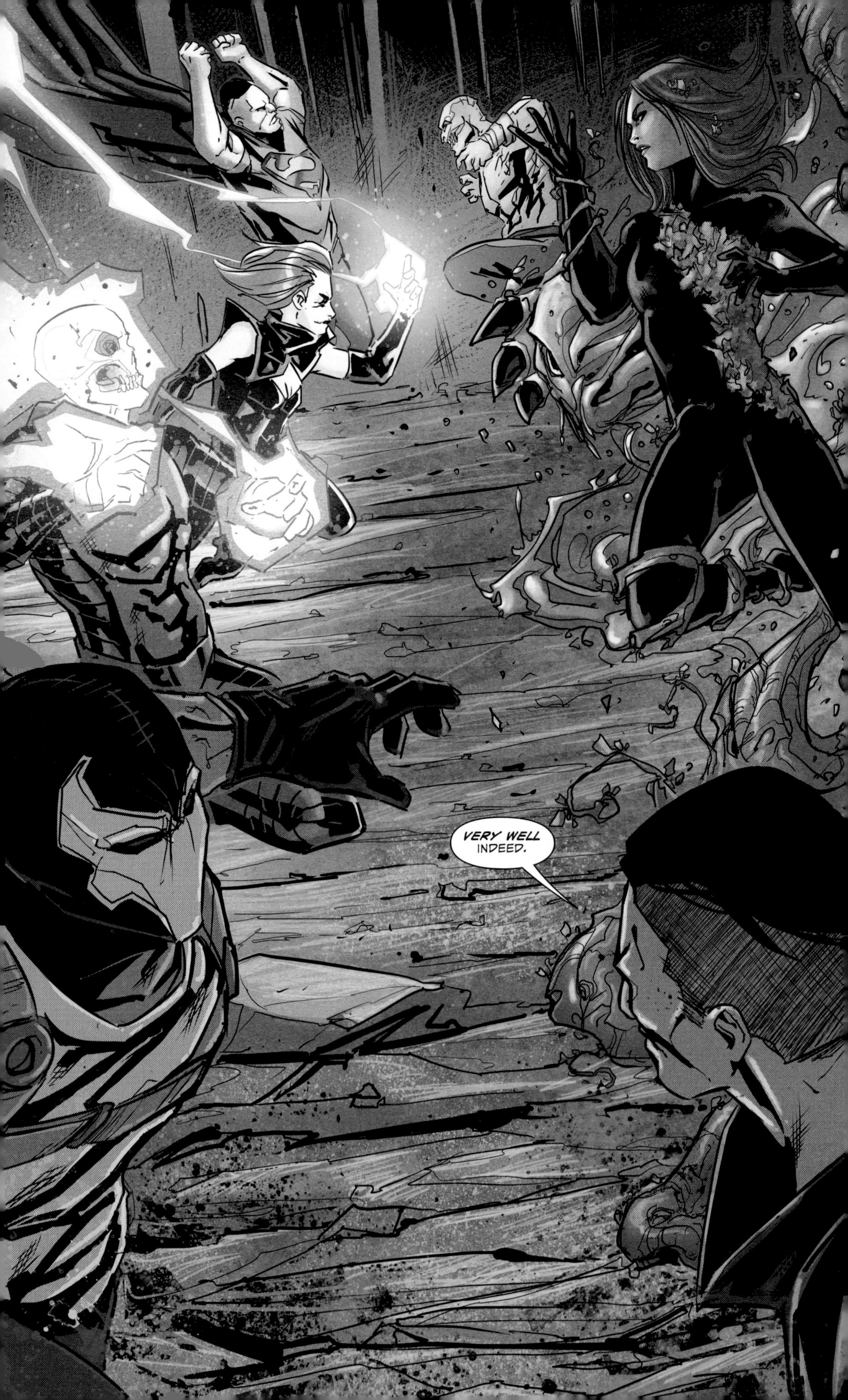
VERY WELL INDEED.

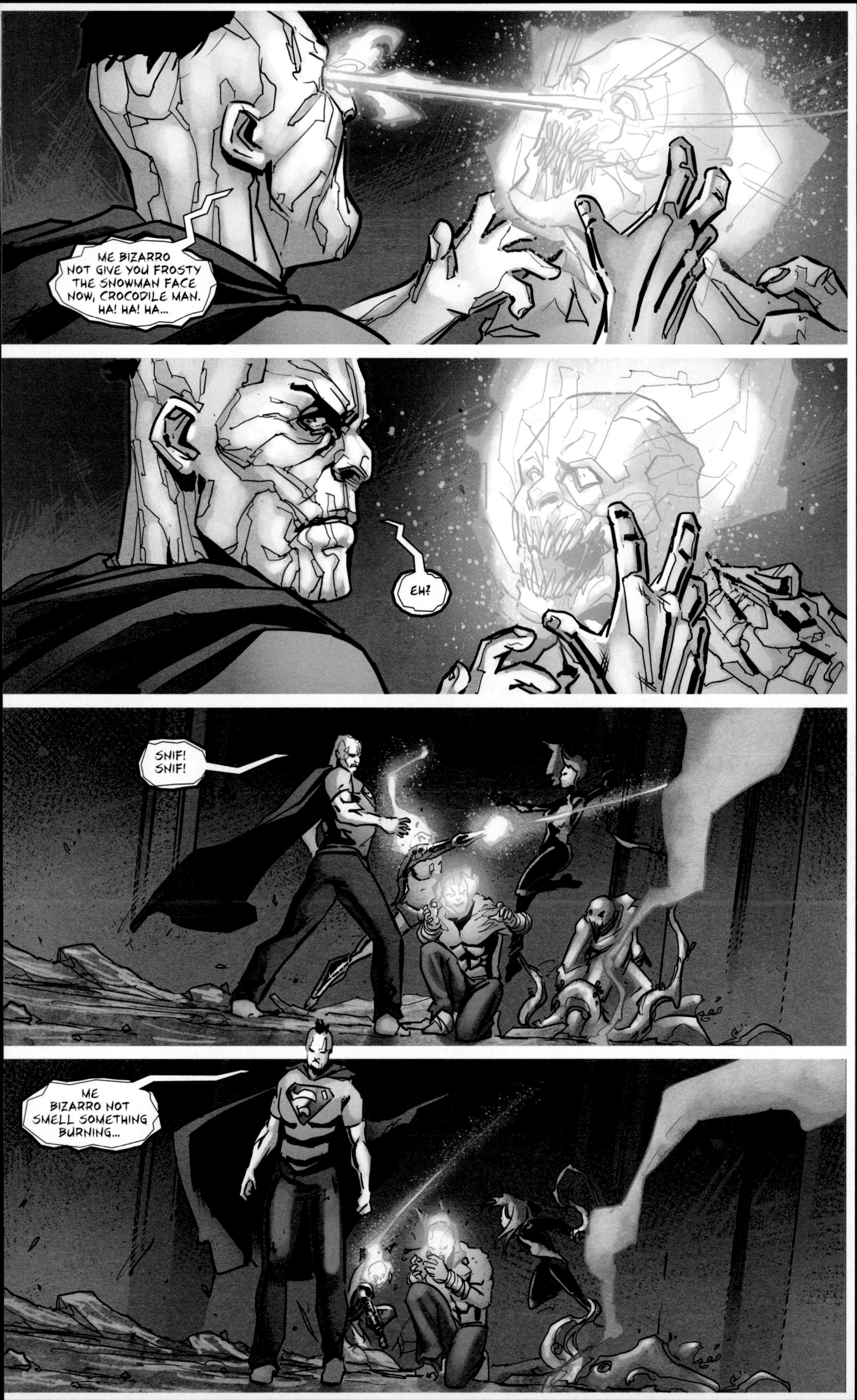
ME BIZARRO NOT GIVE YOU FROSTY THE SNOWMAN FACE NOW, CROCODILE MAN. HA! HA! HA...
EH?
SNIF! SNIF!
ME BIZARRO NOT SMELL SOMETHING BURNING...

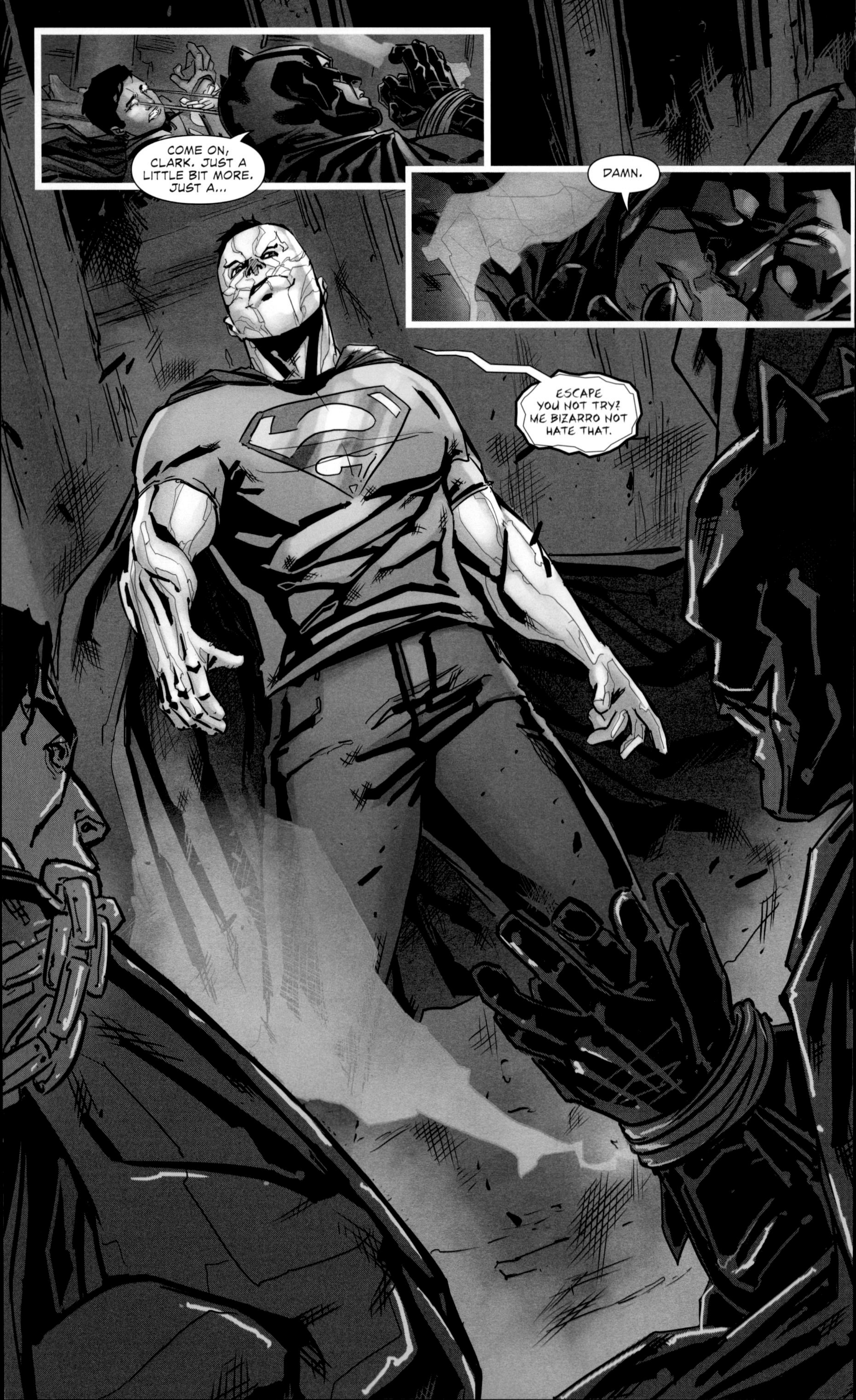
COME ON, CLARK. JUST A LITTLE BIT MORE. JUST A...
DAMN.
ESCAPE YOU NOT TRY? ME BIZARRO NOT HATE THAT.

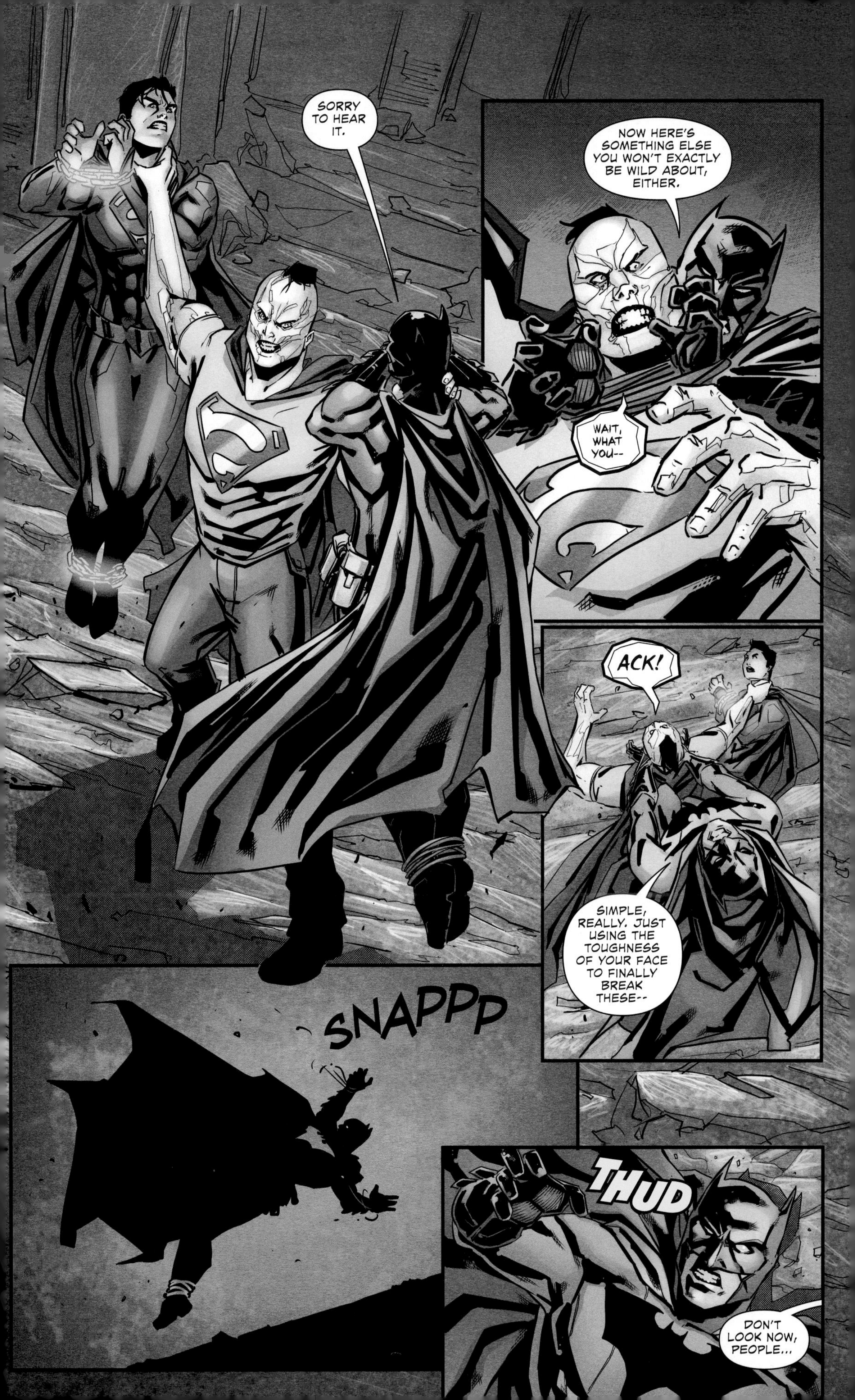
SORRY TO HEAR IT.
NOW HERE'S SOMETHING ELSE YOU WON'T EXACTLY BE WILD ABOUT, EITHER.
WAIT, WHAT YOU--
ACK!
SIMPLE, REALLY. JUST USING THE TOUGHNESS OF YOUR FACE TO FINALLY BREAK THESE--
SNAPPP
THUD
DON'T LOOK NOW, PEOPLE...

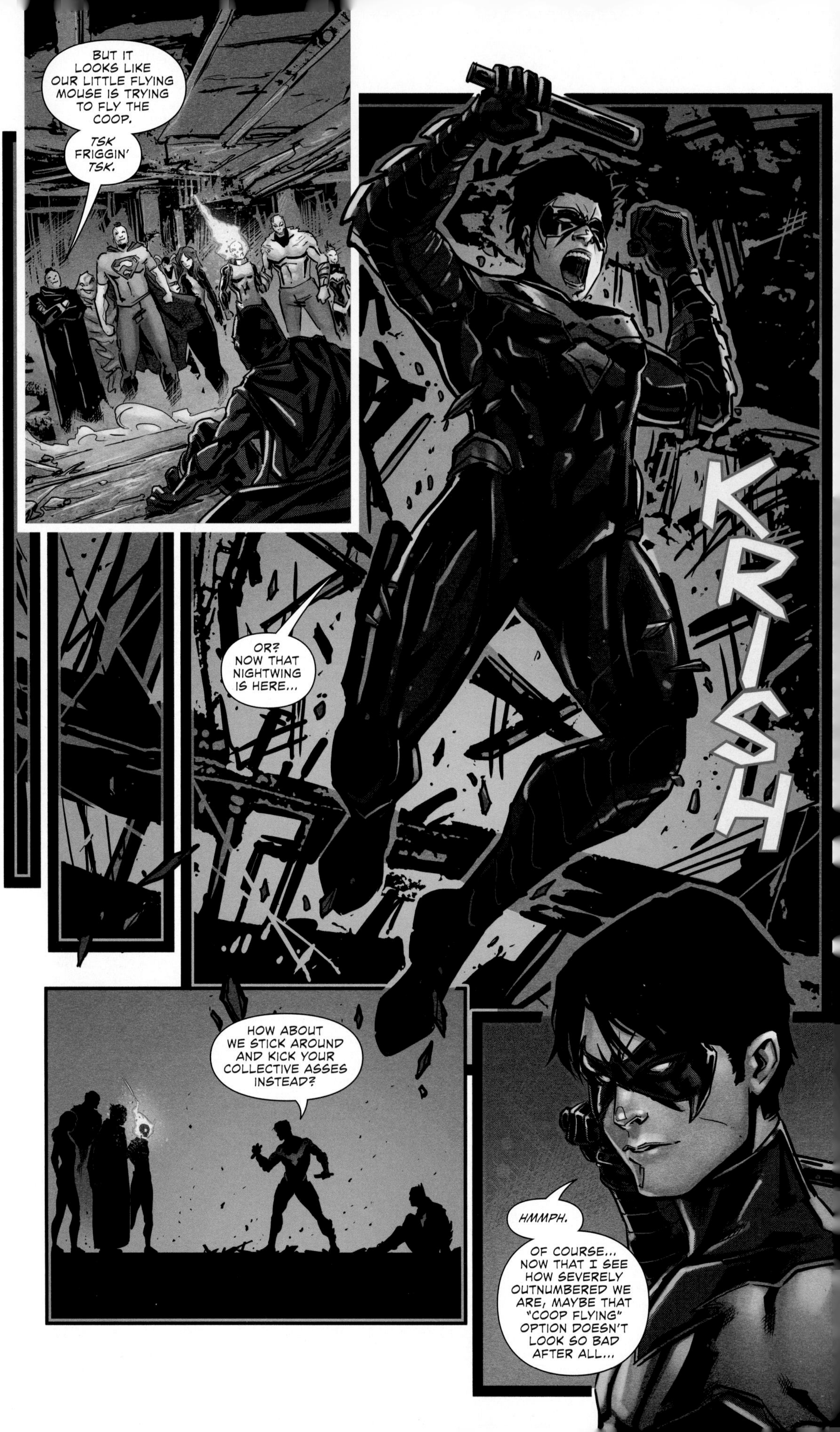
BUT IT LOOKS LIKE OUR LITTLE FLYING MOUSE IS TRYING TO FLY THE COOP.
TSK FRIGGIN' TSK.
OR? NOW THAT NIGHTWING IS HERE...
KRISH
HOW ABOUT WE STICK AROUND AND KICK YOUR COLLECTIVE ASSES INSTEAD?
HMMPH.
OF COURSE... NOW THAT I SEE HOW SEVERELY OUTNUMBERED WE ARE, MAYBE THAT "COOP FLYING" OPTION DOESN'T LOOK SO BAD AFTER ALL...

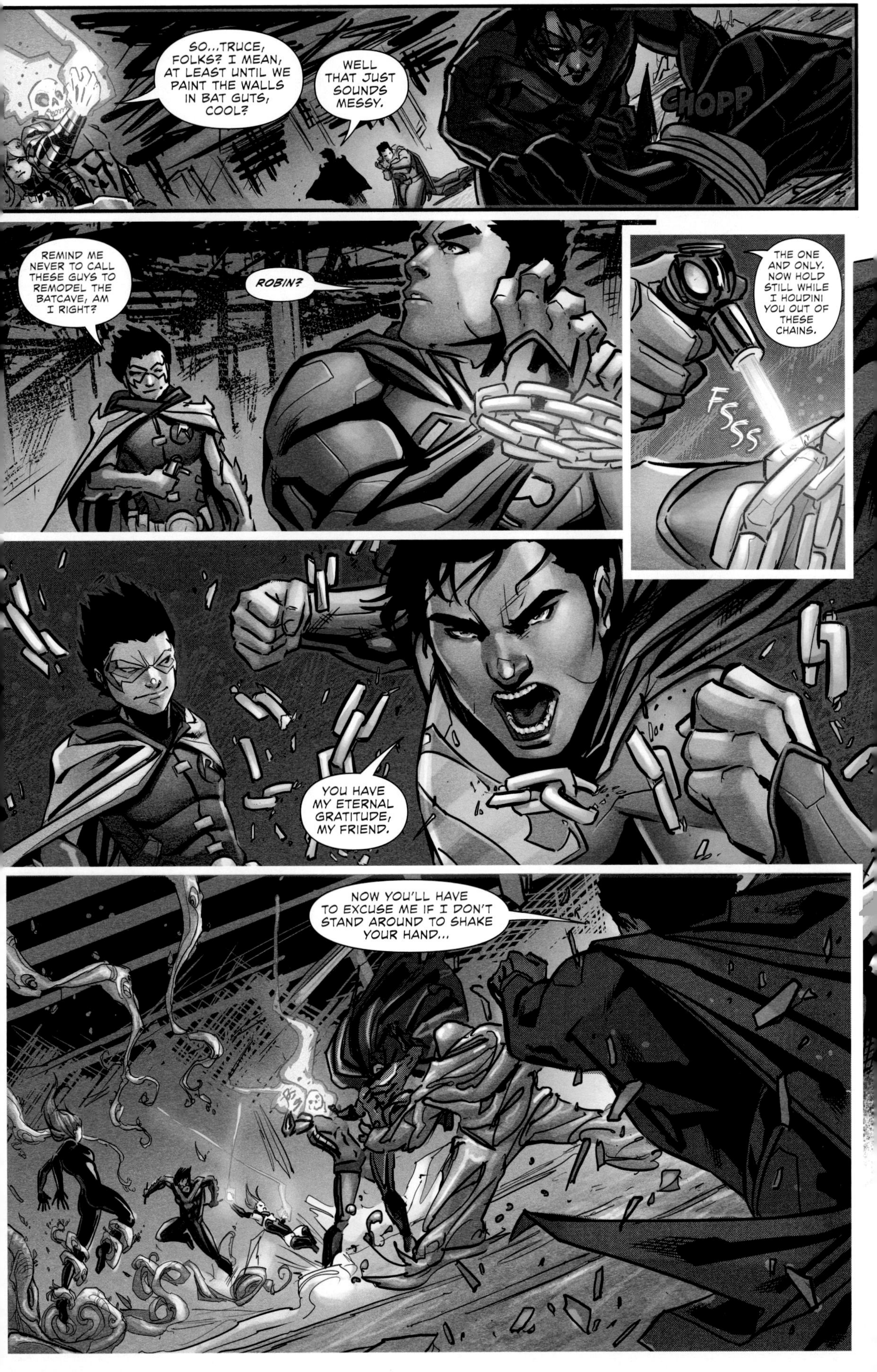

SO...TRUCE, FOLKS? I MEAN, AT LEAST UNTIL WE PAINT THE WALLS IN BAT GUTS, COOL?
WELL THAT JUST SOUNDS MESSY.
CHOPP
REMIND ME NEVER TO CALL THESE GUYS TO REMODEL THE BATCAVE, AM I RIGHT?
ROBIN?
THE ONE AND ONLY. NOW HOLD STILL WHILE I HOUDINI YOU OUT OF THESE CHAINS.
FSSS
YOU HAVE MY ETERNAL GRATITUDE, MY FRIEND.
NOW YOU'LL HAVE TO EXCUSE ME IF I DON'T STAND AROUND TO SHAKE YOUR HAND...

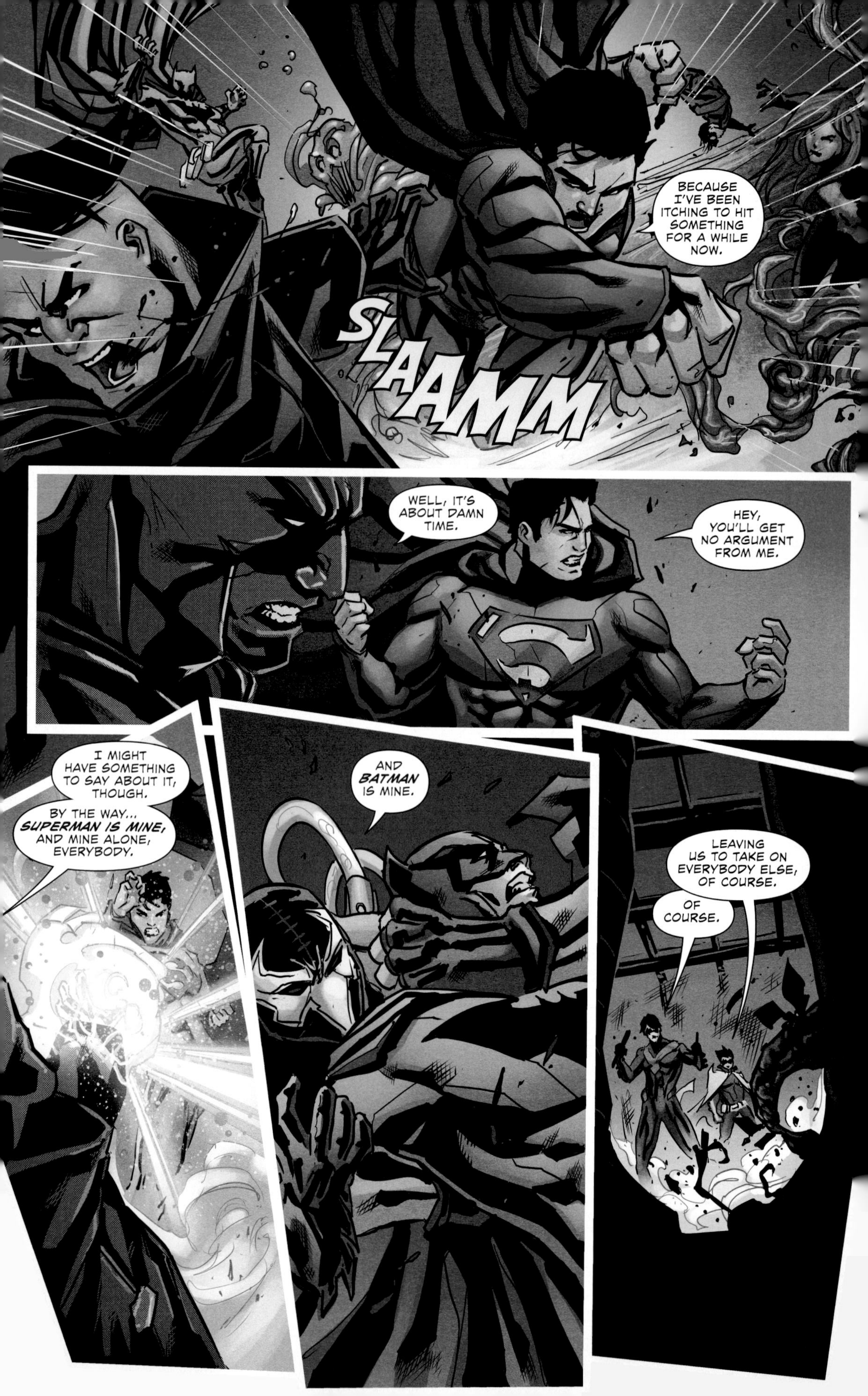
BECAUSE I'VE BEEN ITCHING TO HIT SOMETHING FOR A WHILE NOW.
SLAAMM
WELL, IT'S ABOUT DAMN TIME.
HEY, YOU'LL GET NO ARGUMENT FROM ME.
I MIGHT HAVE SOMETHING TO SAY ABOUT IT, THOUGH.
BY THE WAY... SUPERMAN IS MINE, AND MINE ALONE, EVERYBODY.
AND BATMAN IS MINE.
LEAVING US TO TAKE ON EVERYBODY ELSE, OF COURSE.
OF COURSE.

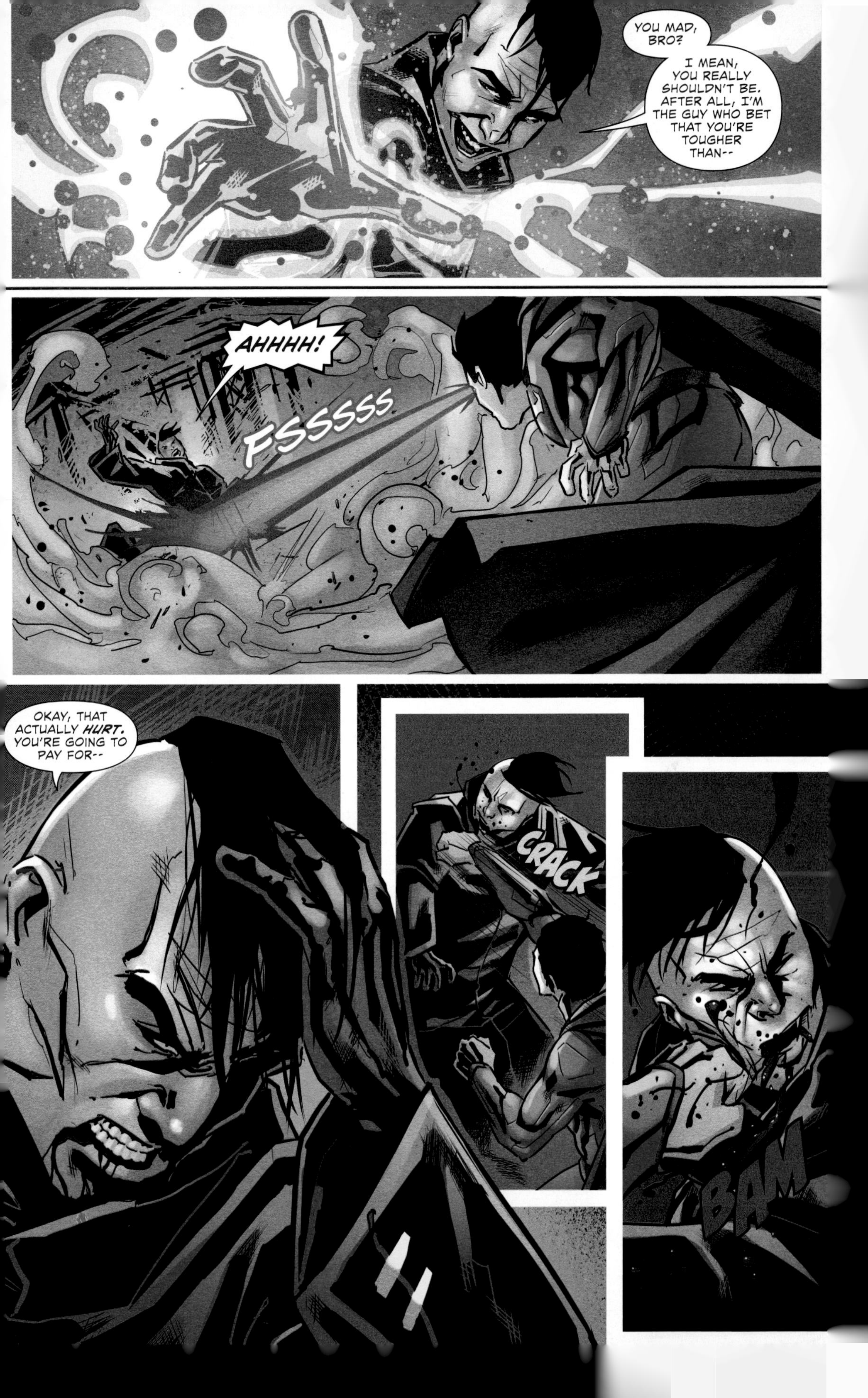
YOU MAD, BRO?
I MEAN, YOU REALLY SHOULDN'T BE. AFTER ALL, I'M THE GUY WHO BET THAT YOU'RE TOUGHER THAN--
AHHHH!
FSSSSS
OKAY, THAT ACTUALLY HURT. YOU'RE GOING TO PAY FOR--
CRACK
BAM

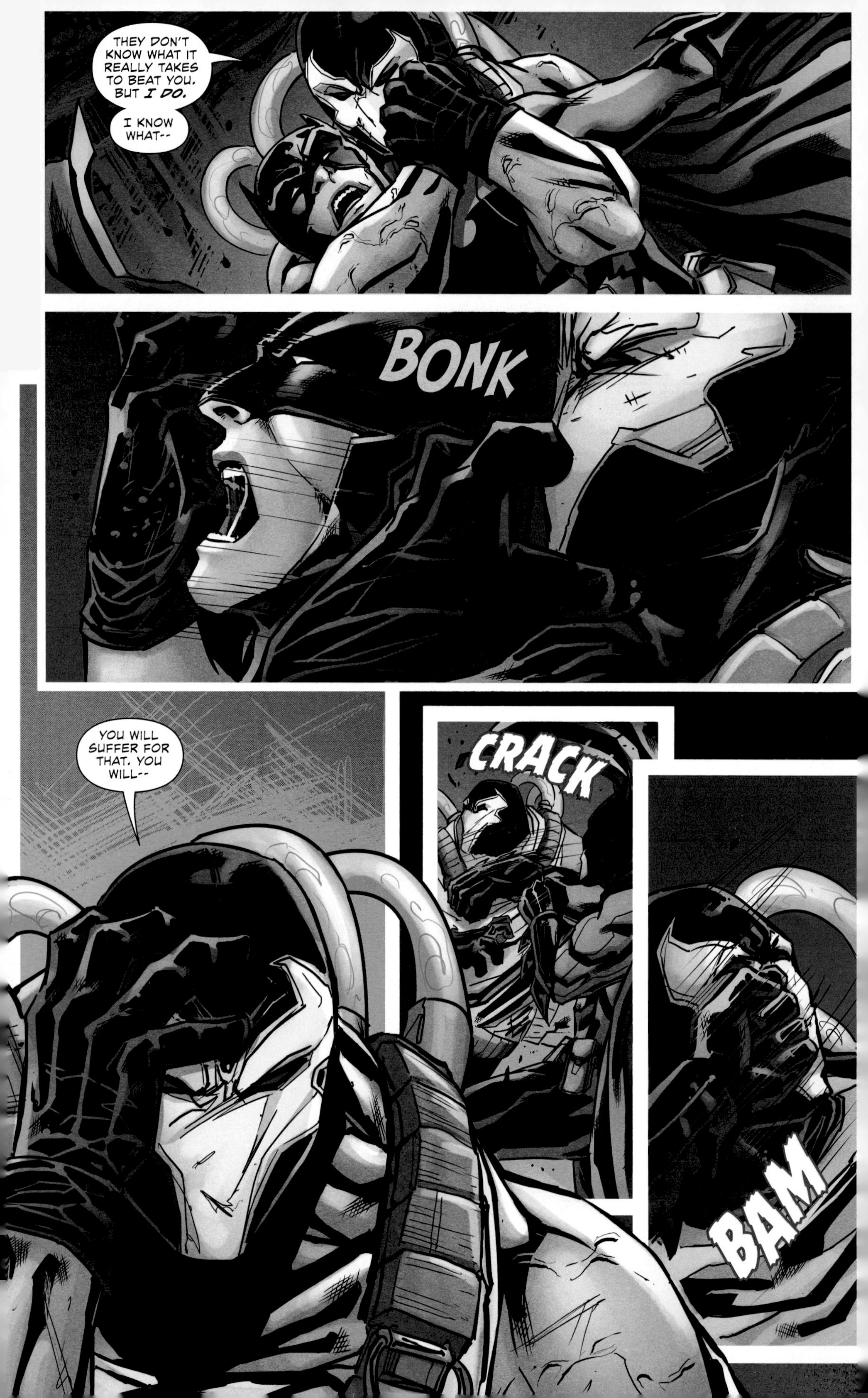
THEY DON'T KNOW WHAT IT REALLY TAKES TO BEAT YOU. BUT *I DO.*
I KNOW WHAT--
BONK
YOU WILL SUFFER FOR THAT. YOU WILL--
CRACK
BAM

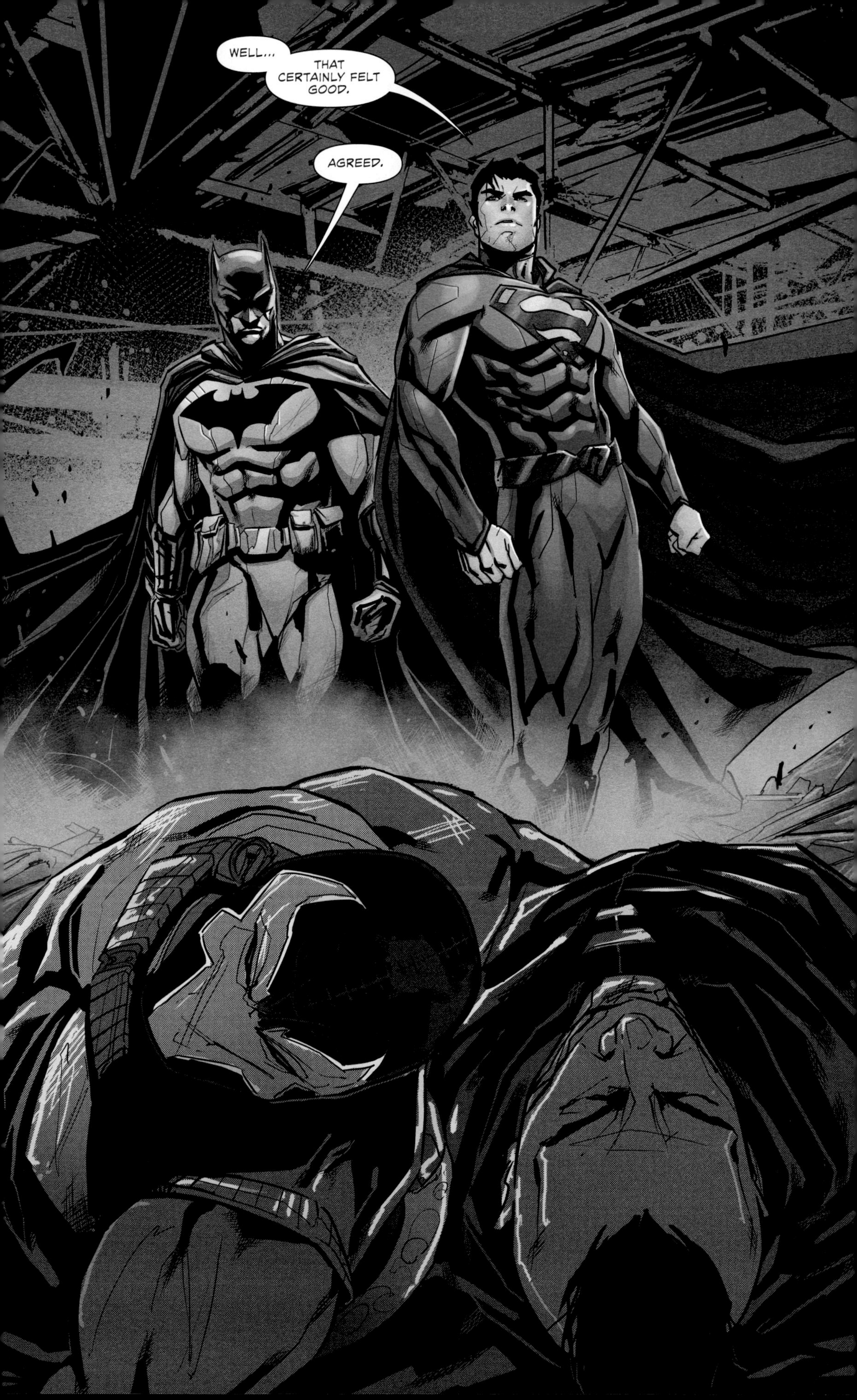
WELL...
THAT CERTAINLY FELT GOOD.
AGREED.

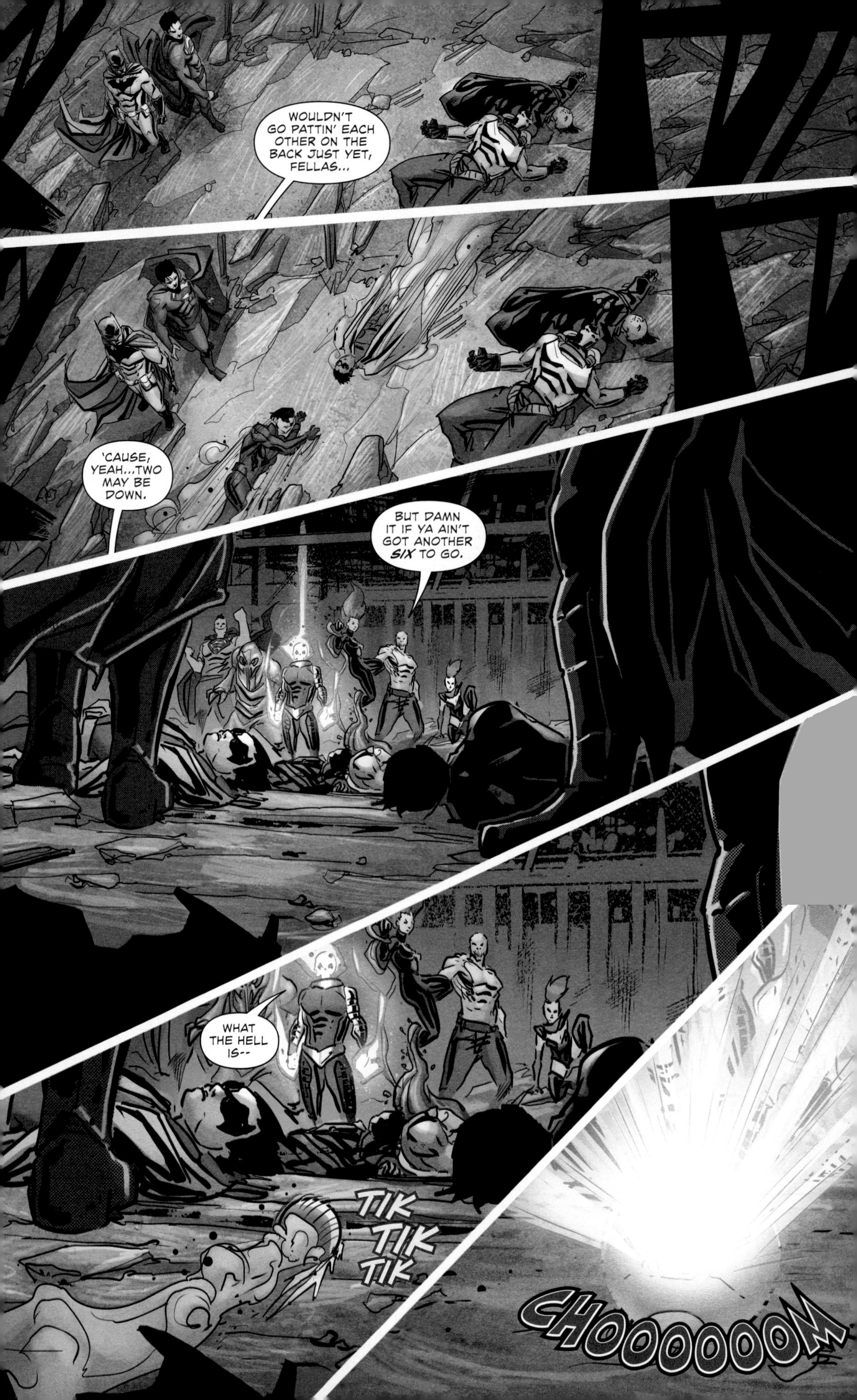
WOULDN'T GO PATTIN' EACH OTHER ON THE BACK JUST YET, FELLAS...
'CAUSE, YEAH...TWO MAY BE DOWN.
BUT DAMN IT IF YA AIN'T GOT ANOTHER SIX TO GO.
WHAT THE HELL IS--
TIK TIK TIK
CHOOOOOOM

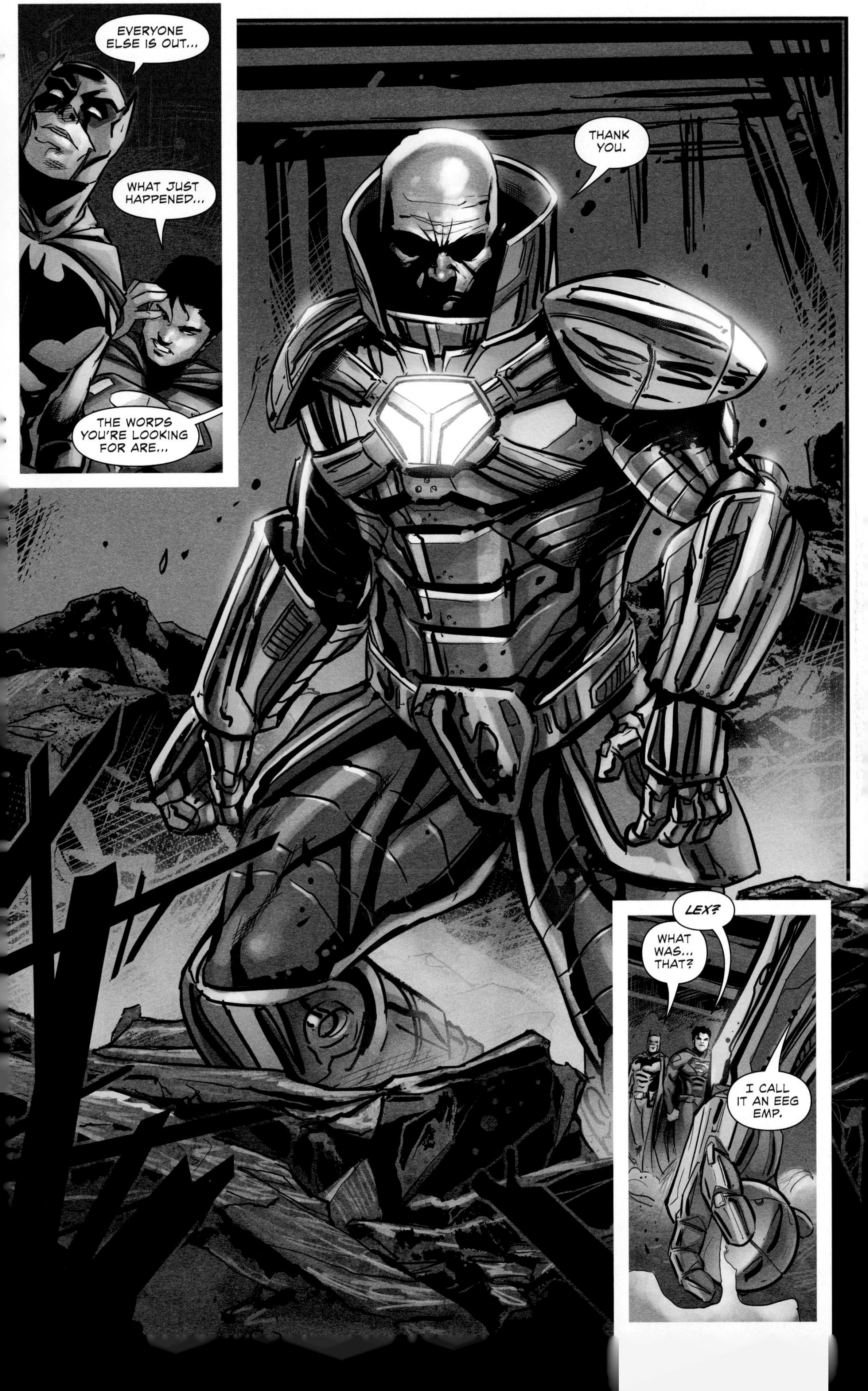
EVERYONE ELSE IS OUT...
WHAT JUST HAPPENED...
THE WORDS YOU'RE LOOKING FOR ARE...
THANK YOU.
LEX?
WHAT WAS... THAT?
I CALL IT AN EEG EMP.

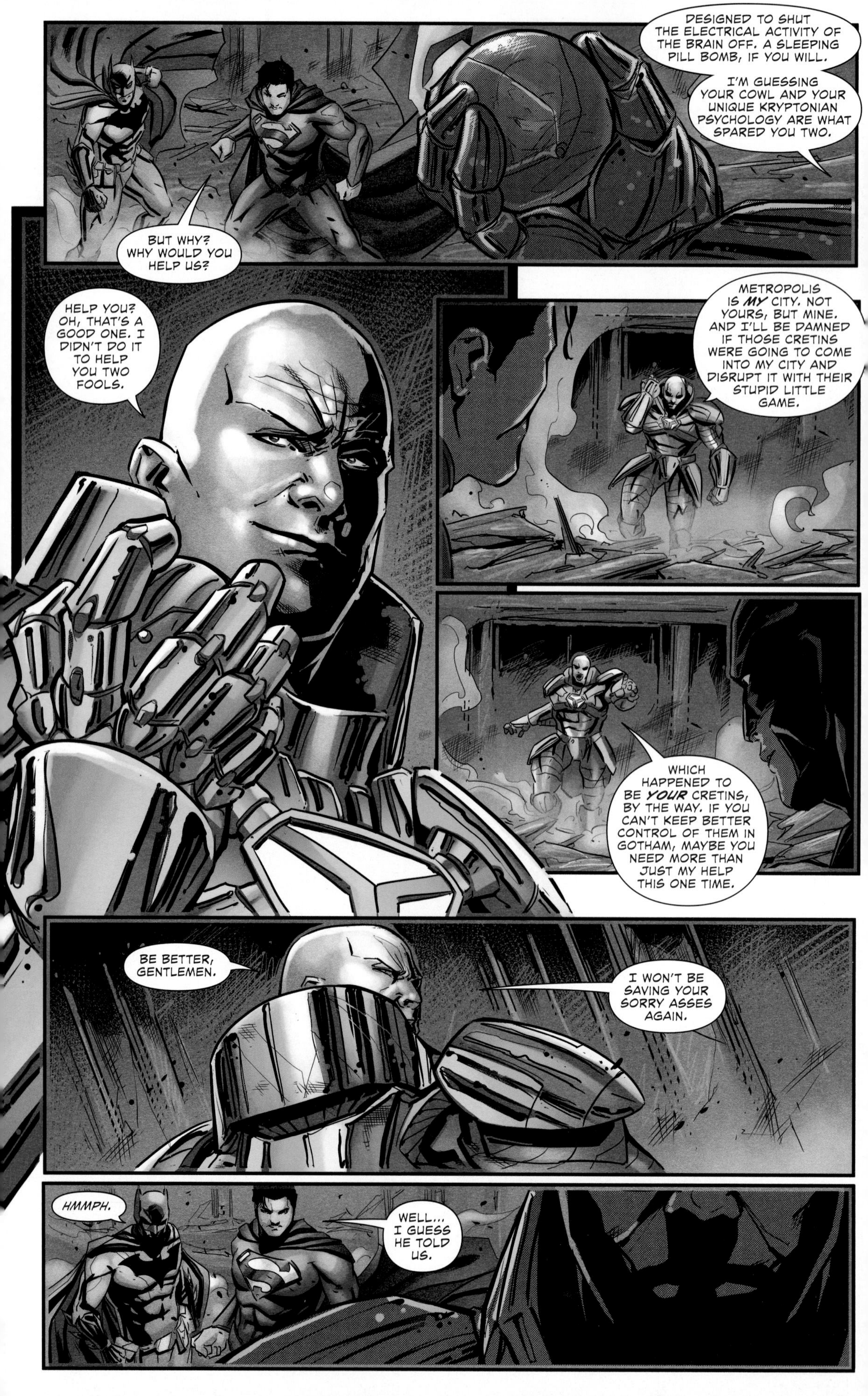
DESIGNED TO SHUT THE ELECTRICAL ACTIVITY OF THE BRAIN OFF. A SLEEPING PILL BOMB, IF YOU WILL.
I'M GUESSING YOUR COWL AND YOUR UNIQUE KRYPTONIAN PSYCHOLOGY ARE WHAT SPARED YOU TWO.
BUT WHY? WHY WOULD YOU HELP US?
HELP YOU? OH, THAT'S A GOOD ONE. I DIDN'T DO IT TO HELP YOU TWO FOOLS.
METROPOLIS IS *MY* CITY. NOT YOURS, BUT MINE. AND I'LL BE DAMNED IF THOSE CRETINS WERE GOING TO COME INTO MY CITY AND DISRUPT IT WITH THEIR STUPID LITTLE GAME.
WHICH HAPPENED TO BE *YOUR* CRETINS, BY THE WAY. IF YOU CAN'T KEEP BETTER CONTROL OF THEM IN GOTHAM, MAYBE YOU NEED MORE THAN JUST MY HELP THIS ONE TIME.
BE BETTER, GENTLEMEN.
I WON'T BE SAVING YOUR SORRY ASSES AGAIN.
HMMPH.
WELL... I GUESS HE TOLD US.

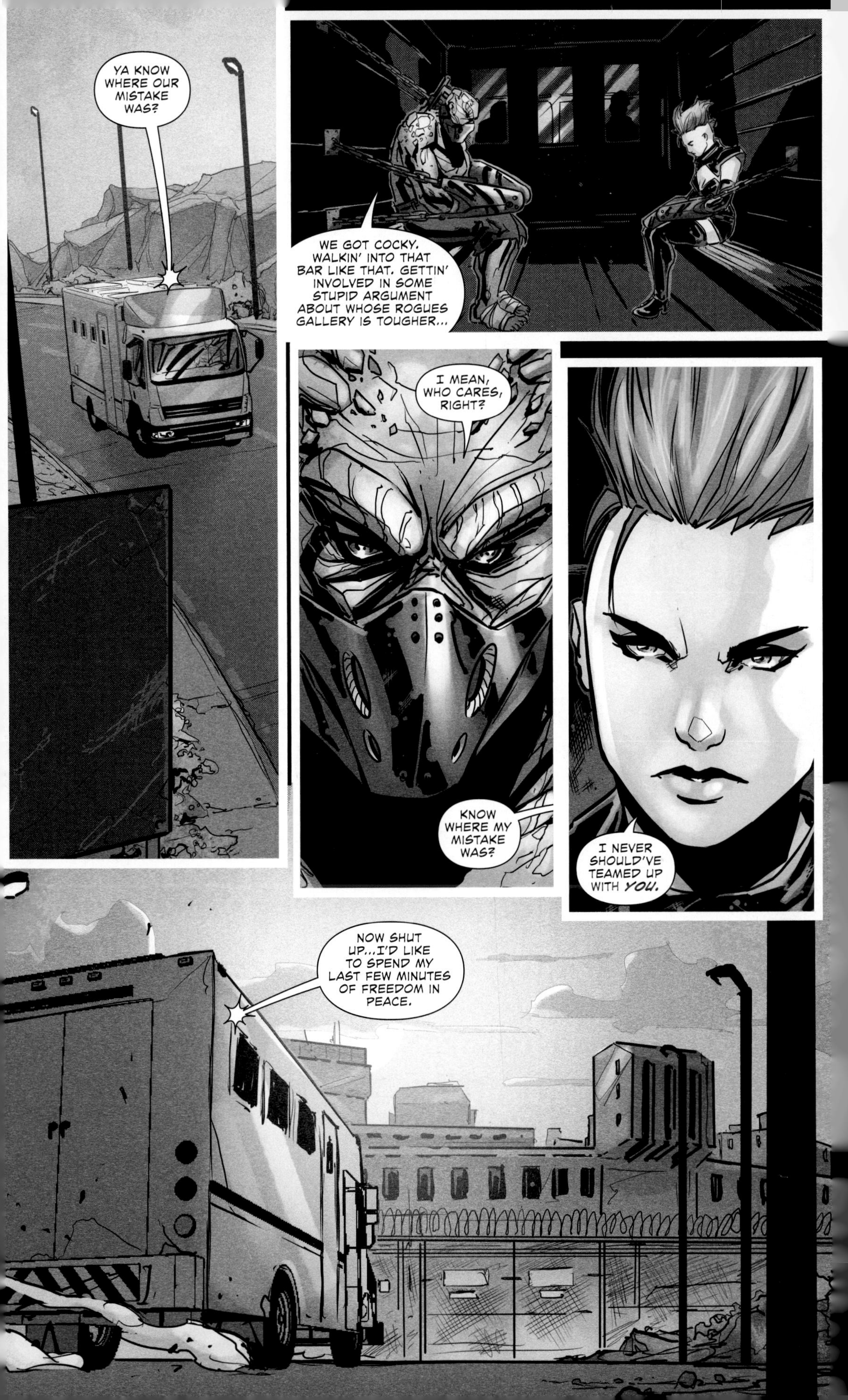
YA KNOW WHERE OUR MISTAKE WAS?
WE GOT COCKY. WALKIN' INTO THAT BAR LIKE THAT. GETTIN' INVOLVED IN SOME STUPID ARGUMENT ABOUT WHOSE ROGUES GALLERY IS TOUGHER...
I MEAN, WHO CARES, RIGHT?
KNOW WHERE MY MISTAKE WAS?
I NEVER SHOULD'VE TEAMED UP WITH *YOU.*
NOW SHUT UP...I'D LIKE TO SPEND MY LAST FEW MINUTES OF FREEDOM IN PEACE.

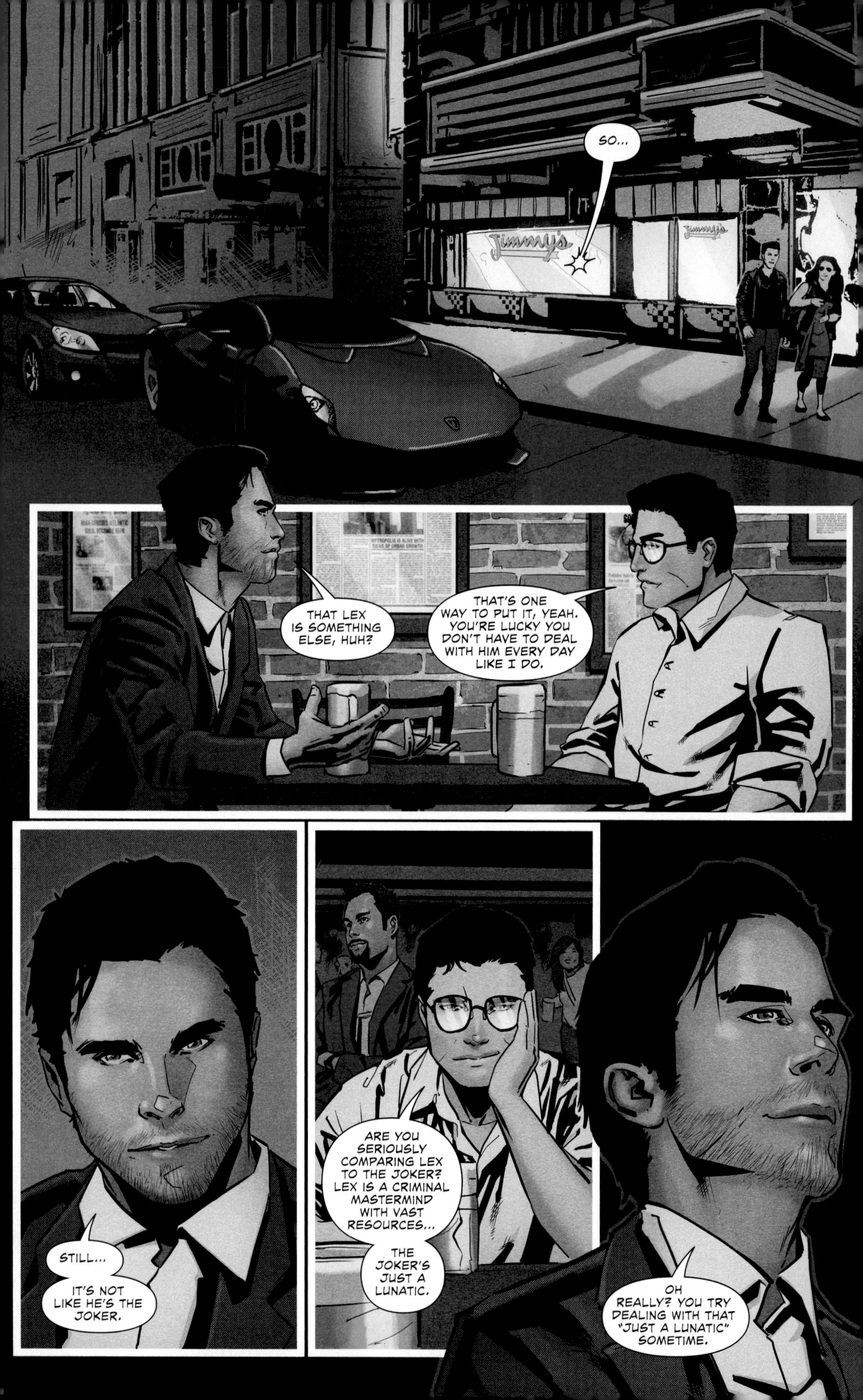
Jimmy's
SO...
THAT LEX IS SOMETHING ELSE, HUH?
THAT'S ONE WAY TO PUT IT, YEAH. YOU'RE LUCKY YOU DON'T HAVE TO DEAL WITH HIM EVERY DAY LIKE I DO.
STILL...
IT'S NOT LIKE HE'S THE JOKER.
ARE YOU SERIOUSLY COMPARING LEX TO THE JOKER? LEX IS A CRIMINAL MASTERMIND WITH VAST RESOURCES...
THE JOKER'S JUST A LUNATIC.
OH REALLY? YOU TRY DEALING WITH THAT "JUST A LUNATIC" SOMETIME.

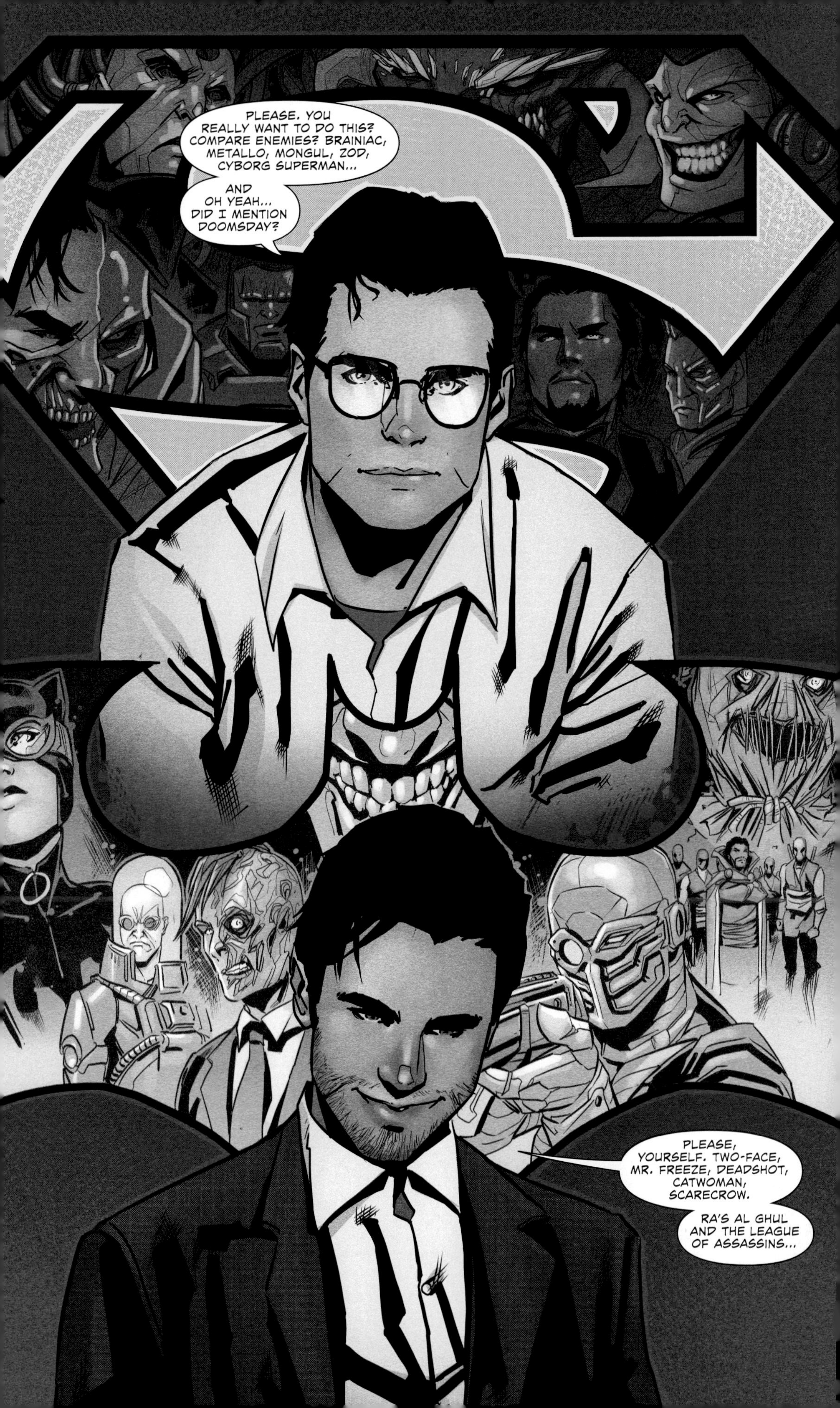
PLEASE. YOU REALLY WANT TO DO THIS? COMPARE ENEMIES? BRAINIAC, METALLO, MONGUL, ZOD, CYBORG SUPERMAN...
AND OH YEAH... DID I MENTION DOOMSDAY?
PLEASE, YOURSELF. TWO-FACE, MR. FREEZE, DEADSHOT, CATWOMAN, SCARECROW.
RA'S AL GHUL AND THE LEAGUE OF ASSASSINS...

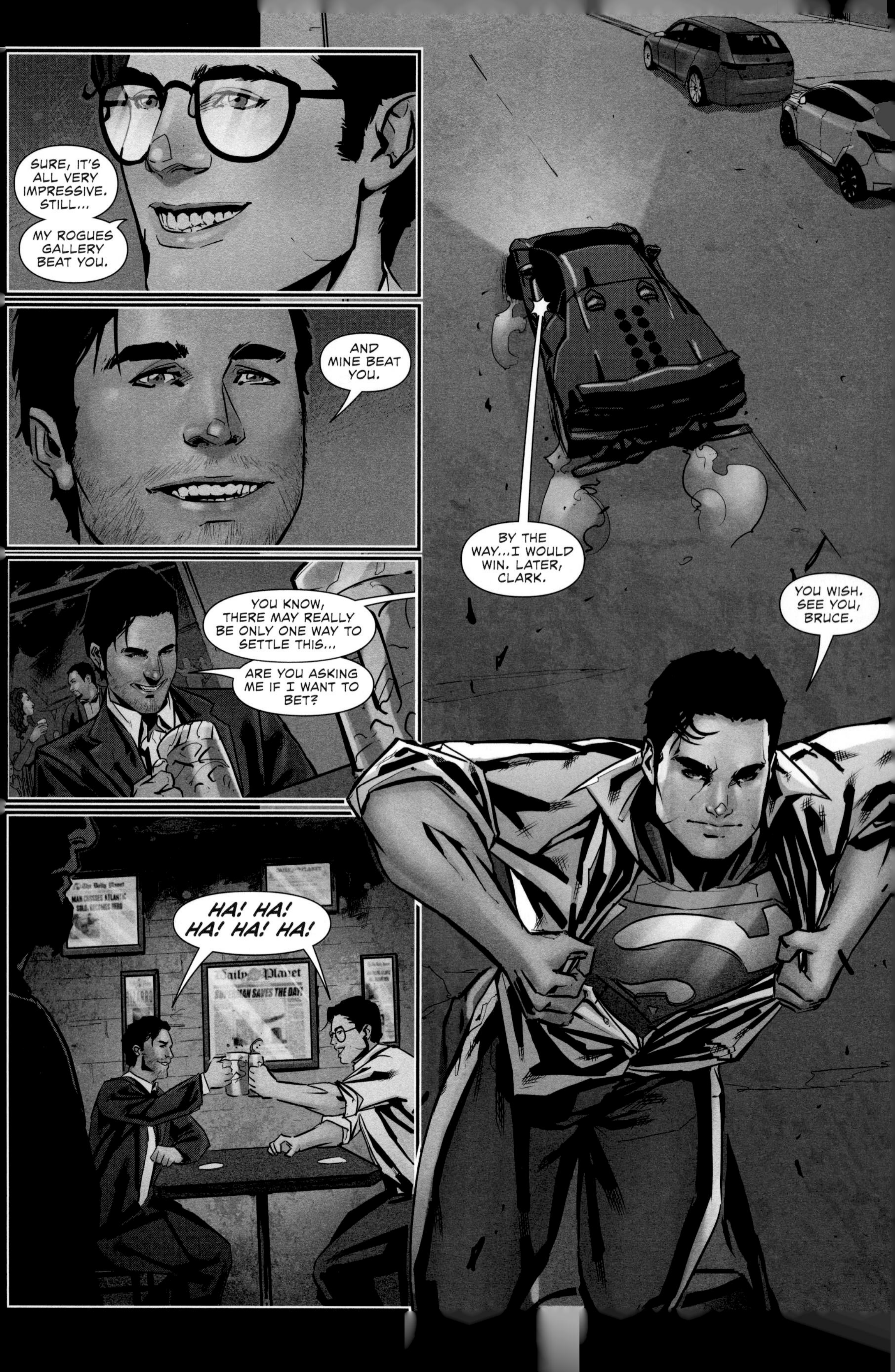
SURE, IT'S ALL VERY IMPRESSIVE. STILL...
MY ROGUES GALLERY BEAT YOU.
AND MINE BEAT YOU.
YOU KNOW, THERE MAY REALLY BE ONLY ONE WAY TO SETTLE THIS...
ARE YOU ASKING ME IF I WANT TO BET?
HA! HA! HA! HA! HA!
BY THE WAY...I WOULD WIN. LATER, CLARK.
YOU WISH. SEE YOU, BRUCE.

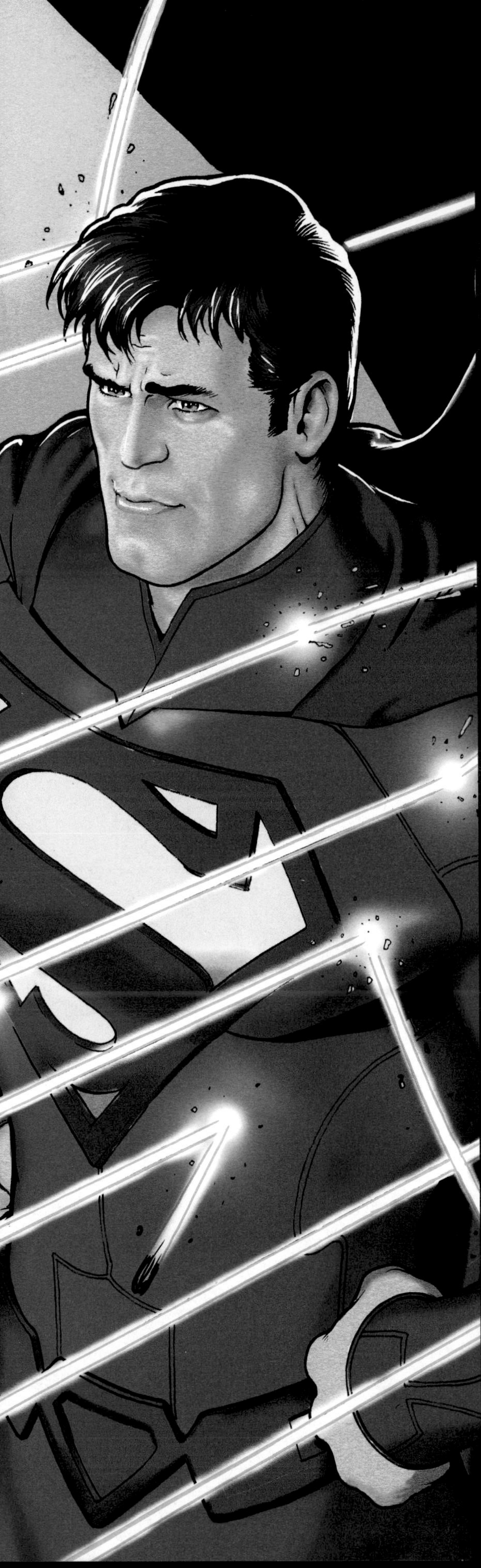

VARIANT COVER GALLERY

BATMAN/SUPERMAN #28
COLORING BOOK VARIANT COVER
BY FREDDIE E. WILLIAMS II

BATMAN/SUPERMAN #29
VARIANT COVER
BY NEAL ADAMS AND JOSH ADAMS
WITH ALEX SINCLAIR

BATMAN/SUPERMAN #30
VARIANT COVERS BY KEVIN MAGUIRE

BATMAN/SUPERMAN #31
VARIANT COVER BY
JOHN ROMITA JR. AND KLAUS JANSON
WITH DAVE McCAIG

BATMAN/SUPERMAN #32
SECOND PRINTING
COVER BY YANICK PAQUETTE
WITH NATHAN FAIRBAIRN

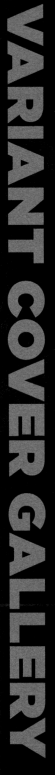

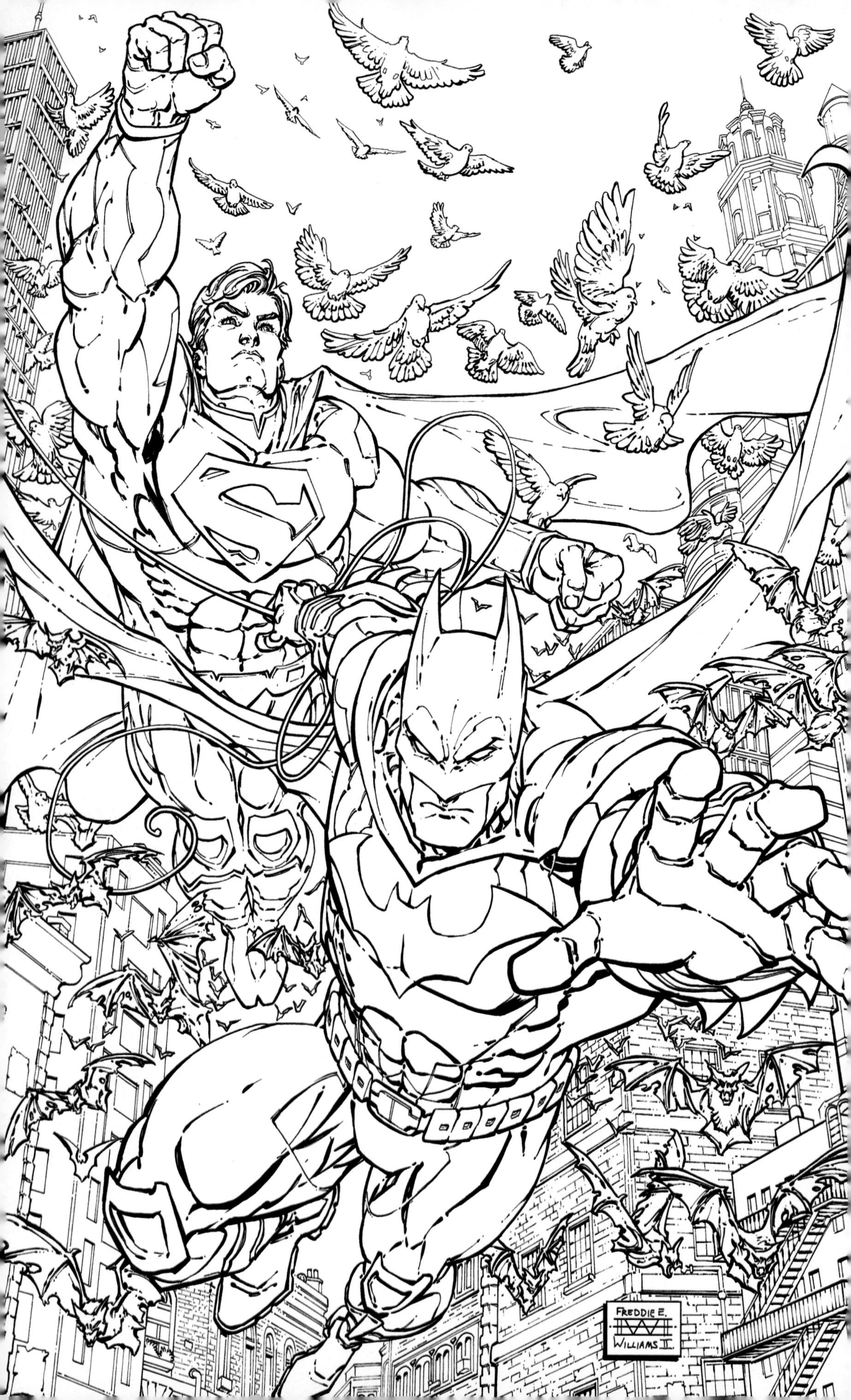
FREDDIE E.
WILLIAMS II

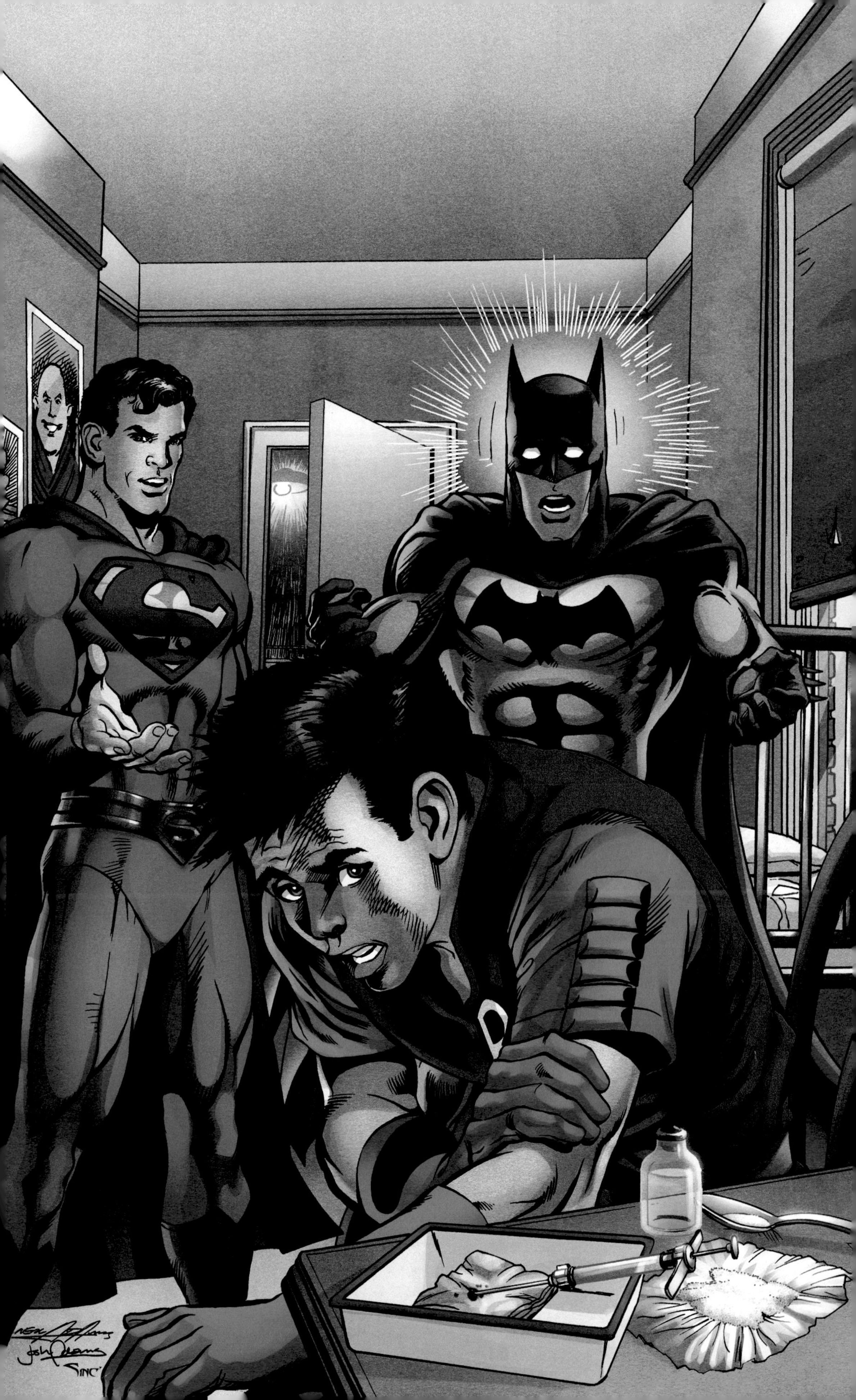

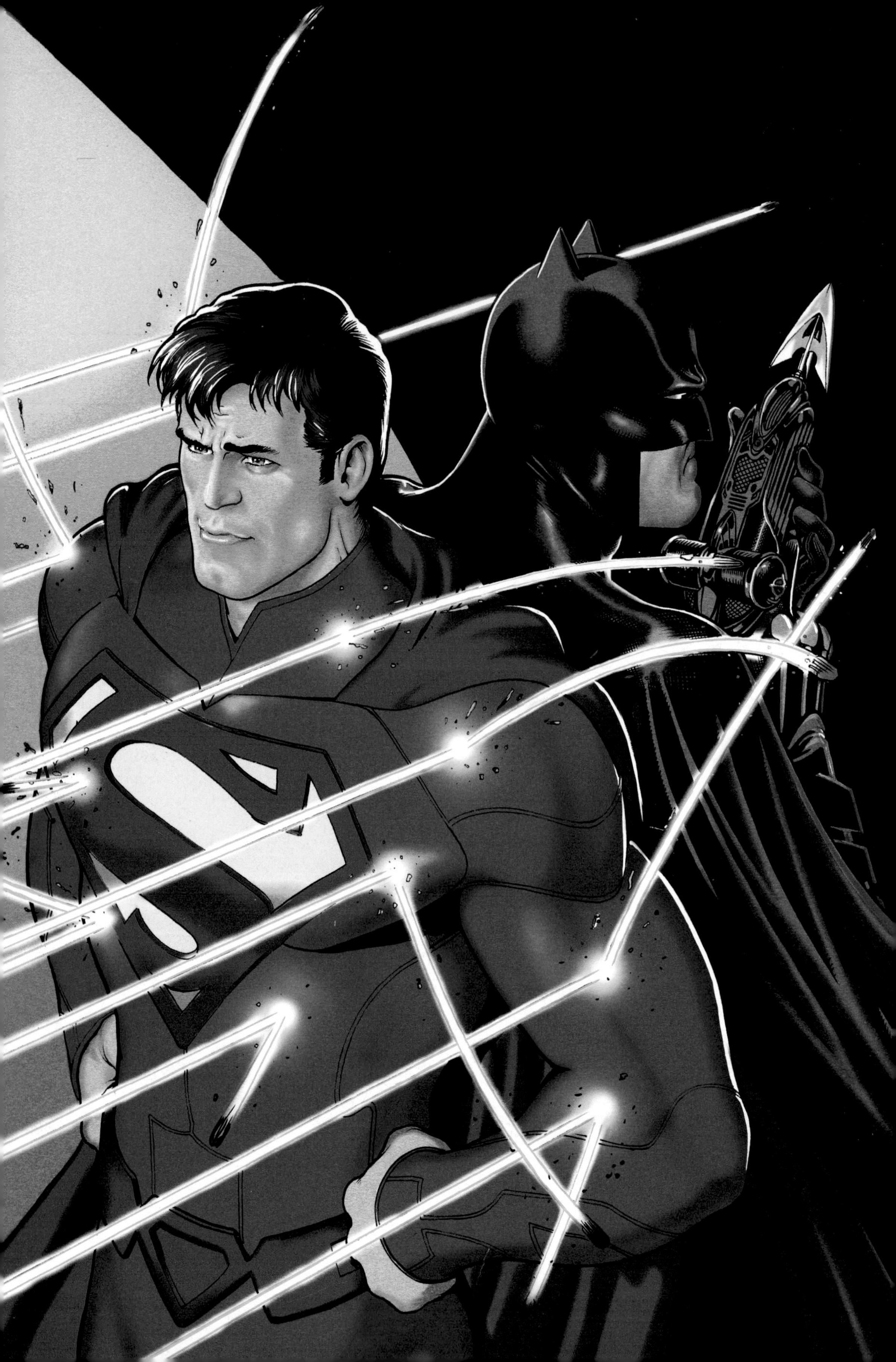

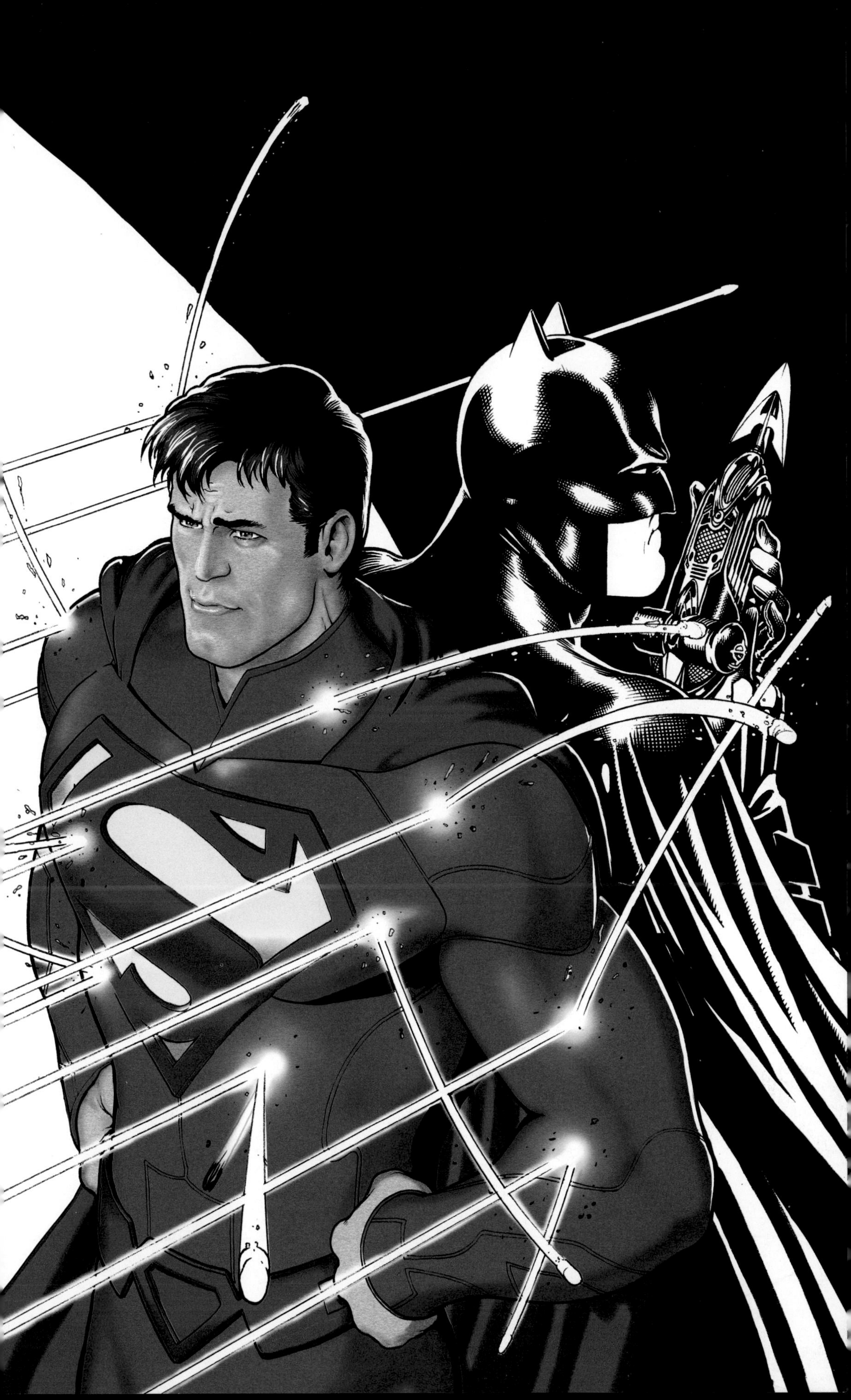

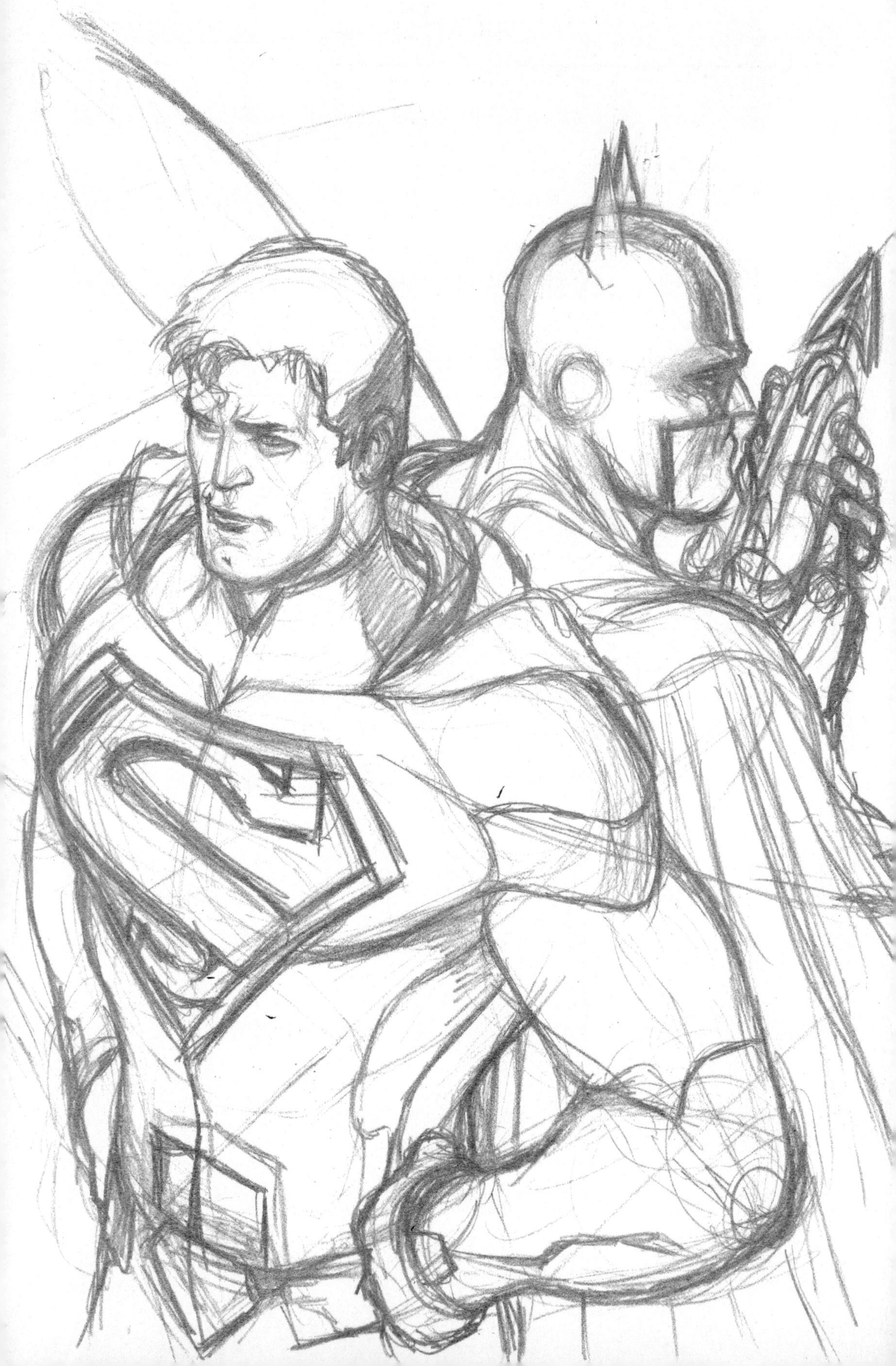

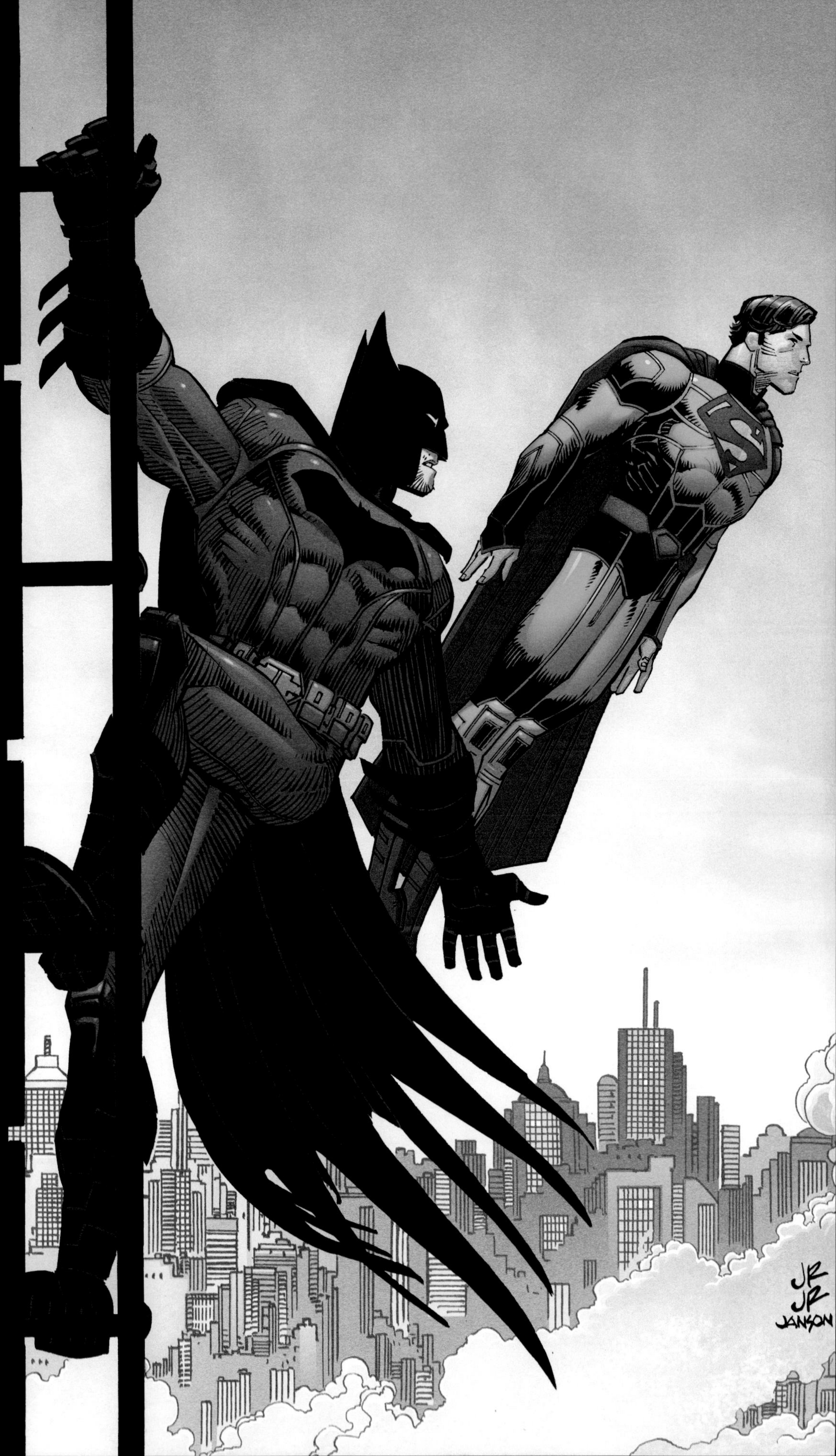
JR
JR
JANSON

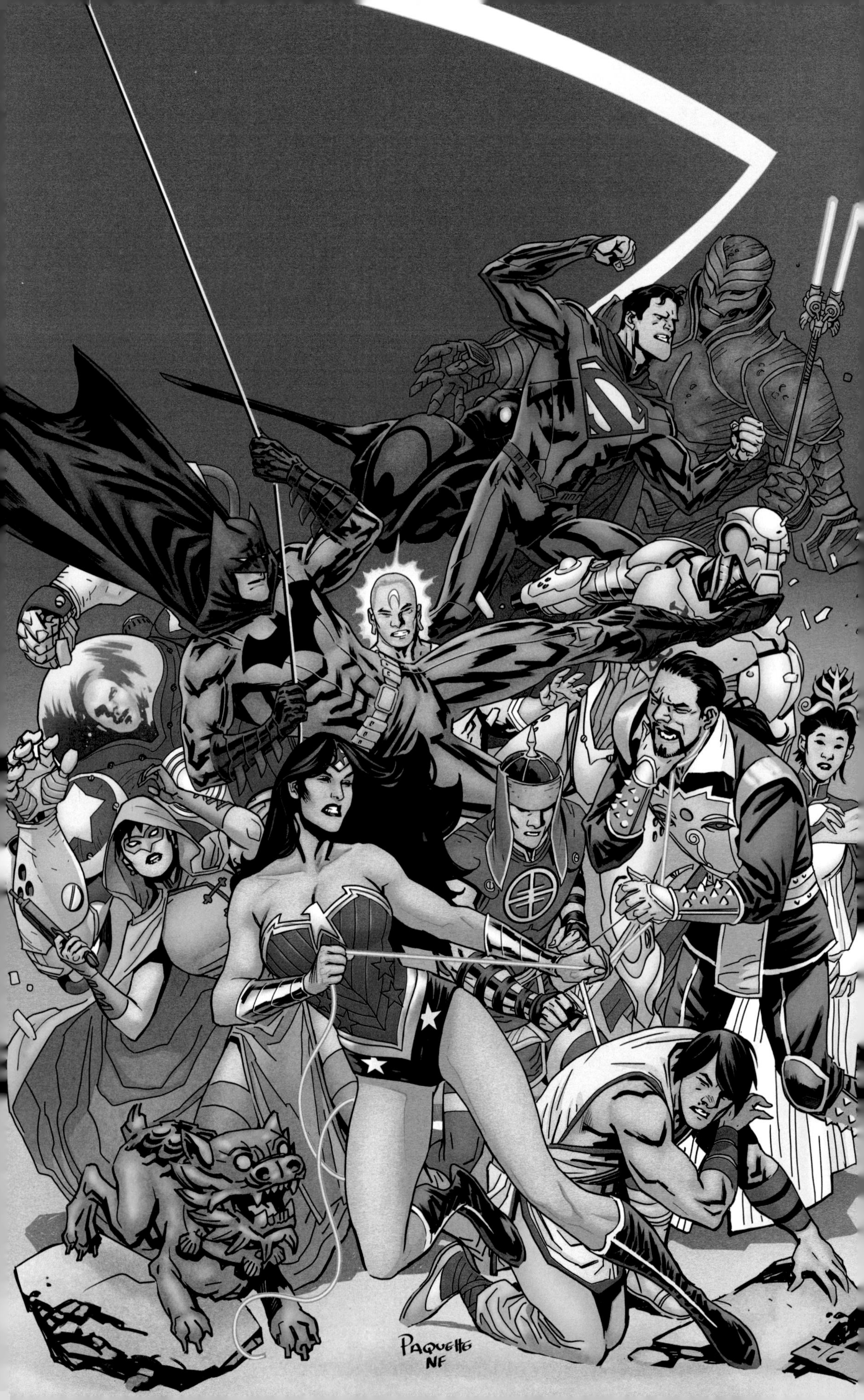
PAQUETTE
NF

DC UNIVERSE REBIRTH
BATMAN
VOL. 1: I AM GOTHAM
TOM KING
with DAVID FINCH

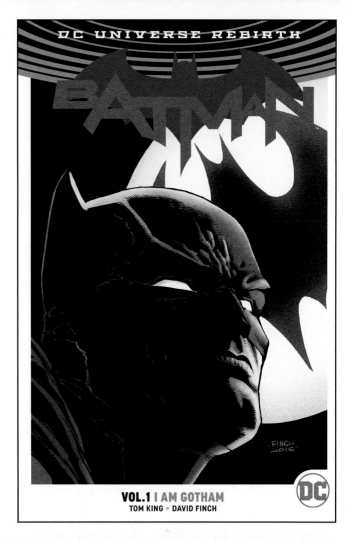

VOL.1 I AM GOTHAM
TOM KING * DAVID FINCH

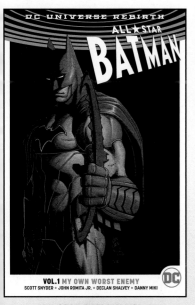

ALL-STAR BATMAN VOL. 1:
MY OWN WORST ENEMY

NIGHTWING VOL. 1:
BETTER THAN BATMAN

DETECTIVE COMICS VOL. 1:
RISE OF THE BATMEN

"That gorgeous spectacle is an undeniable part of Superman's appeal, but the family dynamics are what make it such an engaging read."
— A.V. CLUB

"Head and shoulders above the rest."
— NEWSARAMA

DC UNIVERSE REBIRTH
SUPERMAN
VOL. 1: SON OF SUPERMAN

PETER J. TOMASI with PATRICK GLEASON, DOUG MAHNKE & JORGE JIMENEZ

VOL.1 SON OF SUPERMAN

PETER J.TOMASI ★ PATRICK GLEASON ★ DOUG MAHNKE ★ JORGE JIMENEZ ★ MICK GRAY

**SUPERGIRL VOL. 1:
REIGN OF THE SUPERMEN**

**ACTION COMICS VOL. 1:
PATH OF DOOM**

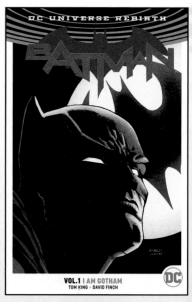

**BATMAN VOL. 1:
I AM GOTHAM**

"Welcoming to new fans looking to get into superhero comics for the first time and old fans who gave up on the funny-books long ago."
– SCRIPPS HOWARD NEWS SERVICE

JUSTICE LEAGUE

VOL. 1: ORIGIN
GEOFF JOHNS and JIM LEE

**JUSTICE LEAGUE
VOL. 2: THE VILLAIN'S JOURNEY**

**JUSTICE LEAGUE
VOL. 3: THRONE OF ATLANTIS**

READ THE ENTIRE EPIC!

JUSTICE LEAGUE VOL. 4:
THE GRID

JUSTICE LEAGUE VOL. 5:
FOREVER HEROES

JUSTICE LEAGUE VOL. 6:
INJUSTICE LEAGUE

JUSTICE LEAGUE VOL. 7:
DARKSEID WAR PART 1

JUSTICE LEAGUE VOL. 8:
DARKSEID WAR PART 2

"The art is beautiful. The writing is terrifyingly spectacular...one of the darkest, most enjoyable Gotham City sagas in recent memory."
– IGN

"Scott Snyder, with rotating artists Jock and Francesco Francavilla, has solidified the title as the place for serious crime fiction in the Bat-universe."
– A.V. CLUB/THE ONION

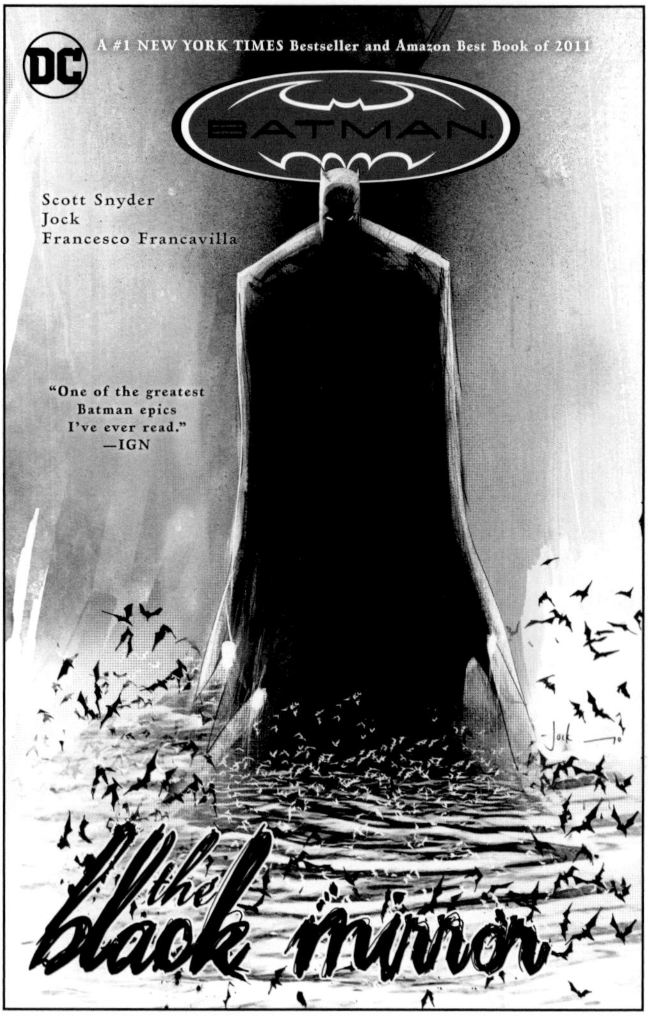
A #1 NEW YORK TIMES Bestseller and Amazon Best Book of 2011
BATMAN
Scott Snyder
Jock
Francesco Francavilla
"One of the greatest Batman epics I've ever read." —IGN
the black mirror

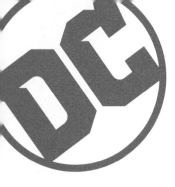

SCOTT SNYDER
with JOCK and FRANCESCO FRANCAVILLA

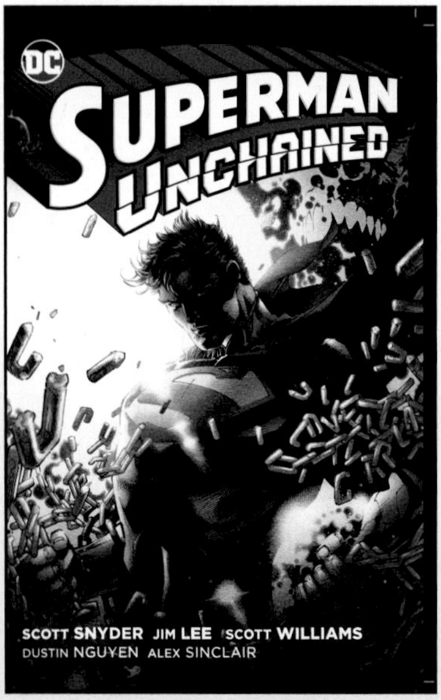
SUPERMAN UNCHAINED
SCOTT SNYDER JIM LEE SCOTT WILLIAMS
DUSTIN NGUYEN ALEX SINCLAIR

SUPERMAN: UNCHAINED
with JIM LEE and others

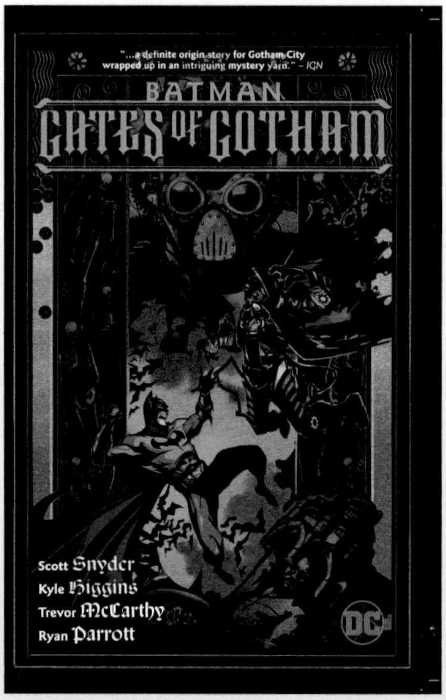
"...a definite origin story for Gotham City wrapped up in an intriguing mystery yarn." – IGN
BATMAN
GATES OF GOTHAM
Scott Snyder
Kyle Higgins
Trevor McCarthy
Ryan Parrott

BATMAN: GATES OF GOTHAM
with TREVOR MCCARTHY and others

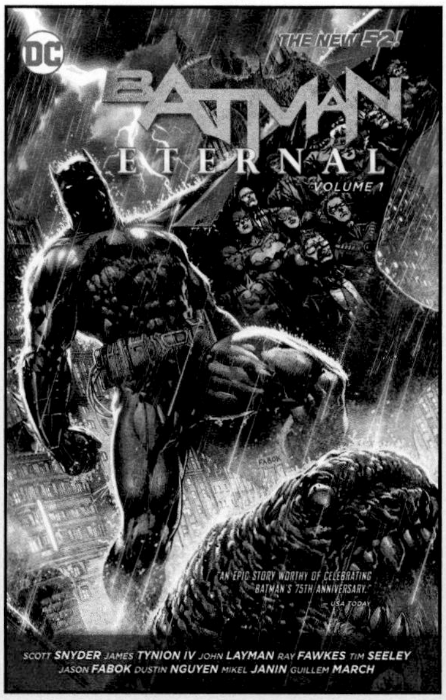
THE NEW 52!
BATMAN
ETERNAL
VOLUME 1
SCOTT SNYDER JAMES TYNION IV JOHN LAYMAN RAY FAWKES TIM SEELEY
JASON FABOK DUSTIN NGUYEN MIKEL JANIN GUILLEM MARCH

BATMAN: ETERNAL
with JASON FABOK and others

Get more DC graphic novels wherever comics and books are sold!